The Mind of the Holocaust Perpetrator in Fiction and Nonfiction

Erin McGlothlin

WAYNE STATE UNIVERSITY PRESS
DETROIT

© 2021 by Wayne State University Press, Detroit, Michigan 48201. All rights reserved. No part of this book may be reproduced without formal permission.

ISBN 978-0-8143-4834-5 (Paperback); ISBN 978-0-8143-4614-3 (Hardback); ISBN 978-0-8143-4615-0 (Ebook)

Library of Congress Control Number: 2020945975

Wayne State University Press
Leonard N. Simons Building
4809 Woodward Avenue
Detroit, Michigan 48201-1309

Visit us online at wsupress.wayne.edu

Cover art by Czechoslovak-Jewish Holocaust survivor Adolf Frankl, who shares this statement: "Through my work I have created a memorial for all nations of the world. No one, regardless of religion, origin or political conviction, should ever again suffer such—or similar—atrocities." Please see www.adolf-frankl.com. Artwork © 2020 Artists Rights Society (ARS), New York / VG Bild-Kunst, Bonn.

The Mind of the Holocaust Perpetrator in Fiction and Nonfiction

Praise for *The Mind of the Holocaust Perpetrator in Fiction and Nonfiction*

"Erin McGlothlin's extraordinary study not only offers sharply insightful readings of journalistic accounts and novels that seek to depict the inner lives of Nazi perpetrators but also presents a most compelling methodology for analyzing such depictions of the perpetrator in works of literary fiction, investigative journalism, and other textual modes. This wonderfully lucid, fiercely intelligent, and beautifully written book is must-reading for anyone studying the representation of the Holocaust or engaging with efforts to understand and portray the mindsets of perpetrators of historical atrocities."

—Gary Weissman, author of *Fantasies of Witnessing: Postwar Efforts to Experience the Holocaust*

"In this extremely innovative and important study, McGlothlin poses crucial new questions about the ways in which fiction and nonfiction texts depict the inner worlds of Holocaust perpetrators. Her careful analysis reveals how these texts give us the impression of 'reading the minds' of agents of extreme violence, while at the same time narrative filtering strategies establish a crucial distance, to prompt our ethical reflection on the Holocaust's legacy."

—Sue Vice, professor of English Literature, University of Sheffield, UK

"McGlothlin offers sophisticated, nuanced, and cogent interventions into scholarly conversations about (a) how to come to terms with the Holocaust; (b) narrative ethics, empathy, identification, and mind-reading; and (c) the relations between fiction and nonfiction. A must-read for anyone involved—or at all interested—in these vital conversations."

—James Phelan, coeditor of *After Testimony: The Ethics and Aesthetics of Holocaust Narrative for the Future*

"In this much-anticipated work, McGlothlin draws on her considerable knowledge of narrative theory to offer the most substantial and sustained exploration of the literature of perpetration in English to date. Expertly bringing together fictional and nonfictional representations of Nazi perpetrators, McGlothlin takes us through an ethical minefield with nuance and sensitivity. The careful work of reading undertaken here is itself a strong argument for the value of literary studies in confronting some of the most significant and troubling areas of human history and culture."

—Michael Rothberg, author of *The Implicated Subject: Beyond Victims and Perpetrators*

"Erin McGlothlin's book is a rigorous and insightful study of the complex dynamics of representing the mind of the Holocaust perpetrator in both fiction and nonfiction. It displays a rare combination of a sense of history and a talent for nuanced narrative analysis."

—Hanna Meretoja, professor of comparative literature, University of Turku

In memory of my mother, Velma Ruth Weiser McGlothlin (1930–2019), at whose bedside I sat as I was writing the last pages of this book. Her boundless love, wisdom, and good humor are among the greatest gifts I have had the fortune to receive.

Contents

Acknowledgments   xi

Introduction   1

Part I: Probing the Mind of the Holocaust Perpetrator in Nonfiction

Introduction to Part I   47

1. Mind-Reading Eichmann   67
   Hannah Arendt's *Eichmann in Jerusalem*, Harry Mulisch's *Criminal Case 40/61, the Trial of Adolf Eichmann*, and William L. Hull's *The Struggle for a Soul*

2. Interpellating the Perpetrator   133
   Gitta Sereny's *Into That Darkness*

Part II: Imagining the Mind of the Holocaust Perpetrator in Fiction

Introduction to Part II   175

3. Perpetrators on the Run   195
   Edgar Hilsenrath's *The Nazi and the Barber* and Jonathan Littell's *The Kindly Ones*

4. **The Perpetrator Mind Divided** 249
   Martin Amis's *Time's Arrow* and *The Zone of Interest*

Epilogue 299

Works Cited 309

Index 331

Acknowledgments

I am indebted to several units at Washington University in St. Louis (WU) for their support of this book. The Department of Germanic Languages and Literatures and the Dean of Arts and Sciences provided the necessary financial resources and time to develop and complete this project, while the WU Center for the Humanities offered additional assistance in the form of a Mid-Career Faculty Fellowship. I feel fortunate to work at an institution that values my research.

I am grateful to my departmental colleagues—in particular, my erstwhile chair, Matt Erlin—for their unflagging encouragement at all stages of my research, but above all in the final months. A number of other individuals offered significant logistical support, including WU former subject librarian Brian Vetruba, who kept ten paces ahead of me in the search for relevant materials; Barb Liebmann and Cecily Hawksworth, whose superb administrative skills helped keep me on track; Corey Twitchell, Brooke Shafar, and Amy Braun, who provided first-rate research assistance during their time as graduate students at WU; and Phyllis Lassner and Elizabeth Baer, who were instrumental in moving the book toward publication. I am very appreciative of their efforts. I'd also like to acknowledge Mitch Reyes, who gave helpful feedback on my book prospectus, and Jim Phelan, who helped me develop my arguments about narrative empathy. Additionally, I would like to thank the participants of the WU Reading Group in Cognitive Narrative Theory, the WU Faculty Seminar on Memory and Violence, the WU Summer Faculty Writing Retreat, the GSA Seminar on Affect and Cognition in Holocaust Culture, and the ACLA Seminar on Perpetration in Contemporary Representations of the Holocaust, all of whom helped me to refine my ideas.

Their general esprit de corps—along with the support and encouragement of my undergraduate and graduate students—inspired me to complete this project. Further, I offer my most heartfelt thanks to my trusted colleagues near and far, including Jennifer Kapczynski, Michael Richardson, Susanne Vees-Gulani, Anika Walke, Cathy Keane, Stephanie Kirk, Gerd Bayer, Hanna Meretoja, Gary Weissman, Katja Garloff, and Ervin Malakaj. I am very appreciative of their intellectual generosity, unremitting collegiality, and good cheer. In particular, I am grateful to Brad Prager, to whom I continually turn for advice and feedback and who unfailingly guides me each time in the right direction.

To Daniel Magilow and Agnes Mueller, I offer heartfelt thanks for their incisive review of the manuscript and helpful suggestions for improving it. I would also like to recognize the efforts of the first-rate staff at Wayne State University Press, including Annie Martin, Kathy Wildfong, Marie Sweetman, Emily Nowak, Kristin Harpster, and Kristina Stonehill. We in the humanities are fortunate to have such a committed team behind our efforts. I further would like to express my appreciation to Anne Taylor, who brought excellent editing skills to bear on the manuscript, and Anna-Rebecca Nowicki and Walter Grünzweig, who were helpful in procuring the cover image.

For their love and support, I wish to thank my family: my brother, Drew; my sister, Cara, my brother-in-law, John, and my dear niece, Abi; my stepson Ben and his fiancée, Samantha; my stepson Dylan and his girlfriend Carly; and my parents-in-law, Roberta and Larry. To my beloved husband, Mark, I offer my deepest gratitude for his generous encouragement, his assiduous lightheartedness, and his abiding love.

Introduction

"What could they be thinking about all this?"

In an essay from 2006 titled "Questioning the Perpetrators: To Give and to Take," the acclaimed Hungarian journalist Gitta Sereny reflects on fundamental questions that have long occupied writers engaged with the phenomenon of Holocaust perpetrators: How can we understand the mindset and motives of the people who planned and implemented the genocide? What constitutes their inner lives, and how do they relate intellectually and emotionally to their own histories of violence? To Sereny, best known for her extended interviews in the 1970s with Franz Stangl, former commandant of the National Socialist killing centers at Sobibór and Treblinka (at which collectively well over one million European Jews were killed), and Albert Speer, former Reich minister for armaments and war production, the project of comprehending the internal experience of the men who perpetrated the Holocaust poses myriad challenges:

> Questioning perpetrators, let me say it right away[,] is difficult, demanding and immensely costly, to oneself and to others—which is, of course, one reason why so few people have done it. What it requires first of all, is the acquisition of knowledge: it is entirely irresponsible to touch, even marginally, upon this kind of historical or social "journalism" without a background of real knowledge in history, law and psychology. That of course you can gain by education and experience. But there is need for more fundamental decisions

which, once made, will almost inevitably profoundly affect the way you lead your life. For you must first of all be prepared to commit unlimited time. What motivates you cannot be just an ambition, or even a desire, but a need inside yourself to know[,] to understand. You need to be capable of opening your mind to even the worst, the most unbearable things human beings can do, and manage the consequences, both in yourself and to a degree [in] "the other"—the person who thus confides in you—your subject, I will call them. ("Questioning the Perpetrators" 121)

Sereny describes here the driving force behind the arduous and mentally and emotionally taxing interviews she conducted over the years in preparation for her two book projects, *Into That Darkness: An Examination of Conscience* (1974; about Stangl) and *Albert Speer: His Battle with the Truth* (1995), for which she questioned not only prominent top- and mid-level figures in the National Socialist regime and its bureaucracy of genocide but also low-level perpetrators: her interviews were impelled by an almost irrepressible internal impetus to comprehend the mindset and experience of men whose actions had made them evil in the eyes of the postwar world. She wanted, she explains, to probe the mind of these perpetrators, to fathom their mental life and their motivations, and to discern "how what happened in and through Nazi Germany could happen, i.e. how individual men could do or be brought to do what individual Germans and Austrians had done" ("Questioning the Perpetrators" 125), namely, commit—or play a role in the commission of—genocidal violence against Jews and other groups. Moreover, she distills here, from her collective endeavors to read the minds of these perpetrators through strenuous one-on-one dialogues, a set of principles for interviewing ethically challenging "subjects." For Sereny, the project of questioning the Holocaust perpetrator requires not only entering into an unsettling relationship with an "other" but also being willing to "open [one's] mind to the worst" and to sit over a protracted period of time and engage in intensive intercourse with someone who, though "just a man[, n]ot an obviously evil man" (126), committed "monstrous things" (127). In short, Sereny's need "to know [and] understand" the crimes against humanity that were committed in the Third Reich, the Holocaust, and the Second World War requires her to project herself into the mind of a person who perpetrated them in an attempt to comprehend his experience from the inside, to explore not only "what he *knew*" but also "what he *felt*" (128), and to consider the narrative of his crimes as recounted from his own perspective. Only through such an internal view, writes Sereny, might it be "possible for us to see and consider the act in the context of the circumstances which produce or permit it" (126).

To be sure, as Sereny acknowledges, the intersubjective approach she brings to her interview practice, which in its quest for understanding is predicated on a willingness to accept, at least in part, the perpetrator's viewpoint and frame of reference, is an intricate undertaking that at the same time necessitates a kind of buffer or filter that helps her to manage the exercise of reading the mind of the perpetrator and to avoid merging his perspective with her own:

> But whatever the relationship one creates, what is always essential, and only possible to achieve with experience and discipline, is to retain distance—spiritual, emotional independence from the subject, a kind of neutrality. Intellectual involvement is right; sympathy and compassion are natural and not to be suppressed, as otherwise you risk your own humanity. Empathy, however, is dangerous and needs to be—not suppressed, but—withdrawn back to the limits which you have set; the distance which you must always maintain. ("Questioning the Perpetrators" 124)

According to Sereny's methodology, the interviewer's willingness to open her mind to the perspective and experience of the perpetrator of violence must at the same time be tempered by an essential measure of distance to prevent unconditional fusion with and uncritical acceptance of the subject's viewpoint and understanding of his crimes (an outcome that, in her view, would imperil the interviewer's own moral position). Sereny describes her practice of questioning Holocaust perpetrators as a flexible, variable, and delicate operation in which the interviewer must both advance into precarious territory and withdraw "back to the limits" that have been previously determined; only through such peripatetic movement between empathetic understanding and detached neutrality is the interviewer able to explore, illuminate, and critically evaluate the internal experience of men whom she views with "ambivalence" (in the case of Speer) or even "aversion" or "abhorrence" (in the case of Stangl) ("Questioning the Perpetrators" 128). By virtue of a method that manages the subject's perspective and self-understanding through the deliberate deployment of buffering, filtering, and distancing strategies, Sereny's interview process, which she makes manifest in both books, thus alternately compels and forecloses identification—both on her own part and on the part of her reader—with the ethically challenging figure of the Holocaust perpetrator.

As a journalist, Sereny exploits the properties of nonfiction in her portraits of Stangl and Speer. But the fundamental questions that drive her work have provided the raw material for fictional narratives as well. Appearing in 2006, the same year as Sereny's essay, Jonathan Littell's novel *Les Bienveillantes* (*The Kindly Ones*, 2009) features the narrative perspective of an SS officer, Maximilien von Aue. In a manner not unlike Sereny's need to understand the Holocaust perpetrators whom she interviews, the fictional Aue attempts to fathom the mental state of the shooters of the Einsatzgruppe to which he is attached as an intelligence officer and which, beginning with the invasion of the Soviet Union in the summer of 1941 and with the aid of local Ukrainians, massacres many tens of thousands of mostly Jews. Writing from a temporal standpoint decades after the war, the narrating I describes what the experiencing I thought as he witnessed for the first time a mass execution of Jews organized by the SS but implemented by Ukrainians.[1] He reports,

> I thought about these Ukrainians: How had they gotten to this point? Most of them had fought against the Poles, and then against the Soviets, they must have dreamed of a better future, for themselves and for their children, and now they found themselves in a forest, wearing a strange uniform and

---

1 Susan Rubin Suleiman points out that Aue claims with this quote to have thoughts that he simply could not have had at the time: "This kind of reflection—together with the historical information contained in these few sentences about Ukrainians enrolled in the German army during the invasion of Russia and used in the murder of Jews—is clearly retrospective, even though it seems to be occurring at the moment; the use of free indirect discourse to report Aue's thoughts marks a temporal and cognitive gap between the narrator and his former self" ("When the Perpetrator Becomes a Reliable Witness" 8).

killing people who had done nothing to them, without any reason they could understand. What could they be thinking about all this? Still, when they were given the order, they shot, they pushed the bodies in the ditch and brought other ones, they didn't protest. What would they think of all this later on? (Littell, *The Kindly Ones* 85–86)

Not having a common language through which he can query the Ukrainian recruits about their reactions to their experience, and separated from them by virtue of his rank and observer status, Aue is forced to speculate from afar on their mental state; he tries to infer from their actions what they might be thinking with regard to the brutal tasks they are ordered—or at least encouraged—to perform. The internal experience of these shooters—along with that of the SS and Wehrmacht officers and soldiers who participate in numerous subsequent massacres of entire Jewish communities through the rest of the summer and fall—becomes an enigma on which Aue fixates but whose meaning he cannot ascertain: he is aware that the extreme violence the men commit must register in some way on a psychic or emotional level, but he is unable to penetrate the riddle of their minds. Although he observes and reports to the reader the men's behavior during the massacres they perpetrate, he is distinctly incapable of mediating their mental states as they engage in their violent actions.

As Aue continues to observe the mass shootings of his Einsatzgruppe (an activity in which he will later take a direct part himself), he begins to include himself in his conjecture:

> I was thinking. I thought about my life, about what relationship there could be between this life that I had lived—an entirely ordinary life, the life of anyone, but also in some respects an extraordinary, an unusual life, although the unusual is also very ordinary—and what was happening here. There must have been a relationship, and it was a fact, there was one. True, I wasn't taking part in the executions, I wasn't commanding the firing squads; but that didn't change much, since I often attended them, I helped prepare them and then I wrote the reports; what's more, it was just by chance that I had

> been posted to the Stab rather than to the Teilkommandos. And if they had given me a Teilkommando, would I too have been able, like Nagel or Häfner, to organize the roundups, have the ditches dug, line up the condemned men, and shout "Fire!"? (95)

Aue's rumination about himself mirrors in essential ways his speculation about the thinking of the Ukrainian shooters; just as he tries to imagine how the Ukrainians might react upon finding themselves dislodged—"without any reason they could understand"—from their everyday lives and suddenly thrust into the position of mass killers, Aue attempts to bridge in mental terms his "ordinary life" and his daily complicity in—although not direct commission of—mass atrocities against the entire Jewish populace, including women, children, and the elderly. One might expect that he would be far more successful in discerning and communicating his own mind here than in mediating the mental experience of the shooters he observed from a distance; indeed, given his status as an autodiegetic (or what is commonly known as "first-person") narrator, we as readers assume that he has complete access to his own interiority, even if he chooses not to fully relate it to us. However, like the mental state of the Ukrainians, his mind—at least as it relates to his experience as a complicit observer to mass killing—remains a remote and elusive mystery to him. Several pages later, after the description of additional mass executions, he states,

> And what about me? . . . I was trying to see what effect all this would have on me. I was always observing myself: it was as if a film camera were fixed just above me, and I was at once this camera, the man it was filming, and the man who was then studying the film. Sometimes that astonished me, and often, at night, I couldn't sleep; I stared at the ceiling; the lens didn't leave me in peace. But the answer to my question kept slipping through my fingers. (107)

Trifurcated into the positions of actor, observer, and observational instrument of his own experience, Aue attempts here to infer his own mental state from the outside, reading himself for clues as to what he might be thinking or feeling, since he is unable—by his account, at least—to actually perceive such processes and outcomes of thinking and feeling from the inside. But as much as he observes himself (and observes himself observing), he fails to determine his own mental reaction to the genocide that he plays a part in perpetrating. Despite his copious and comprehensive narration—his account, which focuses chiefly on the years 1941–45, runs to almost one thousand pages—and his willingness to relay the most minute details of the horrific mass executions and the conversations about them he has with colleagues, he is no more able to narrate his own motivations for and the psychic effects of his complicity with genocidal violence than he is to report on the experience of the Ukrainian men, whom he does not know and with whom he shares no common language. Whether due to psychic denial, traumatization, or disingenuousness—on the part of either Aue the experiencing character or Aue the retrospective narrator—he simply cannot or resolutely will not directly represent to either himself or the reader his mental processing as it relates to the horrific violence of which he is daily a part. Because his narration withholds such information, we as readers must thus infer his mindset from the indirect evidence that is filtered to us.

Through emphatically different means and divergent discursive orientations (nonfiction vs. fiction), Sereny's and Littell's texts both demonstrate the complex dynamics inherent to the project of representing the mind of the Holocaust perpetrator, a figure that in the contemporary cultural imagination has come to represent one of the most notorious agents of extreme violence. Albeit from two antithetical historical and referential positions (a fictional SS officer complicit in the commission of genocide and an actual postwar journalist bent on understanding the motives of real men who were agents of mass killing), the narrators of both texts demonstrate strikingly similar approaches to the issue of understanding and mediating the uncomfortable and morally questionable perspective of men who planned, coordinated, or carried out the destruction of Europe's Jewish communities. On the one hand, both Sereny and the fictional Aue indicate a fervent desire (or, in Sereny's case, "a need") to understand the inner experience and mental framework of apparently ordinary men who engaged in extraordinary brutality and violence; they wish to understand both what might propel men to commit or participate in mass killings and how such acts imprint themselves afterward on their self-understanding, their narratives of their history of violence, and their relationships to the human community. On the other hand, both texts demonstrate problems and obstacles inherent to the project of reading the mind of the Holocaust perpetrator; for Sereny, the issue is the dangerous potential for identification with the perpetrator, whereas in Aue's case it is the various psychic and narrative mechanisms that block access to the perpetrator's mindset. Taken together, the two texts manifest the complex dialectical operations that govern attempts—whether fictional or nonfictional—to depict the inner experience of agents of extreme historical violence. This representational dynamic evinces both a desire for unmediated access to the perpetrator's consciousness—which would, as Robert Eaglestone argues, finally explain the "why" of the evil posited by the perpetrator's behavior (*The Broken Voice* 29)—and an awareness of the impossibility and even undesirability of unqualified representation of the mind of a figure whom, as I have claimed elsewhere, postwar culture has deemed "an incomprehensible Other whose personal motives lie outside the norms of human discourse" ("Theorizing the Perpetrator" 213). In other words, the projects of mind-reading undertaken by Sereny and by Littell's narrator Aue embody two antithetical impulses: they seek to reveal the contents of the perpetrator's mind and at the same time, through particular strategies of filtering, they work to occlude it.

The Mind of the Holocaust Perpetrator in Fictional and Nonfictional Discourse

From their different discursive and referential positions—fiction and nonfiction—Littell's novel and Sereny's interview projects represent disparate but related attempts to construct the internal experience of the Nazi perpetrator, a figure that in the contemporary cultural understanding has been regarded not only as ethically anathematic but also often the very embodiment of concrete evil. Their texts belong to a larger body of artistic works—including fiction and creative and journalistic nonfiction—that seek to probe the minds of a cohort of historical actors who provoke discomfort in contemporary audiences but who are critical to a fuller understanding of the Holocaust. With their concentration on the subjective perspective of such historically culpable and morally reprehensible figures, these works generate particular ethical, aesthetic, and historical questions: How do literary and journalistic texts construct the mind of the Holocaust perpetrator, a paradigmatic figure of violence in the postwar era? What is our ethical relationship to artistic works—both fictional and nonfictional—that ask us to imagine the motives of genocidal murderers and to consider the Holocaust from their point of view? What strategies do they employ to depict the consciousness of their perpetrators, and how do such narrative techniques function to produce or inhibit reader and viewer identification? How exactly do these texts negotiate the perpetrator's difficulty in finding adequate language to narrate his own history of committing extreme violence—or his unwillingness to tell of his experience at all? How can such works render the mind of Holocaust perpetrators without either reducing them to the well-worn trope of monster or transforming them into objects of unreflective sympathy? How do imaginative texts that attempt to portray the consciousness of such historically, emotionally, and ethically charged figures negotiate the often tenuous line between insightful provocation and historical bad faith? And, finally, how do we as readers and critics attend to the interpretive challenges posed by these representations of the mind of the Holocaust perpetrator without elevating him to the status of focal figure in the story of the Holocaust, uncritically accepting his account of his crimes, or even tacitly exonerating him for them—and thereby losing sight of our ethical obligation toward the victims and survivors and their experiences and narratives? By focusing on the disquieting interiority of the perpetrator, do we hazard the risk, as Sybille Schmidt puts it, "that the perpetration and the annihilation of the victim are repeated on a symbolic level" (100)?

In this book, I will address these critical questions by closely examining cultural depictions of Holocaust perpetrators in imaginative and journalistic discourse from the early 1960s to the present that imagine their inner experience, a mode of representation that constitutes, as Jenni Adams argues, a "vexed critical and representational arena" ("Introduction" 4), given that it has conventionally—and until relatively recently—been deemed shockingly transgressive or even outright taboo. By endeavoring to reproduce the mind of the Nazi perpetrator and to account for his subjective view of his participation in genocidal crimes, these seminal texts humanize him, transforming him from the archetype of evil into a complex psychological and moral subject. The evolution of this mythical construct in recent decades is indicative of a shift in how we have come to view perpetrators and how our understanding of them is at least as informed by cultural representations, which often employ considerable creative license in their narrative portraits of both real-life and fictional perpetrators, as it is by historical research, which draws a rigorous but also more generalized view of the men who perpetrated the Holocaust based on meticulous investigation of the historical record. It also bespeaks new modes of engagement with the uncomfortable moral and ethical questions raised by our increasing willingness to take on the perpetrator's perspective (if only provisionally) and to view the events of the Holocaust through his eyes.

Since the 1940s, perpetrators have been a central focus of historical research on the Holocaust; the last three decades in particular have seen a wave of pathbreaking, illuminating, and nuanced work by historians, psychologists, and sociologists that has been dubbed the "new perpetrator research" (Wennberg 31). In the discourse on the Holocaust in literary and cultural studies, however, attention to the representation of perpetrators has been a quite recent phenomenon. From its inception in the 1970s until the first decade of the twenty-first century, the scholarly study of Holocaust literature devoted the greater part of its attention to representations that frame the subjective experience of the Holocaust on the part of those who survived it rather than those who planned, administrated, and executed the genocide, an imbalance that, while understandable for ethical reasons, left unanswered important questions about cultural constructions of an important group of historical actors who played a constitutive role in the events. When literary scholarship did turn to representations of Nazi perpetrators, it typically tended to view them through an external, often myopic, lens, which often cast the perpetrators as evil, unfathomable Others. In an essay that appeared in 2010 (but was composed in 2005), I speculated about whether "there exists an unwritten but nevertheless powerful taboo that prohibits or at least regulates representations of perpetration" ("Theorizing the Perpetrator" 213), especially those that feature "the perspective of the perpetrators—in particular, the *narrative* perspective of the perpetrators, meaning their subjectivity, motivations, thoughts, and desires" (213). While I acknowledged that "literary texts themselves often maintain this unwritten discursive prohibition," I argued that the "greater force for upholding the taboo comes rather from the scholarly criticism on the literature of the Holocaust, which . . . overwhelmingly prefers to frame the experience of the Holocaust in terms of the victims' suffering" (213).[2] Fifteen years after the composition of those sentences, I perceive the scholarly situation quite differently, as it has transformed greatly in the relatively short interval. As insightful scholarship by Jenni Adams, Sue Vice, Elana Gomel, Robert Eaglestone, Brad Prager, Joanne Pettitt, Debarati Sanyal, Matthew Boswell, Susanne Luhmann, and a number of others demonstrates, there is now both a flourishing discourse on the representation of the perspective of Holocaust perpetrators in literary and visual culture and sustained attention to the ambivalent relationship that contemporary culture maintains to such fraught figures. As Saira Mohamed argues with reference to the glass box in which the former SS lieutenant colonel Adolf Eichmann was confined during his 1961 trial, which she sees as a metaphor for postwar culture's reification of perpetrators as monsters, more recent explorations of the perpetrator in both the cultural and the scholarly imagination have begun to consider him "as a fully thinking, feeling human being," allowing for a much more nuanced conceptual relationship to this figure: "When we look at the perpetrator outside of the caged context of objectification, we realize that he is someone we can recognize—almost accidentally, against our urges—as human, a man rather than a monster" (1162).

The new wave of literary research on the representation of Holocaust perpetrators has focused in particular on prominent recent fictional texts that transgress the implied taboo on narrating the Holocaust from the standpoint of the men and women who played a role—whether instrumental or incidental—in the marginalization, persecution, and mass killing of Europe's Jews. Littell's *The Kindly Ones* has been cited as the most notorious example of a greater corpus of contemporary historical fiction that

---

2 For an in-depth discussion on the role of the taboo in Holocaust representation in general and in depictions of perpetrators in general, see Matthew Boswell's excellent essay. Boswell writes, "Much like the taboo on imaginative works of Holocaust representation, the taboo against imagining the consciousness of perpetrators becomes evident through the controversies that surround its transgression" (190); moreover, he argues that "taboos against Holocaust representation make transgressive literary practice almost inevitable: the very existence of a discourse about the taboo implies that *the transgression has always already been made*" (192).

constitutes what Richard Crownshaw calls the "turn toward the figure of the perpetrator" (75); according to Sanyal, it belongs to "an international cultural phenomenon that examines the figure of the perpetrator in a wide range of contexts" (most notably the Holocaust but also other historical incidents of mass violence and oppression), prompting her to ask whether such works "signal . . . the dawn of an 'era of the perpetrator'" (185–86). This recent cultural orientation, which features what Jeremy Metz calls "unfettered literary representations of victimizers" (1037), has been championed by critics, especially in the case of Littell's novel, as an "unprecedented attempt to render the interiority of a bona fide 'Nazi'" (Curthoys 463). However, as Sereny's interviews with Stangl and Speer demonstrate—and as will become clear in this study—the cultural construction of the internal experience of Holocaust perpetrators is not at all a new phenomenon. While it is true that, over the course of the last two decades, a relative profusion of fictional representations focusing on the inner lives of former Nazis has appeared, first-person fictional accounts of Holocaust mass murderers date back as far as the immediate postwar period.[3] Moreover, creative and journalistic nonfictional texts and documentary films that probe the mindset of actual former perpetrators (which, as I will argue in the introduction to part 1 of this study, can be seen as popular successors to the wave of psychological studies of high-ranking Nazis and the "Nazi personality" conducted in the immediate postwar period) were particularly abundant in the 1960s, 1970s, and 1980s, a time when the inner experience of the men who perpetrated the Holocaust—particularly notorious figures like Adolf Eichmann but also lesser-known persons—occupied the cultural imagination. For these reasons, I concur with Sanyal, who concludes that "the turn to perpetration and complicity in our era of the witness is thus not a novel phenomenon" (187). Sanyal considers the current profusion of perpetrator representations instead "a *return*" (187), following a recession of such concerns "from the 1960s to the 1990s" (187), to "existential and ethical preoccupations" (186) with questions of complicity and perpetration, particularly on the part of French intellectuals in the immediate postwar

---

3 In her comprehensive historical study of what she calls "perpetrator fiction," Joanne Pettitt traces a longer history of the genre, including texts narrated from the perspective of a perpetrator. I discuss her findings in the introduction to part 2.

period. I, on the other hand, perceive rather a longer, mostly continuous trajectory in cultural representations of the mind of the Holocaust perpetrator that, while not without fallow periods or moments of disconnection, links the earlier body of nonfictional biographies and documentary films about actual perpetrators, such as Sereny's book projects on Stangl and Speer and Claude Lanzmann's interviews with former perpetrators featured in his 1985 masterwork *Shoah*, with the more recent wave of fiction of which Littell's text is emblematic. Moreover, as I will argue in this book, although they are often read as diametrically opposed to each other, these two discursive orientations with regard to the representation of the subjectivity of perpetrators—fiction and nonfiction—not only are connected historically and thus should be seen as two facets or roughly successive stages of a common cultural phenomenon, but also share a number of aesthetic and narrative properties and are in fact mutually informative and constitutive: on the one hand, nonfictional biographies of perpetrators employ narrative strategies and frameworks derived from fictional genres, while on the other hand, fictional representations of the mind of the perpetrator are modeled not only on the insightful historiography of Holocaust perpetrators of recent decades but also on nonfictional engagements with perpetrators, such as Sereny's and Lanzmann's interviews. As I will demonstrate, more recent fictional novels featuring perpetrators as narrators employ narrative strategies that reproduce some of the effects generated by the mediating figure of the interviewer or interpreter in the nonfictional texts, thereby assuming and at the same time critically transforming the latter's representational approaches. I thus perceive not only a *historical* connection within this greater corpus of texts, whereby journalistic and nonfictional engagement with real-life perpetrators gradually gives way to fictional exploration, but also a *structural* and *aesthetic* one.

Textual Strategies: The "Filter" versus the "Swerve"

In their attempts to infer and represent the consciousness of perpetrators of mass atrocity in the Holocaust, Littell's fictional narrator Aue and the journalist Gitta Sereny manage, as I have argued, both to manifest and to obscure what they infer to be the mental mechanisms of men who perpetrated the genocide. In Sereny's case, this involves the construction of a buffer that allows her to maintain critical distance from the mindset of the men whom she interviews, while for Aue, the distance appears to inhere in his own alienated perspective. From markedly different referential, experiential, and historical positions, the two narrators—one real, the other invented—thus epitomize a particular representational dynamic that I see operative in the larger corpus of fictional and nonfictional renderings of the mind of Holocaust perpetrators, whereby such texts work in earnest to make transparent the mental life of their subjects and at the same time inevitably—and somewhat reflexively—contrive to obfuscate it. Central to this dynamic is the way in which the internal perspectives of the perpetrators are conveyed through narration via particular techniques and formal features that induce and encourage and at the same time forestall and impede processes of empathetic identification with such ethically charged figures. My study here will investigate four canonical and lesser-known nonfictional works that attempt to trace the history of the Holocaust through the narrated experiences of individual actors in the National Socialist program of extermination of European Jewry alongside four prominent fictional texts that do the same. As I will demonstrate in my reading of these texts, in the project of constructing the mind of the Holocaust perpetrator—whether fictional or nonfictional—there subsists a certain tension that revolves around the ethics of representation and identification. On the one hand, each text offers a relatively mimetic representation of the subjectivity of its violent protagonist that is psychologically plausible; in this way it encourages audience identification on a number of levels (an issue that I will address in more detail later in this introduction). On the other hand, the narratives of violence I analyze also work to obscure the perpetrator's mind, revealing anxieties about the project of undistorted representation they profess to undertake and the potential danger of reader identification enabled by their depiction of the perpetrator's perspective. In particular, these texts utilize an array of what I term *filtering strategies* to interpose the reader's access to the perpetrator's consciousness; such filters are generated by the deployment of particular narrative devices, the corruption of narrative functions (such as the breakdown of narratorial identity or doubling), the adoption of conventional generic forms or masterplots, or practices of focalization, and the perception of the thoughts of another that cognitive scientists refer to as "mind-reading" (the latter of which I will also explicate later). The self-conscious filtering strategies produced in each of the texts function as buffering mechanisms to alternately compel and foreclose identification, drawing the reader directly into the perpetrators' experience and at the same time retarding or attenuating her affective and cognitive connection by inhibiting access to the perpetrators' consciousness. In so doing, not only do these texts thus make us keenly aware of the process by which they mediate to us and we in turn consume particular perspectives with regard to the thoughts, desires, feelings, reflections, and moral positions of figures who engage in genocidal violence, but they also demonstrate both the hazards and the benefits of representational practice itself, within which, as Hanna Meretoja argues, inheres both "ethical potential and . . . risks" by virtue of the ways in which it both "enable[s] experience and delimit[s] it" (2).[4]

In the nonfictional texts I investigate—Hannah Arendt's *Eichmann in Jerusalem: A Report on the Banality of Evil*, Harry Mulisch's *Criminal Case 40/61, the Trial of Adolf Eichmann: An Eyewitness Account* (*De Zaak 40/61: Een Reportage*), William L. Hull's *The Struggle for a Soul*, and Gitta Sereny's *Into That Darkness*—all of which were written in the 1960s and 1970s, the minds of real-life perpetrators are rendered in a conspicuously mediated fashion through commentators, who record and analyze the perpetrators' performances of self-disclosure in interviews and court proceedings and in the process imagine their inner perspectives through practices of mindreading. In such texts, operations of filtering are located both in the mediating figure of the interviewer/interpreter, who functions as a discursive buffer between the reader/viewer and the perpetrator under consideration, and in particular narrative conventions (such as the detective story or the confessional) through which the writer chooses to frame his or her encounter with the perpetrator.

---

4 Employing an approach she terms "narrative hermeneutics," which "treats narratives as culturally mediated practices of (re)interpreting experience," Meretoja is interested above all in the "ethical potential of storytelling," meaning not only its ethically constructive value but also its capacity for ethically problematic deployment. She proposes the concept of a "hermeneutic narrative ethics," "which acknowledges that narrative practices can be oppressive, empowering, or both, and provides resources for analyzing the different dimensions of the ethical potential and dangers of storytelling" (2). While my focus in this book is much narrower than Meretoja's, I align my own perspective on the relationship between experience, narrative representation, and ethics with hers.

In the four works of fiction explored in this book—Edgar Hilsenrath's *The Nazi and the Barber* (*Der Nazi und der Friseur*), Jonathan Littell's *The Kindly Ones*, and Martin Amis's *Time's Arrow, or, The Nature of the Offense* and *The Zone of Interest*—filtering strategies include particular narrative devices, such as vocal pathology or temporal instability, that function to either disfigure the plausibly mimetic rendering of the perpetrator's mind or prevent it from materializing in the first place. In this group of texts, such stratagems constitute the fictional counterpart to (or even translation of) the mediating figure of the interviewer or interpreter in the nonfictional texts, thereby steering in analogous fashion the audience's interpretive possibilities and modulating its connection to the perpetrator-protagonist. More recent fictional representations of the mind of the Holocaust perpetrator not only emerge as the historical successors to the wave of nonfiction books and films of the 1960s, 1970s, and early 1980s but also assume, and at the same time critically transform, the representational approaches employed by the earlier referential texts.

At first glance, my argument regarding the textual strategies of filtering in fictional and nonfictional encounters with the interiority of Holocaust perpetrators resembles Robert Eaglestone's notion of the "swerve," which, according to Jenni Adams, is "Eaglestone's vocabulary for the description of a phenomenon by which texts which at first promise to provide insight into the behaviour and motivations of Holocaust perpetrators ultimately diverge from this endeavor" ("Glossary of Major Terms and Concepts" 322). In *The Broken Voice: Reading Post-Holocaust Literature* (2017), Eaglestone, one of the few literary critics to consider fictional depictions of Holocaust perpetrators alongside nonfictional ones, writes,

> There are many historical and biographical accounts of Holocaust perpetrators, and even some memoirs: there are growing numbers of serious fictions, too, which focus on perpetrators. In these, what are we taught about evil? Yehuda Bauer writes that if "we, at some future date, know the exact way the murder was implemented, what will that knowledge give us? We will know who, what, and when, but we will not have asked the really important question: Why?" It is almost universally the case that these historical or fictional accounts do *not* seem to explain evil but leave our speech

broken, with nothing to say. Why do they fail to "penetrate the personality" of perpetrators, fail to answer the question "why" satisfactorily? Even accounting for evasion and mendacity, and for some of the more mundane difficulties of communication, the accounts of perpetrators and their fictional counterparts seem shallow and unproductive. (29)

According to Eaglestone, both nonfictional writing about perpetrators, which he subdivides into "perpetrator testimony" (in the case of autobiographical writing or transcribed interviews, such as the ones conducted by Sereny) or "accusatory biography" (as in Arendt's book on Eichmann),[5] and fictional texts featuring perpetrators as characters promise through their very premise to reveal and explain the evil embodied in the perpetrators' actions and histories; in other words, they claim to address and even pose an answer to the colossal "Why?" question that dominates post-Holocaust culture and thought. However, in Eaglestone's view, such texts inevitably end up reneging on that promise by "swerving" away from a bold, uncompromised, or essential illumination or explanation of that evil. In the case of the nonfictional texts, this deviation from the project of revelation is the result of the text's disclosure of the perpetrator not as a complex moral

---

5 Eaglestone labels texts such as Sereny's books on Stangl and Speer "perpetrator testimonies," a designation that I consciously eschew for two reasons. First, the term obscures the very mediation of the interviewer and author. Eaglestone does acknowledge and explore this aspect: "Work on perpetrators is done by or with other writers, or with very unusual pressures—a sort of 'second person' testimony. In most cases testimony is explicitly dragged out of the 'author' and many—the most celebrated—are written not by the perpetrator but about and with the perpetrator, willingly . . . , unknowingly . . . , or unwillingly" (*The Broken Voice* 42). Contra to Eaglestone, however, I argue that it is precisely the presence and pressure of the mediating, interpreting figure in such texts that preclude them from constituting—or at least being read as—testimonies in the strict sense of the term. The information and affect they communicate originate less in the statements of the perpetrator than they do in the interposition of the narrator or interviewer who depicts the perpetrator and reads his mind. Second, I follow Raya Morag, who makes an explicit "distinction between the victim's testimony and the perpetrator's confession" (3) and thus acknowledges the epistemological, ontological, and phenomenological differences between the two discourses. Even when the confession in question is a failed or inadequate one (which is the case, as we will see in the first two chapters, particularly in nonfictional texts, but also in fictional ones), the perpetrator's communicative act is better classified as confession than as testimony.

subject but as a "nobody" who evades "memory, empathy, roots, and responsibility" (*The Broken Voice* 40) and who thus remains "incomprehensible" (43); in the fiction, the swerve occurs through a failure to meaningfully engage with the inner life of the perpetrator-protagonist or through clichéd language, subplots, and narratives that compete with "the 'genocidal' story" (62). Taken as a whole, this body of literature, in Eaglestone's opinion, avoids rather than clarifies the evil embodied in both the perpetrator's past acts and his present self-understanding (or lack thereof).

While my analysis coincides with or resembles Eaglestone's with regard to some of the stratagems employed by both the nonfictional and the fictional representations of the perpetrator's minds—for example, the figure of the interlocutor or mediator in the nonfictional texts and the role of competing narratives in the fictional texts—my conclusions about this body of literature and its representational strategies differ from his in several essential respects. To begin with, the success of these texts does not hinge for me, as it does for Eaglestone, on their ability to explain evil. For one thing, the more I work on and read about evil, the less I feel I understand what is meant by it, especially but not exclusively in the context of the Holocaust. Philosophers who break down the meaning and constituent parts of evil are able to make some headway with the idea,[6] but, as a cultural concept, it functions more as an emotional signal toward a sense of the ineffable (which is largely how I see it in this case) than as a stable or even helpful designation; more often than not, the evocation of it transports us away from possible understanding rather than bringing us closer to it. Moreover, I am equally unclear about what Eaglestone means by "evil," which he declines to define, leaving it in his otherwise precise and astute analysis an amorphous, obscure, and indeterminate abstraction. As with his question "Why?," which, in its boundlessness and lack of specificity, is unable to delimit the possible scope, shape, or magnitude of the answer it seeks, the word "evil" functions in Eaglestone's analysis as a signifier so capacious as to be functionally meaningless. In this way, "evil" becomes a charged code word—or

---

6 In particular, I find Lars Svendsen's phenomenological approach to evil quite illuminating: "Evil is not a substance, a thing, but rather a *characteristic* of things, events, or actions. Evil is *not* something definite and well defined, nor does it have an essence. 'Evil' is a broad concept we use to describe actions and suffering. In fact, the idea refers to such manifold phenomena . . . that it can appear to be so broad as to lose all specific content" (24–26).

even transcendental signifier—for something Eaglestone intently seeks but is unwilling or unable to define; likewise, he is unable to locate in the texts he examines a satisfying explanation for the "Why?" that evil poses. I read Eaglestone's desire to locate evil and his attendant frustration at not finding it as symptoms of the ways in which the Holocaust—in this case, the existence and ethical conundrum of the perpetrator and his crimes—continues to challenge our epistemological, linguistic, and historical frameworks of understanding, at least when one formulates the question in such expansive, unimaginable, and thus unattainable terms.[7] By elevating the notion of evil to the commodious level of the metaphysical, Eaglestone thus guarantees the failure of both the perpetrator texts to represent and explain their subjects' actions, motivations, and understanding and his own endeavor to extract from them an answer to the question "Why?" Given the stakes of Eaglestone's attempt to locate evil, it is not surprising that he regards all of the texts he investigates as failures; indeed, one might ask whether the expectations he brings to his reading could at all be solved or satisfied by any one text and, if so, what such a text might look like. Is it in fact reasonable to expect that people—whether historical or fictional—with a history of such extreme violence might be sufficiently psychologically candid, truthful, and self-reflective to the extent that they would (or could) adequately satisfy both our questions about how they could have engaged in atrocities and our desire for a comprehensive and credible explanation? Several of the perpetrators—both nonfictional and fictional—portrayed in the texts I will analyze in the following chapters are astonishingly frank about their pasts, yet critics have uniformly censured them for their perceived self-interest, their inauthenticity, their psychic denial and deflection, and their self-pity.

---

7 In this, it is perhaps instructive to follow the lead of the eminent Holocaust historian Raul Hilberg, who, in the interview featured in Claude Lanzmann's *Shoah*, claims, "In all of my work I have never begun by asking the big questions, because I was always afraid that I would come up with small answers; and I have preferred therefore to address these things which are minutiae or details in order that I might then be able to put together in a gestalt a picture which, if not an explanation, is at least a description, a more full description, of what transpired" (DVD disc 2, chap. 6). As Emil Fackenheim writes of this scene (and of Lanzmann's method of interviewing perpetrators), "The 'small' questions concern *how* they did it, the 'big' question is *why*. Never once in his film does Lanzmann ask the criminals he interviewed why they did it, and with good reason" (192).

In my view, no degree of candor and self-interrogation would be adequate either to dispel our skepticism regarding their accounts or to quench our yearning for an absolute, conclusive, and definitive explanation. And what could any individual perpetrator possibly tell us that would in any sufficient way explain the causal meaning of the prodigious crimes of the Holocaust and the inchoate, radical sense of evil we connect with them? In this regard, Eaglestone's quest for a satisfactory answer to the question "Why?" appears to be an unrealizable fantasy for something that simply does not and cannot exist. It is therefore no wonder that he perceives in the texts that he analyzes a decided and irrevocable swerve from the question that, in his view, they claim to address.

Eaglestone's notion of the swerve is thus grounded in assumptions and motivations that differ greatly from those that prompt my notion of filtering; whereas Eaglestone looks to the narratives about perpetrators to give a sufficient explanation of evil, I am interested in how such texts manage to indicate—but in no way fully capture—the interiority of their subjects despite—or perhaps even because of—cultural expectations about the nature and scope of the evil with which such figures are charged. In other words, Eaglestone predicates his evaluation of the texts he investigates on whether or not they explain evil; he constructs thereby a binary in which the texts are either unqualified successes (an admittedly theoretical position, since he is unable to locate any that fit this description) or abject failures (a conclusion that is curiously belied, e.g., by his insightful reading of the nuances of Littell's text). His notion of the "swerve" thus represents the unidirectional movement from one pole of the binary to the other, expressing his pessimism about the potential for both fiction and nonfiction to interrogate in any acceptable way the nature of the evil they purport to illuminate. By contrast, my metaphor of choice, "filter," rejects the dichotomy between success and failure and the notion of irreversible trajectory from one side of the binary to the other; it therefore relocates the focus from the either-or question of whether a text is successful or a failure to an investigation of the dynamics and degrees of the representational process itself, which, rather than fixed or immutable, is motile, variable, divergent, and often contradictory. In its verb and substantive forms, "filter" denotes both the process and the instrument of the partial obstruction (and thus also the partial forward movement) of the flow of a material or force, indicating thereby neither complete blockage (the equivalent of failure) nor unhindered circulation (the analogue of success). In terms of the representational strategies employed by the texts under consideration here, the concept of filtering thus expresses an ambulatory dynamic that moves at different moments among various points on the spectrum between dichotomous positions, allowing the texts to disclose, in part and in sundry stages, the mental constitution of the men they represent and, simultaneously, to undermine, interrupt, or impede actively this process of revelation and illumination through particular narrative strategies. In this way, in contradistinction to Eaglestone's theory of the swerve away from evil, whereby in the perpetrators' texts "the subjectivity of the perpetrators had to be self-erased" (*The Broken Voice* 58), thus leaving behind no possible comprehension (whether on the part of the perpetrators themselves or that of their interlocutors or interpreters) of their motivations or self-awareness, my concept of the filter emphasizes the ways in which these texts both yield and withhold insight into their mental life. By virtue of their employment of such dynamic filtering strategies, the texts broach the ethical dilemma of imagining and understanding the perspective and self-understanding of the perpetrator without solving it or neutralizing its problematic implications.[8]

What Do I Mean by "Holocaust Perpetrator"?

At this point, I find it useful and even necessary to define what I mean by "Holocaust perpetrator," as the term bears not only particular historical connotations that determine how we understand people who were responsible for or participated in genocidal violence but also powerful affective resonances that govern how we interpret cultural representations of them. At the same time, it can be employed in frustratingly vague and counterproductively all-encompassing ways, unifying under a single umbrella concept what historically was a much more diverse phenomenon. Moreover,

---

8 My notion of the filter thus resembles, in part, Matthew Boswell's brief but insightful revision of Eaglestone's concept of the swerve in his reading of Littell's text: "Rather than constituting an avoidance of truth or the 'why,' such a 'swerve' might be regarded as a way of orientating a particular readerly (and literary) relationship to the 'why'" (194–95).

the label has a tendency to reify its referent, a problem inherent to the ways in which it has come to be used in the discourse on the Holocaust. Whereas the term "perpetrator" conventionally has been defined by what a person *does*, in the context of our current cultural understanding of the Third Reich and the Holocaust, it can also denote who one *is*; in other words, it is often used as a shorthand to designate a stable and unchanging category of person rather than as a variable signifier whose referent is located principally in actions and behavior in particular moments and contexts. This is particularly true for popular discourse and cultural depictions. With their conventional characterization of the men (and women) who perpetrated the Holocaust as abstract, mythical figures and their conflation of the seemingly incomprehensible intent, scale, and degree of the violence associated with the genocide—a quality that is often then given, as I discussed earlier, the affectively resonant but conceptually recondite term "evil"—with the human beings that played a role in the commission of that violence, such representations tend to attribute identity tautologically; in other words, a Holocaust perpetrator is identifiable by virtue of being defined as a Holocaust perpetrator.[9] In a sense, in this study I adopt such a shorthand myself; I investigate here depictions of the mind of the Holocaust perpetrator in texts that from the outset prominently denote the person or persons they feature as Holocaust perpetrators. The focus on the internal experience of such figures both in the texts themselves and in my evaluations of the texts thus converges more around questions of identity, self-understanding, and the mental and emotional incorporation and narration of one's history of

---

9 Raul Hilberg argues that the effects of having organized or committed mass violence transform the identity of the perpetrator after the fact in essential ways: "The process of destruction was deliberate, and that once he [the perpetrator] had stepped into this maelstrom, his deed would be indelible. In this sense, he would always be what he had been, even if he remained reticent or silent about what he had done" (ix). At the same time, however, Jürgen Matthäus warns against defining the people whom we designate as perpetrators exclusively through the particular acts that qualify them as such: "It can be assumed that adults, in becoming perpetrators, do not lose their other defining characteristics or sever their social ties unless one adopts a narrow, biologistic definition close to the old thesis of the homicidal maniac which, for all we know, applies to very few of the hundreds of thousands of agents of genocide. The more we restrict our analysis to the incriminating act, the greater the risk of severing causal and chronological connections with other, no less relevant aspects of the past" (210).

violence than it does on the actual contextual factors that contribute to the attribution of that figure as a perpetrator. In other words, we as readers (and I as a critic) accept that a figure is a Holocaust perpetrator because the text deems him one. This is, of course, counter to the ways that historians tend to define and classify perpetrators, which demonstrates an important distinction between the sources and methods of their scholarship and those of the cultural critic: whereas it is unlikely that, in the historical sources analyzed by historians, the persons referred to are considered within the context of a particular document to be perpetrators (or historically considered themselves to be such[10]), in cultural texts written after the Holocaust (and after the development of the very concept of the Holocaust perpetrator), this is a given. Historians thus have to identify their perpetrators; for cultural and literary critics, they come to us ready-made.

At the same time, however, it is important in the analysis of literary representations of perpetrators to be mindful of the ways in which historians have struggled to define in historical terms the concept of the Holocaust perpetrator. As the Holocaust historian Mark Roseman argues,

> Only in the last few years has the term "perpetrator" entered the vocabulary of studies of the Holocaust. Its appearance has been in some ways paradoxical. On the one hand, the deployment of the term—rather than the more neutral "functionary," or the less specifically Holocaust-related "Nazi"—is a sign that after fifty years the perpetrators are finally being taken seriously as a phenomenon. The term has justified itself in one sense, too, in identifying the "unsettling" (Alf Lüdtke) scope for individual decisions, initiative and energy evident all the way down the hierarchy. Responsibility, though unevenly shared, was nevertheless shared across the ranks. . . . On the other hand, the explosion of new research, and the discovery of the sheer diversity of the groups involved, has opened up to question as never before whether there is such a thing as *the* perpetrator. ("Beyond Conviction?" 93)

---

10 As Hilberg points out, "An administrator, clerk, or uniformed guard never referred to himself as a perpetrator" (ix).

Roseman points to the ways in which the institutionalization and widespread adoption of the concept of the "Holocaust perpetrator" both make it legible as a historical dynamic and reduce it to a simplified category that belies the historical specificity of and heterogeneity among the people to whom it is applied. In an effort to signal the complexity of the activities and agents that historians understand to qualify under the category of perpetration, Roseman conceptualizes the term along two axes:

> Horizontally, historians have recognized the huge diversity of institutions and organizations involved—the very significant number of civilian bodies (particularly in the Occupied East), the many military units, from the *Feldpolizei* to ordinary military regiments, the large range of different criminal and regular police units, and all this in addition to the more familiar Party and SS organizations. The result is to complicate enormously our sense of who a perpetrator was. . . . Moreover, historians have expanded their horizons vertically, too, in looking at individuals right down to the grass roots, instead of the narrow elite cadres to whom attention was previously restricted. The more we descend to ground level, the less distinctive the profile is. In that sense, the intensive search for the perpetrator has demonstrated that there *is* no single phenomenon. ("Beyond Conviction?" 94)

Here, Roseman highlights the ways in which diverse groups and individuals played a role—whether instrumental or minor, central or peripheral, recurrent or singular—at various junctures and stages of the operation of the "Final Solution." The two axes that he outlines here demonstrate both the breadth of the category—that it can be applied both to groups we conventionally associate with the implementation of the Judeocide (such as the SS) and to factions and individuals who until fairly recently have not been seen as culpable for it—and its depth, meaning that it can be applied throughout the entire length of the military and bureaucratic chain of command and the strata of German society (and, as demonstrated by the Ukrainian shooters in Littell's novel, the societies of the occupied countries as well). Such ubiquity and diversity with regard to the historical actors complicate attempts—whether on the part of scholars or of artists—to frame culpability and responsibility in unequivocal terms and to attribute a singular mentality to the mind of the Holocaust perpetrator (as, e.g., the title of this book implies).

In their introduction to the first issue of the *Journal of Perpetrator Research*, Kara Critchell et al., working along Roseman's vertical axis, provide a helpful taxonomy for distinguishing the kinds of people involved in the state-sanctioned perpetration of genocide (including, but not limited to, the Holocaust) and the types of actions in which they engage:

> Perpetration can be approached from at least three analytical perspectives: macro (top-level architects), meso (mid-level organizers), and micro (low-level killers). The macro level refers to the context of high political office: the structures and the context of the political helm that wields supreme authority inside a state and is responsible for the decision-making processes that launch mass killing. The meso level consists of those developments right below the highest level: mid-level political and administrative elites, the internal agencies that assume the tasks to divide labour and organize the machinery of killing, the (para-)military bosses who press buttons, and the mechanisms of mass mobilization for the destruction of the victim group. The micro level, then, is about the lowest socio-ecological level: the individuals who become involved in the violent process, either as direct or indirect perpetrators. (11)

The framework posited by Critchell et al. provides a useful shorthand for the more variegated landscape that Roseman sketches, allowing us to group individuals and institutions along his horizontal axis into three concentrated positions on his vertical one, thus providing the differentiation that Roseman calls for while at the same recognizing that even very diverse actors can be aggregated into general subgroups. Moreover, the three levels they delineate are helpful for thinking about the history of cultural representations of perpetrators as well. As I will briefly sketch out in part 1 of this book, initial attempts to read the mind of the perpetrator (along with the early historiography of the Holocaust and the Third Reich)[11] focused almost exclusively on the macro level of Hitler and his "henchmen," the major Party and military officials who were tried at Nuremberg. With the trial of Adolf Eichmann in 1961, this focus migrated to the meso level (even if the Israeli prosecutor Gideon Hausner tried to paint Eichmann as the decisive architect of the "Final Solution");[12] with Sereny's and Lanzmann's projects in the 1970s and 1980s, with the new perpetrator research of the 1990s and beyond,[13] and with some of the recent fiction depicting perpetrators, individuals at the micro level were also placed under scrutiny.

---

11 According to Claus-Christian W. Szejnmann, "Perpetrator historiography [in the late 1940s and early 1950s] uncritically followed the interpretation that blame and responsibility for the Holocaust lay with a few top Nazi leaders, in particular Hitler.... The spotlight on Hitler simplified the dynamics and complexities of Nazism, and the notion of an 'evil monster' diverted attention from the responsibilities of others" (30).

12 Matthäus writes that, during this time, historians like Hans Mommsen and Martin Broszat moved "analytical attention away from its 'Top Three'—Hitler, Himmler, Heydrich—towards different functional elites in the bureaucracy, military and judiciary, their interaction and, ultimately, towards German society at large" (205), while in the work of Raul Hilberg, "the middle-ranking bureaucrat stood out" (202).

13 Both Szejnmann and Matthäus date the emergence of what has been called the "new perpetrator research" to the early 1990s, "when mainstream scholarship and the public in Germany were ready to confront the National Socialist past head-on for the first time and debate it as never before" (Szejnmann 36) and a number of seminal texts were published that "put the problem of perpetrator motivation where it had never been before: at the top of the historiographic agenda" (Matthäus 206). In particular, Christopher Browning's pioneering work *Ordinary Men: Police Reserve Police Battalion 101 and the Final Solution in Poland* (1992) provided "a stunning revelation" (Matthäus 206) and "a real breakthrough" (Szejnmann 37) in its analysis of microlevel killers, although Szejnmann and Matthäus also mention other important interventions: Daniel J. Goldhagen's 1996 *Hitler's Willing Executioners: Ordinary Germans and the Holocaust*, which, though confirming "stereotypical and uncritical assumptions" (Matthäus 207) and "simplistic interpretations" (Szejnmann 38), provoked widespread public debate on the role of microlevel perpetrators in Germany; the "Crimes of the Wehrmacht" exhibit designed by the Hamburg Institute for Social Research (1995–99); and Götz Aly's *Endlösung: Völkerverschiebung und der Mord an den europäischen Juden* (1995). Szejnmann writes that "after Browning, Goldhagen and Aly had thrown down the gauntlet to their peers, Perpetrator Studies became a 'boom' subject amongst a new generation of historians" (40).

Roseman's conceptual axes of the extensive and pervasive existence of and diversity among perpetrators and the hierarchical taxonomy offered by the editors of the *Journal of Perpetrator Research* offer important distinctions and qualifications for the umbrella term "Holocaust perpetrator," allowing me to offer a more precise definition for the ways I will use the term throughout the book. By "perpetrators" I mean the people to whom historians ascribe responsibility for the implementation of the Holocaust, whether as important administrative figures who conceptualized and coordinated the "Final Solution," SS commandants and guards who supervised concentration and death camps, or lower-level soldiers and police who participated in mass shootings and other atrocities.[14] I use the term here to designate both well-known historical actors that figure in the cultural imagination as archetypes of evil and fictional characters based on these real-life perpetrators. Although, of course, Hitler himself belongs in the broader category of perpetration, I have consciously chosen to exclude representations of him from my study, as my focus is directed at the everyday men who played a concrete part in the actual implementation of the Judeocide (whether administratively or physically) rather than the iconic figures (the exception to this limitation being Eichmann, an ordinary perpetrator transformed into an icon). The image of Hitler in the contemporary cultural imagination, which posits him as the inhuman, ineffable embodiment of pure evil, exists on a very different plane than those in the fictional and nonfictional representations of the men who perpetrated the genocide on the ground. While a number of older and more recent texts, such as Timur Vermes's 2012 novel *Er ist wieder da* (*Look Who's Back*, 2014) and the David Wnendt film version from 2015, have attempted to demythologize and humanize the figure of Hitler, the challenge such representations face are

---

14 Throughout this book, I refer to perpetrators (as both characters and historical persons) mostly with the masculine pronoun. Although recent historical research into Holocaust perpetration by Gudrun Schwarz, Wendy Lower, Susanne Luhmann, and others has demonstrated that a not insignificant number of German women were involved in the perpetration of the Holocaust in various ways and to various degrees, historically speaking the number of female perpetrators was miniscule compared to the number of male perpetrators. Moreover, few literary and filmic representations of perpetrators that have attempted to explore the interiority of their protagonists have featured female perpetrators. (Pulp and popular depictions of female Nazis from the 1950s on have pointedly not depicted the subjective perspective of these characters.)

quite different than those encountered by the texts I analyze here. Moreover, a number of insightful studies have already addressed fictional and nonfictional depictions of Hitler, including Alvin H. Rosenfeld's *Imagining Hitler* (1985), Ron Rosenbaum's *Explaining Hitler: The Search for the Origins of His Evil* (1998), Gavriel David Rosenfeld's *The World Hitler Never Made: Alternate History and the Memory of Nazism* (2005) and *Hi Hitler!: How the Nazi Past Is Being Normalized in Contemporary Culture* (2015), and Michael Butter's *The Epitome of Evil: Hitler in American Fiction, 1939–2002* (2009).

Narrative Dynamics, Devices, and Conventions

In my analysis of the various ways in which filtering strategies operate in fictional and nonfictional representations of Nazi perpetrators, I find particularly useful the methodological tools of narrative theory, which gives scholars a rich vocabulary and conceptual apparatus for investigating how the consciousness of a character is constructed through narration. By looking at how texts employ such narrative techniques as voice, or what we designate less technically as narrative perspective, and focalization, meaning the ways in which third-person narratives depict events through the consciousness of particular characters, along with such dynamics as narrative reliability, reader identification, and the cognitive operation of inferring and projecting another's mind, I analyze how the texts structure the consciousness and awareness of their Holocaust perpetrators and in the process mediate to the reader particular interpretations of the perpetrators' thoughts, motivations, memories, and self-image (either—in the case of some of the fictional texts—during the act of violence or afterward, in the narration of that violence). At the same time, I show how particular narrative devices and textual conventions serve to suppress, conceal, or camouflage the character's consciousness, effectively impeding the kinds of identification initially promised by the text's intimate rendering of the character's subjective thoughts. In each chapter, I identify different manifestations of filtering that facilitate a particular understanding of the role of the perpetrator in our cultural narratives of Holocaust violence. The complex operations of disclosure and obscuration mobilized by such filtering mechanisms thus engage the reader in regulated exercises of identification in which she is both aligned with and alienated from the perpetrator's subjective perspective.

In particular, three narrative dynamics are integral both to my corpus of texts and to the trajectory of historical and aesthetic connections that I perceive in it: the relationship between fiction and nonfiction, the cognitive processes of Theory of Mind and mind-reading at work in these texts, and the operations of empathy and identification on the part of the reader. All three of these dynamics have been the focus of recent narratological theorization; my investigation of how they play out in the chosen texts demonstrates the advantages of (re)considering these works from our present cultural and scholarly moment.

Fiction/Nonfiction

The first narrative dynamic that informs my analysis of representations of the perpetrators' perspective is the discursive distinction between fiction and nonfiction. In delineating my study according to these two major types of discourse, I focus on how the generic conventions and limitations of each determine in a specific manner its psychological and narrative portrayals of its subjects. To be sure, fiction and nonfiction are two distinct discursive orientations that are distinguished by their respective referential relationships, their generic and narrative properties, and the practices of reading they necessitate. In particular, they diverge with regard to their epistemological and ontological perspectives vis-à-vis the history of the Holocaust (direct historical reference vs. fictional license), their particular temporal standpoints within Holocaust discourse, and their diversiform techniques for rendering their protagonists (principally homodiegetic or so-called first-person narration vs. heterodiegetic or third-person narration). Such aspects predicate in a specific manner each text's psychological and narrative portrayal of the mind of the Holocaust perpetrator; it is thus important not to conflate fictional representations with nonfictional ones.[15] At the same time, there are compelling reasons for considering these two types of violent narratives as part of a common cultural endeavor. First, both groups of texts strive to humanize their perpetrator subjects and in

---

15 According to Brian Richardson, "No matter how closely it tries to imitate nonfictional discourses, narrative fiction is always a very different kind of speech act. Its functions, intentions, and effects diverge substantially from those of nonfiction. Nonfiction is falsifiable and can be tested against other nonfictional accounts of the same events; fiction can never be falsified by real-world sources" ("Antimimetic, Unnatural, and Postmodern Narrative Theory" 22–23).

this way engage their readers by providing an unconventional lens through which they can consider the events of the Holocaust. Moreover, both manifest and illustrate the tensions and exigencies that reflexively arise with narrative attempts to depict the consciousness of Nazi perpetrators, provoking critical questions about the ethical and representational nature of such narratives. Second, although they are often seen as diametrically opposed, these two discursive orientations—the fictional and the nonfictional—are mutually constitutive and informative. As I argue above (and will discuss in further detail in the introductions to parts 1 and 2), there is in fact an unmistakable relationship between the two in both historical and aesthetic terms. Not only am I able to trace a rough historical trajectory in representations of the consciousness of Nazis, whereby the wave of nonfictional biographies of the 1960s and 1970s that followed the trials of perpetrators in Israel and Germany gradually gave way to the boom in fictional portraits that began in the 1990s, but I also find that representations of the mind of fictional Holocaust perpetrators share some of the aesthetic qualities and narrative frameworks found in nonfictional attempts to render and understand the mind of real-life perpetrators.

The connections between fiction and nonfiction are conventionally assumed to be unidirectional; that is, fiction is presumed to take up and transform the referential narratives that circulate in the real world. This is particularly the case with Holocaust fiction, which invariably derives to some degree from famous and lesser-known nonfictional narratives of the experiences of victims, survivors, perpetrators, bystanders, and other implicated parties. Thus, for example, Martin Amis consciously fashioned his fictional doctor Odilo Unverdorben after the former Auschwitz doctors whom the psychiatrist Robert Jay Lifton studies in *The Nazi Doctors: Medical Killing and the Psychology of Genocide* (1986). Moreover, as I will discuss in a moment, fiction models itself on the kinds of intersubjective encounters—particularly those that involve inferring and projecting the mind of another—common to nonfiction, particularly literary journalism. Little work has been done on the phenomenon of influence in the other direction, that is, from fiction to nonfiction. However, as recent narrative theory has shown, the links between fictional and nonfictional modes of writing are much stronger than conventionally assumed in literary studies, especially in the subdiscipline of narratology. According to Suzanne Keen, "A common sort of narrativity is shared by fictional and nonfictional narrative texts, especially memoir, biography and autobiography, and *testimonio*, as well as narrative history" (13), even though their formal similarities "have typically been either over-looked or glossed over" (10). Moreover, nonfictional discourse, while referential, is not the organic and inartificial antipode to fiction that it is often assumed to be; as Ina Schabert argues, "The composition of a factual as well as that of a fictional text is controlled by a concept of its author, a theory, a prejudice, a convention, a myth of coherence" (7). In other words, according to Monika Fludernik, referential discourse (which she calls "factual narration") often exhibits a "constructed and carefully crafted quality . . . [that] allows for, though it does not regularly invite, an attitude of aesthetic appreciation" (122). Fludernik contends that narrative theory in particular has neglected the study of factual narrative, which constitutes in her view "a missing narratological paradigm" (117); "in the spirit of a prolegomena" (117), she calls for "a poetics of factual narration" that

> may include a variety of subjects such as consideration of structural shaping (with moments of suspense and other factors of information management), stylistic issues, sound patterns, imagery and strategies of repetition, periphrasis or syntactic features like inversion and the choice of tense, all the way down to the use of dialogue or focalization (providing access to people's minds). (122)

A number of features that Fludernik cites (and that are conventionally associated with fiction) are at work in the corpus of nonfictional texts investigated here, including "structural shaping," style, repetition, dialogue, and focalization, along with a number of aspects she does not name, such as experimentation with voice and generic convention. Thus, while the influence of nonfiction on fiction may be more obvious, nonfiction also adopts many of the strategies we conventionally ascribe to fiction in its aesthetic shaping and narrative rendering of the referential world.

Mind-Reading and Theory of Mind

Particularly the last issue Fludernik names, the facilitation of "access to people's minds," constitutes the second narrative dynamic I investigate in this study, as it directly relates to the ways in which fictional and nonfictional texts each approach the question of the interiority of their subjects. In this, I follow David Herman, who disputes prevalent notions in classical narratology that hold that fictional representations of consciousness are vastly different from our imagination of actual minds:

> From one direction, dichotomous treatments of fictional and actual minds can be questioned via research suggesting that readers' knowledge of fictional minds is mediated by the same kinds of reasoning protocols—namely, reasoning about people's *reasons for acting*—that mediate encounters with everyday minds. In this sense, fictional minds are accessible but not transparent. A second argument, trending in the opposite direction, can also be grounded in recent work in the sciences of the mind. Now the claim is that, contrary to the assumptions of Exceptionality, people do in fact experience others' minds, encountering the I-orginarity of others in everyday settings as well as fictional narratives. Everyday minds are not transparent, but they are accessible. ("Introduction" 11).

As Herman argues (and as is borne out by cognitive science), analogous processes of apprehending the minds of others are at work in fiction and nonfiction (even though the resulting minds differ with regard to their actual reference in the real world). Such operations are endemic to narrative in general, which "functions as a resource for constructing one's own as well as other minds" (Herman, "Storytelling and the Sciences of Mind" 308).[16] In particular, recent work in cognitive narratology has demonstrated the importance in both discursive orientations of what cognitive scientists call Theory of Mind (ToM). According to Bertram F. Malle and Jess Scon Holbrook,

---

16 Stefan Iversen takes issue with part of Herman's argument, asserting that, while there are in fact similarities between real and fictional minds, how we apprehend each of them differs in essential ways: "But saying that fictional minds are not the only kind of mind to which we have access through attribution is not the same as saying that our understandings of fictional and real minds are completely similar. Other differences may still be in effect—for instance, differences resulting from the fact that the fictional mind is invented and the real mind is not" (146).

Most fundamentally, ToM refers to the network of concepts and assumptions people make about what "minds" are and how they relate to behaviour. Central elements in this network include the concepts of agency and intentionality, the distinction between observable behaviour and unobservable mental states, and distinctions among a number of specific mental states, such as belief, desire, intention, and various emotions. . . . ToM is not a set of cultural beliefs about mind and behaviour. Rather, it comprises a conceptual framework, a set of fundamental distinctions, requisite for developing any cultural beliefs about how minds and behaviour work. . . . ToM provides the conceptual assumptions and distinctions on which a variety of psychological processes (inference, simulation, empathy, etc.) rely, and concepts and processes together constitute the person's ability to grasp mental states. (630)

ToM thus indicates both the ability to interpret and explain (correctly or incorrectly) others' actions by attributing to them particular mental states and the operation of that capacity; it is not to be confused with any particular individual's "theory" or narrative of another person's mind, meaning the given product of the employment of that facility. The routine functioning of ToM is known in cognitive psychology as "mind-reading"; humans deemed neurotypical engage effortlessly in the process of mind-reading in everyday social and private settings primarily on an unconscious level but also at times on a conscious one.[17] Moreover, as narrative theorist Lisa Zunshine

---

17 According to Malle and Holbrook, "An emergent topic is the question of whether ToM is employed primarily consciously or unconsciously. If ToM is the conceptual framework on which a number of different psychological tools rely, then the answer is twofold. As a conceptual framework, ToM is normally unconscious (though it can be made conscious by specifically asking people about their conceptual assumptions). Among the cognitive mechanisms that operate on those concepts, some are conscious, some are not. Among the conscious ones, we can list active simulation of the other's mental states, search for prior knowledge about the behaviour, the agent, or the context, and specific attempts to detect subtle signs in the agent's outward behaviour that might reveal inward states. The list of unconscious processes is longer: tracking gaze and body orientation, parsing the behaviour stream into intention-relevant

argues, ToM is an integral part of the functioning of literature—particularly fiction, although her insights can easily be applied to nonfiction as well—both on the part of the reader, who reads the minds of the characters whom she encounters in a text, and on the part of narrators and characters themselves, who infer the minds of other characters:

> One preliminary implication of applying what we know about ToM to our study of fiction is that it makes literature as we know it possible. The very process of making sense of what we read appears to be grounded in our ability to invest the flimsy verbal constructions that we generously call "characters" with a potential for a variety of thoughts, feelings, and desires and then to look for the "cues" that would allow us to guess at their feelings and thus predict their actions. Literature pervasively capitalizes on and stimulates Theory of Mind mechanisms that had evolved to deal with real people, even as on some level readers do remain aware that fictive characters are not real people at all. (10)

As Zunshine reminds us, the conclusions that readers and characters draw from their exercises in mind-reading may be faulty, incomplete, or downright erroneous; in fact, the deficient or inaccurate deployment of mind-reading can make the types of conflicts on which literature thrives possible. For that reason, Zunshine points out the essential difference between the process of mind-reading or ToM, which cognitive scientists consider successful when functionally operative, and the result that derives from it, which may or may not accurately identify the mental states of the person in question: "Mind-reading is thus effortless in the sense that we 'intuitively' connect people's behavior to their mental states . . . although our subsequent description of these mental states could run a broad gamut from perceptively accurate to profoundly mistaken" (16).

Throughout this book, I will refer to ToM and mind-reading as operations that undergird the endeavor on the part of the texts' authors, interlocutors,

---

units, empathy by emotional contagion, reading of facial and body expressions that transparently indicate the underlying mental state, and projection of one's own beliefs and perceptions onto another person" (631).

and narrators to deduce and represent the minds of the perpetrators they struggle to understand. As cognitive scientists Glenn R. Reeder and David Trafimow argue, as humans we deploy mind-reading to attribute motivation and causality to another person's often incomprehensible actions: "Perceiving a motive enables the perceiver to make sense of behavior patterns that might otherwise appear as random 'noise'" (107). The exercises in reading the perpetrators' mindset and motives represented in the texts under investigation here are thus connected to a larger project of interpretation that, by elucidating possible causal and motivational factors, aims to ascertain how such men could involve themselves in genocide. In nonfiction, mind-reading is taken up by the author-interviewers and author-interpreters, who actively endeavor to delineate the ethical and experiential contours of the men whom they undertake to analyze; in fiction, on the other hand, the exercise in mind-reading is conducted by the perpetrator himself, who struggles to ascertain and mediate his own mind (or who, as in Amis's *Time's Arrow*, may be dissociated from the perpetrator consciousness and forced to interpret or narrate his experience from the outside). I follow the definition of "mind" put forth by David Herman, who views it as "the nexus of brain, body, and environment or world" ("Storytelling and the Sciences of Mind" 317) that "is ongoingly accomplished in and through its production and interpretation" (308). In this way, I recognize mind not as a concrete, independent object that exists prior to its narration but rather as an entity that is constructed through the efforts of the interpreter and framed by particular psychological and cultural assumptions. My use of the terms "Theory of Mind" and "mind-reading" thus underscores the fact that the effort of apprehending and mediating the mind of another involves processes of interpretation based on a range of verbal, corporeal, gestural, and behavioral cues. My analysis of the construction of the mind of the perpetrator in fiction and nonfiction aims to be cognizant of the cognitive processes behind judgments about others' characters, attitudes, beliefs, and desires. At the same time, however, I do not apply specific aspects and theoretical paradigms from cognitive science so much as foreground the role of interpretation and construction in textual attempts to comprehend the mindset of persons whose actions challenge ethical and moral norms. In the case of nonfiction, the mind of the perpetrator is constituted through the interlocutor's intersubjective engagement with the subject in face-to-face encounters or through the interpreter's intensive analysis of his public performance. In the fictional texts, it comes into being in the—often alienated or dissociated—narration of the perpetrator himself. In each portrait, what emerges is not a mechanical or positivistic reconstruction of the perpetrator's mental life but the creative production and figuration of the mental gestalt of a man whose actions have made him seemingly alien and unfathomable.

Empathetic Identification

The third narrative dynamic on which my analysis focuses is the phenomenon of empathy. As I argue throughout this book, the narrative mediation of the mind of the perpetrator has become an increasingly accepted mode through which the post-Holocaust reader can engage imaginatively with the legacy of the Holocaust. By virtue of its ability to shock and outrage, such a representational approach can perhaps break through the sense of paralysis and numbness that one often experiences when confronted with the sheer scale and horror of the Holocaust. However, in rendering the mind of the perpetrator in a more direct manner (as do the fictional texts) or offering a more oblique window into the perpetrator's psychology (as in the journalistic works), both modes of representation also run the real risk of allowing or even encouraging their readers to identify with the perpetrator-protagonists. The inherent potential for identification and empathy posed by this corpus of texts (a danger that, as I discussed earlier, Sereny perceives also in face-to-face encounters with real-life perpetrators) provokes critical questions about the ethical status of such narratives: What happens to readers when they perceive the events of the Holocaust through the ethically challenging and even transgressive perspective of its perpetrators? How do texts that feature such uncomfortable and morally questionable perspectives stimulate particular affective processes, such as character identification and empathy? If, as Jenni Adams argues, the corpus of Holocaust literature compels a "conventional pattern of identification . . . in which the reader identifies with the victim" ("Reading (as) Violence" 34), what happens to this structure of identification when the narrator or focalized character is a perpetrator rather than a victim? In rendering the mind of the perpetrator, how do narratives negotiate the risk of allowing or even encouraging their readers to identify with the perpetrator-protagonists?

In a 2016 article in *Narrative* ("Empathetic Identification and the Mind of the Holocaust Perpetrator in Fiction"), I attempt to address these questions by considering how fictional texts construct and compel empathetic and identificatory responses to narrators and characters who are Holocaust perpetrators. Drawing on recent research on narrative empathy by Suzanne Keen, Patrick Colm Hogan, Eric Leake, Fritz Breithaupt, and others, I suggest that we regard the issue of empathetic identification in representations of perpetrators not as a total or uniform phenomenon that implies either full alignment or wholesale rejection but rather as a complex issue that can refer to a number of related phenomena in an imbricated field of response that fluctuate throughout the reading process. I further propose a taxonomy of five modalities of identification along cognitive, emotional, and ethical axes that can be used to describe not only degrees of identificatory response but also experiences of blocked identification, disidentification, or alienation. The categories of identification I outline here have been developed specifically with regard to fiction; however, they can be applied, with some modification (which I will discuss in the introduction to part 1), to nonfictional depictions of perpetrators as well.

On the extreme end of the field of response is located what I term *existential identification*, which involves the reader's basic recognition of the perpetrator as a human agent involved in particular historical circumstances. For any given representation of a perpetrator's consciousness to function, the reader must at a minimum partake in existential identification; by putting the perpetrator's experience at the center of the narrative and by provoking questions regarding his motivations for his violent behavior, the text thus makes possible the reader's recognition of the basic human qualities of the perpetrator-character. In a sense, almost any narrative depiction of the consciousness of a victimizer, even when deploying satire or unnatural (antimimetic) distancing devices, will engage the reader's existential identification, for such representations locate the character at the center of his own story and thus require that his experience be seen as more than one-dimensional. In this way, the very act of mediating or focalizing the perpetrator's perspective (i.e., presenting events as filtered through his consciousness) compels some degree of empathetic identification on the part of the reader.

I call the second possible aspect of the reader's relationship to the perpetrator *perspectival identification*, which refers to the measure of the reader's readiness to view the events of the narrative through the eyes of the perpetrator-protagonist and to exclude some or all alternate points of view. Part of the effect of perspectival identification, as my term suggests, is achieved through the text's assignment of narrative perspective, or voice, and how this perspective illuminates the mind of narrators and characters. The operations of homo- and autodiegetic (first-person) narration and—in texts that employ heterodiegetic (third-person) narration—focalization, by virtue of their narrow and sometimes highly manipulative lens, can have a significant impact on how a reader views the events of a narrative, which then can have bearing on the degree of her identification with the narrator or characters. What this means in terms of narratives that are narrated by or focalize the perspective of perpetrators is that certain experiences associated with the Holocaust—the bureaucratic administration of the genocide, the perpetrators' experience of mass killings—are narrated at the expense of others, namely, the radically opposite experience of the victims. In short, these texts ask us to accept the perpetrator as a witness to the events of the Holocaust and to follow his chronicle of them, a form of acceptance that has been standard practice in historiography but has been slow in coming to literary explorations of the Holocaust.

My third type of response is a subcategory of perspectival identification I call *reliability-dependent identification*, which pertains to the extent of the reader's belief in and evaluation of the perpetrator's version of the events, phenomena that are related to issues of narrative reliability and causality. Reliability-dependent identification intensifies the process initiated by perspectival identification: already implicit in the reader's readiness to assume the perpetrator's viewpoint is a degree of willingness to give a measure of credence to the perpetrator's account and understanding of his history and his willingness or ability both to give a factually accurate account of his participation in crimes and to acknowledge on a psychological level his complicity in them. The question of reliability inheres in particular in texts that feature perpetrator-narrators, whose accounts we receive from the beginning with skepticism by virtue of their very status as victimizers. The reader's recognition of the Holocaust perpetrator as a violator of moral and ethical standards may rely at least in part on the knowledge she brings to the text, which allows her to compare the perpetrator's description and interpretation of the events with accounts of victims and historians and to identify moments in which the perpetrator fudges the facts, mischaracterizes the events, or downplays particular experiences to defer responsibility for them. For this reason, issues of unreliability in texts narrated by Holocaust perpetrators are what Per Krogh Hansen has identified as extratextual in nature in that they rely on the reader's ability to recognize "the narrator's misinterpretation of commonly known historical facts" (334). At the same time, representations of perpetrators may also contain aspects of intratextual unreliability, which relates to internal tensions generated by the discrepancy between the narrator's professed account and interpretation of events and cues supplied through his narration by the implied author that call his version into question.

The fourth aspect concerns the degree of the reader's emotional alignment with the perpetrator-narrator's thoughts, feelings, and interpretations of the events, which I term *affective identification*. This form takes into account the reader's emotional engagement (and even identification) with characters with whom she presumably does not share an emotional state and for whom she might feel significant moral repugnance, such as genocidal killers. One way that texts encourage such emotional reaching out is by encouraging the reader's affective identification with the perpetrator: not with regard to his feelings about his crimes (although such identification may, of course, take place in this area, especially if the perpetrator displays reluctance to commit the atrocities or remorse for having done so) but for his emotional life outside his identity as a victimizer, which is much more available to the reader for identification. Affective identification for perpetrators can furthermore be facilitated by the text in such a way that the reader suddenly becomes aware that she is advocating for the perpetrator as the ostensible hero, which can cause discomfort and a degree of cognitive dissonance. In particular, she may find herself rooting for him in his attempt after the war to escape detection for his crimes; the realization that one is holding one's breath and hoping for the escape of the villain can be in such situations quite disconcerting and destabilizing.

Finally, I call the fifth possible form of reader identification with the perpetrator *ideological identification*, which refers to the strength of the reader's alignment with the perpetrator's moral and ethical worldview and his justifications for his own behavior. This aspect lies at the opposite end of the field from existential identification and involves a form of identification that undergirds all the other aspects I have listed. In other words, if a reader identifies with the perpetrator-protagonist along ideological or ethical lines, then she will be more willing to view the events through his perspective, give credence to his account of them, and align emotionally with him. As Jenni Adams astutely argues, alarm regarding the literary representation of the consciousness and narrative perspective of Holocaust perpetrators is concerned principally with the dangers of ideological identification, which she describes as "an unspoken anxiety regarding contagion: the fear that the reader, disarmed by the illusory understanding offered by the text, is susceptible to infection by Nazi ideas. . . . This fear of contagion arguably underlies the unease surrounding imaginative engagements with perpetrator perspectives, engagements potentially facilitated by the techniques of narrative fiction—rendering such fiction a particular ground for ethical contention" ("Reading (as) Violence" 28–29). With regard to the representations of Holocaust perpetrators I investigate here, which reflect the recognizable pedagogical and ethical aims of the implied author even as they flirt with transgressive depictions of perpetrators, ideological identification exists only as a potentially dangerous but abstract specter and not as a likely possibility for the reader. Barring the potential of a gross misreading of these narratives on the part of the reader (a possibility that is real, but one that the texts' authors attempt to prevent through paratextual explanation and contextualization), such ideological identification on the part of the reader could only be made possible by texts that attempt to achieve fascist or antisemitic aims or otherwise glorify violence or genocidal hatred. Although critics have objected to the perpetrator narratives on the grounds that they might "infect" the reader with dangerous Nazi ideas about racial domination and violence, I think the opposite is the more likely danger: that the humanizing representations of perpetrators will be taken by the reader to be naturalized psychological portraits of individuals and that she will fail to see the ideological dimensions of the perpetration of the Holocaust at all.

The five phenomena I have elucidated here engage a range of cognitive, affective, and ethical dimensions that are often subsumed under the broader categories of empathetic identification; by disaggregating them we are able to see the ways in which readers can connect in differing ways to particular characters and their histories of violence at various moments of the reading experience. One can imagine for each of these identificatory phenomena a potential range of response, meaning that any given reader might experience with any given text intense identification in one area, weak identification in a second, and disidentification or alienation in a third, underscoring the potential variability and complexity of identification from one reader and from one representation to the next and demonstrating the dialectical character of identification. Moreover, some of these aspects of identification the reader brings to the text, and some develop at particular junctures of the reading process in response to narrative strategies that encourage or facilitate reader response. A reader's overall identificatory response to perpetrator-characters thus may depend not only on the strength of her alignment in the five areas I have elucidated but also on particular moments or stages in the narrative's progression that facilitate or retard—particularly as a result of filtering mechanisms—such connection. For this reason, to assume that identification is either fully present or wholly absent disregards the dynamic character of narrative progression, the variability and complexity of the relationship between readers and characters, and the idiosyncratic nature of an individual reader's engagement with representations of the inner experience of perpetrators.

By means of the complex operations of revelation and occlusion made possible through what I identify as strategies of filtering, each of the texts under investigation here involves the reader in carefully controlled exercises in identification and alienation, enabling her to engage in complex negotiations with the history of the Holocaust without allowing her to fully identify with the perpetrator and his actions and emotions. The reader thus moves back and forth through the field of possible identificatory response, finding herself at some moments empathetically aligned with the perpetrator's perspective and self-understanding, a cognitive and affective position that facilitates an understanding of how an ordinary person becomes an agent of mass murder, and at other times distanced from it, which creates a space for critical ethical reflection. These fictional and nonfictional representations of the consciousness of Holocaust perpetrators walk a treacherous tightrope stretched between a mode of identification that naturalizes the mind behind state-sanctioned racial violence and a view of Holocaust perpetrators that reifies them as abstract embodiments of radical evil. It is at times a razor-thin line, to which the potential for dangerous identification with genocidal murderers and failed ethical empathy is an inherent tension. But when mobilized in ethically successful ways, such textual exercises in identification and alienation become models for ambivalent empathy, allowing readers to engage in innovative ways with the uncomfortable moral questions provoked by considering the events of the Holocaust from the victimizer's point of view and rendering possible new modes of evaluating the human dimension of the perpetration of genocide.[18]

Overview of Chapters

This study, which considers representations of the perspective and mindset of Holocaust perpetrators according to two major types of discourse—the fictional and the nonfictional—is divided into two parts. Part 1 investigates canonical and lesser-known nonfictional works that attempt to trace the history of the Holocaust through the narrated experiences of individual actors in the National Socialist program of extermination of European Jewry. Part 2 examines four prominent fictional texts that take considerable imaginative license in their depiction of the perspective of their invented perpetrator-narrators. I have eschewed in the organization of the chapters a top-down, symmetrical approach, preferring instead a more diversiform mode of configuration that emerges from my analysis of the texts themselves. For that reason, while one of the chapters (chapter 2) will focus on only a single text, the others will employ a comparative method in analyzing two or more texts alongside one another.

The two chapters of part 1 are concerned with the biographical construction of real-life perpetrators produced during the period of the development of Holocaust discourse in the 1960s and 1970s. The nonfictional texts analyzed in this part of the study feature attempts by journalists, intellectuals, and a clergyman to create portraits of real-life perpetrators either through

---

18 As Hanna Meretoja argues, such exercises in what she terms "perspective-taking" (a term that she links to my notion of empathetic identification) are "not only about feeling with or for the other, but also about imagining the processes that lead certain individuals to act in certain ways. So long as we cannot imagine the experience of the subjects who took part in the events, we tend to regard atrocities like genocides as simply incomprehensible or monstrous. By imagining the experiences of the perpetrators and bystanders, we are more likely to be able to engage in complex ethical reflection on how such events concern us, implicate us, and place ethical obligations on us, instead of thinking that what they did has nothing to do with us" (131).

the medium of the face-to-face interview or through journalistic analyses of the documents and testimony presented at the Eichmann trial. In comparison to the large number of Holocaust survivors who generated verbal and written testimony, very few Holocaust perpetrators spoke publicly (outside the courtroom, at least) about their participation in Nazi crimes, and even fewer wrote autobiographical texts about their experience. The resounding silence on the part of former perpetrators can be attributed to a number of factors, chief among them their refusal to acknowledge the extent of their participation in genocidal crimes and the resistance of the available narrative frames of autobiographical discourse to express the history of the subject's engagement with violence. In the absence of candid autobiographical examinations written by the perpetrators themselves, important figures in the discourse on Holocaust memory, such as Hannah Arendt and Gitta Sereny, undertook earnest attempts to illuminate the mind and motivations of individual perpetrators. In the introduction to part 1, I trace the historical trajectory of such nonfictional explorations of the inner life of Holocaust perpetrators and introduce some of the formal and structural strategies deployed by this mode of writing, which include both conventions commonly associated with fiction and aspects germane to journalistic and nonfictional discourse, such as the intersubjective relationship between author and subject. As I show in the two chapters of this part, their interviews and analyses of perpetrators not only provide a nuanced perspective on the inner life of the men who implemented the Holocaust but also demonstrate the critical interventional role of the interviewer or interpreter in the perpetrators' performances of self-disclosure. My analysis focuses in particular on how the practice of mind-reading and frameworks of knowledge, interpretation, and narration employed in these texts function as filtering strategies that alternately reveal and obscure the perpetrator's consciousness.

Chapter 1 focuses on three of the numerous biographical portraits of Adolf Eichmann that appeared shortly after his 1961 trial in Israel: Hannah Arendt's *Eichmann in Jerusalem: A Report on the Banality of Evil* (1963), Harry Mulisch's 1962 *De Zaak 40/61: Een Reportage* (*Criminal Case 40/61, the Trial of Adolf Eichmann: An Eyewitness Account* [2005]), and William L. Hull's *The Struggle for a Soul* (1963). My analysis of the three texts both illuminates the diversity in the interpretations of Eichmann's mind based on his statements and behavior during and shortly after his trial and contextualizes these portraits within more recent research by Bettina Stangneth and others that highlights the ways in which Eichmann self-consciously performed versions of his identity for different audiences. Arendt and Mulisch, both of whom were very well-known writers and intellectuals, covered the Eichmann trial as journalists and produced illuminating accounts of Eichmann designed to dispute the public image of him as the embodiment of monstrous evil. However, while Arendt focuses narrowly on Eichmann's mind as a product of his clichéd use of Nazi language, Mulisch looks to Eichmann's face for physiognomic clues about his character. Hull, a Christian missionary in Israel, provided spiritual counsel to Eichmann in the weeks before his execution and wrote his account shortly afterward, framing his engagement as a desperate attempt to rehabilitate Eichmann's soul. I argue that Eichmann functions in the book as a surface projection for that which Hull desperately yearns to locate in the Nazi war criminal but also is relieved *not* to find: a Christian conscience. Taken collectively, these three texts show radically disparate perspectives on Eichmann's mind and demonstrate the extent to which this figure has become a screen onto which postwar culture discharges its anxieties and desires.

In chapter 2, I investigate Gitta Sereny's journalistic masterwork *Into That Darkness: An Examination of Conscience* (1974), which constructs the biography of Franz Stangl, the commandant of Sobibór and Treblinka. Sereny's book is based in part on her extensive research on the two extermination camps (about which at the time relatively little documentation existed) and her interviews with the few survivors of the camps, those camp guards who were willing to speak about their experiences, and Stangl's family members. But the central focus of the book is an extensive set of interviews Sereny conducted with Stangl in the spring of 1971, while he was in a Düsseldorf prison serving a life sentence for joint responsibility for the murder of at least nine hundred thousand people. *Into That Darkness* thus seeks to provide a mosaic-like image of the mind of a man who supervised the gassings of hundreds of thousands of European Jews. My analysis focuses on the ethical implications of Sereny's intersubjective encounter with Stangl and her active role in shaping his biography. In particular, I investigate how she frames Stangl's story according to specific masterplots—that of the detective story and the confessional form—that allow her to construct his experience as a narrative of eventual ethical epiphany.

In the second part of the book, I turn to the depiction of the consciousness of Holocaust perpetrators in fictional discourse, a mode of representation that, as the temporal distance from the events of the Holocaust increases, has become more prominently employed by writers seeking alternative entry points into the topic in an attempt to puncture the sanctified aura that has come to characterize it. In the introduction to part 2, I argue that well-known fictional representations of the mind of perpetrators, most of which have appeared within the last two decades, take up and transform some of the structural devices of the nonfictional texts from the 1960s, 1970s, and early 1980s that I discuss in part 1, particularly the figure of the interlocutor or interpreter. I further introduce some of the pertinent narrative dimensions of this body of literature, such as the dynamics of narrative unreliability and the tension between mimetic and antimimetic modes of fictional representation. In the two chapters of this part, I investigate four prominent texts that feature the narrative voice of perpetrators, all of which, on account of the transgressive quality of their imaginative impulse, caused a critical sensation when they were first published. Each of the four texts employs particular strategies of obscuration that operate to filter the mind of its narrator, preventing the perpetrator from fully understanding or acknowledging his motives for his crimes and in the process handicapping the reader in the same endeavor as well.

Chapter 3 concentrates on one older and one more recent fictional representation of the consciousness of perpetrators, Edgar Hilsenrath's *The Nazi and the Barber* (*Der Nazi und der Friseur*), published in English translation in 1971 and in the original German in 1977, and Jonathan Littell's novel *The Kindly Ones* (2009; *Les Bienveillantes*, 2006). Both texts, I argue, utilize filtering strategies in the form of a doubled or mediated narrative perspective. Hilsenrath's satirical novel is narrated by Max Schulz, a member of the SS who, after the war, takes on the identity of Itzig Finkelstein, his former best friend and one of his many Jewish victims, and narrates his tale from the perspective of a Holocaust survivor. Max thus purposely filters the story of his violent past through the radically opposite voice of the innocent victim. Hilsenrath self-consciously highlights both the text's construction of this filter and Max's hubristic assumption of the voice of the victim by employing a heterogeneous narrative strategy that plays with perspective and focalization. The narrative situation functions as an analogue to the novel's plot, reproducing on the level of narration the interminable processes of equivocal transmutation and escape that Max undergoes as a character. Littell's text, on the other hand, provides the most detailed and direct fictional representation of the mind of the perpetrator to date with its mimetic, first-person, detailed narrative of an SS officer. The novel's complex narrative approach foregrounds the ways in which fictional narratives of perpetration require a certain intermediary filter as an interface between historical and imaginative discourse. Critics have identified two dominant discourses in *The Kindly Ones*, the historical-testimonial and the personal-sexual. I locate in the novel a third order of discourse as well: the discourse of dreams, hallucinations, and repressed knowledge, all of which seriously mitigate Aue's status for us as a reliable narrator and infect the historical eyewitness discourse, thereby complicating the larger historical narrative and the documentary effect it produces.

In chapter 4, I take a close look at two texts by Martin Amis that foreground the narrative perspective of Holocaust perpetrators. *Time's Arrow* (1991) tells the story of a German doctor at Auschwitz and his postwar life in the United States under an assumed identity. I locate the filter in this text in its narrative anomalies, which include both the technique of inverted temporal narration and the dissociated narrative perspective of the perpetrator-protagonist, whereby the narrator is split apart from the consciousness of the body in which he is housed. With these disruptive narrative strategies, *Time's Arrow* creates for the reader a window into the mind of the perpetrator, albeit one that is distorted by the narrative's temporal pathology and the narrator's inability or unwillingness to recognize the horrific events in which he participates. In his 2014 novel *The Zone of Interest*, Amis departs from this strategy of dissociated narration within one perpetrator-figure to distribute, in a much more mimetic manner, the narrative voice among three distinct characters, two of which are Holocaust perpetrators with differing degrees of culpability for genocide. I argue that the novel pits the two ethically dubious perpetrator-narrators against each other in a bid for the reader's ambivalent identification, in the process rendering one of its narrators a very human figure by portraying the other with the standard vocabulary of banal evil.

I end my study with a brief epilogue that discusses the potential for comparison between cultural representations of the mind of the Holocaust perpetrator and images of perpetrators of violence more generally.

Probing the Mind of the Holocaust Perpetrator in Nonfiction

Fathoming the "Nazi Mind" in the Postwar Era

The construction of the mind of the Holocaust perpetrator in the larger cultural imagination has a long and varied history that dates to the origins of Nazism. Beginning with the rise of National Socialism as a mass ideological movement and the subsequent establishment of Hitler's dictatorship in Germany, and with increasing frequency after the onset of the Second World War, scholars and writers of nonfiction outside the Third Reich engaged in concerted exercises of mind-reading aimed at apprehending what Daniel Pick has termed the "Nazi mind" as a distinct political, social, and psychological orientation.[1] An example of such an effort can be found

---

1 Pick is careful to historicize this term as a projected ideal rather than a reified concept: "It would be tedious to place the phrase 'Nazi mind' in scare quotes each time it is used in this book; it is intended as a shorthand to indicate the notion that such an (elusive) psychological object existed and could be recovered in some shape or form. This expression is one way to convey the psycho-political quarry that so many researchers keenly pursued during and after the war" (3). For a good (if by now somewhat dated) historical overview

in Harwood L. Childs's 1938 introduction to *The Nazi Primer: Official Handbook for Schooling the Hitler Youth*, his translation of a 1937 Hitler Youth manual. Childs scrutinizes the handbook for clues that would reveal the mindset and goals of National Socialism:

> What are Hitler's intentions? Does Germany want war? What will satisfy Hitler's colonial and territorial aspirations? Is anti-Semitism an essential part of his program, or does it reflect merely the state of mind of a few extremists within the party? What do National Socialists mean by the Nordic race and why do they claim it is superior? Are they really anti-Christian? How do they reconcile their drive for large families with claims for more territory? How are they trying to make Germany economically self-sufficient? Do National Socialists really have a unified, systematic philosophy, and if so, what is it? (xiii)

While Childs's early study, undertaken before the advent of Germany's expansionist war and eliminationist genocide, does not equate the Nazi movement with criminality and the perpetration of mass violence, it does indicate an understanding of National Socialism as a particular mental state that must be probed and interpreted. Childs's project to read the mind of the Nazi movement through its educational program for its youth was but one of a number of prewar projects in the United States, Great Britain, and Europe that aimed to infer a social and psychological worldview from the artifacts of its culture; they usually focused on the "Nazi mind" as a collective national consciousness whose dimensions were simultaneously ideological, cultural, and psychological rather than on the individual psyches of

---

of the history of early psychological study of Nazism, see *The Quest for the Nazi Personality: A Psychological Investigation of Nazi War Criminals* by Eric A. Zillmer et al., especially chapter 1, "The Quest for the Nazi Personality" (1–19). James Waller also provides a good overview of early sociopsychological studies of the "mad Nazi" in *Becoming Evil: How Ordinary People Commit Genocide and Mass Killing*. Waller writes, "Early attempts at understanding the perpetrators of the Holocaust were a search for homogeneity. In other words, they were a search to defend our general belief that *all* Nazis were very similar to each other and very different from each of us" (76).

the leaders and followers of the Nazi movement. More systematic attempts to "analyse the fantasies exploited in Nazi ideology" (Pick 3) commenced only with the outbreak of the war, when it became a strategic necessity for the Allies not only to read the "hive mind" of Nazi Germany but also, on a more individual level, to "map the minds of leaders and followers" (3) and ascertain in particular the motives of the Nazi leadership.[2] A wave of "British and American inquiries into the psychic life of the Nazis" (1) was undertaken most notably by behavioral scientists working for the US Office of Strategic Services, many of whom were émigrés "of Jewish or German descent, or both" (Hoffman, "American Psychologists and Wartime Research" 265), and by British military psychologists associated with the Tavistock Clinic.[3] Their work to outline "Nazi psychopathology" was, as Louise E. Hoffman writes, "heavily psychoanalytic" in its orientation (268);[4] while it was heavily invested in reconstructing the psychic life of Hitler and other high-ranking leaders, it also explored "the mentality that was said to be typical in particular organizations (such as the SS)" and profiled "the entirety of those who became enthralled by Hitler" (Pick 3).

In the immediate postwar period, as historian Robert Gellately argues, "there was enormous interest in 'what made those Nazis tick'" (xx).[5] What

---

2 A further group that was urgently invested in ascertaining and evaluating the motives of both the National Socialist leadership and lower-level perpetrators and in trying to predict their actions—in short, in mind-reading them—was constituted by their victims. For an excellent analysis of the ways in which victims inferred the minds of their persecutors, see Roseman, "Holocaust Perpetrators in Victims' Eyes."

3 According to Pick, the wartime and postwar psychological investigation of "the Nazi mind" was exclusively an American and British endeavor (8–9).

4 Pick writes, "It would be a mistake, of course, to credit psychoanalysis as the only discipline that sought to engage with Nazi psychopathology. Just as Freud had deliberately blurred the lines between the study of the psychology of the individual and of the wider social group, and alluded freely to classical literature, history, and anthropology, others, caught up in the wartime struggle, blurred the lines between Freudian psychoanalysis, general psychiatry, medicine, and various brands of modern psychology derived from sources quite distinct from Freud" (12).

5 While Allied military psychologists and psychiatrists in the early postwar period showed marked interest in the psychological traits of Nazis, a concurrent counter-discourse also pathologized the German mind but discouraged attempts to understand it, as for example in the 1945 American short propaganda documentary *Your Job in Germany*, written by Theodore Geisel (who wrote children's books under the pen name Dr. Seuss) and directed by Frank

had in the main been an attempt on the part of American and British forces to infer the National Socialist mindset and to map its psychological coordinates from a remote distance was transformed into one-on-one encounters, as military psychologists and psychiatrists suddenly gained access to German prisoners of war, especially the Nazi leadership that was put on trial in Nuremberg. Best known for their work with the defendants at Nuremberg are G. M. Gilbert, who wrote *Nuremberg Diary* (1947) and *The Psychology of Dictatorship: Based on an Examination of the Leaders of Nazi Germany* (1950), and his colleague Douglas M. Kelley, who published *22 Cells in Nuremberg: A Psychiatrist Examines the Nazi Criminals* (1947); together the two men administered Rorschach inkblot and other tests to the twenty-two defendants. Leon Goldensohn, also a prison psychiatrist and medical doctor on the team at Nuremberg, likewise conducted interviews (often with Gilbert in the role of translator) with high-ranking Nazis awaiting trial, although his extensive account, which was edited by the historian Gellately, was first published only in 2004 as *The Nuremberg Interviews: An American Psychiatrist's Conversations with the Defendants and Witnesses*. As Gellately pointedly stresses, all three of these men had planned book projects from the beginning of their encounters with Nazi defendants. They thus saw the prisoners under their care "as subjects to be studied, and rather secondarily, if at all as patients" (Gellately xxii), they did not feel bound by the restrictions of doctor-patient confidentiality, and they were not concerned about the ethical issues of making public either the content of their private conversations with the prisoners or their assessments of the men's mental condition. These three men became "the envy of [their] professional peers and the many reporters [who were] eager to interview the defendants" (Gellately xx), and their conclusions about "the 'pathology' of the leading Nazis" aligned with the general cultural conceptions about Nazi perpetrators at the time, which attributed to them what Mark Roseman calls "psychological deformation" ("Beyond Conviction?" 85). Indeed, according to Ervin Staub, the "psychological assessment [of the defendants at Nuremberg] was based on a hypothesis of their mental illness" (75).

Capra. The film cautioned US soldiers to avoid fraternizing with or adopting an empathetic perspective vis-à-vis Germans in Allied-occupied Germany: "The Nazi Party may be gone, but Nazi thinking, Nazi training and Nazi trickery remain."

The psychiatric and psychological analyses of the Nuremberg defendants helped develop a profile of the men who wielded the most power in the Third Reich, an endeavor that was further advanced by early biographical and historical analyses of Nazi leaders, such as Hugh Trevor-Roper's *The Last Days of Hitler* (1947) and William L. Shirer's *The Rise and Fall of the Third Reich* (1960), the latter of which included a chapter titled "The Mind of Hitler and the Roots of the Third Reich" (80). At the same time, such projects were unable to account for the mindset and behavior of lower-level perpetrators, whose initiation of or participation in atrocities both were more direct and yielded fewer tangible benefits. In an attempt to account for the ways in which average Germans were persuaded to carry out the will of the Nazi leaders and ideologues, efforts to explain in psychological terms the moral debasement of Nazism returned in the decade or so after the trials at Nuremberg to a focus on the collective "Nazi mind" with studies such as *The Authoritarian Personality* (1950) by Theodor W. Adorno, Else Frenkel-Brunswick, Daniel J. Levinson, and R. Nevitt Sanford, which "became an instant landmark in the field of social psychology" (Waller, *Becoming Evil* 81) and was one of a number of books that, according to Judith M. Hughes, endeavored to "write [the] psychohistory" (2) of the rise of fascism and the Holocaust. What was missing in these studies was an engagement with the actual men who perpetrated the Holocaust on the ground. In other words, books such as *The Authoritarian Personality* or Hannah Arendt's *The Origins of Totalitarianism* (1951), along with shorter texts such as Adorno's "Freudian Theory and the Pattern of Fascist Propaganda" (1951), could provide an explanation for the structural, political, ideological, or mass psychological factors that drove millions of Germans to support the Nazi regime and further hundreds of thousands to implement its genocidal policies, but they could not account for why a particular individual chose to engage in violence and how he understood and related to his wartime behavior. This oversight was reflected in the historical scholarship as well, in which, according to Guenter Lewy, "the Holocaust was often described as the work of an efficient extermination machine, a crime, as it were, without criminals"; this "structuralist or functionalist approach . . . concentrated on the regime's bureaucratic machinery to the exclusion of individual perpetrators" (3).

At the same time, in the first decade or so after the Holocaust, the dearth of psychological, journalistic, and historical writing about the individual

Holocaust perpetrator was mirrored by the absence of a substantive body of autobiographical writing by former perpetrators themselves that might have shed light on their mental states. In contrast to the profuse number of testimonial narratives and the small but burgeoning corpus of autobiographical texts by Holocaust survivors that appeared in the first two decades after the Holocaust (the most prominent of which were works by Primo Levi, Liana Millu, Robert Antelme, Elie Wiesel, and Charlotte Delbo, among others), candid autobiographical accounts by perpetrators, whether prominent or lesser known, were rarely published. Notable exceptions from the immediate postwar period include the memoirs of Hans Frank, the former governor-general of the occupied Polish territories, and Rudolf Höß, the notorious former commandant of Auschwitz, both of which were written while the men were awaiting trial and execution in Nuremberg and Kraków, respectively; from the late 1960s through the early 1980s, Albert Speer published three autobiographical accounts of his experiences in the Third Reich as well.[6] However, their texts are extraordinary in the canon of Holocaust literature; as Christopher Browning, the Holocaust historian whose 1992 book *Ordinary Men: Reserve Police Battalion 101 and the Final Solution in Poland* has become one of the most influential analyses of the dynamics of violence among lower-level perpetrators, argues, "Unlike the survivors, of course, the perpetrators did not rush to write their memoirs after the war. They felt no mission to 'never forget.' On the contrary, they hoped to forget and be forgotten as quickly and totally as possible" ("German Memory, Judicial Interrogation, and Historical Reconstruction" 28). Apart from their wish to forget, perpetrators may have remained silent about their participation in genocide for a number of possible reasons: they may have wished to avoid criminal prosecution; they may have hoped to keep their violent history secret from friends, relatives, and neighbors; they may have downplayed or denied their crimes to themselves; or they may simply have had difficulty finding adequate language to talk about their criminal acts and their moral and ethical failures. In any case, the paucity of autobiographical accounts by perpetrators that narrated firsthand and from the subjective perspective the experience of the individual actor in the collective implementation of mass violence and

---

6 For an insightful reading of confessional discourse in Höß's memoir, see Alan Rosen.

murder left a lacuna in the cultural imagination of the inner workings of individual perpetrators.

This situation changed radically in the early 1960s with the Israeli trial of Adolf Eichmann, which became, as Jeffrey Shandler argues, "a threshold event" (81) in Holocaust memory culture as "the first major public effort to conceptualize the Holocaust as a discrete chapter of history, distinguished from larger narratives of World War II or the Third Reich, and defined as a phenomenon centered around Nazi efforts to exterminate European Jewry" (84). The Eichmann trial inaugurated a dynamic era of cultural fascination with the mental life of individual perpetrators and concerted efforts to read their minds that continued for two decades. Unlike the Nuremberg trials, which had centered on multiple defendants who had collectively represented an agglomeration of the crimes associated with the Third Reich and the total war it pursued, including crimes against peace, war crimes, and crimes against humanity, the Eichmann trial disaggregated the genocide of the Jews from general crimes of war and moreover focused on one particular man's role in its administration and his attitude regarding the Holocaust atrocities in which he played a part. In this way, it crystallized in the cultural imagination the concept of the everyday Holocaust perpetrator, whose mentality was a fundamental aspect of the crimes for which he was charged, and at the same time initiated what Roseman terms a "shift from the monster to the mundane" ("Beyond Conviction?" 87). Suddenly, journalists, psychologists, and intellectuals had an ordinary perpetrator before them who, though he had not precisely been in the trenches of the genocide, had not—unlike the defendants at Nuremberg—been at a significant remove from them either. Moreover, Eichmann seemed to embody the entire conundrum of how the Holocaust was perpetrated, in Zygmunt Bauman's words, "in the heart of the most civilized part of the world" (xi); his apparent normality was at troubling odds with the actions that he had initiated and sanctioned. A media event of global proportions, Eichmann's capture and the ensuing trial generated a massive wave of nonfictional writing, with many dozens of articles, analyses, biographies, and book-length meditations devoted specifically to analysis of Eichmann's mind, the most famous of these being Hannah Arendt's *Eichmann in Jerusalem: A Report on the Banality of Evil* (1963). Such widely disseminated works not only established Eichmann as the paradigmatic perpetrator but also provided a framework for nonfictional exploration of the mind of the individual Holocaust perpetrator. In chapter 1, I will discuss Arendt's text along with two other in-depth portraits of Eichmann, Harry Mulisch's *Criminal Case 40/61* (1962) and William L. Hull's *The Struggle for a Soul* (1963). In all three texts, as we shall see, Eichmann's mind is rendered textually in a dialogical manner through the overt mediation of the narrating author, who functions as a sort of interface or interpretive buffer between the reader and Eichmann and who filters his or her representation through particular epistemological and phenomenological frameworks that simultaneously disclose and impede access to the perpetrator's mind.

With the Auschwitz trials (1963–65), the Bełżec trial (1963–65), and the Treblinka trials (1964–65, 1970), the 1960s and early 1970s saw a marked increase in the trials of Holocaust perpetrators in West Germany (which in 1958 had mounted the Ulm Einsatzkommando trial, the first major trial of Nazi crimes under West German law), yet no single perpetrator emerged from these trials to become the subject of public fascination or the focus of the cultural imagination on the level of that which had developed around Eichmann, in part because the West German trials did not become the kind of worldwide televised media event that the Eichmann trial had become and because the defendants were not as notorious as Eichmann had been. At the same time, however, penetrating portraits of individual perpetrators emerged in the journalistic work of Gitta Sereny, who published a widely read account of her weeks-long interview with former Sobibór and Treblinka commandant Franz Stangl as long-form journalism in 1971 and then as a more comprehensive biography titled *Into That Darkness: An Examination of Conscience* in 1974, a classic text of Holocaust literature that will be the subject of chapter 2. Sereny aims in particular to illuminate the inner life and conscience of Stangl and "to assess the circumstances which led up to his involvement . . . with the most total evil our age has produced . . . , for once not from our point of view, but from *his*" (*Into That Darkness* 13); at the same time, Sereny herself, as a mediating figure, also becomes an important focal point of the book. In preparation for writing *Into That Darkness*, Sereny further managed to interview three of Stangl's former SS colleagues at a time when former perpetrators were as a rule resolutely mute about their Holocaust experience, at least outside the courtroom. In the late 1970s, Sereny also interviewed Albert Speer, former Reich minister for armaments and war production; as she writes in the book that followed, *Albert Speer: His Battle with the Truth* (1995), her "principle aim . . . , throughout, was to learn to understand Speer" (14). Later in the same decade and into the early 1980s, the filmmaker Claude Lanzmann located and interviewed individual perpetrators as well, although usually men who were on a lower level in the military, SS, or bureaucratic hierarchy. Five of thirteen of those filmed interviews appear in part in Lanzmann's 1985 masterpiece *Shoah*.[7] Lanzmann's and Sereny's penetrating encounters with perpetrators were unparalleled in their intimate access to and representation of their subjects' minds, demonstrating the critical interventional role of the interviewer herself or himself in the perpetrators' performances of self-disclosure.

At the same time, however, Sereny's and Lanzmann's interviews with former perpetrators—alongside a small number of contemporaneous, intensive engagements with former Nazis, such as the films of Marcel Ophüls (*Le Chagrin et la Pitié* [*The Sorrow and the Pity*, 1969], *The Memory of Justice* [1976], and *Hôtel Terminus: Klaus Barbie, sa vie et son temps* [*Hôtel Terminus: The Life and Times of Klaus Barbie*, 1988]) and Robert Kramer (*Notre Nazi* [*Our Nazi*, 1985])—represent both a singular aberration in and the pinnacle of the history of the popular (i.e., not written for a small cohort of expert historians), nonfictional analysis of the psychology of individuals who had been Holocaust perpetrators.[8] In the wake of the

---

7 For analysis of Lanzmann's perpetrator interviews, see McGlothlin, "Listening to the Perpetrators in Claude Lanzmann's *Shoah*," "The Voice of the Perpetrator, the Voices of the Survivors," and "In Search of Suchomel in *Shoah*: Examining Claude Lanzmann's Post-Production Editing Practice."

8 The popular, nonfictional exploration of the mental space of perpetrators in the two decades after the Eichmann trial was not, according to Roseman, reflected in the historiography of the period, especially in Germany: "The 1970s and early 1980s continued to be characterized by an emotional unwillingness to engage with the reality of perpetrating murder" ("Beyond Conviction?" 90). Moreover, in Holocaust Studies in general, there was little interest in the psychic life of the men who were complicit in the crimes of the Holocaust. According to the psychologist Bruno Bettelheim, who shortly before the war was imprisoned in Dachau and Buchenwald for nearly a year, "I restricted myself to trying to understand the psychology of the prisoners and I shied away from trying to understand the psychology of the SS—because of the ever-present danger that understanding fully may come close to forgiving. I believe there are acts so vile that our task is to reject and prevent them, not to try to understand them empathetically" (61).

Probing the Mind of the Holocaust Perpetrator in Nonfiction | 55

roughly twenty years following the Eichmann trial that constituted the heyday of this cultural engagement with particular perpetrators, the number and notoriety of nonfictional, non-scholarly texts that attempted to explore and construct the mind of Holocaust perpetrators began to wane, likely the result of the gradual passing of the perpetrator generation and increasing reticence among former perpetrators to speak about their experience in the context of a culture of ubiquitous Holocaust memory, both in Germany and globally.[9] The cultural engagement with the mind of Holocaust perpetrators henceforth has generally taken one of two forms: either rigorous academic study or fictional exploration. The former, which Rebecca Wennberg terms the "new perpetrator research" (31) and which commenced in the early 1990s in North America with the publication of Christopher Browning's pioneering study *Ordinary Men* and in Germany with the emergence of a wave of insightful studies produced by the "neuere Täterforschung," or recent perpetrator scholarship (Bajohr), has encompassed a surge in groundbreaking, illuminating, and nuanced work on perpetrators by historians, psychologists, sociologists, philosophers, political scientists, scholars of religion and of medicine, and, most recently, scholars of literature, culture, and film. This massive body of interdisciplinary research attempts to track the diversity of perpetrators with regard to temporal, geographical, and generational coordinates, class,

---

9 As I briefly mentioned in the introduction, Debarati Sanyal delineates a slightly different history in her investigation of the dynamics of postwar French memory of the Holocaust, arguing that intellectuals were highly invested in the early postwar years in "understanding the phenomenon of perpetration" (186). In her account, "the turn to perpetration and complicity in our [present-day] era of the witness is thus not a novel phenomenon but a *return*" (187). Sanyal further argues that the cultural focus on perpetration and complicity receded from the 1960s to the 1990s (187). I concur with the first of these two claims, namely, that cultural interest in the dynamics of perpetration and the mentality of perpetrators has a longer history than is often claimed by scholars of Holocaust literature (who almost uniformly see the current "boom" in representations of perpetrators as a new phenomenon). With regard to her second claim, however, I depart from her history. The trajectory I am tracing here, which is more broadly defined than Sanyal's account (which is limited to postwar French "existential and ethical preoccupations" [186] with what was at the time the very recent war and genocide) and at the same time more narrowly focused on examinations of the mental character of Holocaust perpetrators, maintains very different temporal vectors. Where Sanyal perceives a waning in the wake of the Eichmann trial, I discern two decades of sustained (if limited) attention.

and social environment; ideological beliefs and degree of antisemitic and racist outlook; psychological disposition; self-understanding; and post-Holocaust cultural representation. It further considers the behavior of perpetrators within a matrix of "dispositional, situational, and social factors" (Browder, "Perpetrator Character and Motivation" 491). Some of the studies that belong to this corpus—such as Ulrich Herbert's 1996 book *Best: Biographische Studien über Radikalismus, Weltanschauung und Vernunft 1903–1989*, which profiles Werner Best, a former department head of the Reichssicherheitshauptamt (Reich Security Main Office), and which Frank Bajohr calls "wegweisend" (pathbreaking)—present astute biographical profiles of individual perpetrators, but they have not jumped the barrier between the academy and the nonacademic world and entered into the greater cultural imagination in the same way that the more popular—although equally rigorous and meticulously researched—nonfictional portraits by Arendt and Sereny have done. For this reason, I argue that, while the new perpetrator research has undoubtedly been influenced by the nonfictional journalistic representations of perpetrators of the 1960s and 1970s (especially that of Arendt, whose postulate regarding the alleged banality of Eichmann served as a provocation to historians, many of whom labored in their work to dispute it), it cannot be viewed as the proper successor to that tradition.[10] The pride of that place, I contend, goes to more recent fictional representations of the mind of the perpetrator, which assume and at the same time critically transform the representational approaches employed by their earlier nonfictional counterparts, whereby the mediating figure of

---

10 According to Timothy Schroer, while the new perpetrator research has produced a great deal of insight regarding perpetrators' motives and the complex social context in which they operated and how it influenced individual and group behavior, it has been less successful in ascertaining the men's emotional reactions to the genocidal actions in which they engaged, both in the moment and in postwar life: "Historians have dedicated considerable attention to understanding the perpetrators' motives for murdering their victims. They have not dedicated the same attention to understanding how the perpetrators felt about what they were doing. Doubtless many would argue that it is unproductive to make the attempt. Given the mendacity of the perpetrators and the extremity of their crimes, the difficulty of getting at the truth must not be underestimated. Nevertheless, this effort to come uncomfortably close to the feelings of the perpetrators of the Holocaust brings to light fundamental assumptions about how human beings operated as they engaged in genocide, assumptions that are worth probing" (47).

the authorial narrator or interviewer is transformed into particular narrative devices.[11] Such fictional counterparts to the nonfictional exercises in mind-reading the Holocaust perpetrator explored here in part 1 will be the subject of part 2.

Narrative Strategies and Nonfiction

By positing the idea that nonfictional attempts to imagine the mind of the Holocaust perpetrator have gradually been superseded by fictional explorations that carry on the same project, I trace a historical connection between the nonfictional and fictional texts under investigation here. Beyond this linkage, however, I perceive additional dimensions of correspondence between the two types of discourse, particularly with regard to the structural and aesthetic properties employed by this group of texts. Whereas, as I will argue in part 2, the fictional texts take up and transform some of the narrative strategies of nonfiction in their renderings of the interiority of their protagonists, the nonfictional texts I investigate in this part avail themselves of what we often think of as fictional—or, at very least, literary—techniques in order to shape their narratives of the minds of the real men on whom they focus. In particular, they use the fundamental properties of storytelling and narrative worldmaking to construct out of the "raw flux" (Abbott 22) of events, episodes, actions, interactions, and emotional phenomena in each perpetrator's life a comprehensible narrative replete with meaningful causal relationships, intelligible motives, coherent behavior, and legible mental attitudes.

---

11 An important exception to this trend is the relatively recent group of documentary films that explore the mindset of former perpetrators or other persons complicit with the Nazi regime, such as André Heller and Othmar Schmiderer's *Im toten Winkel: Hitlers Sekretärin* (*Blind Spot: Hitler's Secretary*, 2002), which focuses on Hitler's former secretary Traudl Junge; Günter Schwaiger's *Hafners Paradies* (*Hafner's Paradise*, 2007), which features an interview with former SS soldier Paul Maria Hafner; Walter Manoschek's . . . *dann bin ich ja ein Mörder!* (*If That's So, Then I'm a Murderer*, 2012), which investigates a former SS man's participation in a massacre of forced laborers; and Christian Krönes et al.'s *A German Life* (2016), which takes up the story of Goebbel's former stenographer Brunhilde Pomsel. The ubiquity and popularity of such films not only testify to filmmakers' desires to call to account the rapidly shrinking pool of persons complicit in the crimes of the Third Reich but also demonstrate the seismic shift in the media landscape that has occurred since the 1970s.

In this, of course, these texts are no different than any story of the life of a real person, which necessarily follows processes of construction analogous to those found in nonreferential or fictional narratives. Indeed, according to Jerome Bruner, the very notion of a person's "life" is in fact a narrative construct:

> The mimesis between life so-called and narrative is a two-way affair: that is to say, just as art imitates life in Aristotle's sense, so, in Oscar Wilde's, life imitates art. Narrative imitates life, life imitates narrative. "Life" in this sense is the same kind of construction of the human imagination as "a narrative" is. It is constructed by human beings through active ratiocination, by the same kind of ratiocination through which we construct narratives. When somebody tells you his life . . . it is always a cognitive achievement rather than a through-the-clear-crystal recital of something univocally given. In the end, it is a narrative achievement. (13)

In Bruner's view, the very notion of a person's life proceeds from the narration of that life. Moreover, once perceived as a distinct phenomenon (i.e., once apprehended by language), a person's life exists as a product of "the narrative models [a particular culture] makes available to describing the course of a life" (15), meaning the lexica, plot structures, character types, and interpretive frameworks that circulate within a given culture to make sense of experience: "And the tool kit of any culture is replete not only with a stock of canonical life narratives (heroes, Marthas, tricksters, etc.), but with combinable formal constituents from which its members can construct their own life narratives: canonical stances and circumstances, as it were" (15). By virtue of this broad and recurrent circulation of particular generic templates, a culture is thus able to perceive and narrate life experience in ways both personally and socially comprehensible. Furthermore, each singular act of characterizing and communicating a person's life experience utilizes and at the same time contributes to the collective canon of legible narrative blueprints; thus, "the ways of telling and the ways of conceptualizing that go with them become so habitual that they finally become recipes for structuring experience itself" (31).

The texts I will explore in the following two chapters, all of which attempt to apprehend and narrate the experiences and mental attitudes of real-life perpetrators of violence in the Holocaust, are also subject to the dynamic that Bruner terms "life as narrative." The texts by Arendt, Mulisch, Hull, and Sereny all resort by necessity to what Hanna Meretoja calls "culturally mediated models of narrative sense-making" (79) in order to construct comprehensible accounts of the lives of men whom they seek to understand. However, given the subject of their biographical portraits—the inner lives of men whose experience lies ostensibly outside the bounds of conventional ethical norms—a certain paradox also attends the texts' narrativization of the perpetrators' lives. On the one hand, they register what Arendt terms the "unprecedented" (*Eichmann in Jerusalem* 267) situation of the men whose minds they seek to illuminate and whose participation in a genocide so unrivaled in scale and seemingly unparalleled in routinized brutality poses a considerable challenge to traditional moral categories and familiar historical frameworks. As Sereny reports saying to Stangl, "Things had happened to and inside him which had happened to hardly anyone else, ever" (*Into That Darkness* 23), a sentiment echoed in various ways by the authors of the other texts as well, who take on the demanding task of translating the singular, preternatural quality of the perpetrators' experience for an audience to whom it appears remote and incomprehensible. On the other hand, while several of the texts under discussion—particularly Arendt and Mulisch—develop innovative and unconventional strategies to represent the paradoxically anomalous quality of the crimes committed by these rather ordinary men, they also seek commonly intelligible narrative vehicles through which they can make the perpetrators' experience legible to both themselves and their audiences. They thus reach for—sometimes deliberately, at other times reflexively—what Bruner calls "recipes for structuring experience," particularly, as we will see, familiar generic conventions and formal frameworks not uncommonly attributed to fiction, such as narrative masterplots associated with genre fiction and creative practices of mind-reading; in this way, they demonstrate, according to Jens Brockmeier, how "everyday [nonfictional] narrative practices continuously absorb resources from literary, dramatic, and filmic discourses, and from the popular arts" (124). Such "multi-layered exchanges" (124) between the conventions of fiction and nonfiction in turn necessitate practices of reading able to recognize and account for the effects of the texts' recourse to what Brockmeier calls "a shared cultural canon of narrative conventions" that "cuts across the putative divide between fiction and nonfiction" (125). By closely attending to the ways in which the texts embed their constructions of the mind of the Holocaust perpetrator within narrative frameworks and scripts that predicate particular epistemological and affective interpretations, such reading practices not only clarify the processes by which the authors construct the minds of the men they seek to understand but also acknowledge the reciprocal nature of fiction and nonfiction in how we construct and make sense of historical lives.

At the same time, however, while these nonfictional explorations of the mindset and motivations of Holocaust perpetrators avail themselves of formal and structural strategies that we conventionally associate with fiction, they are not themselves fictions, and we should be careful not to conflate them with fictional accounts of perpetrators, even those (e.g., Martin Amis's novels) that take actual historical figures as their models. For that reason, it is equally important to attend to the texts' ontological, referential, and historical specificity. As Daniel W. Lehman argues, "Nonfiction depends on a materiality of its characters' bodies and on a reference to outside events that is more powerful than most forms of fiction" (3); in particular (and to state the obvious), not only are the characters in this corpus of texts real people who were at one time involved in the concrete historical events of the Holocaust, but their authors are also actual persons who met personally with their subjects or engaged intimately with their histories from a remove. The stakes of their projects to represent the interiority of the perpetrators under examination are thus of a much different nature than those of the fictional texts.[12] While both modes of writing—fictional and nonfictional—are bound to some degree of referentiality in their depictions of the Holocaust and its aftereffects, the authors of the nonfictional texts have much less freedom to invent people and events, to creatively reframe motivations and causality, and to grant apparently unrestricted access to the thoughts and feelings of the perpetrators they endeavor to depict than

---

12 The distinction between fiction and nonfiction is particularly important for readers, who according to Stefan Iversen, "ascribe different ontological statuses to fictive and non-fictive consciousnesses"; therefore, such ascriptions "often dictate different interpretational strategies" (160).

do either the authors or the narrators of fictional representations (especially autodiegetic fictional narrators, who presumably—but not necessarily [as in Amis's *Time's Arrow*]—are able to disclose the contents of their own minds). Even when these texts creatively reconstruct or even misrepresent aspects of the perpetrators' lives and narratives, they are still subject to the referential conventions of nonfiction.

While these nonfictional texts confront particular limitations by virtue of their referential status, however, they also demonstrate some of the complexities of nonfictional discourse, especially "the way that writers of nonfiction implicate themselves within the text" (Lehman 38), particularly through the cultivation of an explicit and interventional authorial persona. All of the texts examined here feature not the ostensibly omniscient, impersonal, neutral perspective of the heterodiegetic reporter of "objective" facts but the deeply invested and implicated presence of a homodiegetic narrator whose involvement in the story he or she tells becomes an integral part of the narrative itself. This is particularly true in the case of Sereny and Hull, both of whom become protagonists within the diegesis of their interviews with the respective perpetrators, but it applies to Mulisch and Arendt as well, whose attendance at and personal engagement with the Eichmann trial become an integral part of their narratives. (While Arendt is perhaps the most conventionally objective of all the author-narrators represented here, the presence of her ironic and at times even sardonic voice permeates, as Norberg, Berding, Steitz, and others have pointed out, *Eichmann in Jerusalem*.) Moreover, the authors examined in this part not only construct explicit narrative personae in their texts but also commit themselves to exacting dialogical and intersubjective relationships with their subjects, either as interviewers in face-to-face encounters (Hull, Sereny) or as interpreters who evaluate the perpetrator from a distance (Arendt, Mulisch). Intersubjectivity, or the interaction between two or more subjects, "concerns how one is mentally connected with and distinguished from others" (May 169). While it is often described as a "shared understanding" (Anderson 468) between parties, it does not necessarily denote full correspondence between two subjectivities and can in fact emphasize the areas in which they diverge. For this reason, it is better described as *"the sharing of experiential content (e.g. feelings, perceptions, thoughts, and linguistic meanings)"* (Zlatav et al. 1); whereas the past participial form "shared" denotes the outcome of alleged agreement, the gerund form "sharing" emphasizes the process of interchange, which may or may not result in concurrence and in fact can include discordant encounters, such as some of the ones described in the nonfictional texts examined in this part. According to Lynn Abrams, who writes about interviews between oral historians and their subjects with respect to the latter's life stories (an enterprise in critical ways similar not only to the face-to-face interviews with perpetrators conducted by Hull and Sereny but also to the dialogical engagements at a distance by Arendt and Mulisch), intersubjectivity "describes the interaction—the collision, if you will—between the two subjectivities of interviewer and interviewee. More than that, it describes the way in which the subjectivity of each is shaped by the encounter with the other" (58). Such encounters thus have not only consequences for the self-understanding of the persons being interviewed and for the narratives of their life that are produced via the dialogue between interviewer and interviewee, but also an impact on the interviewers themselves: the authorial personae are transformed as well by the dialogical interaction of the engagement. Valerie Yow terms this phenomenon in the context of oral history research "interview effects," which can include "motives for doing the project, feelings about the narrator [or interview subject], interviewer's reaction to the narrator's testimony, and intrusion of the interviewer's assumptions and of the interviewer's self-schema into the interviewing and interpretive processes" (56). With regard to this particular corpus of texts, the operations of intersubjectivity are at work in a number of dimensions, including the authors' affective, cognitive, and ethical investment in their projects to scrutinize the mind of their subjects, the dialogical relationships (whether direct or indirect) they cultivate with the perpetrators to produce a narrative about their participation in genocidal violence, their self-reflexive meditations on how their experiences with the perpetrators impinge on their own selfhood, and the story that emerges from synthetic cross-pollination between the perpetrators' narration or self-performance and the authors' cathectic ties to their projects.

An additional aspect of such intersubjective investment is the operation of empathy, which is fundamental to the authors' projects of mind-reading their subjects. Indeed, empathy is closely correlated to Theory of Mind and the faculty of mind-reading; according to Jonathan Dvash and

Simone G. Shamay-Tsoory, while Theory of Mind—as both facility and process—denotes "the attribution of mental states to others" (282), empathy refers both to "an individual's ability to understand and feel the other" and "the reactions of one individual to the observed experiences of another" (283). Empathy—especially in its cognitive form—is predicated on the operation of mind-reading; we thus empathize with another to the extent that we can attribute mental states to that person. However, mind-reading may not necessarily lead to empathy: "The ability to infer the thoughts and feelings of others is critical for appropriate and effective social interactions and discourse comprehension, but it is not sufficient. Belief understanding does not guarantee emotion understanding; emotion understanding does not guarantee empathy; and empathy does not guarantee sympathy as manifested by kindness to people" (282). For this reason, although the authors of all of the nonfictional texts discussed in this part engage, as I have argued, in exercises in mind-reading in their projects of constructing the mind of the perpetrator, the operation of empathy plays out to differing degrees in their interactions with their subjects. Arendt, for example, engages in both extensive acts of mind-reading and operations of empathy in her analysis of Eichmann; however, her empathetic stance is undercut by her caustic irony and her insistence on Eichmann's mindlessness. Mulisch's portrait of Eichmann, on the other land, is characterized by a relatively high empathetic disposition; Mulisch even notes at one point that "the boundaries between him and me are lapsing" (159). As Eichmann's spiritual adviser, Hull performatively simulates empathy with Eichmann through his concern for the state of his soul, yet he obstinately refuses to consider Eichmann's experience from within his own frame of reference; his empathetic connection thus resembles at least in part what Nils Bubandt and Rane Willerslev term "tactical empathy," which they define as "the emotional and cognitive projection of oneself into the perspective or situation of another for deceptive purposes" (13). Despite Sereny's warning that empathy "is dangerous" ("Questioning the Perpetrators" 124), her position vis-à-vis Stangl, on the other hand, is fundamentally empathetic; in fact, as Rachel Rosenblum argues, "Sereny's empathy is a serious weapon" in its resolution to force Stangl "to occupy a subjective position which, until then, had remained empty" (1326–27). The empathetic relationship that develops in these texts thus varies appreciably with regard to both kind and degree, demonstrating the considerable diversity in the authors' approaches to their respective subjects.

Taken together, the four texts that I examine in detail in the following two chapters demonstrate the facile and malleable potential of nonfictional discourse for exploring the complex inner lives of figures whose histories of violence pose challenges to attempts to understand their behavior, attitudes, and memories. In their quest for an appropriate vehicle through which they can represent experiences and mental attitudes commonly regarded as incomprehensible or ethically provocative, the authors of these texts adopt and reshape narrative conventions often associated with fiction, thereby expanding the capacity of nonfiction to imagine phenomena that resist empirical validation. As mediating figures who are tasked with translating the perpetrators' minds for their readers, these authors also consign themselves to intersubjective and empathetic relationships with their subjects. The portraits of the perpetrators that emerge in these texts thus reveal as much about the historical conditions of their construction, the representational dynamics that shaped them, and the commitments of their authors as they do the contents of the minds of men who perpetrated genocidal violence.

1

Mind-Reading Eichmann

Hannah Arendt's *Eichmann in Jerusalem*, Harry Mulisch's *Criminal Case 40/61, the Trial of Adolf Eichmann*, and William L. Hull's *The Struggle for a Soul*

The Paradigmatic Perpetrator

Apart from Adolf Hitler, the single most thoroughly documented, painstakingly analyzed, and frequently represented perpetrator of the Holocaust has been Adolf Eichmann, the notorious midlevel SS bureaucrat who played a central logistical role in the deportation of Europe's Jews to the National Socialist ghettos and killing centers. By virtue not only of the copious witness testimony from his 1961 Israeli trial (including his own protracted deposition) but also of the thousands of pages of his autobiographical writing and transcripts of his exhaustive pretrial interrogation, there exists a massive Eichmann archive to which historians, social scientists, writers, and filmmakers can turn in pursuit of answers to their questions about the nature of the mind of the Holocaust perpetrator. Moreover, because of the global attention commanded by the spectacle of his trial and on account of high-profile analyses of the proceedings—the most prominent of which is Hannah Arendt's bestselling masterwork *Eichmann in Jerusalem: A Report on the Banality of Evil* (1963)—Eichmann has become, in the words of historian David Cesarani, "an icon of the twentieth century, of the Nazi regime and the genocide it waged against the Jews" (1), around whom an entire mythology has developed. At the same time, however, Eichmann's extraordinary notoriety is perplexing, particularly given the characterization of him that has taken root in the public imagination as a result, above all, of Arendt's work, which declared him "an average, 'normal' person, neither feeble-minded nor indoctrinated nor cynical" (*Eichmann in Jerusalem* 26). The notion of Eichmann's alleged normality, which Arendt famously and enduringly inscribed into the global discourse on the Holocaust with her memorable designation "the banality of evil," thus reflects an apparent twofold paradox: not only does the particular form of evil represented by Eichmann's person and by his diligent and fastidious facilitation of the deportation process deviate radically, as Arendt argues, from conventional notions of criminal diabolism, but his exceptional and abiding infamy is also at odds with his averred ordinariness, with his intermediate rank, and with the somewhat secondary (albeit not trivial) role that he played in the broader conceptualization of the Judeocide.[1] Despite or perhaps even precisely because of these contradictions, Eichmann continues to fascinate both scholars and artists, who continually and compulsively plumb the depths of his alleged normality, looking for answers to questions that resist easy clarification; their collective attempt to read Eichmann results, as Kara Critchell et al. argue, in "an irreducibly complex web of representations, translations, and (re-)mediation" (20).[2]

The extensive dialogue on Eichmann that has developed in the decades since his trial, which constituted a watershed moment for the revelation of the crimes of the Holocaust and one of the only public trials to feature direct testimony from a perpetrator, has had such a profound and lasting effect on the discourse on the Holocaust and the crimes of National Socialism that one cannot even begin to speak about individual perpetrators without at least mentioning Eichmann. The worldwide televisual broadcast of the

---

[1] According to Cesarani, "Eichmann was not a policy-maker: his function was operational. His role in the follow-up to the Wannsee Conference shows that he could influence policy, but only within restricted parameters" (119).

[2] Bettina Stangneth identifies over eight hundred scholarly titles pertaining to Eichmann's historical role in the Holocaust, his capture, and his trial (541). She does not list creative works that explore Eichmann's person, but the number of such texts is certainly not miniscule.

trial and the massive media coverage it galvanized not only transformed him into "a metonym for the entire history of the Nazi persecution and mass murder of the Jews as well as its legacy" (Cesarani 1) but also firmly established through his case a paradigmatic archetype of Holocaust perpetration, namely, the figure of the "desk murderer," the *génocidaire* who generates and manages the extensive bureaucratic substructure of mass murder but who is able to maintain a clean conscience by virtue of never committing a physically violent act himself.[3] Indeed, Cesarani credits Eichmann's trial and the discourse that developed in response to it (in particular, Arendt's book) not only with establishing the prototype of the perpetrator of state-authorized industrial genocide but also with signaling "the birth of 'Holocaust studies,' an unforeseen and oblique legacy of the trial" (325). And the surge of Eichmann representation and analysis shows no signs of subsiding. In particular, the last ten to fifteen years have witnessed a revitalization of sorts in what one might term "Eichmann studies," a designation I use in a not entirely tongue-in-cheek manner to refer to the recent boom in scholarly literature and popular representations that attempt not only to clarify Eichmann's pivotal historical role in the coordination and implementation of the Holocaust but also—and more prevalently—to probe the psychological and sociological dimensions of his participation in the genocidal crimes of National Socialism and their juridical and philosophical implications. The professed goal of the great majority of these depictions is to decipher from his crimes and his attitudes about them what sort of person Eichmann was and how he thought, positing interpretations regarding his personality, character, and psychological makeup. In short, almost half a century after his execution in 1961, a flourishing literature continues to read Eichmann as a text that can still provide novel insights about the man in particular and his relationship to the perpetration of genocide in general. Moreover, such representations posit Eichmann as the paradigmatic perpetrator, placing

---

3 According to Alan Milchman and Alan Rosenberg, "The desk killer is a high-level functionary in a vast bureaucratic organisation who does his killing from behind a desk, from which he plans and organises mass murder. He never sees the faces of those he consigns to death, his victims, who are no more than so many numbers on official forms. His work is a matter of logistics, of implementing policies decided by the ruling circles of the state apparatus. . . . The desk killer is the quintessential high-level bureaucrat functioning according to the requirements of the evolving genocidal universe" (215).

him at the very center of post-Holocaust attempts to understand the minds of the men who perpetrated the Holocaust. The figure of Eichmann is thus fundamental to the history of perpetrator representation.

The Paradigmatic Eichmann

Just as one cannot speak about Holocaust perpetrators without referring to Eichmann, one cannot likewise discuss the Eichmann phenomenon without also mentioning Hannah Arendt (1906–75) and her extremely influential study of Eichmann, which tackles the concept of evil, a category that had been—and continues to be—unquestionably central to the discussion of Holocaust perpetration. *Eichmann in Jerusalem* comprises above all an inquiry into the dynamics of representation. In particular, Arendt grapples with how to locate, define, and interpret the particular variant of evil associated with Eichmann and his crimes and how to render a model of his mind that would reconcile the indisputably maleficent quality of his role in the Holocaust with his character, which Arendt believes was incompatible with conventional notions of evil. Eichmann, she argues, was not a "monster" (*Eichmann in Jerusalem* 54), "not Iago and not Macbeth" (287), as especially the Israeli prosecutor Gideon Hausner deliberately portrayed him,[4] but "an average, 'normal'" (26), rather unexceptional man of his own historical moment. In Arendt's view, Eichmann's mentality was characterized by "self-deception, lies, and stupidity" (52); by "an inability to *think*, namely, to think from the standpoint of somebody else" (49); and by a reliance on empty jargon and baroque linguistic formulations that served to disguise the absence of and function as proxy for cognitive and ethical depth. In its sheer thoughtlessness, Eichmann's mind thus reflected, according to Arendt, the "systematic mendacity that had constituted the general, and generally accepted, atmosphere of the Third Reich" (52).[5]

---

4 In a series of articles published after the trial in the *Saturday Evening Post*, Hausner writes that Eichmann was "a dangerous, perverted, sadistic personality with an unlimited capability of using fellow men as inanimate objects for the attainment of his goals," who was nevertheless "legally sane and responsible for his actions" (20).

5 According to José Brunner, Hausner's and Arendt's opposing representations of Eichmann's mentality established the lines of the ensuing discourse on the figure: "Much of the debate on Eichmann's psyche, particularly as it emerged

The importance of Arendt's contribution to and influence on the development of the scholarly and artistic discourse on Eichmann over the last several decades cannot be overstated; indeed, most of the recent wave of scholarly works and artistic representations assume as their basic orientation point her supereminent interpretation of Eichmann's mind and his motives—or apparent lack thereof. In the arena of popular representation, for example, Rony Braumann and Eyal Sivan's 1999 creative documentary film *The Specialist* and Margarete von Trotta's 2012 feature film *Hannah Arendt*, to name just two of a slew of cinematic explorations of various aspects of Eichmann's life, feature creatively manipulated archival footage from the trial and reproduce Arendt's thesis of Eichmann's banality as a primary explanatory and narrative framework. And much of the current scholarly surge in Eichmann studies has originated in and benefited from a parallel renewed interest in Arendt and her works, including her coverage of the Eichmann trial, from scholars ranging from Seyla Benhabib to Judith Butler and José Brunner.[6]

In particular, two major historical analyses have worked to rejuvenate and reevaluate the discourse on Eichmann, particularly as it has been framed by Arendt. David Cesarani's compelling 2004 biography *Becoming Eichmann: Rethinking the Life, Crimes, and Trial of a "Desk Murderer"* vehemently rejects Arendt's thesis of Eichmann's banality. In Cesarani's view, because Arendt was not present for enough of the trial to make any informed conclusions about Eichmann's character, she fashioned a powerful interpretation of his character and motives that "was to a large extent predetermined and mythological" (4); that, despite its recognition of Eichmann's superficial

---

at his trial, is structured along the Hausner-Arendt dichotomy: he is portrayed either as a demonic character or as a banal individual" (3).

6 The title of Richard J. Golsan and Sarah M. Misemer's 2017 volume, *The Trial That Never Ends: Hannah Arendt's "Eichmann in Jerusalem in Retrospect,"* pointedly refers to this phenomenon of recurrent interest. In his review of the historiography of the Eichmann trial of the last two decades, Michael Löffelsender writes, "With regard to the Eichmann trial, one can say that the historical and legal scholarship to date is in general still very focused (perhaps too much so) on engaging with Hannah Arendt's interpretations rather than on generating new lines of inquiry" ("Mit Blick auf den Eichmann-Prozess lässt sich konstatieren, dass sich sowohl die geschichtswissenschaftliche als auch die rechtshistorische Forschung insgesamt bis heute sehr und vielleicht zu stark darauf fokussiert, sich mit den Deutungen Hannah Arendts auseinanderzusetzen, statt neue Fragestellungen zu generieren," 247, my translation).

mimicry of conscience, did not take into account the self-interested, calculatedly variable, and strategically performative quality of Eichmann's self-presentation; and that crucially ignored Eichmann's overtly antisemitic beliefs.[7] Most recently, Bettina Stangneth's masterful 2011 tome *Eichmann vor Jerusalem: Das unbehelligte Leben eines Massenmörders* (*Eichmann Before Jerusalem: The Unexamined Life of a Mass Murderer* [2014]), which engages in a synthetic reading of thousands of pages of documents from the pretrial era, including transcripts of interviews with Eichmann and Eichmann's own autobiographical writings, has made a game-changing intervention into Eichmann studies. Stangneth takes up and develops Cesarani's argument regarding the performative aspects of Eichmann's "deliberately banal façade" (257)[8] at the trial, analyzing the ways in which Eichmann self-consciously constructed and performed versions of his identity in multiple texts and public venues in the decades prior to the trial performance that Arendt witnessed and that thus has so dominantly shaped the discourse on and representations of Eichmann. As Stangneth argues, "Eichmann acted out a new role for every stage of his life, for each new audience and every new aim" (xvii), shaping his performance in particular to the expectations of his respective audiences and the discursive requirements of the context.[9] Like Cesarani, Stangneth controverts some of Arendt's

---

7 According to Cesarani, "Arendt, by contrast, never disentangled the courtroom performances from the history that was being recalled within the legal context" (330). Further, he argues that "Hannah Arendt made a similar assumption about Eichmann's demeanour and built a philosophical edifice on it. But Eichmann's disinterested pose was part of the defence strategy: to avoid any display of a violent temperament or giving any justification for the view that he attacked his work with passion. At the same time, his studied indifference was of a piece with his conduct during the months of interrogation . . . ; he gave the impression of someone emotionally dead or profoundly repressed" (257–58).

8 Hausner writes that "Eichmann carefully constructed a picture of himself that was best calculated to save his life" (22); Stangneth argues that the identity he created was "the perfect mask. The ideological warrior became the paper pusher in a remote office, mass murder became a confusing collection of paper transactions" ("die perfekte Maske. Aus dem Weltanschauungskrieger wurde der Papiersortierer im abgelegenen Büro, aus dem Massemord eine unübersichtliche Sammlung von Aktenvorgängen," quoted in Newmark 115, my translation).

9 In their recent edited volume on Arendt's text, Golsan and Misemer frame the question of the appropriateness of Stangneth's focus on the performative quality of Eichmann's testimony: "One of the challenges Stangneth's *Eichmann Before Jerusalem* itself faces is reconciling the author's claim that Eichmann was

conclusions, particularly her "characterization of Eichmann's 'inability to speak' and 'inability to *think*'" (268). At the same time, however, Stangneth takes issue with Cesarani's allegation that Arendt's abbreviated presence at the trial resulted in a superficial familiarity with his testimony and other trial documents, claiming that Arendt in fact "was one of the most thorough readers of the interrogation and trial transcripts, which she took back to the United States with her" (529-30). Stangneth acknowledges that Arendt recognized the highly performative and indeed theatrical dimensions of Eichmann's self-presentation at the trial but argues that Arendt's thesis was flawed because her political-philosophical approach led her to assume that he was an unconscious, superficial, and inflexible mimic (in Arendt's words, "a clown" [*Eichmann in Jerusalem* 54]) who was unable to control—particularly along linguistic lines—his own self-production, rather than an accomplished and opportunistic performer who crafted his appearance and narrative for different audiences according to what he perceived were their interests, desires, and prejudices.[10] In Stangneth's view,

---

a consummate actor and was performing at every stage of his life to please those around him. If this is the case, why would he not have been 'performing' his racial hatred and fanaticism to please his Nazi superiors?" (14). Their statement presumes that Eichmann, had he consciously (or unconsciously) performed his identity for his superiors, would have chosen a different version of self than the one he historically presented in order to please them. But such a conclusion assumes that the superiors whom Eichmann most wished to please, especially Reinhard Heydrich, chief of the Reich Security Main Office (Reichssicherheitshauptamt, or RSHA), and Heinrich Müller, head of the Gestapo and Eichmann's boss at the RSHA, valued overt or irrational displays of "racial hatred and fanaticism" over ambition, efficiency, obedience, and professionalism, the qualities Eichmann worked to project both in his Third Reich–era career and at the trial. In fact, those men may have tacitly encouraged and even modeled the very performance of identity that Eichmann deployed at his trial; as Richard Evans (276) and George C. Browder (*Hitler's Enforcers* 41–42) have both argued, Heydrich and Müller put a premium on the rational, efficient accomplishment of their racial-ideological goals. Cesarani implies that Eichmann's behavior at the trial, particularly his responses to the three German-born Israeli judges, projected the same sort of professional deference that had characterized his relationships with his Nazi superiors, minus, of course, the inherent ideological or antisemitic attitudes that informed those relationships (299).

10 According to Stangneth, "Hannah Arendt chose the method of understanding that she was familiar with: repeatedly reading Eichmann's words and conducting a detailed analysis of the person speaking and writing, on the assumption that someone speaks and writes only when they want to be understood. She read the transcripts of his hearing and the trial more thoroughly than almost

Arendt's text is itself an essential component in the larger narrative of Eichmann's self-representation and its public reception: "One of the most significant insights to be gained from studying Adolf Eichmann is reflected in Arendt: even someone of average intelligence can induce a highly intelligent person to defeat herself with her own weapon: her desire to see her expectations fulfilled" (xxv). Both Cesarani and Stangneth note the ways in which contemporary discourse on Eichmann is inextricably bound to Arendt's reading of him; Cesarani writes, "Ironically, . . . *Eichmann in Jerusalem*, more than the trial itself[,] shaped Eichmann's legacy. Anyone writing on the subject today works in the shadow of Hannah Arendt" (15), while, according to Stangneth, ever since Arendt's book appeared, "every essay on Adolf Eichmann has also been a dialogue with Hannah Arendt" (xxii). (Tellingly, Cesarani and Stangneth each choose metaphors—"shadow" and "dialogue"—that reflect their respective mostly negative and reservedly positive assessments of Arendt's book.) Arendt's assessment of Eichmann is thus taken as a primary or original reading, an Eichmann Urtext that necessitates a kind of Talmudic exegesis and that continues to be the focus of analysis and debate in a wide range of disciplines. Even the work of those scholars, like Cesarani, who labor to dispute Arendt's conclusions has the paradoxical consequence of maintaining her text's centrality for representations of Eichmann. As Mark Lilla argues, "As sometimes happens in the world of ideas, it is those who think least of *Eichmann in Jerusalem* who keep it alive by dragging its author out for what is by now ritual trial and conviction. This is how the book survives."[11]

My aim here in this chapter is not to take sides in the heated debate about whether Arendt, with her famous banality thesis, was correct in

---

anyone else. And for this very reason, she fell into his trap. Eichmann-in-Jerusalem was little more than a mask. She didn't recognize it, although she was acutely aware that she had not understood the phenomenon as well as she had hoped" (xxiii).

11   Seyla Benhabib reads the periodic reemergence of scholarly interest in Arendt's portrait of Eichmann as the expression of the lasting traumatic effect on contemporary discourse of the Holocaust in general and the Eichmann trial in particular: "The trauma of the Holocaust of European Jewry is so deep in us that like a wound that one scratches before it has healed, it will keep bleeding. Hannah Arendt's *Eichmann in Jerusalem* scratches where it has not healed and probably never will. This is why the controversy will 'die down, simmer,' but 'erupt' again and again, in Irving Howe's wise words" ("Whose Trial" 221).

her assessment of the historical Eichmann. Among scholars of history, at least, that matter has largely been settled; as the eminent Holocaust historian Christopher Browning judiciously characterizes the current assessment, "For the record, let me state that I consider Arendt's concept of the 'banality of evil' a very important insight for understanding many of the perpetrators of the Holocaust, but not Eichmann himself. Arendt was fooled by Eichmann's strategy of self-representation in part because there were so many perpetrators of the kind he was pretending to be" (*Collected Memories* 3–4).[12] Instead of rehashing well-established arguments in an attempt to reconcile Arendt's portrait with Eichmann's role and behavior both during the Holocaust and in his trial, I aim rather to examine the cultural construction Arendt creates and mediates with her notorious model of Eichmann's mind and to analyze how and with what means she does so. Moreover, while the diverse recent approaches to Eichmann continue to place Arendt at the center of their analysis, I wish to decenter Arendt slightly in my examination of cultural mediations of Eichmann, for however much we may be overshadowed by or in perpetual dialogue with *Eichmann in Jerusalem*, it is important to note that influential readings of Eichmann precede the publication and immediate notoriety of Arendt's book. For this reason, I find it fruitful to situate her 1963 assessment alongside two other notable biographical portraits that emerge from his trial and that appear shortly afterward: Harry Mulisch's 1962 *De Zaak 40/61: Een Reportage* (*Criminal Case 40/61, the Trial of Adolf Eichmann: An Eyewitness Account* [2005]), and William L. Hull's 1963 *The Struggle for a Soul*. Much like Arendt, the well-known Dutch writer and intellectual Mulisch covered the Eichmann trial as a correspondent and produced an illuminating account of Eichmann designed to dispute the public imagination of him as the embodiment of monstrous evil. His book is a collection of the reports he published in the Dutch prominent weekly magazine *Elseviers Weekblad*

---

12 As Daniel Conway points out, part of the problem with Arendt's banality thesis (and one that contributes considerably to historians' objections regarding its applicability to Eichmann) is that the concept is inadequately explained or theorized by Arendt herself (68). Conway proposes to "render a sympathetic construction of what Arendt had in mind when she referred to the 'banality of evil'" (68), an aim that also aptly describes the projects of other contemporary defenders of Arendt who wish to rehabilitate her text in light of criticism from historians such as Cesarani.

before, during, and after the trial. Neither Mulisch nor Arendt interacted personally with Eichmann; both writers were thus forced by necessity to base their accounts exclusively on their observations and interpretations of his physical demeanor, behavior, and statements at the trial and on their reading of the documents. Hull's relationship to Eichmann, on the other hand, took a rather different form, which had important consequences for his account. A Christian missionary working in Israel, Hull endeavored to provide spiritual counsel to Eichmann in the weeks before the latter's execution and shortly thereafter wrote his book about their encounter. Not unlike Sereny's depiction of Stangl (which I analyze in the next chapter), Hull's portrait of Eichmann is thus based on his representation of the intensive intersubjective engagement between confessor and confessant. The epistemological and discursive foundations for the three texts' respective interpellations of Eichmann thus differ in important ways. At the same time, however, all three constructions of Eichmann's mind are significantly shaped by Eichmann's own self-representation at his trial and—in the case of Hull—in private meetings, which, as Cesarani, Stangneth, and Christian Gerlach have argued, was strategic and variable depending on the specific context of his statements and his particular aims at the moment.[13] My analysis of these three texts both illuminates the diversity in the inferences and interpretations of Eichmann's mind based on his statements, demeanor, and behavior during and shortly after his trial and contextualizes these portraits within the more recent research that highlights the ways in which Eichmann self-consciously performed versions of his identity for different audiences.[14] As I will demonstrate, each of the three mediating

---

13 According to Gerlach, Eichmann's testimony was often self-contradictory and "mix[ed] truth, outright lies, dissimulation, and other tactical maneuvers" (429). For that reason, he argues that it cannot be taken at "face value" (429), particularly by historians. Gerlach identifies in Eichmann's heterogeneous statements public and private "strategies of legal defense and self-justification" (428) that were shaped in response to his immediate context. Christopher Browning has also argued with regard to Eichmann's own writing, "Even more than most memoirs, the Eichmann testimonies, both before and after capture, are self-consciously calculated attempts at self-representation, self-justification, and legal defense" (*Collected Memories* 8).

14 Although the work of Cesarani, Stangneth, and Gerlach focuses on what Christopher Browning terms Eichmann's "strategy of self-presentation" (*Collected Memories* 3) in his biography, autobiography, and testimony, it does not do so from the specific standpoint of theories of performativity as articulated by

figures—Arendt, Mulisch, and Hull—locates Eichmann's mind in discreet aspects or operations of his performed identity: Arendt constructs Eichmann as a product of his own banal language, Mulisch renders Eichmann's mind through his ironic reading of Eichmann's facial features and expressions, and Hull constructs Eichmann's conscience through his narrow and obsessive focus on what he sees to be the state of Eichmann's soul. Taken collectively, these interpretations written by two eyewitnesses and an interlocutor show radically disparate perspectives on Eichmann's mind, creating a kaleidoscopic lens, rather than a comprehensive profile, through which they collectively filter his acts of self-presentation. I find these texts helpful not for determining who the "real" Eichmann was but rather for demonstrating the ways in which contemporary observers of Eichmann's performance attempted to infer and project a coherent cognitive and emotional entity—a theory of his mind, if you will—from his physical appearance, his behavior, and his statements. For that reason, while such assessments may be of partial—or perhaps even, in the case of Hull's text, dubious—historical value, I argue they are critically important for showing how Eichmann's interpellators employed processes of mind-reading in their attempt to craft meaningful narratives about his motivations. Moreover, despite the striking disparity in their relative notoriety (Arendt's book has become a classic of Holocaust literature and political philosophy, Mulisch's account has maintained—outside the Netherlands, at least—a limited readership consisting mostly of scholars in Holocaust Studies, and Hull's

---

J. L. Austin and Judith Butler. At the same time, however, their assessments of Eichmann's strategies align with Leigh A. Payne's work on the confessional performances of perpetrators of authoritarian state violence, which she analyzes from the perspective of Austin's speech act theory. According to Payne, "When perpetrators confess to authoritarian state violence, not only do they read a carefully prepared script, they also act it out. They imbue their performance with political meaning through what they say, how they say it, and where and when they make their confessional performance" (227). Aligning with Gerlach's skepticism with regard to the "face value" of Eichmann's testimonial statements and Stangneth's method of synthetic analysis of Eichmann's diverse written texts and acts of verbal self-representation, Payne further argues that "researchers face the challenge of examining how perpetrators and their 'handlers' lie in their performance through appearances, gestures, and text. This involves comparing performances by the same perpetrator on different stages and tracing media and archival accounts to determine the degree of continuity or disruption with earlier or later performances" (234). I discuss Payne's work in further detail in chapter 2.

book has been largely forgotten altogether), all three texts demonstrate how the myth of Eichmann developed and circulated and reveal the extent to which this archetype of genocidal perpetration has become a screen onto which postwar culture discharges its anxieties and desires.[15]

Eichmann as Linguistic Surface: Hannah Arendt's *Eichmann in Jerusalem* (1963)

Despite its notoriety as the preeminent inquiry into Eichmann's role in the Holocaust, his understanding of his crimes, and his disposition, *Eichmann in Jerusalem* aims its attention only partly on Eichmann's character. The scope of Arendt's book is rather much broader, aspiring additionally to describe and critique the course and movement of the trial, the judgment, and Eichmann's execution;[16] to analyze the juridical and political ramifications of the trial (especially for the young state of Israel, which Arendt sees as negatively exploiting the trial, and for the development of an international juridical response to genocide); to track Eichmann's career throughout the years of the Third Reich; to establish a timeline and causal connections for the deportations of Europe's Jews to concentration camps and killing centers that Eichmann was so centrally involved in planning; to discuss what she controversially sees as the collaborative role the *Judenräte* played in negotiations with Eichmann with regard to the deportations (an indiscriminately general and historically ill-informed conclusion that in the view of both many of her contemporaries and scholars today betrays a callous indifference to the plight of the victims and the untenable situation in which the National Socialist regime placed them); and particularly to reflect on the dimensions of totalitarianism revealed by Eichmann's case. Arendt's assessment of Eichmann's mind is thus embedded

---

15 Stangneth writes, "Like a mirror, [Eichmann] reflected people's fears and expectations, whether they were fearing for their own lives or hoping he would confirm a theory of evil" (367).

16 According to Leora Bilsky, Arendt was especially critical of the Israeli prosecution's didactic presentation and its reliance on the emotional effects provided by "witnesses of suffering," the over one hundred Holocaust survivors who were called to testify at the trial, many of whom had never met Eichmann or been aware of his existence and whose testimony could thus not directly contribute to establishing his culpability (161).

in her larger framework of discussion of Eichmann's function as an actor within the totalitarian state of the Third Reich; for this reason, although her book places Eichmann at its center, the individual, idiosyncratic aspects of his psychology and biography are made subordinate to her analysis of him as a "phenomenon" (*Eichmann in Jerusalem* 287) who represented not a psychological aberration or "'exception within the Nazi regime'" (26) but rather the embodied implementation of its totalitarian logic. As Moishe Postone argues, "In spite of appearances, however, Arendt's book is neither primarily a report on the Eichmann trial, nor a historical analysis of the Holocaust. Rather, it should be read as an extension and elaboration of her investigation of totalitarianism, which she regarded as the central problem of the twentieth century" (190). Arendt's concentration on the dynamics of totalitarianism as they played out in Eichmann's case directs her to examine primarily both his function within the genocidal project of the "Final Solution" and the ways in which totalitarianism manifested functionally within his personality. In other words, as a political philosopher, Arendt is interested above all in Eichmann's mental character as a reflection of the ideological worldview, the ethical principles, and the behavioral habitus of National Socialism rather than in his particular individual psychological makeup, meaning his emotional history, his relationships with others, his deep-seated motivations, and his psychic processing of his past (a perspective that she derisively describes as "the comedy of the soul experts" [26] in reference to both the psychiatrists who examined him in prison and the apostolic minister Hull). For this reason, although her analysis does indeed produce some astute insights with regard to his mental constitution, Arendt prefers to portray Eichmann more as a representative—albeit extreme—prototype of a "new type of criminal" (*Eichmann in Jerusalem* 276), namely, the thoughtless totalitarian bureaucrat whose crimes were strikingly unmotivated by any particular animus toward the victims—in Daniel Conway's words, the "criminal devoid of criminal intent" (72)—and less as an idiosyncratic amalgamation of conflicting psychological dynamics.[17] As Arne Johan Vetlesen argues, Arendt's "intellectualist bias" (106)

---

17 According to José Brunner, Arendt disdained any overtly psychological approach to understanding Eichmann's mentality and behavior: "Note Arendt's choice of the term 'comedy' to describe Eichmann's alleged examination by a team of mental health professionals. In her eyes, the 'soul experts' were putting

and her philosophical penchant for generating sweeping "analytic categories" (106) cause her to ignore Eichmann's particular emotional or psychological disposition in favor of a method of mind-reading that gives priority to his "purely cognitive" (122) characteristics.[18]

Proceeding from her view of Eichmann as a totalitarian actor rather than an individual psychological entity, Arendt sees him as representing, according to Daniel Conway, "the uniquely modern evil that is produced and mobilized by totalitarian regimes" (72). This new variant of evil resists conventional understandings and frameworks of malevolent or monstrous criminality as embodied, for example, in the Shakespearean villains Iago, Macbeth, and Richard III, three figures against whom Arendt juxtaposes Eichmann, in that it no longer proceeds from discernable and immediate personal motives, emotions, or passions that connect a criminal directly and

---

on an act and a laughable one at that. This remark reflects Arendt's dismissive attitude towards psychologists, psychiatrists, and their crafts. . . . Clearly, there was no place for psychology in the philosophical mode of understanding pursued by Arendt. . . . As opposed to psychologists, whose interest she defined as focused on the discovery of structures assumed to exist in the hidden 'inner world' of a personality, Arendt's understanding was directed exclusively at the diversity of visible and audible phenomena. . . . In Arendt's view, focusing on the mind's hidden structures or forces is as misguided as focusing on the body's internal organs: both yield monotonous results that are irrelevant to an understanding of the beautiful and abundant multiplicity of human existence" (16). Ravit Reichman takes up a similar position, arguing that Arendt's avoidance of psychological interpretation is connected to the particular generic perspective and framing of the textual form she adopts for her analysis: "Her approach, in keeping with the genre-free form of the report or the chronicle, sets out to describe individuals' surfaces rather than their depths in order to arrive at a more sweeping analytical and aesthetic position. If the past is an outline or chronicle, then the person—in outline form—is a silhouette" (148).

18 Seyla Benhabib links what Vetlesen terms Arendt's "intellectualist bias" in *Eichmann in Jerusalem* with Arendt's own history with the Third Reich and her emotional investment in the trial: "Arendt herself was a survivor, and her 'Olympian distance'—as Ralph Ellison once named it—may have also been a defence mechanism against the traumatic possibility of falling into the hands of the Gestapo. . . . Arendt, who rejected psychoanalysis, would most likely be offended by this interpretation, yet there is so much evidence in her language, in the construction of narrative voice in *Eichmann in Jerusalem*, that reveals a storm raging within her, that this reading is hard to resist. Arendt's much-misunderstood sarcasm as well as her thinly veiled contempt for Eichmann himself were like layers of additional skin that she had to clothe herself in so that she could provide one of the first and most dramatic accounts of the destruction of European Jewry" ("Whose Trial?" 210–11).

often obsessively to his victims (such as political gambits and power machinations or hatred, betrayal, and rage).[19] Rather, it emerges through Eichmann's unquestioning identification with the totalitarian state's program of persecution and his self-important role within it; an abstract, depersonalized relationship with the victims of that project; an obtuse lack of interest in and empathy for their fate; and an absence of moral imagination that would have allowed him to have considered taking any action that opposed the state's genocidal objectives. Eichmann's evil, as Arendt sees it—and she clearly regards Eichmann's crimes as proceeding from a definite form of evil, however unimaginative and thus mundane—cannot be described "in metaphysical terms as ultimate depravity, corruption, or sinfulness" (Benhabib, "Whose Trial?" 219), the characteristics with which evil has been defined for millennia in Western thought (traits that, not incidentally, the Israeli prosecutor Hausner had tried to pin incongruously onto Eichmann). Arendt famously and controversially describes this new manifestation of evil, which—or, more precisely, *whom*—she saw as inextricably bound to totalitarian practice, as "banal." With that descriptor she refers not to the evil embodied in Eichmann's crimes during the Holocaust but to that which inheres in Eichmann's commission of them, which she views as lacking the villainous intent or malevolent character conventionally associated with agents of evil (a fundamental distinction that especially early critics of her texts failed to perceive).[20] With her concept of the "banality of evil" (one

---

19 According to Brad Prager, "It is not by accident that [Arendt] often refers to Shakespeare" (74) and employs in her analysis "theatrical analogues" (77); in fact, he argues, she regarded the trial as "judicial theater" (78) and "understood the entire courtroom to be participating in a performance—it was a room in which everyone had a part to play" (78). Daniel Conway maintains that, unlike Eichmann, the three Shakespearean villains mentioned by Arendt "fascinate by virtue of their psychological and affective complexity" (74). He further argues that Iago, Macbeth, and Richard III "project themselves imaginatively into their crimes and into the resulting suffering of their prospective victims" and function as "*agents* in the full, robust sense of that term" (74–75). Eichmann, by contrast, "lacked the imagination needed to 'prove a villain,' which ensured that he never would become one" (74). For this reason, "on the world-stage envisioned by Shakespeare, Eichmann might be cast as a knave, stooge, or fool, but he would not qualify as a genuinely evil villain" (74).
20 Richard J. Bernstein refers to the "hysterical fashion" of the statements of Arendt's early critics, who believed that "the very phrase 'the banality of evil' was offensive" in that "it seemed to trivialize not only what Eichmann had done but the full horror of the Shoah" (128–29). Seyla Benhabib acknowledges

that she admittedly conceptualized in *Eichmann in Jerusalem* only in part and later attempted to further define and qualify), Arendt thus opens up a distinction between crime and criminal, highlighting "the gap between the deeds and the doer" (Vetlesen 86) and manifesting "the dilemma between the unspeakable horror of the deeds and the undeniable ludicrousness of the man who perpetrated them" (*Eichmann in Jerusalem* 54), namely, a man who "had no motives at all" (287). In so doing, she divests the agent of evil of his dramatic character and diabolical associations and tethers him to the everyday reality of his participation in the minute decision-making process and painstaking administration of programmatic genocide.[21]

One year after the appearance of *Eichmann in Jerusalem*, Arendt writes in a letter to her old friend Gershom Scholem in response to his pointed criticism of her text,

> It is indeed my opinion now that evil is never radical, that it is only extreme, and that it possesses neither depth nor any demonic dimension. It can overgrow and lay waste the whole world precisely because it spreads like a fungus on the surface. It is "thought-defying," as I said, because

---

Arendt's difficulty in pinning down exactly what she meant by the phrase but at the same time takes the early critics to task for willfully distorting its intent: "Arendt forced the English language into a procrustean bed to convey her own complex, and perhaps even ultimately inconclusive, reflections on the issue of 'personal responsibility under dictatorships.' She did not mean that what Eichmann had helped to perpetrate was banal or that the extermination of the Jews, and of other peoples, by the Nazis was banal. It takes either a great deal of hermeneutic blindness and ill will or both to miss her meaning in the usage of this term, even if one may disagree with the assessment of Eichmann's psychology. The phrase the 'banality of evil' was meant to refer to a *specific quality of mind and character* of the doer himself, but neither to the deeds not to the principles behind those deeds" ("Arendt's *Eichmann in Jerusalem*" 74).

21 Devin O. Pendas provides what I find to be an insightful definition of what Arendt means by banal evil in the case of Eichmann: "Such evil is banal in a dual sense. First, it is not grandiose. It has about it not the slightest whiff of 'satanic greatness.' Consequently, it is a purely unromanticized evil. . . . This is an evil so banal that, Arendt's own protestations to the contrary, it becomes radical. Second, this thoughtless, unmotivated evil is banal in that it is mundane and ordinary as well. Like the logic of everyday life in modernity itself, evil is banal both because it is general, typical, and unexciting *and*, in Arendt's more technical sense, because there is a systematic and increasing disconnect between individual motivation or will and collective action" (82–83).

thought tries to reach some depth, to go to the roots, and the moment it concerns itself with evil, it is frustrated because there is nothing. That is its "banality." Only the Good has depth and can be radical. ("'Eichmann in Jerusalem': An Exchange of Letters" 56)

In defense of her assertion of Eichmann's banality, which she sees as proliferating laterally "on the surface" but not penetrating into the "depth," Arendt reveals here her proclivity to read Eichmann as manifesting a superficial externality rather than a subterranean dimensionality, an aspect of her analysis that a number of scholars have pointed out and that is in part a result, I suggest, of her avowed eschewal of a psychological approach to her subject.[22] Judith M. Hughes maintains that Arendt "had no wish to plumb [Eichmann's] depths. Actually, she took it for granted that he had no depths" (151), while Valerie Hartouni argues that "in Arendt's reading, . . . there was no hidden or hideous evil lurking beneath or behind the defendant's nondescript exterior, no mask to be removed or depths to be unearthed or examined" (72). José Brunner, who has most closely addressed this aspect of Arendt's analysis, writes that, for Arendt, "the essential was not beneath the surface; rather the surface of human conduct itself revealed the uniqueness, plurality, and splendor of life" (16). He attributes this position to Arendt's "phenomenological outlook," an understanding of mind that is "directed exclusively at the diversity of visible and audible phenomena" and leaves "no room for mental archeology, which seeks the forces active in the dark recesses of the psyche, encoded in external appearances" (16). For

---

22 Critics who have investigated Arendt's focus on Eichmann's "surface" include Judith M. Hughes, Valerie Hartouni, José Brunner, Daniel Conway, Lars Svendsen, Ravit Reichman, Brad Prager, and Yasco Horsman. As Hughes argues, "Arendt's appraisal of Eichmann, his 'extraordinary shallowness'—a close cousin to his 'sheer thoughtlessness'—made any further inquiry into his psyche pointless. And so she abandoned the psychological field—prematurely" (137). According to Prager, "Plumbing his unplumbed depths . . . would have been fruitless. The man remained, in her eyes, a surface onto which the prosecution and the public could only project. . . . She avoided writing about things that she could not see, in particular the perpetrator's elusive psychological depths" (77–78). Conway writes, "For Arendt, the question of the *real* Eichmann, the actor behind the masks, the schemer behind the schemes, was simply a nonstarter" (83).

this reason, "her observations on the defendant in the glass booth centered on what could be seen and heard, that is, his appearance and utterances at the trial and the protocol of his interrogations" (16). In other words, while Arendt is highly aware of what Daniel Conway calls "Eichmann's penchant for theatricality" (82) and in fact, as Brad Prager argues, presents him "as an actor among actors" (85), she takes "his appearance as all there [is] to him" (Brunner 20) rather than regard it as a sign inviting her to excavate Eichmann's subterranean levels for evidence of the possibility of other, more enigmatic versions of a self.[23]

While, as Brunner argues, Arendt is a penetrating—if sparing—observer of Eichmann's "visible ... phenomena" (16), meaning his physical demeanor and body language (an aspect of her interpretation I will touch upon briefly later), and a meticulous analyst of his actions and decisions while a member of the SS, she filters Eichmann's mind and character almost exclusively through his verbal expression, both during his trial testimony and in the documentation of his pretrial interrogation. Indeed, Eichmann's verbal expression constitutes the primary aperture through which Arendt is able to infer his mind, which is perhaps not surprising, given the attention she, as a philosopher, devotes to the role of language in comprehending another's mental states. Especially in "An Expert on the Jewish Question," the third chapter of *Eichmann in Jerusalem* and the part that contains her most extensive and incisive analysis of Eichmann's character, Arendt pays close attention not only to *what* Eichmann said in his statements, meaning the

---

23 Brunner further argues—convincingly, in my opinion—that, despite Arendt's insistence that Eichmann was "normal," her characterization of him connotes him as Other: "In contrast to Hausner, she constructed Eichmann's mind as marked by a crucial absence; she attributed neither depth nor contradiction to it, neither murderous passions nor a hatred of life nor a devotion to death. However, there also was a surprising similarity between Arendt's conception and Hausner's that neither might have appreciated. Both of them presented Eichmann in a reductionist mode; ... both sought to reduce Eichmann's mind to one dimension: either to a demonic urge to annihilate the Jews or to a horrifyingly banal thoughtlessness. Both of them suggested that Eichmann had no conscience, lacked empathy and traditional standards of morality, and felt no guilt despite his murderous deeds. Moreover, in spite of Arendt's repeated emphasis on the ordinariness and normalcy of Eichmann's personality, her rhetoric constructed a deep divide between the defendant and ordinary, normal people.... Arendt may have described him as a monster, despite her intention not to do so" (20–21).

historical content of his testimony, but also—and more acutely—to *how* he said it, meaning the linguistic means by which he shaped his own testimonial performance. Eichmann's surface, Arendt argues, was actualized above all in language—in particular, his weak command of the German language, which Shoshana Felman calls his "quasi-parodic German" (204)[24]—meaning the verbal façade through which he encountered the world and through which he testified to his role in the Holocaust. Rather than expressive of an extant and immotile internal nature, Eichmann's language, according to Arendt, determined his character and defined his social function in the world. In a frequently quoted passage that constitutes her most focused examination of Eichmann's speech (and his mental character in general), Arendt writes:

> The German text of the taped police examination, conducted from May 29, 1960, to January 17, 1961, each page corrected and approved by Eichmann, constitutes a veritable gold mine for a psychologist—provided he is wise enough to understand that the horrible can be not only ludicrous but outright funny. Some of the comedy cannot be conveyed in English, because it lies in Eichmann's heroic fight with the German language, which invariably defeats him. It is funny when he speaks, *passim*, of "winged words" (*geflügelte Worte*, a German colloquialism for famous quotes from the classics) when he means stock phrases, *Redensarten*, or slogans, *Schlagworte*. It was funny when, during the cross-examination conducted on the Sassen documents, conducted in German by the presiding judge, he used the phrase "*kontra geben*" (to give tit for tat), to indicate that he had resisted Sassen's efforts to liven up his stories; Judge Landau, obviously ignorant of the mysteries of card games, did not understand, and Eichmann could not think of

---

24 The Israeli police captain Avner Less, who conducted 275 hours of pretrial interrogation of Eichmann between May 1960 and February 1961, writes that "his [Eichmann's] German was hideous. At first I had a very difficult time understanding him at all—the jargon of the Nazi bureaucracy pronounced in a mixture of Berlin and Austrian accents and further garbled by his liking for endlessly complicated sentences which he himself would occasionally get lost in" (vi).

any other way to put it. Dimly aware of a defect that must have plagued him even in school—it amounted to a mild case of aphasia—he apologized, saying, "Officialese [*Amtssprache*] is my only language." But the point here is that officialese became his language because he was genuinely incapable of uttering a single sentence that was not a cliché.... To be sure, the judges were right when they finally told the accused that all he had said was "empty talk"—except that they thought the emptiness feigned, and that the accused wished to cover up other thoughts which, though hideous, were not empty. This supposition seems refuted by the striking consistency with which Eichmann, despite his rather bad memory, repeated word for word the same stock phrases and self-invented clichés (when he did succeed in constructing a sentence of his own, he repeated it until it became a cliché) each time he referred to an event or incident of importance to him. Whether writing his memoirs in Argentina or in Jerusalem, whether speaking to the police examiner or to the court, what he said was always the same, expressed in the same words. The longer one listened to him, the more obvious it became that his inability to speak was closely connected with an inability to *think*, namely, to think from the standpoint of somebody else. No communication was possible with him, not because he lied but because he was surrounded by the most reliable of all safeguards against the words and the presence of others, and hence against reality as such. (*Eichmann in Jerusalem* 48–49)

Like the Israeli judges Moshe Landau, Benjamin Halevy, and Yitzhak Raveh, the Israeli interrogator Avner Less, and other observers of the trial, Arendt recognizes in Eichmann's testimony a rote, routinized, and ritualized relationship to language, which the judges collectively designated "empty talk" and Arendt classifies as "cliché." However, whereas, according to Arendt, the judges believed that Eichmann deployed his "empty talk" strategically to disguise more complex and mendacious motives that lay beneath the surface of his inane speech, Arendt is convinced that Eichmann exercised his ridiculous and noticeably repetitive language in part to contrive the effect of depth that in reality did not exist. He spoke in a limited repertoire of garrulous clichés, in Arendt's view, to perform the role of the punctilious, principled, and scrupulous functionary who was being called to account for situations in which, in his opinion, he had behaved impeccably and indeed admirably, considering what he characterized as the difficult circumstances in which he found himself.[25] His verbal expression was a script of sorts, consisting of formulaic "stock phrases" that he recited almost word-for-word in different contexts and for different audiences; in effect, it was deployed as a sort of locutionary liturgy to denote cognitive and emotional depth and to allow Eichmann to convince himself and others that he possessed a conscience and a moral framework for his actions. In reality, however, as Arendt argues, it functioned as a smokescreen that camouflaged Eichmann's near-total deficiency in what she calls "thought," by which she means not his general cognitive aptitude[26]—although she was convinced he possessed "rather modest mental gifts" (*Eichmann in Jerusalem* 135)—but rather his "total inability ever to look at anything from the other fellow's point of view" (47–48).[27] Eichmann's language not

---

25 "What makes these pages of the examination so funny is that all this was told in the tone of someone who was sure of finding 'normal, human' sympathy for a hard luck story" (Arendt, *Eichmann in Jerusalem* 50).
26 Arendt writes in her postscript to the book, "It was sheer thoughtlessness—something by no means identical with stupidity—that predisposed him to become one of the greatest criminals of that period" (*Eichmann in Jerusalem* 287–88).
27 Scholars demonstrate slightly divergent understandings of what Arendt means with her concept of thoughtlessness. For Pendas, it designates a moral category: "'Thoughtlessness' in this context does not mean ignorance. Arendt is quite clear that Eichmann knew full well he was sending Jews to be killed. His thoughtlessness was of an altogether different character. What Eichmann was unable to think through was the moral implications of this killing" (81). For Vetlesen, on the other hand, it is emotional: "I am prepared to claim that what Eichmann epitomizes is not so much thoughtlessness as *insensitivity*. The capacity he failed to exercise is emotional rather than intellectual or cognitive; it is the capacity to develop *empathy* with other human beings, to take an emotional interest in the human 'import' of the situation in which the persons affected by his actions found themselves" (105). Conway, for his part, sees it as chiefly a cognitive failing: "For the sake of clarity, we might say that Eichmann certainly was capable of *thinking*. . . . What he could not do, however, was to think *imaginatively*, i.e., from the experience and point of view of those who were most likely to raise a credible objection to his present or proposed course of action" (80).

only expressed his thoughtlessness but also capacitated it and actualized it in the first place; together they worked in tandem as a "mechanism that had become completely unalterable" (50) and that allowed him to live "in perfect harmony" (52) as a law-abiding citizen and administrator in the Third Reich. As Conway argues, "The familiar clockwork of his duty-bound conscience" and his "non-negotiable reliance on clichés, stock phrases, and language rules" functioned as a circular economy to guarantee "that he was unlikely ever to attain escape velocity from the closed system of his thoughtless existence" (79).

Eichmann's idiom of recurrent and recycled cliché, which Arendt describes with a sort of bitter sardonicism as "macabre humor" (*Eichmann in Jerusalem* 50) on account of its grimly humorous effects, took two forms.[28] On the one hand, Eichmann's language was characterized, as he himself admitted, by his reflexive recourse to "officialese," the bureaucratic vernacular both in which he discharged his duties as the principle coordinator of the deportation of Europe's Jewish populations to ghettos, concentration camps, and killing centers and in which he remembered and described his past in the present moment. With his bureaucratic idiolect, Eichmann, in Arendt's view, constructed himself as the obedient, scrupulous, efficient, and hands-on bureaucrat—"a functionary who adored his functionality" (Prager 77)—whose ultimate responsibility (and, it merits overtly mentioning, culpability) for the orders and actions he discharged in his role as *Obersturmbannführer* was, however, reassuringly limited (a representation of himself that he clearly thought would be positively evaluated by the judges). Moreover, through his articulation of his personal and public history in the language of bureaucratic regulation, he was able to "safeguard" his actions and moral self from possible self-reproach or even awareness of liability; his employment of the calcified officialese, which was

---

28 As Kerstin Steitz argues, Arendt's recognition of the grim humor of Eichmann's trial performance is one of the aspects of her text that most troubled readers when it appeared: "Arendt's critics found that the humorous aspects and intonations of her report lacked the propriety and gravity one expects from material dealing with the Holocaust. Since her critics considered laughter and seriousness as binary oppositions and therefore as mutually exclusive, they failed to realize that Arendt's irony and humor were part of her political rhetoric, which was intentionally provocative and had serious goals in mind" (133). Steitz connects Arendt's ironic perspective to a larger German and German-Jewish tradition of provocative speech.

characterized by abstraction, euphemism, circumlocution, jargon, convoluted sentence structure, objective or dehumanizing formulation, and preference for the passive voice, thus became the means by which, according to Cesarani, he erected a "carapace ... around his past" (244).[29] On the other hand, as Arendt notes, Eichmann also resorted to decidedly nonbureaucratic "winged words," meaning his own self-invented, bastardized variant of the linguistic repository particularly of German Classicism and Romanticism, which Eichmann used as a sort of self-proclaimed credential for membership, despite his limited education, in the *Bildungsbürgertum*, the German educated bourgeoisie.[30] These phrases, which gave him, as Arendt cites him, an "extraordinary sense of elation" (*Eichmann in Jerusalem* 53) whenever he used them, allowed him to "lay out his hermetic interpretation of the world and abandon himself to the pathos of his own language" (Stangneth 231), an ostentatiously affected relationship to language that characterized Nazism more generally. At the same time, his self-conscious use of his "winged words" indicated that he himself was very aware of the performative dimension of language, which created (rather than merely expressed) something every time he employed it. Through repeated recitation of his "winged words," out of which he constructed what Jakob Norberg calls "chains of pre-articulated sentences" (754) and "the templates of simplified narratives" (756), Eichmann forged, in Arendt's representation of him, a particular relationship to his role in National Socialism, fashioning a life narrative for himself "within quotation marks" (756).[31]

---

29 Istvan Shlomo Kulcsar, the Israeli psychiatrist who, prior to the trial, administered a battery of psychological tests that were then analyzed by the psychologist Shoshanna Kulcsar, writes in *Der Spiegel* in 1966: "[Eichmann's] language, just as his world view, was lifeless, mechanistic, formalistic and dehumanized" ("Seine Sprache ebenso wie seine Weltanschauung waren leblos, mechanistisch, formalistisch und entmenschlicht," 176, my translation). Geraldine Horan reads Eichmann's use of "officialese" as evidence of his continued identification with National Socialism (57).

30 According to Arendt, "In court, Eichmann gave the impression of a typical member of the lower middle classes, and this impression was more than borne out by every sentence he spoke or wrote while he was in prison. But this was misleading; he was rather the *déclassé* son of a solid middle-class family" (*Eichmann in Jerusalem* 31–32).

31 Citing from Eichmann's autobiographical writings, Arendt presents a stunning example of his penchant for "winged words" in his recitation of his own biography: "Today, fifteen years and a day after May 8, 1945, I begin to lead my thoughts back to that nineteenth of March of the year 1906, when at five o'clock in the

In her attempt to describe Eichmann's "regurgitat[ion]" (Norberg 756) of formulaic and hackneyed idioms, which in her view constituted a kind of language pathology, Arendt attributes to him "a mild case of aphasia" (*Eichmann in Jerusalem* 48), implying that Eichmann's ability to vocalize speech was impaired, preventing or making difficult his ability to speak. However, the opposite was actually the case; with his "empty talk," Eichmann suffered rather from a kind of logorrhea (or what Stangneth calls "his torrent of words" [422]), causing him to speak incessantly, whether in the Sassen interviews, in the interrogations with Less, at his trial, or during (as I shall discuss later in this chapter) his discussions with the Reverend Hull.[32] What was impaired in Eichmann, as Arendt's analysis makes clear, was not the form or physical organ of his speech but rather its content, which consisted almost exclusively of citation or mimicry. Eichmann, as Arendt reads him, was unable to operate as a linguistic subject and the author of his own speech; for this reason, he also can be regarded as having suffered from a kind of xenoglossia, or production of a language that is unknown or not in the possession of the speaker. In effect, he functioned in her characterization not as an answerable agent who generated language to actualize his own independent thoughts but rather as what Norberg calls "a conduit for a jargon" (750) that did not originate in him or belong to him. As Yasco Horsman describes it,

> [Eichmann's] words, even though they come out of his own mouth, *are not really his*; they are what Arendt calls, in *The*

---

morning I entered life on earth in the aspect of a human being" (*Eichmann in Jerusalem* 27). Norberg offers an intriguing and insightful exploration of the ways in which Eichmann's narrative construction of himself at the trial—"his relentless narrativization of his life" (753) and his subordination of "all the events of his life under the elements of a restricted jargon" (751)—imposes limits on Arendt's own possibilities for telling Eichmann's story: "Arendt's intervention is to display explicitly the quotation marks in between which his life played out.... Arendt does not translate what Eichmann says into some other idiom, she does not interpret it, give it another form, and thereby cover over its irredeemable banality. Instead, she puts his inability to speak into circulation, so that it begins to speak its own liability.... Her story of Eichmann's life comes in the form of an elaborate commentary on his uncanny ability to tell a cheap and hackneyed story" (756–57).

32 Stangneth's catalog of the many thousands of pages of autobiographical writings composed by Eichmann (538–43) makes clear that he suffered from a kind of graphorrea as well.

> *Human Condition*, mere speech—empty phrases that do not disclose anything about the speaker. To use the terminology employed by the French linguist Emile Benveniste, Eichmann is not capable of subjectivizing himself in his discourse. When Eichmann uses the first-person pronoun, he seems to be speaking as if in *the third person*; he seems to be merely the mouthpiece of a speech that finds its origins elsewhere. (38)

In Arendt's view, Eichmann functioned as the vocal organ for a bromidic language—"empty talk"—that was meant to signify and simulate the type of autonomous, organic thinking that ideally originates in the human conscience.[33] Lacking a conscience, Eichmann accordingly lacked his own language; the words he uttered at his trial were, as Shoshana Felman argues, adopted to perform the simulation of conscience that was stipulated by the discursive requirements of the criminal trial:

> I see the crux of Arendt's concept of banality of evil not only in the new conception of a criminal without *mens rea* but in the added legal and linguistic factor of the superimposition of a *borrowed (Nazi) language*—of recognizable and structuring *clichés*—on this absence of subjective motive. Eichmann's quasi-parodic German, a German limited to an anachronistic use of Nazi bureaucratic jargon (noticeable during the trial by every native German speaker as the farcical survival of a sort of robot-language), *takes the place of mens rea*. This unintentional *linguistic parody that substitutes for mens rea* is what makes Arendt call Eichmann "a clown" and view in general the German-language version of the trial as "sheer comedy" (a comedy compounded by a farcical, inadequate simultaneous translation into German).... As a parrotlike "clown," Eichmann does not *speak* the borrowed (Nazi) language; he is rather *spoken by it*,

---

33 Juliet Flower MacCannell writes, "According to Arendt's analysis of Eichmann's speech, the 'inner voice' of conscience in Eichmann was perhaps less silent than voiced over" (63).

spoken for by its *clichés*, whose criminality he does not come to realize. This total loss of a sense of reality regarding Nazi crimes is what encapsulates, for Arendt, the utmost moral scandal (the *ventriloquized mens rea*, the criminal linguistic "banality") typified by Eichmann. Eichmann's continued impersonation during the trial (his autistic ventriloquism) of technocratic Nazi language is what incriminates him above all in Arendt's eyes. (204–5)

As Felman sees it, Eichmann's "borrowed" or xenoglossic speech constituted the farcical, ventriloquized performance of mens rea; it is represented by Arendt "in an arc of suspense that stretches over close to 200 pages" (Steitz 137) of *Eichmann in Jerusalem* as a cliché-ridden caricature of the expression of conscience and the awareness of criminal liability that the framework of the criminal proceeding obligated. Further, it indicated that Eichmann operated less as a producer of language and more as its product. In this regard, Felman's metaphor of ventriloquism is aptly instructive: rather than taking on the role of the ventriloquist who controls the performance by manipulating the insensate dummy, Eichmann was the dummy itself, which was forced to mouth words it did not itself vocalize. Arendt thus characterizes Eichmann's mind as the reified outcome of his own speech; rather than performing himself as the active agent of his own linguistic self-presentation, his "empty talk" performed *him*, a view that, taken to its logical conclusions, divests Eichmann of agency with regard to his speech and thus also with regard to his crimes. In Arendt's view, Eichmann was constituted not only by his banal language but also in and through it. His mind was simply a linguistic surface constructed from an aggregation of clichés.

But precisely what kind of language performed Eichmann and produced his mind, in Arendt's view? Felman, Horsman, and Norberg all imply that it was the language of National Socialism—particularly its bureaucratic apparatus—that spoke through Eichmann via clichés and "empty talk." Such a conclusion is logical and plausible, but it may also underestimate the force and insight of Arendt's analysis. After all, as I have previously discussed, Arendt's analysis of Eichmann's testimony locates two distinct features in Eichmann's speech, each of which signified a different order of social discourse in early twentieth-century Germany: "officialese" referred not only to the vernacular of the National Socialist administrative machinery of terror and genocide but also to the language of modernity and of totalitarian movements, which harnessed the bureaucratic organization of the state to their own ends; by contrast, the "winged words" designated the discourse of bourgeois respectability and the language of the educated and middlebrow elite as these emerged in Germany over the course of the nineteenth century, particularly via the German educational system and the development of a German national literature and culture. Eichmann ventriloquized—if erroneously—both of these discourses; Arendt's archeological excavation of his speech reveals that it contained *both* the main vein of the remote and impersonal administrative functionalism of the modern bureaucratic nation-state as embodied in the Third Reich *and* the ideological substratum of middle-class morality, gentility, and rectitude, particularly as it was supported by the "household" (*Eichmann in Jerusalem* 136) appropriation—or even disingenuous or ignorant manipulation—of the cultural and intellectual tradition of Germany's *Dichter und Denker*.[34] Arendt thus implies through her reading of Eichmann's speech that it was not just the bureaucratic-technological discourse of fascism that produced his mind but also the attenuated discourse of *Bildung*, both of which she sees as contributing to the creation of a man who was "terribly and terrifyingly normal" (*Eichmann in Jerusalem* 276). These two languages—one of which can induce things, such as the organization and execution of genocide, to happen; the other of which can allow those things to be conscientiously and indeed morally justified—worked together to generate the type of mentality to which Arendt refers when she writes of the banality of evil. These two languages are "terrifying normal" because they are precisely *not* limited to the vocalization of National Socialism or even to that of

---

34 Arendt's most prominent example of Eichmann's flawed and self-serving citation of the German intellectual tradition is his allusion to Kantian ethics in general and the categorical imperative in particular, for which he gave "an approximately correct definition" (*Eichmann in Jerusalem* 136), to justify his "blind obedience" (135) to orders that resulted in the murder of millions. Arendt finds this episode to be particularly troubling, for it shows how principles that she, as a philosopher, believes to be indispensable to a moral philosophy can be cognitively comprehended and at the same time profoundly and devastatingly misunderstood (136–37).

totalitarianism; rather, they inform modern political, social, and individual consciousness in general. As she writes in the postscript to *Eichmann in Jerusalem*, which she appended to the 1965 revised and enlarged edition of the book, "The essence of totalitarian government, and perhaps the nature of every bureaucracy, is to make functionaries and mere cogs in the administrative machinery out of men, and thus to dehumanize them" (289). Using Eichmann as the paradigmatic example, Arendt makes clear that part of this dehumanization involved replacing the functionary's inner voice of consciousness with the discourses of corrupted bourgeois respectability and the bureaucratic machine in which he operated.

Reading Eichmann's Face: Harry Mulisch's *Criminal Case 40/61* (1962)

Attending the Eichmann trial at the same time as Hannah Arendt—and likely even sitting beside her in the courtroom when the indictment was read[35]—was Harry Mulisch (1927–2010), a Dutch novelist who would go on to become one of the most important postwar writers in the Netherlands. Like Arendt, Mulisch was not a journalist, but he similarly saw his assignment for the *Elseviers Weekblad* as an unparalleled opportunity to probe questions about the legacy of Nazi crimes in the Second World War, a topic that, as he acknowledged later, remained the abiding intellectual and artistic preoccupation of his life.[36] Mulisch collected his dispatches from

---

35 In their brief epistolary exchange (quoted in de Goeij), Arendt and Mulisch acknowledge that they were in Jerusalem at the same time but lament that they did not meet each other. However, according to Bart de Goeij, it is possible that the two writers sat next to each other when Eichmann entered his plea in response to the fifteen counts on which he was indicted (which took place on 17 April 1961), each without knowing who his or her neighbor was. De Goeij remembers a 1995 Dutch television program that showed a picture of Mulisch seated next to Arendt in the courtroom; moreover, he cites as possible evidence Mulisch's entry for that day: "Everybody is hoping for at least one 'guilty.' (When I commented to a female reporter what a relief that would have been for us and the world, she said, 'Don't forget he has children.')" (46).

36 Mulisch writes in his 1975 autobiography *Mijn getijdenboek*, "Such was my situation. I did not so much 'experience' the war; I *am* the Second World War" ("Zo was mijn situatie. Ik heb die oorlog niet zo zeer 'meegemaakt,' ik *ben* detweede wereldoorlog," quoted in Shamir-de-Leeuw 252). Mulisch's personal experience and parentage help to explain his claim to have embodied the complex dynamics of this period in history. His father, an Austrian who had been

the trial, along with entries from his diary during that period, and published them in 1962 as *De zaak 40/61: Een Reportage* (translated in 2005 as *Criminal Case 40/61, the Trial of Adolf Eichmann: An Eyewitness Account*). After *Eichmann in Jerusalem* appeared a year later, Mulisch sent Arendt a copy of the German translation of his book, *Strafsache 40/61*, noting that he "was struck by the resemblance in the theory [Arendt] unfolded" (quoted in de Goeij). Two weeks later, Arendt replied to Mulisch, agreeing that she "too was struck by the resemblance in approach and 'theory'" and that she planned to include quotes from his book in the German translation of hers (quoted in de Goeij). In the postscript, Arendt further writes that Mulisch "is almost the only writer on the subject to put the person of the defendant at the center of his report and whose evaluation of Eichmann coincides with my own on some essential points" (*Eichmann in Jerusalem* 282).

Following Mulisch's and Arendt's own recognition of the affinity between their respective representations of the Eichmann trial, a number of recent Dutch- and English-language critics, including Bettine Siertsema, Joop Berding, Pepijn Corduwener, Debórah Dwork, Matthew S. Weinert, Stephan Landsman, and Fabian Kettner, have read their two books alongside one another,[37] noting the striking correspondence between them. As the similitude between them is well documented, it is not my aim here to do a comprehensive comparative study of their semblance. But I find it instructive to briefly rehearse the compelling convergences. Both writers consider the larger phenomenon of the trial and the role it played in shaping Israeli Holocaust consciousness and the transnational discourse on Nazi crimes and Jewish suffering in the Holocaust. Further, like Arendt,

---

an officer in the First World War, met his mother, the daughter of a German-Jewish banker, in Amsterdam in 1926; nine years after their son was born, they divorced. During the German occupation of the Netherlands, his father became "one of the directors of the notorious Lippmann-Rosenthal bank, which had a key role in the depredation of Dutch Jews and the expropriation of their wealth" (Dwork xiv). Though Mulisch's father would be imprisoned for three years after the war for collaboration with the Nazi regime, through his position in the bank he was able to protect both his son and his ex-wife, the rest of whose family was murdered by the Nazi regime.

37 Indeed, several of the English-language critics read the English translation of Mulisch's text merely as a "supplement" to Arendt's *Eichmann in Jerusalem* (Weinert 184) or as an analysis of the trial that "bolsters Arendt's observations" (Landsman 1076).

Mulisch is keenly aware of the theatrical character of the trial, calling it in an April 1961 diary entry "an artistic creation" (58) that takes place "on a stage" (59); however, also like Arendt, Mulisch does not consider the extent to which Eichmann performs for the particular context of the trial. To be sure, unlike Arendt, who contextualizes Eichmann's character within a larger inquiry into questions of justice, the complex nature of the National Socialist bureaucracy and Eichmann's role in it, and the complicity of the *Judenräte* (among other aspects), Mulisch more forcefully, fixedly, and extensively explores "who Eichmann *was*—not what *he had done*" (Dwork xvi). At the same time, however, both writers actively attempt to grapple with the ironic tensions between the "perfectly ordinary man" (Mulisch 117) that Eichmann seemed to be, the crimes for which he was being tried, and the sensational way in which he was being portrayed at the trial and in the press as diabolically evil. The Eichmann both Arendt and Mulisch encountered in the courtroom was somewhat of a buffoon; whereas Arendt writes, "Despite all the efforts of the prosecution, everybody could see that this man was not a 'monster,' but it was difficult indeed not to suspect that he was a clown" (*Eichmann in Jerusalem* 54), Mulisch claims at the conclusion of the trial, "Not an apotheosis, not a 'genesis of a god' would have been right for him, but more an *apocolocynthosis*, which Seneca once dedicated to Emperor Claudius: 'the genesis of a pumpkin'" (142).

Further, in their conclusions about the unprecedented character of the evil that Eichmann represented, Arendt's and Eichmann's books, as Corduwener argues, "partially overlap" (139). Arendt, as we have seen, sees in Eichmann a "new type of criminal" (*Eichmann in Jerusalem* 276); stresses his thoughtlessness and the banality of his language, motives, and self-understanding; and notes that he was "not Iago and not Macbeth" and thus the obverse of conventional notions of evil. Mulisch, for his part, similarly attempts to pin down Eichmann's normality and his divergence from historical and cultural models of evil; in an article written shortly after the trial, he emphasizes Eichmann's "smallness" and argues that he was "not an 'Anti-Christ' or a 'Genghis Khan'" (161). Indeed, according to Mulisch, Eichmann represented not only a new kind of criminal but "a different human being" (134), whose language—"his linguistic labyrinths" (131), "a torrent of words in a baroque syntax" (127), "the lingo of the tax form and of the written record, multiplied to insanity" (127)—revealed Eichmann to be, at least in his present manifestation, "not so much a human being in trouble as a whirling machine having lost its engineer" (135). Mulisch's characterization of Eichmann with the metaphor of the automaton set into perpetual motion—a "rational tool set up to execute any command whatsoever, without comment" (113), "the mechanical order receptor" (117), a "machine that is good for anything" (119)—resonates with Arendt's characterization of his "inability to *think*, namely, to think from the standpoint of someone else" (*Eichmann in Jerusalem* 49), which she argues was a "mechanism" "triggered in him ... that had become completely unalterable" (*Eichmann in Jerusalem* 50). Like a machine, whose sole raison d'être is to embody the function to which it is dedicated, Eichmann, Mulisch writes despairingly midway through the trial, "could no more step out of his skin than could a crematorium, which also obeyed its structure" (115). His thoughtless, unmodified, automatic thinking and "administrative pedantry" (134), as revealed in the courtroom testimony to which both Mulisch and Arendt attended with growing incredulity and unease, demonstrated his continued identification with the role he had enjoyed during the Third Reich, when, according to Arendt, "he and the world he lived in had once been in perfect harmony" (*Eichmann in Jerusalem* 52). In this way, Mulisch and Arendt render analogous depictions of Eichmann's mind. For Arendt, as we have seen, Eichmann expressed "the essence of totalitarian government," whose object was to transform men like him into workable instruments of a greater administrative mechanism (289); by virtue of his total identification with the authority of this machinery, he considered himself to the end a "law-abiding citizen" who "acted upon orders" not out of personal inclination but out of a sense of duty (135). For Mulisch, in turn, Eichmann not only was the "calm, dutiful civil servant who transports the European Jews to Rudolf Höss's gas chambers" (93) and thereby the immutable embodiment of the "amputated" (114) morality of National Socialism; he also functioned more broadly as "the ideal of psycho-technology" (119) in the modern age, a mechanical "medium without belief or hypnosis" (93), who carried out an order purely because it must be "obeyed, no matter where it is coming from" (111). Moreover, both writers are in agreement that Eichmann was not an anomaly but rather the rule in his environment (whether narrowly totalitarian or more universally modern); as Arendt writes, "The trouble with Eichmann was precisely that so many were like him, and that the many were neither perverted nor sadistic, that they were, and still are, terribly and terrifyingly normal" (*Eichmann in Jerusalem* 276). According to Mulisch, "This living dead person is the prototype of modern man, who created the machine in his own likeness" (117); there are "millions like him ... roaming the earth" (119). For this reason, "we do not have to continue to be wary of criminals; we must continue being wary of perfectly ordinary people. We must keep one eye in the mirror" (117).

While *Eichmann in Jerusalem* and *Criminal Case 40/61* are "astonishingly similar" (*Eichmann in Jerusalem* 281) with regard to their characterization of Eichmann and their conclusions about the unprecedented and—in modern and totalitarian societies, at least—ubiquitous nature of the evil he embodied, there are obvious and essential differences between Arendt's and Mulisch's accounts due chiefly to the particularity of their authors' respective perspectives, their "training and biography" (Dwork xvii), and the generic framing of their reports. As Corduwener writes regarding the books' discrepant approaches, "Arendt remained the philosopher who engaged actively with Eichmann, calling his understanding of Kantian moral philosophy 'outrageous,'" while Mulisch "remained the novelist" whose "personal account is therefore less confrontational and more empathetic" (143). Although Mulisch shares with Arendt keen analytical observations and penetrative insight, his book, Sander Bax argues, is "a complex, hybrid text that contains elements of journalism, essays, philosophy, and literature at the same time" (38), revealing his "chameleonesque authorship" (41). Mulisch thus employs—as we will see in greater detail shortly—a degree of novelistic license in *Criminal Case 40/61*, which allows for perspectives not available to Arendt's purely analytical method.[38] Moreover, while Arendt wrote the entirety of her report in the last half of 1962, a year after the conclusion of the trial and shortly after Eichmann's execution, most of the chapters that appear in Mulisch's book were written during the trial as articles for *Elseviers Weekblad* or as diary entries; only the last few chapters were written after the trial but before Eichmann's execution. For

---

38 As Corduwener writes, "What makes Mulisch's account stand out even more is the fact that it is not exclusively journalistic, but marked by his qualities as a novelist. Eichmann can be seen as the protagonist of the plot that Mulisch hopes to unravel and he uses both imagination and empathy to understand its main character" (137–38).

this reason, his book reads not as a global analysis written from the hindsight of a posterior vantage point (as does, in the main, Arendt's report) but as an ongoing, summative attempt to grapple with the person of Eichmann as the trial plays out in real time. In his short preface to *Criminal Case 40/61*, Mulisch writes,

> "40/61" is the number of the Eichmann case on the roll of the District Court of Jerusalem. In this volume, I give the account of an experience behind this number. An experience is different from a train of thought: it is subject to change. At the end one finds a different person, partly with different thoughts, from at the beginning. Since the account of this changing experience is announced in the first entry, I have not made any corrections anywhere: this was not supposed to be a book about Eichmann, but to remain the double report as it was intended from the start. (1)

Mulisch depicts his coverage of the trial as a metamorphic personal experience and his engagement with the figure of Eichmann as a profound intersubjective encounter, even though he never meets or interacts with the man himself. This encounter not only changes him but also leaves its mark on his writing, which transforms over the course of the trial as well. Most important, as Corduwener's quote above indicates, rather than distance himself from Eichmann by virtue of sardonic hindsight and a fully fleshed analytical framework (as Arendt arguably is able to do), Mulisch draws himself closer to him, developing a paradoxical empathy with him as he watches him endure the trial.[39] As Mulisch writes in September 1961, after the conclusion of the trial but before the verdict was read,

> The Eichmann case is more about me than I know myself, and this connection goes farther than a thematic link with other work that I have written or will write . . . : he is one of

---

39 According to Corduwener, "While Arendt saw Eichmann more as a clown than as a monster, Mulisch seems to take him more seriously and with less disdain. He repeatedly tries to remind us of the humanness of Eichmann by focussing on his behaviour during the trial" (140).

the two or three people who have changed me. Above all, he has *cured* me of many things: of indignation without obligation, for example, but also of much carefreeness. He has also taught me a certain vigilance: my eyes have opened a little wider. I see him, myself, as well as others, in a brighter light. What is remarkable here is that the outlines have become more blurred. The boundaries between him and me are lapsing, between the others and him, between me and the others, but also between him and the dead, between the dead and me, between the others and the dead. . . . This is where speechlessness begins. (159)

Mulisch's engagement with the figure of Eichmann not only triggers a not entirely welcome empathetic disposition in him but also dissolves conventional structures of apprehension and generates new modes of viewing both the object of his study and himself.

Mulisch's reference to the act of seeing with regard to his encounter with the Eichmann trial is not entirely metaphorical; in fact, his book not only features his analysis of Eichmann's character but also is replete with detailed descriptions of his own visual perceptions of Eichmann, particularly his face.[40] For example, in a diary entry from 12 April, he writes,

> Today the courtroom is half empty, and to observe him well, I go sit in the front row, ten feet away from him. . . . Then I have a good view of his eyes. People here wrote that he has snake eyes (*France Soir*), and also that each of his eyes is a gas chamber (*Libération*). But in truth they are soft and somewhat velvety, which is only more horrifying. . . . Sometimes they suddenly shoot sideways, in some sort of a tic. Then his head shudders for a moment, and he sucks his cheeks in, which makes him pull his mouth to the left. In moments like these, he is somewhat like the Eichmann

---

[40] Corduwener argues that Mulisch places great emphasis on the visual in his text: "Mulisch argues we have to understand Nazism by looking at the images, rather than the ideas that led to Nazism. These images run like a red thread through his work" (138).

> we would like to see: an inexplicably merciless face, sending shivers up my spine—a shattered face, simultaneously evoking strong pity. (37)

Focusing on his face and eyes, Mulisch attempts to divine who Eichmann was and what he thought from his countenance. At times, Mulisch concedes, Eichmann conformed to the "image of Satan that the press has created out of [him] in the last few months," which "can be more easily approached theologically than psychologically" (36). At the same time, however, Mulisch argues that Eichmann was irreducibly human: "with Eichmann the theological effect has disappeared with his apparition. He turns out to be human: a somewhat grubby man with a cold, wearing glasses" (37). Eichmann's appearance thus embodies for Mulisch the paradox that his character posed at the trial; as he writes of himself and his fellow journalists, "Slowly everybody here is becoming schizophrenic about Eichmann. We know what he did, although it still has to be proven, but in the cage we see a lonely dying man" (41).

With his keen focus on Eichmann's facial features and expressions and what they revealed about his character, Mulisch pursues in his dispatches and diary entries a particular variant of the cognitive operation of mind-reading grounded chiefly in the interpretation of a person's face and other physical features. This manner of mind-reading through perception of the body and face is related to the Enlightenment-era science of physiognomy, or the systematic study of the correspondence of psychological characteristics to facial features or body structure. Physiognomic theory of the late eighteenth and nineteenth centuries, according to Rochelle Rives, "predicates the expressive strength of the face on its ability to consolidate the interior and exterior dimensions of the human subject" (1366); as Richard Gray explains in his study of modern German physiognomic thought from the Enlightenment to the Holocaust, it involves "the hermeneutic (re-)constitution of the internal character, desires, and dispositions of human beings based on the interpretation of the body as a system of meaningful signs" (xvii). Although physiognomy was deemed well into the twentieth century an objective methodology by many of its proponents, from a contemporary perspective, as Gray's words remind us, it is better understood as an interpretive cultural practice embedded in particular historical contexts; for this reason, it has conventionally presumed an essential link between appearance, psychology, and morality that has often been deployed to construct and support hegemonic racist, sexist, ableist, and classist ideologies and theories of criminality. While the problematic determinant relationship between outer characteristics and inner character posited by physiognomy has been largely discredited by current science,[41] the practice of physiognomic interpretation—or what both Ellen Spolsky and Guillemette Bolens call "kinesic intelligence"—persists as a cognitive process on the level of individuals, who routinely make judgments—often incorrectly and from a heavily biased perspective—about their fellow human beings based on the largely unconscious meanings they assign to facial and bodily features. Moreover, such physiognomic practices are also at play in cultural texts that simulate the ways in which real-life individuals engage in bodily interpretation; they comprise the textual conventions not only of fiction, where narrators and characters infer a figure's interiority from his or her physical characteristics and readers are encouraged to engage in similar acts of interpretation of descriptions of characters' bodies and faces, but also of journalistic portraits and other genres of nonfiction, whereby the author attempts to convey some aspect of the subject's inner life by describing his or her outer appearance. Particularly literary nonfiction and texts associated with the New Journalism of the 1960s and 1970s (to which Sander Bax [34] and Thomas Vaessens [58] have attributed Mulisch's text), which fuse factual reporting on actual historical events and people with novelistic techniques and foreground rather than efface the subjective interpretation of the authorial voice, utilize a variant of Theory of Mind that I, following Spolsky and Bolens, term "kinesic mind-reading." In their attempt to render the inner character of their subjects by describing their facial and bodily features, such texts often self-consciously draw attention to the writer's cognitive and emotional process of reading the human subjects under investigation.

As indicated by Mulisch's reference in the quote above to the ways in which journalists writing in *France Soir* and *Libération* interpreted Eichmann's

---

41 As demonstrated by the work of Lisa Feldman Barrett, the study of the face as a reflection of character has been replaced (or recycled in alternate form) by the cognitive study of the face as a reliable indicator of emotion; indeed, it has become a major focus of cognitive scientists in recent decades (4–12).

eyes, narrative recourse to strategies of kinesic mind-reading is particularly ubiquitous in the numerous nonfictional assessments of Adolf Eichmann that appeared during and after his 1961 trial, which are based not on personal interaction with Eichmann himself but on either firsthand observation or photographs and televisual footage of Eichmann's countenance and behavior during the trial. These portraits attempt to solve what has been called "the enigma" (Landsman 1076) of Eichmann and to reconcile the public image of him disseminated in the media before the trial began, which sensationally characterized him as the embodiment of evil, with the rather mundane appearance and demeanor of the man seated in the glass box in the courtroom.[42] Such attempts at kinesic mind-reading are particularly characteristic of Arendt's assessment, which, according to Prager, perceives in the defendant "nothing more than a series of expressions, statements, and gestures" (77) that demand interpretation. She describes Eichmann as

> medium-sized, slender, middle-aged, with receding hair, ill-fitting teeth, and nearsighted eyes, who throughout the trial keeps craning his scraggy neck toward the bench (not once does he face the audience), and who desperately and for the most part successfully maintains his self-control despite the nervous tic to which his mouth must have become subject long before this trial started. (*Eichmann in Jerusalem* 5)

With her description of his facial and bodily features, Arendt portrays Eichmann as physically weak, cagey, desperate, and comically mediocre, a depiction that she then compounds with her interpretation of his banality. More recently, Marianna Torgovnick, in her 2005 analysis of Eichmann's appearance in iconic images from his trial, both interrogates and confirms the operation of kinesic mind-reading as a reliable source of knowledge about Eichmann's character:

> The pictures. Eichmann's transformation began, I believe, with the pictures. In televised images and in passport-size

---

[42] Mulisch writes in an April diary entry, "I have not met anyone here yet who is not preoccupied with this kind of mental exercise, intended to keep the image of Eichmann as Satan alive for the world" (37).

magazine close-ups, Eichmann's face appeared over and over again, looking not commanding or "toweringly arrogant" as words in *Life* described him, but nondescript. Thin face with sunken cheeks. Some lines, though not deep or dramatic. Sparse hair, sticking up and patted down occasionally by the self-conscious defendant. Middle-aged, middle-European. Ordinary eyes, ordinary build, ordinary though thin and sharp nose, ordinary glasses. Ordinary, ordinary. Except for the mouth, which looked peculiar—like a hole, or alternately, like a twitch or a grimace.... The status of Eichmann's [false] teeth may seem trivial. But trivia can influence the way that visual images help to shape public memory, and even history. Grotesque in its mobility, Eichmann's mouth suggests a man who had developed a facial tic long before the trial began. Knowing this man to have been a Nazi who helped to organize the murder of millions, we cannot help but see guilt at work, or perhaps frustration. Either way, the man looks at once sinister but also ridiculous and contemptible. (64–65)

As Arendt's and Torgovnick's quotes demonstrate, our cultural image of Eichmann as simultaneously mundane, ridiculous, and grotesque—in other words, as both commonplace and exceptionally evil—has originated at least in part in attempts to discern his character from analyses of his face, in particular his facial tic and the contortions of his mouth.

Mulisch brilliantly performs the binary between the malevolent and the mundane embodied by Eichmann's appearance and at the same time deconstructs it in his second dispatch, titled "The Two Faces of Eichmann" and written in March 1961, a month before the trial commenced, when global speculation about Eichmann's character and motives was at its peak. His article performs a study of Eichmann's face by concentrating on a photo (fig. 1) of Eichmann taken in 1960, shortly after his capture in Argentina by the Israel secret police, which presents half of his face bathed in light and the other half cast in shadow and thus distorted. However, rather than simply interpret this photo of Eichmann's face as a source for reliable knowledge about Eichmann's character, Mulisch proposes to conduct a thought experiment—"a little trick" (9)—by bisecting the photo lengthwise through Eichmann's face and constructing from the sundered parts two additional images, each of which is composed of one half of the original image and its mirror opposite (figs. 2 and 3). One of the resulting images (fig. 2) presents Eichmann as fully illuminated, while the other (fig. 3) displays him fully shadowed (10–12). With these two manufactured photos, which, he tells us, are "portraits of men who have never existed and who never will" (9), Mulisch thus makes manifest the dualism that characterizes the public discourse on Eichmann's character. Moreover, the fictional status of these portraits (and thus of Mulisch's mental exercise) is marked by the obvious line that runs down the middle of both fabricated photographs, which emphasizes the artificial sutures that create these two fictional men.[43]

Mulisch's initial interpretation of these two fabricated images follows conventional physiognomic interpretation, which would associate even, harmonious features with psychic consonance and a distorted exterior with interior deformation: "The first impulse is: *that* is the real Eichmann, figure 3: the barbaric, twisted mug of the mass murderer. Figure 2, on the other hand, is very human: a calm face, serious eyes, and a glimmer of a smile around his mouth" (9).[44] However, rather than follow his first impulse and regard these fabricated images as respectively embodying Eichmann-the-ordinary-human and Eichmann-the-Anti-Christ, Mulisch quickly questions this "simple interpretation" (9): "Do modern murderers really have such frighteningly distorted faces?" (13). Mulisch answers this question in the negative. The face in figure 3, Mulisch reasons, does not really resemble the actual Eichmann, whose likeness is rather to be found in figure 2, a factor that "undermine[s] the theory that 2 is the human and 3 is the beast" (13). Moreover, the horridly disfigured face exhibited in figure 3 cannot be seen as embodying the distilled essence of Eichmann's crimes, for Eichmann's transgressions were not that

---

43 Thanks to Sarah Copland of MacEwan University for pointing out the function of the suture line during a discussion at the 2018 Narrative Conference in Montréal.

44 This is the reading of the stark contrast between the two sides of Eichmann's face—one harmonious, the other distorted—proposed by Meir Ronnen, who, in his capacity as illustrator, cartoonist, and art critic for the *Jerusalem Post*, made drawings of Eichmann at his trial: "Interestingly enough, I had discovered that the left side of Eichmann's face was totally different from his quite handsome right side; in a sort of Dorian Gray procedure, his left side had become that of a degenerate villain."

Figure 1

Figure 2

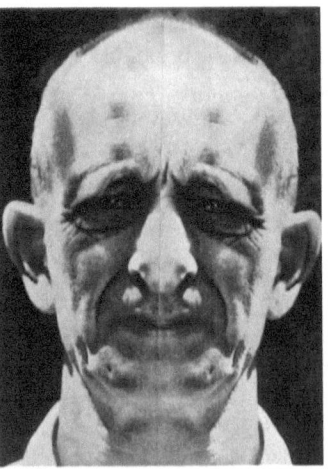

Figure 3

of the conventional evildoer (a figure that, according to our physiognomic expectations, should resemble the horrific face in figure 3) but rather that of the "mechanical order receptor," a fully modern murderer whose lack of conscience leaves his face unlined and grimace-free. Reading against the grain of conventional physiognomic interpretation, which attributes to a grotesque appearance an equally malformed mental and moral state, Mulisch sees the pleasant, more "human" face presented in figure 2 as more fittingly emblematic of Eichmann the technological bureaucrat of genocide, while the face featured in figure 3 reminds him rather of a Buchenwald survivor he met while touring the site of the former concentration camp: "The man who showed me around . . . was the spitting image of figure 3, except his nose was smashed in addition. He was not an ex-camp bully, but one of the oldest prisoners: at the start of Buchenwald in 1938 he was brought in as a Communist. He had been through everything" (14). In the survivor's face—and thus in its likeness in figure 3—Mulisch sees the physical manifestation of the violence the man somatically endured during his time as a prisoner. In Mulisch's view, the face in figure 3, like the one in figure 2, functions thus as a physiognomic archive of the crimes of the Holocaust—crimes that were administered and facilitated in no small part by Eichmann. However, while the visage in figure 2 is a record of the commission of those crimes, the one in figure 3 is the vestige of their effects.

Proposing a much more nuanced reading of these two photographs, Mulisch writes further,

> I believe we will be getting closer to the truth if we see the *witness* in figure 3. Figure 3 is the face that sees what the man in figure 2 does. Figure 2 is the slick, unmoved, merciless face of the killer; figure 3 is the face that observes the killing, filled with horror. Or: if figure 2 is Eichmann, then figure 3 is the face of the world watching him at work. Returning to Eichmann's real face: the right-hand side is the part on which his crimes have had an effect, the side of the heart; the left-hand side is the part that committed the crimes. (14)

With the act of physiognomic or kinesic mind-reading made possible by his "little trick," Mulisch thus not only hemisects Eichmann's photo but also bifurcates the figure of Eichmann himself, characterizing the half that appears placid and impassive as the identity of the perpetrator, whose face betrays no signs of mental disquiet for the crimes he has undertaken, while the "twisted" side is relegated to the victim, whose ruined countenance testifies to and is permanently maimed by the perception of his crimes; it thus functions as a living document of tormented horror. In this way, Mulisch reads the grotesque right-hand side of Eichmann's face not as indicative of the sort of evil that disfigurement conventionally connotes in physiognomic thinking but rather as evidence of Eichmann's atrophied or extinguished conscience, which silently observes but does not intervene in the genocidal crimes committed by its placid, untroubled, obedient Doppelgänger.[45]

With his counterintuitive reading of Eichmann's face made possible by his partition of the pretrial photograph, Mulisch thus both creatively adopts and ironically transforms the textual conventions of much of the media coverage of the trial, which attempted to construct Eichmann's nefarious interiority through acts of kinesic mind-reading.[46] The paradox of this practice and the image it produces becomes the leitmotiv of Mulisch's entire text; by virtue of its disruption of conventional associations of physical harmony with goodness and distortion with evil, Mulisch continually reminds himself and the reader of the ways in which Eichmann and his crimes upend the traditional moral and juridical categories and the seemingly intuitive association between aesthetics and ethics. At the same time, however, Mulisch's exercise in kinesic mind-reading does not remain static throughout his coverage at the trial; rather, at the end of *Criminal Case 40/61* he returns to Eichmann's face and reevaluates his introductory reading of it. In an article from 20 August, written less than a week after the trial adjourned, he writes,

> After spending 398 hours in his capsule, Eichmann disappeared in the wall, probably to come back out only for the verdict. . . . Anyone who has seen Eichmann on TV these

---

[45] In his notion of a split in Eichmann's face and identity, wherein the one half embodies the horrified witness of the crimes of the other half, Mulisch prefigures the fictional conceit that Martin Amis adopts in his perpetrator representation *Time's Arrow*, which splits the protagonist into a perpetrator-actor and his mute, witnessing soul. I discuss this novel in detail in chapter 4.

[46] For a good analysis of Mulisch's use of irony, see Joop Berding.

last few weeks realizes that he was looking into the face of a man who has practically gone insane. The eyes, the mouth, the entire face is in a constant, shivering, pulling motion, but never does so much as an "expression" form on it. Every separate motion is senseless. No motion is connected to another: the man has been shattered into a thousand pieces. This is emphasized by the total immobility of the rest of his body. That is what happens to a human being who is elevated to the Devil. The motions in his face are not indicative that the horrendousness of his crimes has finally sunk in, but of the fact that nothing is sinking in. Really, this man is being punished. I cannot say that he does not deserve it or that I am delighted. It is hideous, first and foremost. (148)

Here, Mulisch adds a third face to the two he divines from his reconstitution of his portrait. Alongside the placid face of the killer and the horrified witness to his crimes is another physiognomic manifestation: that of the defendant who, over the long course of the trial, was continually compelled to embody a kind of absolute evil that is at odds with his own self-understanding and the commission of and motives for his crimes. After all, as Mulisch writes on 13 August, "something was being done to him that he had never expected: he was being turned into a myth. I do not believe that this has ever happened in world history to someone who was less mythical in character" (142). Moreover, the erratic, disconnected movements of Eichmann's face,[47] as described here by Mulisch, signified neither his moral awareness of his crimes nor even his recognition of them as crimes; in other words, they did not indicate the kind of growing realization and acknowledgment on the part of the criminal that the trial was intended to engender. Rather, they constituted meaningless, automatic tics that did not coalesce into an "expression," namely, a legible countenance or body language. What the pressures to personify evil did, according to Mulisch, is shatter Eichmann's face as a coherent, intelligible text, making it no longer accessible to conventional practices of kinesic mind-reading. Mulisch thus suggests here that Eichmann's crimes, behavior, and character

---

[47] For an excellent analysis of Mulisch's description of Eichmann's increasingly spasmodic face, see Bettine Siertsema 185.

not only supersede our conventional categories of evil but also immobilize the very diagnostic tools we have developed to detect and interpret them as such. In this, Mulisch's conclusions parallel the assessment of Jean-François Lyotard, who famously likened the aftermath of the Holocaust to a geological disaster:

> Suppose that an earthquake destroys not only lives, buildings, and objects but also the instruments used to measure earthquakes directly and indirectly. The impossibility of quantitatively measuring it does not prohibit, but rather inspires in the minds of the survivors the idea of a great seismic force. . . . With Auschwitz, something new has happened in history (which can only be a sign and not a fact), which is that the facts, the testimonies which bore the traces of *here*'s and *now*'s, the documents which indicated the sense or senses of the facts, and the names, finally the possibility of various kinds of phrases whose conjunction makes reality, all this has been destroyed as much as possible. (56–57)

In Mulisch's view, much like Lyotard's preternatural earthquake, whose force is so great that it disables conventional methods or tools for registering its scope or making sense of it, Eichmann's crimes and his relationship to them incapacitated established frames of reference for criminality and culpability. Conventional practices of mind-reading thus proved impotent to generate any sort of meaningful account of the kind of criminal Eichmann constituted and the circumstances that catalyzed his willing and eager commission of genocide. As Mulisch writes in an April 1961 diary entry with regard to the prosecutor Hausner, who seemed still to believe that Eichmann's mind was apprehensible, "He apparently still believes in an 'explanation,' while in the same breath speaks of 'breaking through the window of human logic.' Behind this reality there is no more explanation. It is in itself an explanation of what man is. It is the final word thus far" (46–47).

"A Living 'Autopsy' on the Mind of This Man": William L. Hull's *The Struggle for a Soul* (1963)

Also sitting in the courtroom with Arendt and Mulisch during the Jerusalem trial was William L. Hull (1897–1992), a Canadian Christian minister and founder of the Zion Apostolic Mission in Israel. Hull, a former salesman from Winnipeg, had received what he described in an interview in *Time* as "'a very real personal call from God to move to Jerusalem'" and had become ordained as an evangelical minister ("Converting Eichmann"). In the mid-1930s, he had settled in Palestine with, according to Gary Alley, "the express purpose of 'preaching the Gospel throughout the land.'" Despite his zealously evangelical mission in Israel and his fundamentalist Christian belief that "Everyone must come to God through Jesus. There is no other way to be saved" (Hull 70), Hull "stood close to the Israeli elite" (Kieser 134) and had cultivated a good relationship with the Israeli government. Through such connections and "upon the recommendation of the [Israeli] Ministry of Religious Affairs, [he] was selected to unofficially represent the Protestant Christian clergy at the Eichmann trial," in which capacity he "attended the majority of the sessions" (Hull 9) but, unlike Arendt and Mulisch, did not report publicly on them. After the reading of the guilty verdict and the issue of the death sentence in mid-December 1961, Hull, utilizing his network of governmental officials, offered his services as "spiritual adviser" to Eichmann, a post he justified with the argument that "a Protestant spiritual adviser would forestall criticism from certain sections of the Christian world" (7). With the aid of Robert Servatius, Eichmann's defense attorney, Hull's offer to minister to Eichmann during the period of his appeal of the court's judgment was accepted by both Arieh Nir, the commissioner of prisons, and Eichmann himself. Hull thus provided spiritual counsel to Eichmann in the weeks leading up to his execution, an experience that he chronicled in *The Struggle for a Soul* (1963), which he published not long after Eichmann's death and in which he proposes to conduct "a living 'autopsy' on the mind of this man" so that "the source of the evil sickness could be discovered" (xii). Hull offers his reading of Eichmann's mind as a sort of public service, since "the world is entitled to know . . . how a living human being could yield himself to be used as such an awful instrument of destruction" (xii).

With his book, Hull purports to tell "the story that never was told concerning Adolf Eichmann" (xi), namely, his efforts "to bring him to an active faith in Jesus Christ" (13)—a task at which Hull admittedly failed in the end, as Eichmann, though a firm believer in God,[48] rejected the fundamental tenets of Christianity and "died denying any faith in Jesus Christ, any need of a mediator" (xiii). *The Struggle for a Soul* depicts Hull's frequent meetings with Eichmann, during which he attempted to convince him "that Jesus is the only way to God" (52), as a "desperate battle for the soul of this man" (18), a valiant last-minute intervention to preach the gospel to Eichmann to rehabilitate his soul and save him from eternal damnation. To be sure, Hull's book accords, albeit in less sophisticated ways, with Arendt's and Mulisch's assessments of Eichmann with regard to a number of Eichmann's personal characteristics, chief among them his appearance as "just an ordinary little man who had been set in a job, told what to do, and . . . did it in spite of the awful suffering and death which followed his actions" (41); his "garbled" (45) and convoluted employment of language; his function as "only a cog . . . , just a tool, but a willing tool" (3) in the National Socialist genocidal machinery; and the performative quality of his trial testimony and his interactions with others, with whom he was seen as "acting a part" (32).[49] At the same time, however, Hull departs radically from Arendt and Mulisch in his reading of Eichmann's mind and in his understanding of the kind of evil that Eichmann represented:

> It is a frightening and sobering thought to realize that any normal, average man, without being fully aware of the evil

---

48 Eichmann shocked Hull in the first minutes of his initial meeting with him by claiming, "I know God; I have never lost touch with God" (22).

49 In agreement with Arendt's assessment, Hull disputes the idea that Eichmann, in his duties during the Third Reich, had acted out of antisemitic motives. However, his reasoning with regard to this belief issues from his particular evangelical perspective: "Our conclusion to date is that the story of Eichmann was not the tragedy of the Jewish people but rather the tragedy of Christianity. Jews do not need to feel inferior as a race because of the activities of an Eichmann. He was not murdering Jews as such; he was murdering those officially recognized as enemies by the Nazi Party. It would have been the same if the Party had declared their enemy to be Frenchmen, or Arabs, or Hottentots, or Roman Catholics, or all Christians, or anything else. Basically Eichmann's actions against Jews were inspired by Nazi policy rather than by a personal anti-Semitic bias" (110).

of the path he is treading, could be led by Satan to a point where he could even be transformed into an Adolf Eichmann. This is not to excuse Eichmann—there is no excuse for one who yields to Satan—but it is to warn man that *There is a way which seemeth right unto a man but the end thereof are the ways of death*....

Eichmann permitted himself to become the servant of Satan in the guise of the Nazi Party. As such he must needs obey. (41)

For Hull, the type of evil embodied in Eichmann was neither the "uniquely modern" variant suggested by Arendt nor "the ideal of psycho-technology" posited by Mulisch, but "the horrible revelation of the power of Satan" (42), whom Hull sees not as a metaphor for the general human tendency toward turpitude but as a concrete force that seeks to foil God's reign on earth by actively intervening into human affairs and by recruiting followers—both unwitting and enthusiastic—to its cause. Hull thus approached Eichmann's mind through an orthodox evangelical Christian doctrine that understands evil as a perpetually pitched battle between light and darkness, between obedience to God and sin, and between those who recognize the divine status of Jesus (and thus serve God) and those who do not; in his myopic view, the sole solution to the problem of Eichmann's crimes—which in his opinion were merely the symptoms, not the cause, of Eichmann's greater, more profound sin of rejecting Christian doctrine—resided in Eichmann's potential "salvation through faith in Jesus" (50). Although Hull claims that his account of Eichmann's last days contains "much . . . of interest from a psychological standpoint" that could be of use to "psychologists and reporters" (xi–xii), it is narrowly informed by his parochial conception of Eichmann as a person and as a historical phenomenon, which intractably refuses psychological explanations for Eichmann's mindset and his criminal behavior. When asked in a media questionnaire what made Eichmann "tick," Hull reports that he responded,

> To use your expression, what makes Adolf Eichmann tick is the same thing that makes millions of other people tick. Such a man must always be a puzzle to people who do not

> understand the power of Satan. If a man surrenders him-
> self to Satan he becomes his slave and must obey him. Eich-
> mann, by joining the Nazi Party, rejected God and yielded to
> Satan. Man is either influenced for good by God or for evil
> by Satan. Once man chooses there is no limit to the good or
> evil he may do. (75)

Although Hull spent several dozens of hours with Eichmann, the narrow evangelical perspective through which he perceived the former perpetrator significantly restricted his assessment. As Cesarani argues, while *The Struggle for a Soul* offers "almost the only insight we have into Eichmann's inner life, such as it was," it is also "filtered through Hull's conversionist fervor" and thus is of limited value to historians (316). However, viewed from the perspective of cultural production, Hull's filter—his exclusive focus on Eichmann's soul and the state of its accord with Jesus Christ, which represented "the only means whereby [it] could be saved" (79)—functions not simply as a tendentious barrier to Eichmann's mind. Rather, it also operates within Hull's narrative of his ministry as an active force that shapes his construction of Eichmann's mental and spiritual life as a battleground in which "the power of God" was challenged by "the power of Satan" (41).

It is important to note, however, that Hull's ministry to Eichmann was not a one-man show. Hull was accompanied on his pastoral visits by his wife, who served not only as his "co-worker in the gospel work" (13) but also as his German interpreter, as Hull did not speak German and Eichmann had no facility in English. In response to Nir's objection that Ramleh Prison, where Eichmann was held, "was not a fit place for Mrs. Hull to visit" (13), Hull reports that he insisted that, because of the ecclesiastically Christian nature of their intended mission, "only she could properly interpret my thoughts on spiritual matters. A Jewish policeman would not understand what I was talking about and much of the effect would be lost" (13). Throughout the book, Hull refers to his "co-worker" in his ministry only as "Mrs. Hull"; of the admittedly small number of easily obtainable sources and more recent assessments of the book, only the German weekly *Der Spiegel* mentions her given name, Lillian ("Satan in der Zelle").[50] Given

---

50 Oddly, unlike the *Spiegel* article, the *Time* article "Converting Eichmann," which shares some exact formulations with the article in *Der Spiegel* and thus

the gendered practices of the time, Hull's own deeply traditionalist perspective, the reduced role relegated to women in evangelical Christian doctrine, and the conventional devaluation of the work of interpreters and translators (occupations that were—and continue to be—not uncommonly held by women), his punctilious omission of her nominal identity is perhaps to be expected. Furthermore, although he does occasionally give his wife a voice within his text, he downgrades her role in the couple's encounter with Eichmann as one primarily of obedient helpmeet or mechanical linguistic conduit of the more important exchange between the two men, which is almost without exception presented as a series of seamless, direct interactions. William L. Hull's erasure of Lillian Hull's identity and her crucial function in his relationship with Eichmann is mirrored in the press reports from the time, which similarly downplay or efface the role she played in her husband's spiritual guidance of the prisoner. While the *Time* article does state in its second paragraph that Hull's (unnamed) wife "serves as German-English interpreter," she is excluded from the scene painted at its outset, which implies a dramatic, direct meeting between two solo correspondents:

> Twice each week, armed guards escort Pastor William Lovell Hull of Jerusalem's nondenominational Zion Christian Mission into the maximum security cellbock of Israel's Ramla prison. As he enters, a sallow, thin-faced prisoner behind a thick glass partition snaps to his feet, bows and clicks his heels. Then the two men sit down, take up the earphones and microphones through which they communicate and open their Bibles. Pastor Hull then begins another session of trying to bring Adolf Eichmann back to the Christian faith he left in 1937. ("Converting Eichmann")

Lillian Hull's critical function as the sole linguistic and communicative interface between her husband and his spiritual charge is expunged here by the emphasis on the technological media "through which [the two men] communicate." Yet her role in Hull's ministry to Eichmann was central, not marginal, to the very feasibility and functioning of the endeavor; she

---

appears to depend on a common source, does not mention Hull's wife's given name.

was neither a silent observer nor an attendant but rather the linchpin upon which the entire enterprise relied. With his book, William L. Hull provides the authorized account of the ministry and thus also his own particular representation of Eichmann's mind, but Lillian Hull served as an important part of that mediation, albeit one that is left largely unacknowledged in both the text's narrative discourse and its reception. In this respect, *The Struggle for a Soul* appears to embody the conventional autobiographical dynamic in which the author is represented within the text as both the narrating I and the sole (or at least primary) narrated (or experiencing) I. However, the construction of the latter as a singular, autonomous, active entity represented by the Reverend Hull not only suppresses Lillian Hull's function in the narrative but also elides the plural, interactive nature of the couple's joint campaign to counsel Eichmann.

The Hulls met with Eichmann more than a dozen times between 11 April and 31 May 1962, the evening of his execution (which took place shortly after midnight on 1 June). For each meeting they typically prepared a sort of agenda—or even a detailed script—for the discussion, a "series of Bible studies" centered on the topics of "man and salvation" (15). After each encounter they reconstructed in English the dialogue that had taken place and made a systematic record of the exchange. The "day-by-day" (xiv) transcripts the Hulls produced after each meeting form the core of *The Struggle for a Soul*, which is organized into separate chapters devoted to each encounter with Eichmann and presented mostly in the form of reconstructed, "back-translated" (Stangneth 488) dialogue in dramatic format or diary entries written shortly after the events they describe and thus without intimation of either the fate of Eichmann's appeal or the state of his religious beliefs at his execution. These chronicles of the pastoral sessions are supplemented by introductory chapters describing the trial and Hull's attempts to gain access to Eichmann and closing chapters describing Eichmann's hanging and the scattering of his ashes in the Mediterranean, both of which the Reverend Hull attended (but Lillian Hull did not, as it was assumed that it would be an "additional strain" [138] for her to witness the execution).[51]

---

51 The Reverend Hull's discomfort with the extent of his reliance on his wife for communication with Eichmann, which for him clearly signals a transgression of prescribed gender roles, is evident in his description of the couple's meeting with Israeli minister of justice Dov Josef shortly before the execution: "He

The book further incorporates a diversity of other materials related to the ministry, including two letters written by Hull to Eichmann (one of which did not reach Eichmann before his execution); three letters from Eichmann to Hull; a questionnaire designed by Hull to survey Eichmann's religious beliefs; lists of scriptures the Hulls requested that Eichmann review as homework between sessions; a formulated confession written by Hull and intended for Eichmann's signature (but never signed by Eichmann); Hull's correspondence with Israeli officials and the press; and quotations from psychologist G. M. Gilbert, pastor H. F. Gerecke, and Justice Robert H. Jackson, all of whom had counseled or prosecuted Nazi war criminals at the International Military Tribunal at Nuremberg and whom Hull read while awaiting the decision on Eichmann's appeal. Capping off this conglomeration of diverse texts is a short foreword written after the execution that frames and interprets the entire phenomenon from a posterior perspective.

The Struggle for a Soul is thus constituted by an amalgamate assemblage of reconstructed dialogues, diary entries, embedded texts, and a summative foreword, the aggregate of which is repetitive with regard to its narrative of the ministry and creates a curiously anticlimactic effect, as we know from the beginning that the Hulls' "final testing of his soul" (73) was in vain. At times the book reads like a patchwork of unedited texts padded with reiterated detail, unreflective speculation, and aggrandized consequence and quickly thrown together to approximate the form of a reflective book commensurate with the gravity of the topic and at the same time to capitalize on the sensationalistic wave of interest in Eichmann that followed his trial and execution. That *The Struggle for a Soul* appeared less than one

> [Josef] questioned whether Mrs. Hull should be subjected to the additional strain of being at the place of execution. There was no thought of her witnessing the hanging, but I would want to talk with the condemned man before his execution and would need an interpreter. Mrs. Hull assured Dr. Joseph that she would be all right and that she wanted to see the thing through to the end (short of the hanging). 'Very well,' he said, 'I know that you have done social work and possibly this will not be any worse.' None of us realized that it might possibly be the only time in history that a woman officially assisted in counseling a condemned man only minutes before his execution" (138). In this hyperbolic claim, which is somewhat typical of the tone of Hull's book, Hull further effaces the history of women's ministry to men awaiting execution. Since at least the nineteenth century, and in particular in the American Civil War, nuns have served in arenas of armed conflict as spiritual advisers to prisoners of war, including men condemned to execution (Barton 171–72).

year after Eichmann's death[52] lends credence to such a suspicion, as does Hull's attempt to imbue a sense of transhistorical, even divine import to both the trial and the defendant:

> The two most publicized trials in history had found their locale in Jerusalem. In both cases Jews and Gentiles were involved. The first, that of nearly two thousand years ago, involved a Jew, illegally seized by order of the Sanhedrin, then illegally judged, illegally sentenced, illegally slain by a Gentile court.... Here was innocency, a Man Who did nothing but good to mankind.... The greatest Man Who ever lived....
>
> And now—from the supreme height of righteousness we descend, two thousand years later, to the deepest depth of depravity and evil and gaze upon a man, a Gentile, being judged by a Jewish court....
>
> There is something almost sacred about the proceedings. One could imagine that he was sitting in a modern church service, lacking only the organ and the singing. The trial seems to be lifted out of a mundane, worldly setting into the very heavenlies, as though God Himself is judging a guilty world which has produced such a monster as the prisoner at the bar. (2–4)

Hull grandiloquently and bombastically embellishes the significance of the Eichmann trial by elevating it to the status of a consecrated proceeding and positing it as the parallel case to the Roman trial of Jesus; he works thereby to augment his own authority and dominion as a clergyman over the Eichmann case in general and to place it firmly within his particular area of expertise. The effect of his attempted sacralization of the trial, however, is paradoxical, as it transforms at times the inherent weightiness of his subject into sensationalistic hyperbole, which, combined with the repetitive, hastily assembled character of the book and Hull's amplified representation of his ministry, gives the impression of a man preeminently

---

52 Hull's book is listed in the Library of Congress's *Catalog of Copyright Entries* for January–June 1963, 407.

interested in gaining fame as Eichmann's final interlocutor, who alone can deliver the "true story, the content of those conversations which took place in the death cell between the writer and Eichmann, [which] was never disclosed to the press" (xi).[53] This impression is supported by the recollection of Meir Ronnen of the *Jerusalem Post*, who writes over forty years after the appearance of Hull's book,

> Much of the information about Eichmann's speedy execution comes from an unpleasant Christian missionary who insinuated himself into the Eichmann story by volunteering to become his pastor. The Rev. William Hull was a pudgy fanatic who, after gaining access to Eichmann, tried several times to sell me his accounts, for I was then Features Editor of *The Jerusalem Post*. I was sure that Hull was less concerned about Eichmann's soul than in using the opportunity to write a book. Indeed, his book appeared soon after the execution.

With his critique of Hull's allegedly cynical motive for publishing his account, Ronnen implies here that Hull exploited his and his wife's encounter with Eichmann in order to write what he evidently aimed to be a bestselling tell-all about Eichmann's last days. His investment in both advising Eichmann and in providing "a living 'autopsy'" of his mind was thus also informed by a desire to find a marketable narrative vehicle for his account.

Above and beyond the questions of sensationalism and the quick time to publication, however, the fragmentary, slapdash character of *The Struggle for a Soul* not only expresses internal tensions with regard to Hull's stated goals for undertaking his ministry but also indicates a fundamental discord between the Hulls' pastoral program and the narrative that recounts it. This dissonance derives from a fundamental antagonism between the project of

---

53 Hull demonstrates similar self-important bombast about his role in ministering to Eichmann in his quotation of the words of Tzvi Terlo, the Israeli assistant attorney general: "He had a big smile as he remarked to us that my visiting Eichmann was divine irony. 'In all the world,' he said, 'you were the one Christian clergyman or priest who helped the Hagannah to create the State. Now, out of all the clergymen in the world you are the one who is ministering to Eichmann.'" (134).

conversion and that of confession, between the Hulls' intention with regard to what Stangneth calls their "conversion conversations" (487) and the narrative form of those conversations that Hull creates for a wider public. Moreover, the tension between the modes of conversion and confession is further instructive in its disclosure of the ways in which the reverend and his wife inferred Eichmann's mind from what they viewed to be his sins and what they took to be the perversely reprobate state of his soul.

From the beginning of his account, Hull makes clear that his and his wife's ministry to Eichmann was focused above all on the question of conversion, not confession. In his foreword, he writes, "I had not been called in to hear a confession" (xii), a statement Hull uses to authorize and justify his "tell-all," as it allows him to fend off anticipated criticism of his breach of the conventional contract of privacy and confidentiality between clergyman and the person whom he counsels. Hull tackles that potential ethical dilemma head-on, writing in the second paragraph of his foreword,

> The question might be raised as to the propriety of revealing the content of conversations which took place between a man and his spiritual adviser. To some it would be considered unethical. This would have been so if our conversations had been on the level of the confessional, where priest and confessor are alone and the erring one reveals the secrets of his heart and life. Then I would have felt bound to respect the privacy of the man to whom I ministered, even an Adolf Eichmann. But such was not the case. (xi)

By rejecting from the beginning the notion that his "Christian spiritual counsel" (xii) involved either the formal ritual of confession (meaning the Catholic administration of the sacrament of penance and reconciliation, a practice that Hull, a Pentecostal with "a vicious anti-Catholic perspective" [Kidd 89], viewed with evident disdain)[54] or communications of a private

---

54 Yaakov Ariel hints at Hull's anti-Catholicism: "[Hull] remarked that the demand of the Roman Catholic Church for the internationalization of Jerusalem would have ended Protestant evangelical missionary activity, which, he noted, was protected under Israeli rule. A fundamentalist Protestant, Hull preferred to work under a Jewish government than a non-Protestant Christian one" (157).

nature between a "spiritual adviser" and his advisee embodied in the legal principle of clergy-penitent privilege, Hull is able to square in ethical terms his ministry to Eichmann with the detailed account of it he offers to the public. His rejection of the correlation of his pastoral care of Eichmann with the practice of confession in the book's foreword is duplicated in the main body of the account. Hull writes that he explicitly insisted to Nir in advance of his first meeting with Eichmann that his planned pastoral care would not aim "to hear a confession or to give last rites" (13) to the condemned prisoner. As an evangelical Christian in negotiation with the Israeli government, he took pains thereby to clearly distinguish his intentions from the Roman Catholic sacraments. Rather than endeavor to elicit and attend to a confession from Eichmann, Hull writes that his sole goal was to bring Eichmann "to an active faith in Jesus Christ" (13), an undertaking fully in keeping with Hull's evangelical worldview and his adoption of what Veli-Matti Kärkkäinen calls the "robust missionary ethos" (295) of Pentecostalism, which, according to Julie C. Ma, gives utmost "priority ... to soul-winning" (87). For Hull, whose "interest primarily is in the soul of man" (50), what matters most was the urgent question of Eichmann's relationship to Jesus Christ, for "everyone must come to God through Jesus. There is no other way to be saved" (70). (Apparently the hubristic irony of asserting this fundamentalist Christian belief in the presence of Israeli prison guards to a man sentenced for his role in the genocide of millions of Jews was lost on Hull and his wife, the latter of whom says at one point to Eichmann, "We are concerned for any human being who is going to die—is he ready through Jesus Christ to meet God? Even the policemen here, they are not guilty of anything, but if I had the opportunity I would ask them if they were ready to meet God through Jesus Christ" [144]).[55] The crimes for which Eichmann was tried were—at least

---

55 At another point, Hull explicitly states (in the presence of the Israeli guards) his belief that the Jews among whom he lived in Israel would automatically be barred from heaven. When Eichmann queries him, "There are probably three billion people or more in the world today, Jews, Christians, and others. Possibly one third are saved through believing. The other two thirds do not believe. Are they lost?," Hull responds, "Yes, they are all lost" (68–69). As Yona Malachy writes based on information from an article in the Tel Aviv newspaper *Herut*, "In Canada, Hull told the correspondent of a Toronto newspaper that the six million Jewish victims of the Nazis were doomed to perish in Hell, and would not enter paradise, because they had not accepted the belief in Christ.

within the context of the Hulls' ministry—"mundane, worldly" (4) matters and thus somewhat irrelevant; although Hull writes that he and his wife labored to force Eichmann to "realize and confess his guilt" (75) and to challenge him to account for how he "made it possible for people to be killed" (106), Eichmann's legal guilt by and large did not interest them. As Hull reports telling Eichmann on the day he was to be hanged, "We are not concerned about your guilt but as to whether you are ready to meet God" (143). The Hulls thus placed much more emphasis on the necessity for Eichmann to performatively acknowledge Jesus than they did on the importance of Eichmann admitting his crimes; at one point Hull writes that he lectured to him, "Adolf Eichmann, listen well. Some day or some night faith is going to come into your heart to believe on [sic] the Lord Jesus Christ. When it comes get down on your knees and accept Jesus as your Savior. He will forgive your sins and fully pardon you" (104), an exhortation that completely bypassed the need for Eichmann to recognize his own wrongdoing and that, in fact, with its pledge of pardon, promised to undo discursively the proceedings and verdict of the trial. Furthermore, for Hull, Eichmann's guilt was confirmed in full not by the jury verdict but by his continued rejection of Christ. As he writes after his sixth visit,

> Who knows what is in the mind of this man? . . . We have offered him the chance of salvation at this last moment, through Jesus Christ. If he still rejects, has no remorse or repentance for his acts, it will be shown that he was a hopeless case, his sentence was justified, and the world will feel that justice was done. Today many say that he should not be hung. Our approach to him offers a final testing of his soul. If he remains adamant then the whole picture of his guilt is proved true and his death the least expiation he could make for his crimes. (73)

Moreover, he said, Eichmann's sins were not as great as those of the average man who denied Jesus as the redeemer" (105). Malachy reports that Hull's statement elicited "sharp criticism" within Israel and "may have been partly responsible for the final departure of the Rev. Mr. Hull and his family from Israel in 1963" (105).

In Hull's Pentecostal worldview, the "earthly judgment" handed down by the Israeli court "can be nothing" to the "final judgment" of God (8), whose sole criterion for salvation and a full exoneration from worldly crimes is the performative acknowledgment of Jesus Christ, through whom Eichmann's "sins, even all his vile deeds, would be forgiven" (15). In this way, Hull disjoins Eichmann from his crimes, which become a marginal backstory to the more important narrative of the Hulls' "efforts to win the soul of Adolf Eichmann" (xiii).

However, while Hull is not reticent in *The Struggle for a Soul* about his aims for his ministry to Eichmann, which set out "to bring an erring Gentile back to the fold" (102), he is also evidently aware that Eichmann, who had been convicted of crimes against humanity and against the Jewish people, constituted no ordinary target for proselytization. Indeed, to characterize his ministry to Eichmann according to the singular goal of conversion, which places paramount importance on the successful salvation of the sinner's soul rather than on his potential contrition or repentance for his crimes, would have implied the bracketing of Eichmann's role in the Nazi genocide. Moreover, while it is clear that his envisioned audience for his book was composed largely of the "millions of Christians [who] are praying for [Eichmann's] salvation" (141), Hull is also acutely cognizant that the greater part of public interest in Eichmann—especially but not exclusively among Jews—was largely concerned not with whether Eichmann "expressed faith in Jesus Christ" (120) but with his mental disposition (i.e., whether he was intrinsically an evil person), his motivations for his active contribution to the "Final Solution," and the possibility of his acknowledgment of guilt and remorse for his actions. From the beginning of his ministry, Hull writes, he was aware that his conversations with Eichmann could form the basis of a written account with potential mass appeal:

> We felt that if these meetings continued, a story might develop from them that would be of both interest and profit to an inquiring world. Adolf Eichmann's deeds had been so awful, the scale of murder so immense, that the world was at a loss to understand how a human being could harden his heart to a degree enabling him to do these deeds. Possibly our conversations would provide the answer. (27)

Perhaps because of these reasons—Hull's recognition that his audience might disapprove of a narrow report of his attempts to convert Eichmann, his awareness of a general public desire to understand Eichmann's motivations, and his intent to reach a wider readership—Hull embeds his evangelical project in a rhetoric of confession even as he rejects the actual practice of confession. In order to create a dramatic arc—"a story"—in the narrative of his ministry to Eichmann, one that necessitates a book-length text that is able to hold the attention of readers and to impart a moral lesson (albeit through a negative example), Hull shapes his account loosely according to the genre of the confessional autobiography. As Sidonie Smith and Julia Watson explain, confessional autobiography "is addressed to an interlocutor who listens, judges, and has the power to absolve" (192). In its conventional form, which can be traced back to Augustine in the fourth century, the confessional text is "doubly addressed, to God and to a confessor," while in modern versions the role of confessor is assumed by "the human reader who needs a narrative explanation of sinfulness and redemption" (192). Moreover, the confessional address, as Peter Brooks investigates in his book *Troubling Confessions: Speaking Guilt in Law and Literature*, is predicated on the confessant's performative articulation of a sin to a confessor within the context of a complex, intersubjective, "symbiotic" (42) relationship. Christian religious confession, in particular, which has been shaped in large part by Catholic doctrine but also has its Protestant variations (particularly in the form of the evangelical conversion narrative),[56] requires the performative speech act of the verbal admission of guilt in order for the sinner to achieve repentance and be eligible for salvation; this performative aspect is especially important in the "ancient ritual of deathbed confession," which effects the "absolution . . . and reconciliation of the sinner with the human community whose bonds he has so sundered" (Brooks 115).[57]

---

56 Brooks writes of the ubiquitous template of the Catholic rite of confession, "The confessional model is so powerful in Western culture, I believe, that even those whose religion or nonreligion has no place for the Roman Catholic practice of confession are nonetheless deeply influenced by the model. Indeed, it permeates our culture" (2).

57 For further exploration of the theory and practice of confession, especially as it plays out with regard to nonfictional portraits of Holocaust perpetrators, see chapter 2.

The Struggle for a Soul assumes the basic configuration of the confessional autobiography but also transforms the confessor-confessant dynamic and its link to the text's narration; in this case the confession is narrated not from the perspective of the confessant (Eichmann), who addresses his confessor (Hull), but from that of the confessor, who created the confessional scene as well as the conditions under which the confessant was coerced to confess. As the author of Eichmann's confessional text, Hull emplots the ritualistic process of confession as a trajectory of increscent enlightenment with a discernable moral course that is made increasingly manifest with each visit. Of the pastoral plan that he and his wife developed in advance of their first meeting with Eichmann, which they designed as "a series of studies of logical progression on man and salvation," Hull thus writes: "Our objective was first to bring to Eichmann a sense of guilt for his deeds of the past—then a realization of his lost condition, spiritually—then the revelation that through Jesus Christ his sins, even all his vile deeds, would be forgiven" (15). Tracing a dynamic that follows the conventional confessional arc, Hull lays out here the steps he felt were necessary to achieve Eichmann's spiritual revelation, linking what he hoped would be Eichmann's acceptance of Jesus as his savior—Hull's primary objective—to Eichmann's prospective admission of criminal and moral wrongdoing, which would fulfill the rituals of the confessional mode to which he had committed Eichmann. Throughout the series of meetings they conducted with Eichmann, the Hulls emphasized to him the importance and the necessity of the confessional act, exhorting, "If you were led by God now you would repent for all that you did and would now confess" (83). As they began to realize that Eichmann was immovable in his intent not to convert, they became increasingly desperate to convince him to do so. Frustrated by Eichmann's intransigent refusal to admit to any wrongdoing or transgression, Hull presented during his eleventh visit for Eichmann's signature a written preformulated "confession form" (102) containing a four-point list of crimes to which Eichmann was expected to confess, including his responsibility for transporting European Jews to death camps, his failure to make a "real effort to be relieved of [his] command and duties," his continued membership in the Nazi Party until 1945, and his performance of his duties "in a manner which gave little chance for the survival of any Jew who came under [his] jurisdiction" (114). In this, Hull asked Eichmann to confess to crimes for which, at his trial, he had refused to admit guilt. (In response to each of the fifteen criminal charges for which he had been indicted at the trial, Eichmann had claimed, "Not guilty in the sense of the indictment" ["Im Sinne der Anklage nicht schuldig"]). Hull rounded out the "confession form" with two additional statements affirming Eichmann's "faith in the Lord Jesus Christ" and his acceptance of "the Lord Jesus Christ as my Saviour" (114) that he expected Eichmann to undersign. Through the confessional script that he wrote for Eichmann, in which he imagined the possible shape a potential confession from Eichmann might take, Hull conjoined the question of conversion to that of confession, utilizing the latter to achieve the former. Hull not only demonstrated thereby what Hans-Lukas Kieser calls a "dramaturgy of conversion deeply embedded in evangelical tradition" (134) but also staged along with it the ritualistic drama of confession.

Despite the Hulls' strategic employment of the rhetoric of confession in their ministry to Eichmann, however, the latter resolutely declined to play his part in the confessional scene they had orchestrated. Not only did he maintain that he was innocent of any crime for which confession would have been necessary—"I have nothing to confess, I have not sinned. . . . What I did was what I was ordered to do. I was a subordinate" (83)—but he also refused to engage in confessional performance: "I am not interested in making a show of confession before men" (140). Further, he adamantly and "angrily" (115) refused to sign the confessional form that Hull had prepared for him, protesting that "even in the court they did not accuse me of all this. It is not true. . . . I do not have an ounce of guilt" (115–16). At the same time, Eichmann also resolutely resisted the Hulls' concentrated pressure to win him over to "the gospel of Jesus Christ" and to bring him "to a place of repentance and salvation through faith in Jesus" (50). As he writes in his first letter to Hull (which he composed after the Hulls' first visit),

> Yesterday I saw again how wide a chasm separates me from the Evangelical interpretations. . . . In case you should harbor expectations that after a certain number of visits and conversations I will return to the lap of the Evangelical Church, this will never happen. I am sorry that I must spell out what must seem to you discouraging statements, but if I did not I would consider myself a hypocrite. (30)

On the day of Eichmann's execution, when the Hulls stepped up their frantic pressure on Eichmann to acknowledge and express faith in Jesus Christ and, in fact, as Hull's transcript of the visit indicates (138–44), began to hound him relentlessly, Eichmann became equally agitated in his determination to repel their attempts to convert him:

> The sentence was clear. I am going to be hung. Why should I pretend to believe something I don't believe? . . . I do not believe in hell. Those are men's thoughts; there is no hell. . . . Don't tell me that you came thirteen times for me. You did not do me any favor. . . . Don't interrupt me. Let me talk. I wrote you right at the start what I believed and you need not have come. I am under no obligation to you. . . . I do not need a middleman or a mediator. I go directly to God myself. I am very dogmatic on this, so I don't believe in Jesus Christ. (140–42)

In the reaction that Eichmann, according to Hull, exhibited in response to the Hulls' intensified ministry, one glimpses for a moment Eichmann's own viewpoint on his meetings with the Hulls; rather than giving him spiritual succor or helping him to adjust psychologically to his guilty verdict and impending execution, they became for him an extension of the trial in that he was once again forced to defend himself against what he perceived to be injustice. In this case, however, the injustice inhered not in the perceived outrage of being called to account for acts that he "was ordered to do" (83) but in the Hulls' encroachment on Eichmann's religious beliefs.[58]

---

[58] Stangneth writes regarding the Hulls' attempts to browbeat Eichmann into conversion, "One of the grotesque consequences of these 'conversion conversations' is that Eichmann actually appears in a positive light, having put up a respectable defense against Hull's aggressive attempt to convert him. As a reader, you feel something like genuine sympathy for Eichmann in the face of such an odious fundamentalist visitation—something you then hold against Hull personally" (487). Stangneth's description of Hull's missionary zeal here is typical of the occasional sardonicism that characterizes her writing, whereby she briefly—and in my view, refreshingly—abandons the posture of objectivity customary of historiographical style and acknowledges the outrageous ethical incongruities, bitter ironies, and paradoxical empathetic effects created by Hull's portrait of his encounter with Eichmann. She reads here her own reaction

In response to their coercive efforts to force him to confess and convert, Eichmann remained obstinately unchanged in his spiritual position.

For this reason, rather than chronicle either a confession or a conversion, both of which would have constituted a dramatic outcome of the Hulls' efforts, fulfilled the promise of their ministry, and—perhaps most importantly—rewritten the narrative of Eichmann's crimes and his personality, Hull's book records their failure to successfully transform Eichmann through their "gospel message" (xiii). The "story" that Hull had hoped to write, which would have been "of both interest and profit to an inquiring world," thus did not materialize; instead of a satisfying narrative arc or a redemptive resolution to the drama of Eichmann's confessional scene, Hull was left with a record of a series of stonewalled attempts at conversion that could not be massaged into either an evangelical success story or an edifying lesson. But Hull attempts nevertheless to extract some meaning out of his futile endeavor:

> The fact that Adolf Eichmann died denying any faith in Jesus Christ, any need of a mediator, was a tragedy, for no man on earth had greater need of a savior. But one faint ray of satisfaction emerges from the sordid picture—Adolf Eichmann's almost public rejection of Jesus Christ completely dissociated him and his evil deeds from Christianity. Christianity can be held responsible for producing an Eichmann, but not for his doing what he did. As the man in charge of finding a solution to the so-called "Jewish Question," he was completely separated at that time from Christianity and the teachings of Jesus Christ. (xiii)

Although Hull was not able to achieve his objective and provoke Eichmann into expressing faith in Jesus Christ, he was able, in the writing of his account, to derive both solace and significance in Eichmann's refusal to do

---

as much as she reads Hull's narrative and admits a disconcerting empathy for Eichmann induced in her by Hull's single-minded and dogmatic ministry to him. Stangneth is coerced almost against her will into such an empathetic response by virtue of her antipathy toward the ways in which she believes Hull uses his fundamentalist Christian certainty to bully Eichmann.

so. In this way, rather than articulate a crisis in Hull's relationship to his own faith or in his belief that "A world with faith in God and in fellowship with God could never produce an Adolf Eichmann" (111), his account of his failed ministry to Eichmann is at heart "doctrinarily self-confirmatory" (Kieser 134) in that it validates and thus reinforces Hull's prior doctrinal perspective. Hull's reading of Eichmann is thus an example of what Hanna Meretoja terms "subsumptive appropriation," a concept she develops to designate narrative practices that "function appropriatively and reinforce cultural stereotypes by subsuming singular experiences under culturally dominant narrative scripts" (112).[59] Hull subsumes Eichmann's refusal to "come to Jesus" under a paradoxically redemptive narrative script that takes two antithetical forms: misfortune and fortune. On the one hand, Hull sees Eichmann's failure to acknowledge Jesus as cataclysmic, terming it a "tragedy." Apart from the absurdity and indecency of designating Eichmann's fate as tragic (after all, Eichmann's death, in contrast to the deaths of his victims, was the outcome of a legitimate, rigorous court trial and not the result of unilateral, regime-initiated genocidal murder), his framing of his failed ministry as a tragedy elevates his encounter with Eichmann to the status of a literary event, imbues his narrative with consequence and higher import, and allows him to offer his account to his readership as a moral homily. Hull's strategy here further accords profound meaning and elegant, coherent closure to a story—namely, the narrative of the Hulls' misguided efforts to rehabilitate Eichmann's soul—that otherwise would have remained incidental, indeterminate, and lacking in a moral message. On the other hand, with his reinterpretation of the higher significance of Eichmann's rejection of Jesus, Hull is able to transform the failure of his project to convert Eichmann into a kind of success; his reading of Eichmann's soul thus functions as a surface projection for that which Hull desperately yearned to locate in the Nazi war criminal but also is ultimately relieved *not* to find: a Christian conscience. Further, it allows him to perform an outrageous blanket exoneration of Christians and Christianity for the brutal genocide

---

59 Meretoja makes a distinction between what she terms "subsumptive narrative practices," which "simply reinforce problematic stereotypical sense-making practices" (112), and "non-subsumptive practices," which "challenge such categories of appropriation and follow the logic of dialogue and exploration" (112). However, rather than position these two models as a binary, she sees them as heuristic categories that exist on a continuum.

of millions of European Jews, an absolution that brazenly disregards the intimate involvement in mass murder of many thousands of self-identified Christians in planning, implementing, and supporting the Holocaust. In that regard, Hull's mission can be considered—from his own subsumptive perspective, at least—to a certain extent auspicious, even victorious; although he was unable to help Eichmann attain God's saving grace and thus lost his "desperate battle for the soul of this man," he is triumphant in what in his mind was the next best thing: through Eichmann's repudiation of Christian belief, Hull manages to broker a state of unconditional absolution for Christianity.[60]

Eichmann as Reflector

While Hull's book, with its dogmatic and subsumptive perspective, is not nearly as insightful and penetrating as the portraits of Eichmann by Arendt and Mulisch, taken together the three texts offer a fascinating glimpse into the ways in which Eichmann's crimes, his persona, and his performance of identity functioned in very different ways for different interpreters. All three observers of Eichmann shared a common vantage point in space and time, namely, the gallery of the Jerusalem courtroom during the period of Eichmann's trial, yet they each employ frames of reference in their respective projects of reading Eichmann's mind that diverge—sometimes in radical ways—from the schemata brought to bear by the other two. Arendt, as we have seen, perceives Eichmann through a phenomenological perspective, attending very carefully to what she was able to apprehend from Eichmann's performance at the trial, particularly his verbal testimony. Focusing on what she heard and read, she construes Eichmann's mind as the superficial byproduct of the banal language that he employed to generate the effect of a thinking, ethical self. The novelist Mulisch, by contrast, demonstrates discomfort with such phenomenological interpretation, especially that which deduces mindset from physical exteriority. He is both drawn to Eichmann's face as a legible text that begs kinesic mind-reading and at the same time skeptical of any inference of mind that can be made based on

---

60 Thanks to Gerd Bayer from the Friedrich-Alexander-Universität Erlangen-Nürnberg, who pointed out the fact that Hull achieves rhetorical absolution of Christianity even though he was unable to save Eichmann's soul.

physical features and expressions, which in his view dissemble as much as they disclose. For his part, the Pentecostal pastor Hull sees in Eichmann an evangelical commodity; in his zealous focus on the state of Eichmann's soul to the exclusion of all other questions, he reifies Eichmann and reduces the complexity of his criminal identity to the status of a wayward, sinful soul in desperate need of evangelical intervention. Each of the three mediating figures—Arendt, Mulisch, and Hull—thus approaches Eichmann with a distinct set of questions and a particular understanding of the nature of evil and the mindset and motivations of persons who perpetrate it; they each accordingly filter their perceptions of this paradigmatic perpetrator through established but singular frameworks of knowledge and interpretation. Eichmann functions in these three portraits as much as a reflector, illuminating the distinct perspectives and predispositions of each of his mediators, as he does as the focal point of their observations; in that respect, his mind becomes a kind of repository for each commentator's particular investment in his history, identity, and self-understanding. At times, the three readings of Eichmann's mind resonate with each other, producing an aggregate, synthetic profile of a man who, though voluble about his position in the genocidal administration of the Third Reich, resolutely abnegated his functional and moral responsibility for the genocide itself. At other moments, however, the assessments by Arendt, Mulisch, and Hull diverge from or even contravene each other, generating collectively a surfeit of interpretation that exceeds logical application to any given person. The disagreement between their assessments not only indicates the irreducibility of the mind of the Holocaust perpetrator but also reminds us of how unreliable, misleading, and ambiguous the exercise in mind-reading—particularly in the case of a chronic performer and self-mythographer like Eichmann—can be.

2

Interpellating the Perpetrator

Gitta Sereny's *Into That Darkness*

"A Drive to Know"

In spring 1971, journalist Gitta Sereny (1921–2012) sat down for a series of prison interviews lasting over seventy hours with Franz Stangl (1908–71), former commandant of Sobibór and Treblinka, two of the three Aktion Reinhard death camps at which as many as two million European Jews were murdered. A few months prior to their conversations, which Sereny chronicled in her 1974 masterwork *Into That Darkness: An Examination of Conscience*, Stangl had been sentenced to life imprisonment in Düsseldorf for joint responsibility for the murder of at least nine hundred thousand people; less than a day after their final interview in June 1971, he would die of a heart attack. As Sereny notes in her 2001 collection of essays, *The Healing Wound: Experiences and Reflections on Germany, 1938–2001*, the origins of these interviews lay in her frustration with the failure of postwar trials of Holocaust perpetrators (in particular, the West German trials of the late 1960s) to offer plausible explanations for the psychological motives of individual perpetrators beyond facile self-justification:

> When, sometime in 1968, I realized that this was the reason for my frustration, I decided to try to find one perpetrator if possible less primitive and with at least a semblance of moral awareness, who, if approached not as a monster but as a human being, might be able to explain his own catastrophic moral failure. (*The Healing Wound* 88)

With Stangl, Sereny believed she had found just such an open, willing, and—above all—*human* perpetrator. Although Stangl struggled in the "agonized process" (92) of the interviews between an earnest exploration of his participation in genocide and the denial and evasion of personal responsibility and guilt, Sereny writes that "this man showed me as no other could have done the very essence of the process of corruption" (92). In the end, Sereny claims retrospectively that, despite the pain and despair experienced by Stangl over the course of their conversations, "the whole experience was a huge relief to him" (92).

Sereny's interviews with Stangl were taxing not only on the former perpetrator but also on the interviewer herself. As she writes further in *The Healing Wound*,

> It was an experience I might not have given myself had I known what it would do to me. . . . I think my reason for doing the things I do, is and always has been quite simply—or perhaps not so simply—a need, a drive to know. The price one pays (and, selfishly, expects the people one loves to pay) for giving in to this inner need, in shock, in tension and in a very particular kind of fatigue, can be high. Perhaps something that happened when I was about halfway through the conversations with Stangl, can illustrate these tensions. It happened on an evening after I had stayed late talking to the prison director and the Düsseldorf station platform was virtually empty as I waited for my train. I heard the sound of crying . . . of many children crying, it seemed to me . . . for a long time before a freight train, slowing down during its passage through the station, went past us. And as it rolled through—the cries by now, I thought,

desperate—I saw parts of pale small faces pressing against the narrow openings in each car. I'm not given to fainting, but I blacked out. The railway worker who helped me up told me the freight train carried cattle. It was calves, calves crying just like children. I can still hear them now, as I write. (92–93; ellipses in original)

Sereny embarked on the difficult project of interviewing Stangl because of a deep need to understand, in human terms, the motivations and crimes of Holocaust perpetrators. Her reflections on her time spent interpellating Stangl reveal the extent to which she has become entrammeled by her empathic engagement with him. The world of the extermination camp, about which Sereny has diligently researched and seeks to learn more from Stangl, is actualized in her fantasy as a present threat that plays out on the platform in Düsseldorf. Her conversations with Stangl and the troubling knowledge they contain affect her to such an extent that she not only *perceives* the trainload of bellowing calves to be a deportation train carrying children to their death but also *experiences* it as such. This disturbing episode, which Sereny describes three decades after the fact, resembles uncannily an anecdote that Stangl relates to her during their interviews:

"When I was on a trip once, years later in Brazil," he said, his face deeply concentrated, and obviously reliving the experience, "my train stopped next to a slaughterhouse. The cattle in the pens, hearing the noise of the train, trotted up to the fence and stared at the train. They were very close to my window, one crowding the other, looking at me through that fence. I thought then, 'Look at this; this reminds me of Poland; that's just how the people looked, trustingly, just before they went into the tins...'"

"*You said 'tins*,'" I interrupted. "*What do you mean?*" But he went on without hearing, or answering me.

"... I couldn't eat tinned meat after that. Those big eyes... which looked at me... not knowing that in no time at all they'd all be dead." He paused. His face was drawn. At this moment he looked old and worn and real.

> "So you didn't feel they were human beings?"
>
> "Cargo," he said tonelessly. "They were cargo." He raised and dropped his hand in a gesture of despair. Both our voices had dropped. It was one of the few times in those weeks of talks that he made no effort to cloak his despair, and his hopeless grief allowed a moment of sympathy. (*Into That Darkness* 201)

Sereny's terror at the Düsseldorf train station is, both structurally and in terms of content, astonishingly similar to Stangl's own epiphany from the Brazilian train, thus provoking critical questions about the ways in which she internalizes Stangl's testimony. The affective correspondence between the two accounts is also instructive. Sereny is so profoundly disturbed and frightened by the cries of the calves that she loses consciousness. Stangl is likewise so unsettled by witnessing cattle in the slaughterhouse pen that he loses the desire to eat meat. However, Sereny's reaction to and interpretation of the animals in her experience put Stangl's account in stark ethical relief. Sereny faints because she believes—at least momentarily—that the cattle in the train are incarcerated children, whom she links—irrationally but, given the intensity of her engagement with Stangl's testimony, understandably—to the brutal experiences of the people deported to Stangl's Treblinka. Stangl, on the other hand, is discomfited not because he perceives, as Sereny does, that people are being treated like animals but because the cattle in the pen, in his view, are reduced to the same cargo-like status of the Jews who were deported to and murdered in Treblinka. Leaving aside the important but—at least for my purpose here—less relevant issue of the ethical treatment of animals, at stake in Stangl's reaction is the way in which, decades later, he continues to naturalize the murder of hundreds of thousands of Jews that took place under his watch. The agitation he describes to Sereny stems from his recognition that the animals he sees (and who in turn gaze innocently back at him) are degraded to the level of freight to be transported and destroyed—cargo that he at bottom identifies, without irony or awareness of paradox, with the Jewish victims whom he is convicted of murdering.

Sereny's distressing episode at the Düsseldorf train station, which both mirrors and critically departs from the similar incident related to her by

Stangl, is key for understanding her biographical portrait of Stangl, for it reveals both her empathic investment in Stangl's story and her ethical departure from his understanding of his culpability for the genocidal murder at Sobibór and Treblinka. Her interviews with him constitute an intersubjective encounter that she then recounts retrospectively. In her dual narrative roles as diegetic interlocutor within the interview and extradiegetic narrator of the account of the interview, Sereny functions as the self-conscious mediator of Stangl's voice, focalizer of his internal perspective, and translator of his experience. She also becomes an intervening ethical voice in and the active shaping force of Stangl's story. Moreover, Sereny's "drive to know" both the facts of Stangl's crimes and his mindset regarding them, an element she stresses in her anecdote about her distressing experience at the Düsseldorf train station, becomes the guiding principle of her text and has important implications for both how she interpellates Stangl in the interviews and how she frames his story. Sereny utilizes in her production of Stangl's biography particular narrative masterplots and generic conventions, such as those of the detective story and the confession, that shape how she transmits and interprets Stangl's experience as a Holocaust perpetrator. Sereny thus filters Stangl's consciousness through the narrative frames in which she fashions his testimony.

In its effort to shed light on Stangl's moral and mental processing—during his work as a police office in the National Socialist euthanasia center Schloss Hartheim, in his role as commandant of Sobibór and Treblinka, and in his postwar life—Sereny's book about Stangl distinguishes itself from the efforts of her contemporary Claude Lanzmann, who is also known for penetrating interviews of Holocaust perpetrators in the 1970s, many of which appear in his 1985 film *Shoah*. Lanzmann notably resists attempting to understand or empathize with his interviewees (one of whom is Stangl's Treblinka colleague Franz Suchomel, whom Sereny also interviewed for her Stangl book)[1] or to account for how they understood their own actions; according to Jay Cantor, Lanzmann "refuses to enter the Nazis' psychology,

---

[1] Suchomel, "for whom recalling the details of Treblinka has become something of a passion" (Sereny, *Into That Darkness* 205), plays an important role in Sereny's text that has been overlooked in the scholarship. His astonishing frankness about the details of Treblinka and his work there contrasts with Stangl's reticence about his own duties at the death camp.

to grant them inwardness" (34). As Dominick LaCapra has argued, Lanzmann follows a "Warumverbot" with his film, "an absolute refusal of the *why* question and of understanding" ("Lanzmann's *Shoah*" 245), and instead focuses on the *how* of the operations of the extermination machinery; Lanzmann thus adamantly rejects a psychological approach that would allow him to enter into a common mental space with the perpetrators he interviews. Sereny, by contrast, is far less interested in the functioning of Schloss Hartheim, to which Stangl was first posted, and of the death camps Sobibór and Treblinka; in fact, one can glean much more about the organization and daily operations of Treblinka from Lanzmann's grainy covert footage of his interview with Suchomel than Sereny is able to elicit from Stangl. While Lanzmann obsesses over the minute details of the extermination process, Sereny's approach, as he asserts rather dismissively in his 2009 autobiography *The Patagonian Hare*, "seemed to me purely psychological: she wanted to think about evil, to understand how a husband and father can calmly take part in mass murder" (420). Lanzmann thus contrasts Sereny's overwhelming desire to understand Stangl with his own engagement with perpetrators, in which, as he says, "I buttressed with all my might the refusal to understand" (420).[2]

Lanzmann's approach to the Holocaust, which LaCapra describes as "absolutist" in its refusal to understand, psychologize, or find relatable explanations (however partial) for the events of the Holocaust in general and the perpetrators' actions in particular, reflects a poststructuralist skepticism regarding the possibility of identifying meaning in or extracting any communicable explanation from the testimony of those whom he interviews. Sereny's *Into That Darkness: An Examination of Conscience*, by contrast, with its "drive to know" Stangl's mind, follows a decidedly Enlightenment procedure.[3] As the title of the book indicates, her goal

---

2 In the original French of his autobiography, Lanzmann writes, "Je me suis arc-bouté de toutes mes forces au refus de comprendre" (*Le lièvre de Patagonie* 605). Because the translation of this sentence in the published English version—"I braced myself with all my might against the refusal to understand"—implies with its ambiguous use of "against" the opposite of what the French sentence connotes, I have chosen to render my own translation of this sentence.

3 Critics who analyze interviews with perpetrators are divided about the possibility of gaining understanding from their testimony, a split that reflects the philosophical differences between Lanzmann and Sereny. Tzevtan Todorov, who directly compares Lanzmann's and Sereny's approaches, favors Sereny: "Sereny's

is to penetrate what she sees as the opaque obscurity of the actions and reactions of a small group of men about whom very little was known: the commanders of the Nazi extermination camps. By working with Stangl to bring to light not only the facts of his perpetration but also the history of his emotional and moral engagement with his past, she hopes to illuminate "a whole dimension of reactions and behaviour we had never yet understood" despite what she characterizes, as far back as the early 1970s, as "the great number of books and films on the Nazi era" (*Into That Darkness* 13). In short, Sereny endeavors to make Stangl's darkness visible to her readers by laying bare, through his own words, his mind. As she tells her readers in the preface,

> I thought it essential, before it became too late, to try at least once, as far as possible unemotionally and with an open mind, to penetrate the personality of a man who had been intimately involved with the most total evil our age has produced. It was important, I thought, to assess the circumstances which led up to his involvement, for once not from our point of view, but from *his*. (*Into That Darkness* 13)

Her goal, as she states, is to bring her readers into Stangl's mind and to portray the events in which he was so murderously involved from his own

---

attitude is not only more moral than Lanzmann's but also more productive.... she never tried to force Stangl to say one thing or another, for she knew that whatever was said under constraint would be of no value. It is for this reason that Sereny's work takes us farther down the path to knowing and understanding evil than Lanzmann's does" (*Facing the Extreme* 280). Inga Clendinnen agrees that Sereny's approach brings us closer to understanding the perpetrators' motives: "Sereny did not attempt to 'identify' with either Franz Stangl or Albert Speer beyond that first, essential assumption of a shared humanity, yet through her scrupulous work we are brought to understand those two men immeasurably better. I do not pretend that 'understanding' men like Hitler, or Himmler, or Stangl is an easy matter. I would only insist that the problem is not qualitatively different from the problems inherent in understanding any other human beings—and that our understanding of our fellow human beings will not be and cannot be complete" (111–12). Robert Eaglestone, on the other hand, echoes Lanzmann in his assessment of perpetrator testimony, particularly with regard to Sereny's interviews with Stangl: "The attempt to 'penetrate,' to understand the evil is doomed to failure, because, simply, there is nothing to understand" ("Reading Perpetrator Testimony" 132).

perspective, an endeavor that requires a willingness on the part of both interlocutor and reader to try to understand how a man such as Stangl, who, even after his 1970 conviction, continued to see himself as a morally upright person, could not only be drawn into the perpetration of genocide but also excel at it to such an extent as to receive a commendation as the "best camp commander" ("der beste Lagerleiter").[4] For Sereny, such a project of understanding, however, both presupposes a readiness on the part of interviewer and reader to enter into Stangl's mind and demands radical honesty from him, the interviewee. As she reports telling him on the first day of the interviews, after he had spent several hours recapitulating "the arguments, the phraseology, the very words . . . from his and other trials for Nazi crimes" (*Into That Darkness* 22), she was determined that he strive to transcend the pat phrases and polemics that had until this point characterized the perpetrators' speech about their culpability:

> If he . . . preferred to go on in the vein of that morning's recital, then I would listen to him . . . , go back to England, write a little something about the interview, and that would be the end of it. But if, after thinking about it, he decided to help me delve deeper into the past (*his* past, because things had happened to and inside him which had happened to hardly anyone else, ever) then perhaps we could find some truth together; some new truth which would contribute to the understanding of things that had never yet been understood. (*Into That Darkness* 23)

Sereny expresses here a confidence that, together with Stangl, she can uncover a heretofore unidentified truth about the Holocaust and Stangl's role in it, an attitude that reflects her Enlightenment belief not only that the truth is locatable and apprehensible but also that in its identification it has liberating potential for both Stangl and the post-Holocaust world. As I shall later argue, her conviction in this regard has implications for how

---

[4] Stangl was named "der beste Lagerleiter, der den größten Anteil an der ganzen Aktion hatte" (the best camp commander who had the greatest share of the entire action) by Odilo Globocnik, the organizer and supervisor of the Aktion Reinhard program (Berenstein 301–2).

she tells her story of her encounter with Stangl. In her efforts to narrate Stangl's struggle with his past, she reaches for particular narrative forms that help buttress the coming-to-truth effect that she stages in her book. From the outset, Sereny is convinced that she will locate Stangl's truth; she thus shapes her narrative as a quest for truth that will eventually be fulfilled.

Translation and Authenticity

Into That Darkness constitutes an extended biographical project with a long and complex publication and translation history that reflects the highly mediated nature of Sereny's construction of her narrative. Although her conversations with Stangl were conducted entirely in German (one of her native languages), Sereny translated parts of them into English (the language in which she most often wrote) and published them in an article in the *Daily Telegraph Magazine* in October 1971 entitled "Colloquy with a Conscience." Shortly thereafter the article appeared in German in four parts in *Die Zeit*—"Bekenntnisse eines Biedermanns" (Confessions of a petit bourgeois); "Ich war gefangen in der Falle" (I was caught in a trap); "Es war Dantes Inferno" (It was Dante's Inferno); and "War Gott in Treblinka?" (Was God in Treblinka?)—and in other newspapers around the globe. Sereny then expanded her original essay into a book-length analysis that included extensive research and interviews with Stangl's wife, survivors of the camps, camp guards, Polish bystanders to the atrocities, and other witnesses from the period. The English original appeared in 1974 as *Into That Darkness: From Mercy Killing to Mass Murder* (later editions were titled *Into That Darkness: An Examination of Conscience*), followed by translations into French, Italian, Swedish, Spanish, Japanese, Polish, and Portuguese. The delayed German translation appeared first with the Ullstein Verlag in 1979 as *Am Abgrund: Eine Gewissensforschung* (At the abyss: An examination of conscience) and in a second edition with the Piper Verlag in 1995 as *Am Abgrund: Gespräche mit dem Henker* (At the abyss: Conversations with the executioner). While the second edition of *Am Abgrund* lists a translator, Helmut Röhrling, who translated *Into That Darkness* "aus dem Englischen," or from the English (*Am Abgrund: Gespräche mit dem Henker* 3), neither the articles in *Die Zeit* nor the 1979 edition contains references to a translator; nor does Sereny mention the process of translation in the foreword or acknowledgments to either the first German edition or the second, retranslated edition. It is reasonable to assume that, given the absence of an identified translator, Sereny played at least a partial role in the translation and preparation of the articles in *Die Zeit* and the first German edition. Moreover, it is very likely that Sereny (or her possible co-translator) translated directly from her English texts (meaning that the German texts would have been the product of retranslation) rather than consulting interview transcripts and notes and reproducing the original German wording of her questions and the statements of Stangl and the other witnesses.[5]

The convoluted translation and publication history of Sereny's Stangl project and the lack of a clear chain of referentiality between the interview in German, the original English articles and book, and the articles and two book versions in German make it difficult to track the origins of Stangl's statements or to determine how much they have been affected by the practices of translation and retranslation. Sereny's extended interview project, in its multiple variants in both English and German (not to mention its translation into other languages), is thus mediated linguistically on myriad levels; not only does Sereny transcribe Stangl's original verbal statements, but she also translates them into English for her original article in the *Daily Telegraph Magazine* (and later for *Into That Darkness*) and then retranslates them (or has them translated) back into German for the articles in

---

5 As far as I have been able to determine, there are no extant original transcripts of Sereny's interviews with Stangl; Howard Falksohn with the Wiener Library in London, which received Sereny's papers after her death in 2012, reports that it holds neither notes nor transcripts relating to these interviews (email to author, on 2 Dec. 2013). As I discovered to my horror while performing an online search of scholarly and journalistic assessments of Sereny's work, Carlo Mattogno and Jürgen Graf's *Treblinka: Extermination Camp or Transit Camp?*, a publication devoted to Holocaust revisionism (one I therefore omit from my bibliography; it is available at http://holocausthandbooks.com/dl/08-t .pdf, accessed 23 Apr. 2020), takes this apparent absence of extant documentary material to mean that she fabricated part or all of the interviews with Stangl. Mattogno and Graf's interpretation of the absence of Sereny's missing transcripts should perhaps not be surprising, given the penchant of Holocaust revisionists to reject both forms of evidence widely accepted by historians and the testimony of witnesses (whether survivors or perpetrators). But it also shows how they manipulate gaps in the historical record to make specious arguments. After all, much of the historical information (if not Stangl's personal motives) Sereny relates in her book is supported by transcripts from Stangl's trial and widespread historical research.

Die Zeit and then the German editions of the book. Far from representing a direct and undistorted representation of either the tenor of the interviews or the affective and psychological registers of Stangl's responses, the English and the two German versions must be regarded, at best, as significantly mitigating the apparent linguistic transparency and candid forthrightness they appear to convey, for there is no Urtext that can be consulted or to which the English translation and German retranslations can be compared. Of course, *no* text or spoken statement can possess unequivocal referentiality or psychological transparence, given the complex operations of the human psyche, the semiotic mutability of language, and the performative quality of the interview genre. But Sereny's book about Stangl, on account of the long since effaced trails of its original linguistic reference, merits an even greater degree of awareness of the critical role that translation and mediation might play, even if the pathways of translation are difficult or indeed impossible to reconstruct. Her portrait of him is emphatically *not* a simple, straightforward, unfiltered account of a perpetrator's thoughts and feelings about his crimes. The truth that Sereny promises both Stangl and her readers to illuminate is thus from the outset half shrouded by its linguistic mediation on a number of levels. The absence of a textual fountainhead or translational touchstone for her representation of her dialogue with Stangl raises a host of ethical and aesthetic questions regarding the referential and authentic status of her book and presents particular challenges to readers who wish to carefully probe Stangl's statements in it. At the same time, however, by downplaying or even concealing its multilingual provenance and tangled translation history and implying a one-to-one correspondence between Stangl's original verbal statements and his testimony as represented in the texts (in both English and German), Sereny's texts function according to what Yasemin Yildiz calls the "monolingual paradigm," which she identifies as "a key structuring principle" according to which "individuals and social formations" reify the notion of a single authentic, unified language, deny the interplay between languages, and disavow the complex ways in which both human identities and texts are shaped according to multilingual practices (2). By filtering the complex linguistic movements of her text through the highly constructed illusion of monolingual origin, Sereny further underscores the appearance of authenticity and immediacy of Stangl's statements and encourages readers of both the English and German texts to believe they have a view into his mind that is unobstructed by the text's actual multilingual mediation.

In some scholarly assessments of *Into That Darkness*, critics have accepted the conceit of authenticity encouraged by the text, often regarding the interviews as open windows into Stangl's mind and infrequently acknowledging either the ways in which Sereny artfully constructs this life story according to particular narrative schemata or the specific role that language and translation play in her book. Although historians and social scientists who have written about the interviews (literature scholars have for the most part ignored Sereny's book) are, following Sereny's lead, rightly skeptical about Stangl's veracity and candidness about his role in genocide, they tend to regard the book as a whole as an objective account of the encounter between interviewer and interviewee, such that one might find in a controlled laboratory setting. At most, they question Sereny's interpretation of her biography of Stangl based on the testimony she presents, but they ignore critical factors such as her strategic questioning, her orchestration of his testimony, her shaping of the larger narrative, and the complex linguistic interventions and dynamics of translation of her project. John Kekes, for example, summarizes over the course of several pages Sereny's account of Stangl's biography (with little acknowledgment of its intersubjective provenance or dimension) but seems unaware that this story of Stangl's life emerges not primarily from archival research but from interviews that result from Stangl's positioning of himself vis-à-vis Sereny:

> I mean to go further than Sereny has done both in seeking to understand the cause of evil in Stangl's character and actions and in answering the question how it is reasonable for us to see Stangl, regardless of how he saw himself. I rely on Sereny's account of the facts but interpret them differently. (48)[6]

---

6 While Kekes's analysis of the question of Stangl's responsibility is incisive, in my opinion it does not depart as dramatically from Sereny's own interpretation as Kekes claims. In fact, Kekes titles his chapter on Stangl "A Fatal Fusion," a phrase that derives directly from Sereny's text: "The deeper he went into his story, the clearer emerged the picture of the fatal fusion between his own character, and the sequence of events" (*Into That Darkness* 34). Although Kekes takes issue with Sereny's insistent implication that Stangl might have had some

Kekes's focus on Sereny's "account of the facts" (a narrative that relies in large part on Stangl's own presentation of his history) thus not only fails to acknowledge the highly unstable nature of Stangl's self-narrative but also neglects to consider how the mediated biography is crafted by Sereny according to particular generic formulas. Harald Welzer and Johannes Lang, both of whom examine *Into That Darkness* to assert innovative and persuasive social psychological theories about the existence of moral principles in perpetrators and the problematic concept of dehumanization for understanding their behavior, despite their excellent arguments, likewise take Sereny's account at face value as an accurate and mostly objective representation of Stangl's life story, even if they dispute her conclusions about Stangl's self-understanding. Moreover, neither scholar addresses the issue of language and the role of translation in his study. (Welzer, a German scholar whose article on Stangl appeared in English, cites from the 1995 German edition, *Am Abgrund: Gespräche mit dem Henker*, creating his own translation into English rather than quoting from the original *Into That Darkness*. In his quotes, we thus encounter the almost grotesque situation of a tripled process of translation: Stangl's statements are translated from German into English for *Into That Darkness*, Helmut Röhrling retranslates them from English into German for the 1995 edition of *Am Abgrund*, and Welzer retranslates those words back into English for his article. The words that Welzer cites thus stand a full four degrees of separation from those originally uttered by Stangl.) Such approaches, while understandable from a social science point of view, neglect to consider the textuality of *Into That Darkness*. Sereny's book should be subject to the same awareness of constructedness, narratorial positioning, and linguistic provenance that scholars should bring to any text, especially one of life writing that, like Sereny's, is both biographical (in its portraiture of Stangl) and autobiographical (in its self-conscious and often quite subjective presentation of the functions of the interviewer, narrator, and author).

---

choice to opt out of his assignments (he argues that, given the makeup of his character, Stangl could have chosen no other path), his conclusion to my mind is very similar to that of Sereny: "It is reasonable to hold him responsible for his actions, even though without the fatal fusion of his character and circumstances, he might not have done what he did" (59).

Intersubjective Intermediation

Scholars who view Sereny's role as disinterested facilitator of Stangl's factual narrative miss textual cues that negate such a view from Sereny herself. At times, she self-consciously undermines both readers' expectations of objectivity and the ostensibly impartial quality of her narration by inserting herself into the developing narrative and self-consciously producing Stangl's moral and psychological perspective. Sereny is nothing if not a highly invested narrator (as her experience on the Düsseldorf train station platform indicates), and she does not conceal from her readers the fact that she actively shapes both the interviews as they take place and their subsequent framing in the book. Moreover, at times, she strategically makes her English readers aware of the linguistic context in which the interviews are taking place. She refers several times throughout the book to Stangl's native Austrian dialect, into which he slips at particular moments:

> Stangl had a curious habit, which was to become very familiar as our talks went on, of changing from the semi-formal German he usually spoke to the popular vernacular of his childhood whenever he had to deal with questions he found difficult to answer. This was manifestly not a conscious act; nor did it necessarily mean that at those moments he was lying. In fact it was often, on the contrary, when he was telling a very difficult truth that he took this instinctive refuge in the "cosy" language and mannerisms of his childhood. (*Into That Darkness* 29)

In the statements she quotes of Stangl, Sereny does not attempt to reproduce the idiom of his Austrian vernacular, either as a colloquial equivalent in the English original text or as recognizably Austrian speech in the two German translations. Indeed, in the second German edition, the text informs us in a footnote to the passage above that "For the benefit of better readability, such transformations of the linguistic register are not factored into this account" ("Derlei Wechsel der Sprachebene bleiben bei der Wiedergabe zugunsten der besseren Lesbarkeit hier unberücksichtigt," *Am Abgrund: Gespräche mit dem Henker* 30, my translation).[7] In both the English and the German, Sereny thus highlights the process of linguistic mediation even if she does not explicitly point to her role as the translator of Stangl's statements into English. Rather than mimetically approximating his verbal idiosyncrasies, which would enhance the illusion of transparent correspondence between the text and Stangl's mind, she both interprets for us the significance of Stangl's abrupt switch in register (which, after all, would be almost imperceptible to us in both translation and retranslation) and makes us aware of her active role in interposing his testimony.

Sereny further underscores her twofold mediatory position as both interviewer and narrator in the way in which she organizes her book, which alternates between transcribed portions of the interviews with Stangl, in which she functions as a diegetic interlocutor; her conversations with other witnesses; and long extradiegetic passages in which she, as the text's narrator, reflects on Stangl's statements, assesses their truthfulness and accuracy, and muses on the implications of what she has learned. Not surprisingly, the sections that present the interviews with Stangl form the core of the book's inquiry, and Sereny sets them apart formally both from her narrative speculations and from her conversations with other witnesses. While Stangl's remarks in these prison exchanges, like those of other witnesses she interviews, are marked as verbal statements with quotation marks, her direct questions to him in her role as diegetic interviewer are placed in both quotation marks and italics. This formal strategy has consequences for how the reader consumes these passages, allowing her to distinguish her voice within the interviews with Stangl from her extradiegetic interventions about his assertions, which are interwoven with transcribed sections of the interviews and often reflect on research she conducts after Stangl's death. It also noticeably marks her conversations with Stangl from the statements of other witnesses, whose testimony is presented in long discursive passages in which she, as a diegetic

---

7 This footnote in the German edition explains the text's refusal to reproduce Stangl's statements in their original vernacular as a question of readability, but I reiterate the argument that I assert above, namely, that both German editions take as their source text not the transcripts of the original German interviews but rather Sereny's translation of the German testimony in her original English texts. Accordingly, the Austrian character of his statements was effaced in the translation into English and thus in the retranslations into German as well.

Interpellating the Perpetrator | 147

interviewer, is mostly absent. (In the rare moments in which her voice is present in these passages, her questions are set in quotation marks but not italicized). Sereny's method of formally distinguishing her questions in the text—a practice that Anneleen Spiessens has termed with regard to *Une Saison de machettes* (2003), Jean Hatzfeld's account of the Rwandan genocide, "framing activity" (321)—also highlights her important role as intermediary and coproducer of Stangl's testimony; she becomes less the passive transcriber of Stangl's story and more a dialogical partner who also contributes prominently to his narration of that story. Sereny emerges in the interviews with Stangl uniquely positioned as an active character, a role that the author takes pains to distinguish from that of the text's narrator. In this way, Sereny's functions as interviewer, empathic listener, and participant in the artfully staged scene of Stangl's testimony are made manifest to the reader.

In part, Sereny prominently foregrounds both her diegetic function as an interviewing figure and her extradiegetic critique because she is intent on making clear the intersubjective stakes of her project. Far from a disinterested listener, objective biographer, or scientific observer, Sereny is a present force in the diegetic space of the interview; as the substantial portion of italicized text in *Into That Darkness* reveals, rather than passively consuming Stangl's perspective on the events of his past, she actively participates in the interviews by querying, prodding, provoking, and probing his testimony. According to Inga Clendinnen, Sereny's dexterity as an interviewer and her careful interrogative colloquy form the active, dialogical heart of her enterprise:

> Sereny's capacity to pursue and to retain detailed information, to recall the small fact needed to thwart an evasion, is remarkable. But her most useful characteristic is her terrier curiosity. She is curious about everything, and she is never satisfied. . . . Out of that insatiable curiosity comes her fathomless capacity for alert listening and the concentration to note the smallest hesitations, even changes in skin colour and tone, over interviews that sometimes lasted for more than seven hours. She has the forensic skill to analyse elaborate, calculated statements as she hears them, and to

pose a precise and destabilising question in response. And she has what I take to be the key skill of the great interviewer: the ability to engage with her subject so deep inside their own territory that the urge to justify, to explain or simply to gossip with someone "in the know" becomes irresistible. (109–10)

Clendinnen's description of Sereny's strategy as occupying a position "deep inside [Stangl's] own territory" is instructive; it allows us to see the ways in which Sereny is able to elicit responses from Stangl by being willing, within the time and space of the interview, to consider the events of his past from his perspective and from within the framework of historical conditions without merging completely with his point of view. As John Tulloch argues, the success of Sereny's work lies in her decision not to represent Stangl from the outside but to try—as both narrator and journalist—to enter into his world to the extent possible and to tell his story from within: "only by placing herself *within the frame* of her narrative as a moral, historical being, can she establish the relationship with her subject and the accompanying ethical dialogue on which her work depends" (634). Tulloch claims that Sereny's precarious position, in which she is able to view the events through Stangl's eyes and at the same time to retain a measure of ethical distance from his perspective, results from a "restrained exercise of imaginative sympathy" (636), a strategy that encourages Stangl both to speak openly about his crimes and to develop an ethical relationship to them. According to Rachel Rosenblum, Sereny's method of intersubjective engagement, the hallmark of which is a demanding form of empathy, forces Stangl to assume ownership over his past:

> By erasing all intent from an activity he seems to perform almost mechanically; by claiming that he is a mere instrument and by delegating the role of "subject" to the Nazi government, Stangl completely evacuates his subjectivity. The journalist almost forces him into reintroducing it by offering her own affect. She, the listener, somehow obliges Stangl, the speaker, to occupy a subjective position which, until then, had remained empty. Sereny's empathy is a

serious weapon. Not only does it encourage the telling of Stangl's own "ghastly tale," but it calls for the corresponding affect, for the matching of narration and emotion. Faced with another subject, Franz Stangl must recognize himself as one. (1326–27)

Rosenblum perceptively locates the power of the interviews in the complex form of empathic affiliation that Sereny builds with Stangl, a singular, ad hoc, and intensely dialogical (though also necessarily one-sided) alliance between interviewer and subject whereby she provides for him possible models for narrating, relating to, and taking responsibility for his crimes as a perpetrator (regardless of his willingness to follow such models). According to Sereny, however, such a connection, while unique and enormously productive, is also precarious: "The relationship I had established between Stangl and myself was both subtle and exclusive, and very vulnerable, I feared, to intrusion" (*Into That Darkness* 254). Sereny's comment reveals the extent to which the space of the interview, by virtue of the intersubjective demands placed on both interlocutor and interviewee and the difficulty of Sereny's goal of empathically assuming Stangl's perspective and at the same time retaining an external ethical orientation point, is inherently unstable. To achieve the delicate balance required, the interlocutor must be excessively attentive to the vicissitudes of the moment and willing to constantly calibrate both questions and responses. As Sereny explains in a 2006 article about her experience with interviewing perpetrators,

> But whatever the relationship one creates, what is always essential, and only possible to achieve with experience and discipline, is to retain distance—spiritual, emotional independence from the subject, a kind of neutrality. Intellectual involvement is right; sympathy and compassion are natural and not to be suppressed, as otherwise you risk your own humanity. Empathy, however, is dangerous and needs to be—not suppressed, but—withdrawn back to the limits which you have set; the distance which you must always maintain. ("Questioning the Perpetrators" 24)

As Sereny's attempt to maintain a balance between distance and engagement indicates, the scene of the interview is a precarious setting that requires the intersubjective investment of the interviewer who is willing to take on the perspective of the perpetrator and at the same time to mark out a critical space outside of this point of view. It requires, as Tzevtan Todorov argues, a "middle distance [. . . that] must be maintained between evil and the person trying to understand it if that person is to come back and give us an account of his or her descent 'into that darkness'" (*Facing the Extreme* 282).[8] In this way, by departing from what Tulloch calls "classic journalistic objectivity" (634) and by simultaneously delimiting the extent to which she will follow Stangl's point of view, Sereny writes herself into his process of coming to terms with his past. Her self-conscious inclusion of herself in the diegetic interior of the interview as an empathetic but rigorously critical voice makes evident the performative interaction between interlocutor and subject and prevents the reader from detaching Stangl's testimony from the dialogical encounter that produced it. It furthermore encourages the reader not only to reflect on Sereny's conduct and engagement in the interviews but also to actively identify the ways in which she guides and facilitates Stangl's testimony.

In addition to engaging intensively with Stangl as a diegetic interviewer, in her role as narrator Sereny brings the reader into her process by revealing the challenges, impasses, and small breakthroughs she encounters in his narration of his story. According to Tulloch,

> In the case of the monstrous acts that she describes, it is arguable that classic journalistic objectivity is impossible. One cannot achieve a "balance" between the Nazis and their victims and a writer would be irredeemably corrupted by such an effort. Instead, Sereny attempts to establish a direct relationship with the reader as a sort of moral guide or commentator who reports on her complex states of feeling as

---

8 As my opening discussion of Sereny's collapse on the Düsseldorf train platform demonstrates, this "descent into darkness" is at times a taxing and perilous endeavor for Sereny. As she describes it over three decades later, "Questioning the perpetrators, let me say right away[,] is difficult, demanding and immensely costly, to oneself and to others—which is, of course, one reason why so few people have done it" ("Questioning the Perpetrators" 121).

the narrative unwinds. This space allows Sereny to admit to feelings of shock and repugnance as she confronts the material, but also to acknowledge feelings of empathy for her subject. (634)

As Tulloch indicates, to negotiate the monstrosity of Stangl's crimes, Sereny is forced to provide a counterweight to his testimony in the diegesis (i.e., the interview) by fashioning a dialogical counterpart in the extradiegesis (i.e., her account of the interview). Sereny does this by creating a space of interlocution with her readers, to whom she reports the ethical dilemmas of her interaction with Stangl. She foregrounds the intense and often conflicted position of the interviewer, whose ambivalent role requires her not only to seek out, receive, and acknowledge intensely disturbing testimony but also to work against the evasions, denials, self-justifications, and self-illusions such narration inevitably produces. A vivid example of Sereny's ethical intermediation can be found in her description of a particularly unsettling moment in their exchange, when Stangl tells the story of how he was ostensibly thanked tearfully by Blau, one of the Jewish slave laborers (or "work-Jews") at Treblinka, for allowing Blau's father to be shot at the *Lazarett* (the euphemistically named "infirmary" where sick and old deportees were sent immediately upon arrival in the camp, not for medical care but to be shot) rather than murdered in the gas chamber.[9] (Stangl relays this anecdote as evidence of the more enjoyable aspects of his job as commandant, as they afforded him "friendly relations" with the "work-Jews" [*Into That Darkness* 207]). As Sereny writes,

> This story and the way it was told represented to me the starkest example of a corrupted personality I had ever encountered and came very near to making me stop these conversations. I broke off early that lunchtime and went to sit for nearly two hours in a pub across the street, wrestling

---

9 Benjamin Ross's short film *Torte Bluma* (2005) portrays this unsettling encounter between Stangl, played by Stellan Skarsgård, and the prisoner Blau, played by Simon McBurney. The film's screenwriter, Barry Langford, based his script on the anecdote that Stangl relates to Sereny.

> with the most intense *malaise* I'd ever felt at the thought of listening further to these disclosures.
>
> I think the reason I finally did return to the little room in the prison was because I came to realize—perhaps as a result of the intensity of my own reaction—that for a man whose view was so distorted that he *could* tell that story in that way, the relatively simple terms "guilt" or "innocence," "good" or "bad" no longer applied; what was important was that he had found in himself the need—or strength—to speak. Even as I acknowledged my own apprehension at continuing these talks, I also knew for certain, at that moment, that if I did he would end by telling me the truth. (208)

In this moment, Sereny strategically draws the reader into the inner workings of her project, making visible the difficult conditions of its production and her conflicted role as intermediary.

With Sereny's extradiegetic commentary and her concomitant activation of the reader as dialogical partner, her empathic struggle with Stangl's testimony thus becomes the shadow subject of *Into That Darkness*, a narrative layer distinct from both the story of the Holocaust that Stangl narrates and the diegetic scene of their conversations in the Düsseldorf prison. In this way, the book's framework resembles the tripartite narrative structure found in such self-conscious works of collaborative testimony as Art Spiegelman's graphic narrative *Maus*, which features, as I have argued elsewhere, not only the story of Vladek Spiegelman's Holocaust experience and the scene of his narration of that experience to his son but also a "meta-dialogue on the other two narrative levels" that "consists of Art's reflections on witnessing his father's story and on the problems of shaping it into a visual narrative" (*Second-Generation Holocaust Literature* 73, 70). Sereny's reflection here as narrator, while not as artfully developed or strategically designed as Spiegelman's meta-reflection in *Maus* (particularly as the latter plays out in the second volume, which features the hallmark of his approach in the self-conscious image of Art seated as his drawing table), makes clear the extent to which, by interpellating Stangl, Sereny herself cannot help but become implicated in the intersubjective pull of his testimony. Her book thus joins (or rather prefigures, since it is antecedent temporally) an entire subgenre of writing about the Holocaust represented by such diverse texts as *Maus*, Patrick Modiano's *Dora Bruder*, Daniel Mendelsohn's *The Lost: A Search for Six of Six Million*, and, most recently, Laurent Binet's *HHhH*, in which the attempt to reconstruct the biography of a person who experienced the Holocaust (as either victim or perpetrator) compels autobiographical meta-reflection. Although *Into That Darkness* represents in the main a collaborative biography of the perpetrator, it also can be regarded as an autobiographical exploration of what it means to listen to the perpetrator's disclosure of his experience, construct it into a coherent narrative with causality and consequence, and communicate this representation of his mind to a broader public.

Masterplots and Closure

Sereny's passionate "drive to know" about Stangl's crimes, to "penetrate the personality" of the perpetrator and to "find some truth together" with him, as we have seen, galvanizes her desire to interview him and undergirds her biographical project, fortifying her physically, emotionally, and spiritually through the long hours of their conversations and providing her the necessary stamina afterward to continue her research and write the book. Without question, Sereny could not have completed such a massive project and nonfiction masterwork without either her dogged persistence or the activating impulse of her certainty that her quest for Stangl's truth would yield something useful for the post-Holocaust world, a measure of understanding that might help us to recognize a future *génocidaire* in the making. However, Sereny's conviction that there is indeed buried truth in Stangl's biography that can be brought to the surface through rigorous and soul-searching dialogue has important consequences for how she understands and narrates Stangl's story. Her expectation that identifiable truth exists, waiting to be brought to light, establishes the limits of his testimony and shapes the narrative structure and rhetorical arc of her book. Indeed, from the outset of *Into That Darkness*, the value of the interviews is predicated on her anticipation—or, perhaps more accurately, her certainty—that they will yield a profound epiphany on his part. Sereny's book is thus written chiefly toward the moment of Stangl's ethical anagnorisis, a sudden revelatory experience of recognition in which he will connect psychologically and morally to his crimes, undergo a significant transformation as a result of his acknowledgment, and communicate his process of revelation to Sereny, who will then mediate it to the reader. For this reason, following her Enlightenment impulse to both expose the truth of Stangl's crimes and compel Stangl to earnestly and responsibly acknowledge them in more than a cursory way, Sereny chooses particular narrative frames and masterplots for her book that allow for this notion of epiphanic avowal and spiritual conversion. As I shall demonstrate, Sereny molds her narrative according to the rhetorical conventions of the classical detective story and the confession, two genres that fundamentally serve Sereny's project of enlightenment. These genres function in *Into That Darkness* as masterplots that, by virtue of their familiarity and codified stability, orient the reader toward the truth for which Sereny strives both as interviewer and narrator, namely, Stangl's eventual anagnorisis.

According to H. Porter Abbott, masterplots are "recurrent skeletal stories . . . belonging to cultures and individuals that play a powerful role in questions of identity, values, and the understanding of life" (236). They are archetypal narrative codes that unfold according to predictable and identifiable schemata and satisfy certain expectations on the part of the reader. Some masterplots are closely associated with particular literary genres; one thinks of the epic or the Bildungsroman, which are recurrent vehicles for archetypal stories of heroism and individual development, respectively. An important feature of the masterplot is the necessary settlement of important questions, which "brings satisfaction to desire, relief to suspense and clarity to confusion" (64); in other words, masterplots offer closure, which normalizes the world of the narrative according to the codes associated with the masterplot. Closure can, of course, designate the ending of the story, in which the loose ends of the narrative are tied together and unresolved issues are clarified, but the term "can refer to more than the resolution of the story's central conflict" (57); it can also designate the text's satisfaction of the reader's desire. With heavily coded or paradigmatic masterplots, the desire for closure will be strong, since the reader will engage with the text with the preconception that it will offer predictable patterns of closure. Abbott distinguishes between two types of closure: "closure at the level of questions" (60), with which the text resolves uncertainties, and "closure at the level of expectations" (58), with which the narrative satisfies the assumptions and desires that the reader brings to the text based on her recognition of the codes of the masterplot. Of the two masterplots or genres I identify in Sereny's text, the detective story is associated with closure on the level of questions, since that genre is by nature focused on solving uncertainties surrounding a crime, while the confession, a genre whose codes promise the protagonist's self-disclosure and remorse, is a matter of closure on the level of expectations. Closure regarding the detective story, as Eyal Segal argues, is thus essentially epistemological,[10] while the confession offers closure in the realm of ethics. Sereny, as I shall demonstrate, seeks both epistemological and ethical closure. She formulates her biography of Stangl, which is predicated on the assumption that he possesses a certain truth to disclose and to avow, according to the codes of these two masterplots.

The Detective Story and Epistemological Closure

Given Sereny's intense "drive to know" the truth of Stangl's history as a perpetrator, it is not surprising that she shapes her narrative according to the conventions of the detective story, especially considering that the genre is characterized by the quest of the persistent detective determined to solve a crime (although the crimes associated with the Holocaust are, of course, of a vastly different order than the crime featured in a typical murder mystery). The narrative movement of classical detective fiction follows the detective's push toward increasing enlightenment about the particulars of the crime, the final details of which are revealed only at the text's conclusion, often with a surprise ending that, as Segal argues in his study of closure in detection fiction, produces typically strong closure. While the genre, of course, allows for variation, the typical classical detective story is focused in particular on the perpetrator of the crime, whose identity stumps the detective

---

10 According to Segal, "The detective genre—at least in its classical form—can be characterized as essentially more 'epistemological' than 'ethical'" (168). Segal notes that, while confession may occur in detective fiction, "the main role such a confession plays in securing closure may well be that of contributing to the reader's certainty regarding the correctness of the detective's solution of the mystery" (168). The act of confession in the classical detective story thus serves the purpose of epistemology, not ethics. It thus differs greatly, as we shall see, from the role of confession as a generic masterplot.

throughout her quest for truth. As Segal reminds us, "Closure in the detective story is typically created by the successful conclusion of the investigation in uncovering all the important facts relating to the crime mystery and thus filling in all the important curiosity gaps. The most central gap usually relates to the criminal's identity—and hence the popular appellation 'whodunit'" (166). In Sereny's biography of Franz Stangl, however, the identity of the perpetrator of the crimes is known from the beginning; in fact, Sereny seeks Stangl out *after* the trial at which he is convicted for the murder of hundreds of thousands of Jews. For this reason, the paradigmatic focal point of the detective story, with its quest to identify the agent of a criminal act, undergoes an important transformation in her text; the truth that she seeks and the "curiosity gaps" that she creates for the reader concern neither the perpetrator's identity (even though, as *Into That Darkness* chronicles, he spent the decades after the war trying to conceal both his identity and his criminal history) nor the essential facts of his crimes. Rather, the unsolved mystery at the heart of her project concerns information that the criminal proceeding, by virtue of its narrow focus on the objective instance of the crime and its commission, is unable to elicit, namely, Stangl's subjective state during the execution of the crime and his present ethical relationship to his past. As Robert Eaglestone argues in his short survey of postwar perpetrator testimony (which, as he argues, is almost nonexistent, especially in comparison with survivor testimony), narrative accounts of perpetrators, in particular Sereny's books about Stangl and Albert Speer, "are faintly reminiscent of not who but 'whydunnits'" ("Reading Perpetrator Testimony" 129), an assertion that aptly describes Sereny's shifted focus.[11]

Although Sereny relocates the central issue of her inquest from the question of the "who" of the crime to that of the "why" (and, one might argue, also to that of the "how"), she nevertheless crafts her narrative according to some of the rhetorical precepts of the classical whodunnit, which features, as Tzevtan Todorov has argued, "not one but two stories:

---

11 While Eaglestone does not pursue the generic implications of his association of *Into That Darkness* with detective fiction, he does discuss an important feature of perpetrator testimony that links it to the detective story; as he argues, "One symptom of these perpetrator texts is their desire for closure, for an ending" ("Reading Perpetrator Testimony" 127).

the story of the crime and the story of the investigation" ("The Typology of Detective Fiction" 44). In Sereny's "whydunnit," the first narrative refers to the story of Stangl's past as a commandant of two death camps and his mental, emotional, and ethical attitudes toward his crimes, while the second story tracks Sereny's attempts to discover Stangl's truth in the interviews and her later research.[12] By aligning her book with what Peter Hühn terms "the double plot-structure" (453) of the detective story, Sereny thus avails herself of the rhetorical and functional power of the genre, which ascribes to the detective a powerful role in crafting the definitive narrative of the crime. According to Hühn in his analysis of the roles of reading and writing in detective fiction, the classical detective novel centers on the ability and facility of the detective to read the signs of the crime and create a workable narrative of it:

> Described in the terminology of reading, the double plot-structure (the combination of the two stories) can be outlined in the following manner. The initial crime—as long

---

12 It is important to note, however, that Todorov's typology is a separate issue from the narratological distinction I make above between the diegesis of the interview and Sereny's extradiegetic commentary in the role of narrator. My classification according to diegetic level is a structural one that focuses on the interview scene as the primary narrative and Sereny's reflections on that scene as a secondary one. Todorov's framework, on the other hand, helps to distinguish between the principal story of Stangl's crimes and the second-level story of Sereny's attempt to uncover the meaning of these crimes. As Peter Hühn helpfully elaborates on Todorov's model, "The plot of the classical detective novel comprises two basically separate stories—the story of the *crime* (which consists of action) and the story of the *investigation* (which is concerned with knowledge). In their narrative presentation, however, the two stories are intertwined. The *first story* (the crime) happened in the past and is—insofar as it is hidden—absent from the present; the *second story* (the investigation) happens in the present and consists of uncovering the first story. . . . Employing Gérard Genette's and Seymour Chatman's distinction between *story* and *discourse*, one can define the narrative organization of a classical detective novel as follows. The usual constellation of story and discourse (the abstractable preexistent sequence of events and acts versus its mediation in a narrative) occurs twice over: the story of the crime is mediated in the discourse of the detective's investigation; and the story of the detective's investigation, in its turn, is mediated in the narrator's discourse" (452). Hühn's last definition of the structure of the classical detective novel according to the doubled functions of story and discourse seems to me to be the closest approximate to the organization of Sereny's book.

as it remains unsolved—functions as an uninterpretable sign, that is, one that resists integration into the established meaning-system of the community. Because it consists of the destruction of life and tends to discredit the validity of the system, it cannot be ignored. Therefore it becomes vital for the community to uncover the hidden meaning and—by reintegrating the sign—to defuse it. The progress of the plot (that is, the second story) is then presented as a succession of attempts to ascribe meaning to the sign by finding the missing links to the accepted patterns of reality. This interpretive linking invariably takes the form of a narrative, thus employing one of the most fundamental devices for generating coherence and meaning—*telling the story* of the genesis of the crime. This notion of the "genesis of the crime" can be said to imply with particular clarity the essential components of any narrative as a highly organized as well as organizing structure—origin, agent, causal connection, temporal sequence, aim—or in the (incomplete) handy formula often cited in detective novels: the motive, the means, and the opportunity. (453–54)

Although Hühn focuses here on the function of the investigation narrative in detective fiction (which in his analysis here is oddly agentless) rather than on the critical agency of the detective in shaping the story of the crime, we can recognize in his description much of the narrative logic of Sereny's quest to reconstruct Stangl's past and to probe his motivations and mindset with regard to his crimes. By casting herself in the role of detective, Sereny is able to assume the interpretive and generative power of the investigator to create a plausible narrative of the genesis of Stangl's crimes; to ascribe coherence and causality to Stangl's motivations, mental activity, and reactions to his crimes; and to locate meaning in his attempts to come to terms with them. The narrative she creates with this power is meant to solve the enigma of his crimes, to discover their truth, and to bring it to light.

Of course, it is important to note that the Holocaust crimes for which Stangl was convicted, in terms of all of the structuring elements that Hühn ascribes to the detective story (origin, agent, causal connection, temporal sequence, aim) but also with regard to their scope, complexity, and psychological and social implications, vastly exceed the explanatory capacity of the typical detective story. Indeed, as maintained by the decades-long discourse on the alleged incomprehensibility of the Holocaust (one of the most prominent proponents of which being Claude Lanzmann) and demonstrated by the number of texts that have attempted to reconstruct the complex history of the Holocaust (two trends that at first glance seem mutually exclusive but are rather dialectically connected), the Holocaust resists the easy explanation of motive or clear reconstruction of cause and effect that one finds in the classical detective story. As Eaglestone argues, following the incomprehensibility argument and its poststructuralist variants, this is precisely the problem of perpetrator testimony: it promises its readers the possibility of the types of explanation and closure found in such genre fiction as the detective novel, but it cannot deliver that genre's strong narrative closure:

> Each of [the perpetrator texts] seems almost to offer, at the beginning, . . . insight. And yet, when it comes to it, there is no "secret why." . . . For all our hope that the testimony will penetrate the veil of this mystery, it only seems to reveal more veils. Even to ask for an answer is a mistake. . . . The Nazi is simply not amenable to debate or rational discourse, which in turns means that their post-war accounts of themselves simply won't make sense: there will be no "real" to which to penetrate. ("Reading Perpetrator Testimony" 129–31)

Echoing Lanzmann's misreading of the famous Primo Levi anecdote, whereby Lanzmann transforms Levi's story of an Auschwitz guard's cruel refusal to explain the absurd logic of the camp's regulations into an expansive claim about the Holocaust's radical challenge to meaning and understanding, Eaglestone argues that "there is no why" to perpetrator testimony, including that which emerges in Sereny's *Into That Darkness*. While it may be true that no perpetrator account can fully satisfy our desire to understand what the perpetrators were thinking and how and why they engaged in their crimes, Eaglestone implies here that the perpetrator's testimony not only is resistant to meaning but also cannot be shaped narratively in the same ways that other aspects of human experience (including that of Holocaust survivors) can be narrated, in whatever fragmented, faulty, or frustratingly inadequate way. Moreover, his statements ignore precisely the efforts of Sereny, whom he uses in his article as a major example, to find a viable narrative framework with which she can create meaning out of Stangl's experience. This meaning may distort that experience in that it requires that it be reshaped according to the conventions and limitations of the generic frames in which it is cast, but this problem is quite the opposite of the claim that the perpetrator's testimony is inherently impervious to meaning or explanation. Not only is Stangl's experience more than amenable to narrative shaping, but Sereny is also able to find narrative frames that easily contain and transmit it, even if those narrative masterplots inevitably simplify, disfigure, or diminish the complexity of his history in order to conform it to their conventions. Stangl's testimony is as malleable and open to multivalent construction as any other text.

From the beginning of *Into That Darkness*, Sereny thus crafts Stangl's biography according to the masterplot of the detective story, which casts Stangl's life as a sort of mystery that requires investigation, clarification, and solution. One of the most prominent features of the detective novel that Sereny employs in her text is a carefully controlled presentation of the development of her investigation, which allows the reader to accompany her as she reconstructs the crime and gives access to her reasoning at various junctures in Stangl's story. Although her representation of her conversations with Stangl is organized along the chronological lines of his biography, so that the interviews seem to move along a seamless trajectory from Stangl's childhood through the Holocaust and into his postwar life in Brazil, a concomitant underlying structural principle is the narrative of Stangl's gradual but inevitable progression toward enlightenment to which, as Sereny promises her readers, their interviews slowly build. Sereny hints at this eventual "A-ha" moment on the part of Stangl at the beginning, when she objects to his initial "recital" (*Into That Darkness* 23) of the hackneyed arguments that Holocaust perpetrators had advanced beginning with the Nuremberg Trials and convinces him to change his approach to their interviews and to work with her to find a new truth to his crimes. As Stangl says to her,

> "I've thought about what you said," he told me at once, his voice slightly unsteady. "I hadn't understood before— I hadn't understood what you wanted. I think I understand now . . . I want to try to do it . . ."
>
> There were tears in his eyes before we even began to speak of his childhood. (*Into That Darkness* 25)

As implied by Sereny's depiction of Stangl's change of heart, Stangl decides to open up to her and to work with her to uncover buried truth about his past, a truth that will not only help us to understand his involvement in his crimes but also provide, in its exposure, psychological and spiritual relief for him. Sereny's narrative indicates that, through the process of mutual investigation, Stangl and she will be able to solve the mystery that characterizes his story, even if the investigation is occasionally stalled by his difficulty owning up to his past. Through the investigative work of the interviews, as Sereny reports, Stangl gradually begins to acknowledge a buried truth; as Sereny states, musing on two slightly different stories he has told her regarding a visit to the Aktion Reinhard killing center Bełżec: "His giving different versions of events is not too important from the point of view of facts. It is, however, of psychological relevance, for the gradual decrease in evasions, embellishments, and anxiety to project a favourable image of himself reflects significantly and accurately the intensity of his emotion, and possibly the psychological changes these conversations produced in him" (*Into That Darkness* 111).[13] Moreover, as *Into That Darkness* continues, Sereny begins to insert more explicit signposts in the text that

---

13 Sereny's characterization of Stangl's transformation here, whereby he begins to let go of psychological mechanisms he has used to "project a favorable image of himself," resembles what James Waller has described as the psychological process of integration: "This integration tendency implies that we are troubled by inconsistencies between our overt behaviors and internal psychological constellations and motivated to alleviate these inconsistencies to preserve the integrity of the self. The inconsistencies may be alleviated either by (a) modifying our overt behaviors to be congruent with our internal psychological constellations, or (b) altering our internal psychological constellations to be congruent with our overt behaviors. Neither means of preserving the integrity of the self necessitates the creation of a second self or the activation of an altered state" ("Perpetrators of the Holocaust" 16). Sereny implies here that, to resolve his own cognitive dissonance, Stangl has heretofore pursued the latter process, but now he is beginning to follow the former.

signal a coming epiphanic climax to this quest for truth, a sort of narrative foreshadowing of the successful conclusion to the investigation that, as in the classical detective story, tantalizes the reader and keeps her in suspense about the content of the coming revelation. As Sereny writes of Stangl's assertions about his transfer to Treblinka,

> It is probable that Stangl altered the sequence of these events for my benefit so as to convey as much as possible the impression that his reassignment to Treblinka had been "a surprise" to him and that, once again, he "didn't really know" what his function was to be, a myth he kept up throughout his trial and only relinquished in his conversations with me at the very end. (161–62)

The "very end" of the interviews, to which Sereny repeatedly refers and which coincides exactly with the end of *Into That Darkness*, is, in good detective novel fashion, also the scene of the text's epistemological closure. This is the moment in which Stangl, in the presence of Sereny, finally acknowledges the truth that he has denied, displaced, deferred, and evaded throughout the investigation. Moreover, as Sereny states at the beginning of the final section of the book, which introduces this critical scene of anagnorisis, it is also connected with a further type of closure, in which Stangl, having faced his truth, passes away only hours after the last interview: "Perhaps in the end it was easier for [Stangl] to tell the truth because, I think, he knew he would die when he had told it" (*Into That Darkness* 362). By letting us know in advance of revealing the content of this truth that the shock of his anagnorisis would somehow cause his heart attack, Sereny sets the stage dramatically for its revelation and signals to the reader that the investigation has been concluded and the mystery solved. At the same time, however, she delays the revelation of the truth until the last pages of the book, thus continuing to follow the precepts of the detective story, in which, as Segal argues, "the customary caution of not telling the end in advance is regarded as more binding here than in any other genre or narrative form. This testifies to the degree to which the overall narrative structure and effect of the detective story depend upon the ending—and particularly the manner in which the ending produces its typically strong closure" (154). In keeping with the conventions of suspense and closure in detective fiction, Sereny thus reserves the uncovering of the truth of Stangl's crimes until the very end of the text, where it is presented quite literally as Stangl's final word on his past as a perpetrator.

Confessional Performance and Ethical Closure

But what exactly is this final truth to which Sereny continually refers and for which her text has been preparing the reader? At this point, the masterplot of the detective story in *Into That Darkness* morphs into a separate but adjacent narrative frame, namely, the confession, for the truth of Sereny's investigation is delivered in the last pages in the form of Stangl's alleged acknowledgment of guilt. With the term "confession" I mean here two phenomena that are often collapsed together: the speech act of the confession, in which, according to Peter Brooks, "the individual authenticates his inner truth" to an interlocutor, and the narrative masterplot of the confession, which is its textual performance (4). The act of confession has its roots in religious and legal discourses, rituals, and procedures beginning in the Middle Ages, while the confessional narrative traces its generic roots from Augustine through Rousseau and into modern autobiography. Brooks uses the term "confessional model" to refer to their combined effect, arguing that both the verbal act and the written performance of confession are similar in terms of structure and function. While I will also mostly combine the two meanings in my discussion of Stangl's confession to Sereny, it is useful to acknowledge the ways in which the two aspects—the verbal confession and its narrative performance in the text—operate in tandem in *Into That Darkness*. Sereny relies here on the confession as both a recognizable technique in criminal investigation, legal proceedings, and religious discourse and a familiar literary masterplot that shapes the narrative of the individual who is called upon to bare his soul and acknowledge his transgressions.

As Michel Foucault has famously argued, the confession is "one of the West's most highly valued techniques for producing truth"; it is "a ritual of discourse . . . that unfolds within a power relationship" between the confessor, "who requires the confession, prescribes and appreciates it, and intervenes in order to judge, punish, forgive, console, and reconcile," and the confessant, who is "exonerate[d], redeeme[d], and purifie[d]" through the expression of the truth (59, 61–62). The confessional ritual is a technique by which the subject is called upon to police himself, to plumb the depths of his soul, to discover his own wrongdoing, and to articulate it to an interlocutor, whether sympathetic or hostile. The dialogical aspect of the confession is critical to its successful performance; the guilt must be recognized by another to be legitimate. For this reason, as Brooks points out, the "bond of confessor and confessant often is crucial to the production of confession" (35). The confession, as Brooks further argues, functions as a privileged vehicle for the communication of the inner truth of the individual; as both act and genre, it thus is seen as the public expression of the private workings of the self:

> Confession is considered to bear a special stamp of authenticity. From the thirteenth century, when the Roman Church began to require annual confession from the faithful, it has become in Western culture a crucial mode of self-examination; from the time of the early Romantics to the present day, confession has become a dominant form of self-expression, one that bears special witness to personal truth. In an increasingly secularized culture, truth *of* the self and *to* the self have become the markers of authenticity, and confession—written or spoken—has come to seem the necessary, though risky, act through which one lays bare one's most intimate self, to know oneself and to make oneself known. Psychoanalysis, one of the most conspicuous inventions of the twentieth century, offers a secular version of religious confession: it insists on the work of patient and analyst—comparable to confessant and confessor—toward the discovery of the most hidden truths about selfhood. (9)

Through the means of self-expression made possible by the confession, the individual believes to know himself; by virtue of this articulation to others, he is perceived as having a truth to tell. Historically speaking, the self-declaration of truth has been seen as the guarantee of its authenticity. As Foucault's description of the confession as a ritualized production of truth demonstrates, the confession is thus a masterplot with coded conventions to which listeners and readers bring particular expectations; like the detective story, it can offer a high degree of closure. Indeed, the prescribed movement of religious confession (confession-judgment-atonement-absolution) and its secular counterparts demonstrate that confession, in order to be successfully performed, must take particular pathways that are a priori known to both confessant and confessor. Understood on all sides of the confessional process is that truth will inevitably be revealed, bringing closure both to the previously unacknowledged guilt of the individual and to the crime to which he has confessed.

However, although the confessional act is seen as the "prime mark of authenticity" (Brooks 4) in Western culture, its inherently performative nature calls into question the truth that it produces. As Jo Gill argues, the truth of the confessant not only is invalid until acknowledged by the confessor but also does not even come into being until the confessional performance itself:

> Confession, then is not a means of expressing the irrepressible truth of prior lived experience, but a ritualized technique for producing truth. Confessional writing is poietic not mimetic, it constructs rather than reflects some pretextual truth. It is not the free expression of the self but an effect of an ordered regime by which the self begins to conceive of itself as individual, responsible, culpable and thereby confessional. (4)

Rather than existing as a secret that the confessant harbors deep within until it is extracted from him, confessional truth is thus produced by the confessional act rather than compelling it; in this way, the narrative of the confession is predicated on the scene of the confession and the relationship between confessant and confessor. The performance of the confession creates the truth that emerges from it. A fundamental tension thus arises with the confessional performance; the inherently performative and ritualized quality of the confession, in which the confessant produces the truth in the very act of telling it, comes into conflict with the expectations of authenticity and closure that are attached to the confessional process. This tension, too, is an integral part of the confessional dynamic; the possibility exists that the confession is not a revelation of truth but a hollow recital of the truth-producing ritual. As Brooks reminds us,

> Readers of Rousseau have long been aware that the act of confessing does not offer so straightforward or unproblematic an access to the inner being as one might assume. The problem may not be one of error, in any simple sense: study of any autobiographical and confessional text can usually detect some errors of fact, but that does not necessarily invalidate the confession of the "inner being," which has no referential verifiability other than the speech act that makes it known to us. But if that is the case, what is it that is being confessed to? In what sense is the confession true, if its apparent referent is false? What other kinds of truth, what other place of truth, is involved? Herein lies the problem: what is the relation of the act of confessing to the reliability of what is confessed? (19)

As readers of confession, we thus approach the text with a set of contradictory expectations: we expect the confession to be the expression of the individual's inner truth, and at the same time we anticipate that the confession will in some way be shaped, sometimes in deceptive ways, according to the dictates of the confessional scene. Moreover, not only may the form of the confession contain falsehood, but the act of confessing can also actually serve to evade rather than admit guilt. According to Leigh A. Payne, who has studied the confessional performances of perpetrators of authoritarian state violence in Argentina, Brazil, Chile, and South Africa, perpetrators often use the masterplot of the confession to assert control over the public narratives of their crimes; they "may confess . . . without ever admitting the truth or any wrongdoing" (229). As she explains further, "The most common way in which perpetrators confess to their past is through the language of denial or simply by remaining silent, but amnesia, revenge, fiction, sadism, and heroism are other narrative forms that perpetrators use to describe their past actions" (230). The confession can thus be used as a vehicle for the individual's attempt to evade acknowledgment of his crimes and to create an alternative narrative of them; as a tool for discerning truth, it is thus far from epistemologically reliable.

It is helpful to be aware of the conventions of confession, its performative nature, and the epistemological uncertainty of our expectations regarding it as we consider Stangl's anagnorisis, toward which Sereny has built her narrative. By examining the interviews from the perspective of the confessional model, we not only locate in them the truth-producing discursive rituals cited by Foucault and Brooks but also better understand Sereny's intersubjective engagement with Stangl (and his own engagement with her) as a variant of the power relationship between confessor and confessant. Moreover, Sereny quite deliberately exploits the conventions of the confessional masterplot to conclude her portrait of Stangl. As discussed previously, in conformity with the dictates of the classical detective novel, Sereny reserves the "reveal" of Stangl's truth until the end of the text, where she presents it as his final confrontation with and acknowledgment of the truth of his crimes. In what she tells us is her last interview with him, the two talk about various matters and then eventually come to the topic of God, which then quickly evolves into a discussion of Stangl's search for truth during the weeks he and Sereny have spent in conversation. I highlight here some of the most important parts of this last section of text:

> "[. . .] The only thing is, there *are* things which are inexplicable by science, so there must be something beyond man. Tell me though, if a man has a goal he calls God, what can he do to achieve it? Do you know?"
>
> "*Don't you think it differs for each man? In your case, could it be to seek truth?*"
>
> "Truth?"
>
> "*Well, to face up to yourself? Perhaps as a start, just about what you have been trying to do in these past weeks?*"
>
> His immediate response was automatic, and automatically unyielding. "My conscience is clear about what I did, myself," he said, in the same stiffly spoken words he had used countless times at his trial, and in the past weeks, when we had always come back to this subject, over and over again. But this time I said nothing. He paused and waited, but the room remained silent. "I have never intentionally hurt anyone, myself," he said, with a different, less incisive emphasis,

and waited again—for a long time. [. . .] "But I was there," he said then, in a curiously dry and tired tone of resignation. These few sentences had taken almost half an hour to pronounce. "So yes," he said finally, very quietly, "in reality I share the guilt . . . Because my guilt . . . my guilt . . . only now in these talks . . . now that I have talked about it all for the first time . . ." He stopped.

[. . .] "My guilt," he said, "is that I am still here. That is my guilt."

"*Still here?*"

"I should have died. That was my guilt."

[. . .] "But believe me, now I would have preferred to die rather than this . . ." He looked around the little prison room. "I have no more hope," he said then, in a factual tone of voice; and continued, just as quietly: "And anyway—it is enough now. I want to carry through these talks we are having and then—let it be finished. Let there be an end." (*Into That Darkness* 364–65)

Sereny presents here Stangl's final words in their interviews as both a confession and a call for closure to his past. The effort and time he takes to pronounce them, aspects to which Sereny calls attention in her description of his monologue, are meant to denote their weightiness and profundity; as readers we are made aware that, at this moment, Stangl is owning up to something very difficult for him to express. Moreover, as argued above, Sereny signposts to us at the beginning of this final section of the book (362) and at its end (364–66) that Stangl will "tell the truth," which creates a frame of expectation around the heart of Stangl's monologue; Sereny indicates that in this final conversation he faces the long-avoided truth of his past and confesses his guilt for it.

However, the truth toward which the narrative has been building and that Sereny claims Stangl has acknowledged is chiefly the result of the conventions of the confessional *form* that she constructs here; the *content* of his monologue, when examined closely, reveals itself to be hollow. Stangl begins his monologue with a denial of responsibility for his crimes ("My conscience is clear") and an affirmation of his innocent motivations

("I have never intentionally hurt anyone") before admitting a vague situational complicity ("I was there"). When at last he turns to the topic of guilt, he first apportions part of it to unnamed accomplices ("in reality I share the guilt") and then eventually begins to pronounce the words "my guilt," although he struggles to find an appropriate predicate for the subject. When he finally is able to make a substantive declaration about the nature of his guilt ("My guilt . . . is that I am still here"), he refers not to any actual past crimes he committed or in which he was complicit but to an existential dilemma in the present. His vague avowal of guilt not only universalizes his specific situation as an existential human problem but also expresses his own self-pity for having to live out the punitory consequences of his criminal activity ("I would have preferred to die rather than this") but does not acknowledge any particular wrongdoing. His confession is thus not an admission of guilt in any legal or moral sense; indeed, to my ears it still carries the traces of the arguments used at Nuremberg to which Sereny, at the beginning of her interviews with Stangl, so vehemently objects: they "were sometimes close enough to a kind of truth to throw at least some doubt on the *quality* of their guilt" (*Into That Darkness* 23). While it is clear here that Stangl himself believes (or would like Sereny to believe) he has given a confession ("That is my guilt"), his declaration in the final pages marks not a break with his previous denials and evasion but a reiteration of them, paradoxically, in the form of the confession. His admission functions as an example of the confessional performances Payne analyzes, in which a perpetrator's confession may disavow guilt or recognition of wrongdoing. The truth that Sereny promises us throughout the text that she and Stangl will discover together, although packaged by Sereny in this final section as an ethical revelation, emerges here not as a profound anagnorisis but as an iteration of Stangl's difficulty in crafting a narrative of his past that acknowledges more than surface culpability. For the reader, his confession thus operates anticlimactically; the expected culmination of the confession, which, as a result of Sereny's intensive signposting toward it, is supposed to eclipse his earlier testimony, becomes a trite conclusion to an otherwise perceptive glimpse into Stangl's mind. Rather than offering the closure and the satisfaction of the reader's desire promised by the masterplot of the confession, Stangl's words remain ambiguous, revealing not a man who has discovered the truth of his past but a mind that continues to equivocate about it.[14]

Death by Confession

Given the hollowness of the content of Stangl's alleged confession and its anticlimactic effect, one might wonder why Sereny chooses the narrative masterplot of the confession to conclude her text, especially since, rather than creating the closure associated with the narrative of confession, the confession evinces a high degree of ambiguity with regard to Stangl's truth and trivializes some of the more important historical and psychological

---

14 Critics are divided on the issue of whether Stangl acknowledges his guilt in this moment of confession. As Gesine Schwan claims in reference to Stangl's statement about "my guilt," "Stangl did not succeed in stating clearly what he felt in finishing his sentence, but that he tried to confess his guilt is clear" (735). Lars Svendsen sees the admission of guilt as a sort of surface phenomenon: "He recognizes his own guilt, but doesn't seem to grasp the extent of what he admits to be guilty of. . . . The paradoxical thing is that he admits his guilt *and* asserts that his conscious is clean" (157). For Av Richard Blucher, the question of Stangl's acknowledgment of guilt remains an open one, even at the end of the book: "His final conversation with Sereny, when the question of guilt was again raised, remains ambiguous" (52). According to Harald Welzer, "Sereny's own central interest is in the question of the perpetrator's recognition and processing of guilt. She too implicitly assumes that her interviewee secretly experienced a deep sense of guilt, which in turn presupposes that he violated his own moral standards" (24). For Welzer, such problematic assumptions, which he demonstrates to be inapplicable to Stangl's testimony, tell us less about Stangl's moral code and more about Sereny's own expectations regarding Stangl's relationship to his culpability: "Consequently in this connection she disregards not only that he externalized any potential sense of guilt, but also that her 'monster' thesis is substantiated by nothing more than confusing her own normative self-image with that of another person" (24). Welzer's insight here with regard to Sereny's moral presumptions underscores the degree of Sereny's intersubjective investment in her project that I have identified; as he sees it, her profound need to locate a recognizable moral framework in Stangl provokes her to fashion one for him through her narrative. In *Remnants of Auschwitz*, Giorgio Agamben likewise reads this scene as indicative of the failure of conventional narrative frames to express the ethical rupture of the Holocaust, which Sereny is unable to recognize because of her single-minded focus on Stangl's anagnorisis: "It does not signify the emergence of an instance of truth, in which Stangl 'became the man whom he should have been,' as Sereny, solely concerned with her dialectic of confession and guilt, seems to think. Instead, it marks the definitive ruin of his capacity to bear witness, the despairing collapse of 'that darkness' on itself" (99).

dimensions Sereny has previously uncovered in his testimony. One answer for this vexing question might lie in the way in which Sereny interprets Stangl's death, which occurs only hours after his so-called confession. Although we know going into the last section of the book, which stages Stangl's anagnorisis, that he will die after telling the truth of his crimes, Sereny makes an even stronger connection between his confession and his death in the last sentences of her text:

> He had not committed suicide. His heart was weak and he would no doubt have died quite soon anyway. But I think he died when he did because he had finally, however briefly, faced himself and told the truth; it was a monumental effort to reach that fleeting moment when he became the man he should have been. (*Into That Darkness* 366)

In this conclusion, Sereny not only associates Stangl's death with his anagnorisis but claims that the former is a direct result of the latter.[15] Her interpretation is supported with Stangl's final words of his confession, in which he not only claims to have preferred death over imprisonment but also makes a plea for what can be read as death: "Let there be an end." From her perspective after Stangl's death, Sereny thus reads his final statement, which as an admission of guilt, as we have seen, is evasive and hollow, as a sort of premonition of his death, a foreknowledge of it on his part that compels him to face the truth. As a narrator, she thus engages in the practice of backshadowing, which, as Michael André Bernstein argues in the context of post-Holocaust narratives about German Jews before the Holocaust,

---

15 Some critics have endorsed Sereny's implication that Stangl's death was the result (directly or indirectly) of his so-called confession. According to Rachel Rosenblum, for example, "In a way Stangl died from having told his story" (1327). Robert Eaglestone takes the claim even further: not only does Stangl's death proceed from his confession, but the text actually implies that Sereny, through her rigorous questioning, effects his death: "There is more than a hint here—not least from the form itself, the location of this comment in the narrative flow of the text—that Sereny, or Sereny's actions have in fact killed him: and that final sentence—when he became the man he should have been—is very ambiguous" ("Reading Perpetrator Testimony" 128). In any case, the critical view of Sereny's text draws a strong connection between the confessional act and the death that results from it.

"is a kind of retroactive foreshadowing in which the shared knowledge of the outcome of a series of events by narrator and listener is used to judge the participants in those events *as though they too should have known what was to come*" (16). Because Sereny backshadows Stangl's death, interpreting it as a direct, logical, and existentially appropriate outcome of the morally and physically exhausting challenge of acknowledging the truth of his crimes, she emphasizes the import and content of his so-called confession. A lesser admission of guilt could not have explained his death. However, rather than the confession making his death inevitable, it is the other way around: *Stangl's death makes the confession narratively possible as a moment of anagnorisis*. Without his death, his confession could not exist; his death thus offers the closure that his final words, taken alone, cannot offer. Only in tandem can they complete the conventions of the confessional masterplot.

As my analysis of Sereny's narrative of Stangl demonstrates, the masterplots that Sereny chooses to frame her interviews with him shape the narrative expression of her interpellation of him, compelling her to make particular interpretive choices that shape how both she and the reader view him. While her biography of Stangl, a remarkable achievement of its day as one of the first texts to grapple in detail with the mind of an important Holocaust perpetrator, remains of lasting value to historians, psychologists, literary scholars, and anyone who wishes to understand how men such as Stangl became agents of mass killing, it also serves as an important example of how profoundly our understanding of Holocaust perpetrators is shaped by the narrative masterplots we use to narrate their experience. We—and they—filter their stories through known and available frameworks, which means that we delimit them according to the desires we bring to them, both epistemologically and ethically, and our own intersubjective investment in their closure. In so doing, we often employ what Hanna Meretoja terms "subsumptive narrative practices," such as masterplots, that "assimilat[e] new experiences into a pregiven mold" (115). In the case of *Into That Darkness*, Sereny entered into her project with a strong desire to discover something radically new that, in the millions of pages that had been written about the Holocaust, had not yet been expressed, namely, the truth of the perpetrator—his history, his perspective on his crimes, and his remorse for having committed them. While her considerable skills as an interviewer and storyteller allow her to discern important facts and insightful perspectives from Stangl's story and to reveal, at least in the body of his testimony, telling moments of ambiguity in his story, her strong empathetic engagement with her subject and her Enlightenment desire to uncover "some new truth which would contribute to the understanding of things that had never yet been understood" (23) compel her to resort to narrative masterplots that, at times, misshape his testimony, subsume his experience "into a coherent system of representation" (Meretoja 108), and thus also immure the mind her project is aimed at penetrating. With her narrative of Stangl, Sereny thus journeys "into that darkness," but what she brings back into the light turns out to be not Stangl's truth but rather her own desire for it.

 # Imagining the Mind of the Holocaust Perpetrator in Fiction

A Brief Literary History of the Mind of the Holocaust Perpetrator

One of the premises of this book, as I explain in the introduction, is that the recent profusion of what Joanne Pettitt, Robert Eaglestone, and Richard Crownshaw call "perpetrator fiction" proceeds historically and aesthetically from the wave of nonfictional texts of the 1960s, 1970s, and 1980s that explore the mental life of perpetrators. However, while one can trace a clear trajectory in representation in which fictional depictions of the mind of the Holocaust perpetrator gradually supersede nonfictional ones (an unsurprising progression, given that real-life perpetrators—when they could be identified as such—began to die out during this period), this does not mean that fiction exploring this phenomenon did not exist prior to this time. On the contrary, from the beginning days of the Nazi movement, writers (particularly German writers in exile) attempted to render what they saw as a distinct Nazi mindset, as demonstrated, for example, by Bertolt Brecht's portrayal of SA thugs and complicit bureaucrats in his 1938 play *Furcht und Elend im Dritten Reich* (*Fear and Misery in the Third Reich*) or his 1941 imagination of Hitler as a ruthless mobster in *Der aufhaltsame Aufstieg des Arturo Ui* (*The Resistible Rise of Arturo Ui*) or by Heinrich Mann's 1942 satirical depiction of Reinhard Heydrich in his novel *Lidice*. This fascination with the figure of the Nazi continued after the end of the Third Reich; in fact, a not insignificant body of German literature by both postwar authors, such as Heinrich Böll, Günter Grass, and Peter Weiss, as well as more recent writers, such as Peter Schneider, Bernhard Schlink, and Marcel Beyer, renders characters who reflect the fascist, genocidal mentality of the Third Reich, even if it does not often explicitly, as Petra Rau points out (14), represent actual acts of perpetration. (At the same time, neglected in much postwar German fiction, as Ernestine Schlant insightfully argues, is *not* the experience of the perpetrators but the perspective and experience of the victims.) And, of course, as seen from a broader, diachronic, and transnational perspective, Nazis have been the focus of a steady wave of cultural production in the decades since the war, from "high" cultural works, such as Dan Pagis's poem "Testimony," to popular representations with mass appeal, such as Quentin Tarantino's 2009 film *Inglourious Basterds*, to the pulp or lowbrow forms that belong to the phenomenon Daniel H. Magilow, Elizabeth Bridges, and Kristin T. Vander Lugt term "Nazisploitation." While many such works present reified images of perpetrators as the embodiment of ultimate evil, a number of them also engage the reader in exercises in mindreading, thereby mediating a psychological profile—sometimes nuanced, sometimes hackneyed—of their perpetrator characters. Literature written in the voice and from the perspective of Holocaust perpetrators, however, which is what I suspect Crownshaw, Eaglestone, and Pettitt by and large have in mind with the designation "perpetrator fiction," is a much more narrow corpus with an accordingly limited history.[1] Joanne Pettitt discerns three periods in which the production of such texts has been particularly

---

[1] While the term "perpetrator fiction" provides a pithy designation for the texts I investigate in this part of the book, I find it reductive, ill-defined, and so general as to be meaningless and thus prefer to avoid it. After all, any fiction that depicts perpetrators at all—meaning the enormous corpus of post-Holocaust fiction as well as the even larger body of texts about other instances of violence—could satisfy the basic criterion it implies. None of the three scholars whom I have cited—Eaglestone, Pettitt, and Crownshaw—explicitly defines what he or she means with the term, but it is clear that all of them use it to designate mostly fiction narrated from the perspective of perpetrators.

intensive: the early postwar period, the full decade of the 1970s, and a period spanning from the mid-1980s until the present moment. While I find it necessary to make some minor modifications to her historical framework, I find it to be a generally valuable taxonomy for conceptualizing the development of this body of literature.

Pettitt (1), Rau (108), and Aurélie Barjonet and Liran Razinsky (9) each cite Jorge Luis Borges's short story "Deutsches Requiem," which was published in Spanish in 1946, as one of the earliest fictions narrated in the autodiegetic (first-person) mode by a perpetrator.[2] The narrator of the text, Otto Dietrich zur Linde, a convinced Nazi, former sub-commander of a concentration camp, and self-proclaimed "torturer and murderer" (141), faces imminent execution for his crimes. He writes his short confessional text not to "seek pardon, because I feel no guilt," but "to be understood" (142). In this way, Borges's text frames the literary engagement with the mind of the Holocaust perpetrator as a question of understanding, not necessarily of moral evaluation. Borges's story, however, did not usher in a new wave of fiction featuring the perpetrator's voice; in the two decades following the end of the war, only a couple of fictional texts hazarded the representational risks associated with such a viewpoint, including Robert Merle's novel *Death Is My Trade* (published in the original French, *La Morte est mon métier*, in 1952 and in English translation in 1954), a fictionalized rendering of the autobiography of Rudolf Höß, the infamous commandant of Auschwitz; and Romain Gary's *The Dance of Genghis Cohn* (published in the original French, *La Danse de Gengis Cohn*, in 1967 and in English translation in 1968), a comic novel narrated by a dybbuk—the soul of a Jew who perished in the Holocaust—who inhabits the body of the SS officer who murdered him. Pettitt views the small number of texts from this period as constituting an initial wave of literature that demonstrated a "genuine engagement with the perpetrator perspective" (1).

Pettitt perceives the second wave, which began in the 1970s, as part of a "resurgence of interest" (1) in perpetrators following the Eichmann trial. (In this, fictional attempts to project the mind of the perpetrator align with nonfictional ones, which, as I argue in the introduction to part 1, were also

---

2 Pettitt identifies four further texts written between 1943 and 1946 that "portrayed Nazi criminality as a central theme" (1), although it is unclear whether they were written in the voices of perpetrators.

generated in the wake of the perpetrator trials of the 1960s.) In this second wave, the greater number of texts featured Hitler as a "central figure" (Pettitt 1); exceptions include Michel Tournier's *The Ogre* (published in English translation in 1972 and in the original French, *Le Roi des aulnes*, in 1970), narrated by "the strange, monstrous Abel Tiffauges" (Boswell 189), a onetime POW POW of the Germans, who kidnaps children and takes them to a Nazi training school; and the satirical novel *The Nazi and the Barber* (first published in English translation in 1971 and then in the original German, *Der Nazi und der Friseur*, in 1977), written by the Holocaust survivor Edgar Hilsenrath and narrated by an SS guard who murders his Jewish childhood friend in the Holocaust and then later assumes his identity. When it appeared, Hilsenrath's text, which I will analyze in detail in chapter 3, was considered transgressive not only because of its satirical excess but also because a Holocaust survivor presumed to write the story of the perpetrator in the first person (McGlothlin, "Narrative Transgression" 233–35).

Only with "the third wave of depictions" (Pettitt 2), which began in the 1980s, has there been "a steady stream of novels" (2) that engage the perpetrator's perspective; this wave encompasses the "turn toward the figure of the perpetrator in recent historical fiction" (Crownshaw 75) that has been an emerging focus of scholarship on Holocaust literature within the last ten years or so. Pettitt locates the beginning of this period in the publication of David Grossman's *See Under: Love* (published in English translation in 1989 and in the original Hebrew [עיין ערך: אהבה] in 1986); however, while Grossman's text does not feature a perpetrator-narrator, it does render the character of a camp commander, Obersturmbannführer Neigel, in Or Rogovin's words, "as a human being with a developed past and inner life" (74).[3] In terms of autodiegetic narration by the Holocaust perpetrator, however, a better beginning point for this phase is the 1991 publication

---

3 Rogovin sees Grossman's novel as marking a shift in the literary discourse on perpetrators in Israel as well: "Starting with *See Under: Love*, Holocaust perpetrators are characterized through a mode that is sharply, even radically, opposed to the mode used in Hebrew and Israeli fiction published between the mid-1940s and the mid-1980s" (67); in this "new phase in Israeli literary response to the Holocaust . . . , perpetrators are individualized, multifaceted, and humanized characters, and the divide between them and their victims is blurred if not completely erased" (87).

of Martin Amis's *Time's Arrow, or, The Nature of the Offense*, which is narrated in reverse chronology by the sundered soul of a former Auschwitz doctor. Amis's text, which I will analyze in chapter 4, is innovative not only with regard to its depiction of the Holocaust from the viewpoint of a perpetrator but also with its steadfast embrace of antimimetic (meaning conventionally antirealist) formal strategies. In the wake of *Time's Arrow*, a small but regular stream of texts featuring the auto- or homodiegetic narration of perpetrators has appeared, including Ian MacMillan's *Village of a Million Spirits: A Novel of the Treblinka Uprising* (1999), which contains a number of character-narrators, including an SS guard and a Ukrainian auxiliary guard; and Dieter Schlesak's documentary novel, *The Druggist of Auschwitz* (published in the original German, *Capesius, der Auschwitzapotheker*, in 2006 and in English translation in 2011), which, though narrated by a fictional Jewish survivor, contains first-person accounts of actual perpetrators. In the same year that Schlesak's modestly noticed text appeared, Jonathan Littell burst onto the literary scene with his novel *The Kindly Ones* (published in French in 2006 as *Les Bieveillantes* and in English translation in 2009), which features the sustained narrative perspective of an SS officer who tells over the course of one thousand pages the story of his participation in the genocide of European Jews. *The Kindly Ones* has been somewhat hyperbolically hailed as "a new phenomenon in fiction" (Suleiman, "When the Perpetrator Becomes a Reliable Witness" 5) and often mistakenly identified in the abundant scholarly discourse on it "as the first important work of fiction to narrate the Holocaust from the perpetrators' perspective" (von Koppenfels, "The Infamous 'I'" 133). At the same time, Littell's novel, which I will analyze in chapter 3, has without question made its mark on both the literary landscape and the discourse on Holocaust literature. In the last ten years, a number of further texts have appeared, including Douglas Skopp's *Shadows Walking* (2010), a novel about a Nazi doctor that, while narrated by a heterodiegetic narrator, features the protagonist's lengthy letter explaining his actions; Timur Vermes's *Er ist wieder da* (2012; *Look Who's Back*, 2014), a satire narrated by Hitler, who suddenly wakes up in contemporary Berlin; and, most recently, Martin Amis's return to the subject of Holocaust perpetration with *The Zone of Interest* (2014), which features three character-narrators, including two perpetrators, a fictional commandant of Auschwitz, and an

SS officer stationed there. I will look at *The Zone of Interest* along with *Time's Arrow* in chapter 4.[4]

According to Pettitt, "Even as the Holocaust moves further back in history, the fascination with its perpetrators shows little signs of abating" (2). However, at the same time, she discerns in her text corpus a recent shift away from autodiegetically narrated fictional accounts of the experience of Holocaust perpetrators:

> At a time when the Holocaust is beginning to slide out of living memory, a new narratological [*sic*] mode also appears to be emerging so that, whilst the vast majority of early examples of perpetrator fiction concerned themselves with explorations of the point of view of the perpetrators, later works, especially those that form part of what I have identified as the third wave of perpetrator fiction, have demonstrated a tendency to avoid the first-person narrative mode in favour of alternative forms of mediating discourse. Of course, there are exceptions to this pattern: Jonathan Littell's *The Kindly Ones* (2006) and Martin Amis's *Zone of Interest* (2014), for example, both offer first-person accounts of perpetration; however, Amis's earlier *Time's Arrow* (1991), Bernhard Schlink's *The Reader* (1995), David Albahari's *Götz and Meyer* (1998), Lauren[t] Binet's *HHhH* (2009) and Jodi Picoult's *The Storyteller* (2013) all, in one way or another, deny the reader direct access to the thoughts and feelings of the perpetrator. (2)

In an implied response to much of the discourse that claims the allegedly unprecedented character of Littell's novel, Pettitt makes an important point here about the longer history of auto- or homodiegetically narrated fiction about Holocaust perpetrators. In my view, however, it is hasty to conclude that we are seeing a waning of this mode. The "data set" with which Pettitt is working is relatively small, thus making it difficult to determine whether

---

4 In his article on *The Kindly Ones*, Jakob Lothe mentions a further Norwegian novel that features a perpetrator-narrator, Kjartan Fløgstad's *Grense Jakobselv* (2009), which has unfortunately not yet been translated into English.

there is a marked trend in one direction or another. Sophisticated quantitative methods provided by digital humanities scholarship aside, literature resists the kind of simple or one-to-one statistical evaluation Pettitt implicitly applies to it; some texts (like *The Kindly Ones*) attract disproportional notice, while others (e.g., MacMillan's deftly written *Village of a Million Spirits*) are barely registered at all, a situation that becomes all the more complicated when one takes into account factors such as marketing strategy, the language in which the book is written, the question of whether it has been translated into English (the language that seems to be the baseline assumption for Pettitt's study), and its transnational circulation and reception. Moreover, Pettitt's catalog of recent texts, though extensive, is not exhaustive; as demonstrated by the texts I list above, there are a number of recent works featuring the homodiegetic narration of perpetrators that she does not mention. Finally—and this will be a focal point of my argument—some texts, such as *Time's Arrow*, that Pettitt sees as "deny[ing] the reader direct access to the thoughts and feelings of the perpetrator" achieve that effect precisely through experimentation with new forms that challenge the clear divide between heterodiegetic and homo/autodiegetic narration.

On the whole, though, as demonstrated by the corpus of texts that Pettitt identifies as the third wave of "perpetrator fiction," there has been a decided uptick over the last three decades or so in novels that are narrated from the perspective and in the voice of men who play a role in perpetrating the Holocaust. The emergence of this body of fiction represents a perceptible historical shift in the canon of Holocaust literature away from prominent nonfictional works that probe the mind of the perpetrator, such as those by Arendt and Sereny, toward fictional texts that imagine his perspective. There are, of course, practical reasons for this shift. First among them is the conclusion in the late 1960s of the string of perpetrator trials in Israel and Germany that made the identities of a number of perpetrators public knowledge. In fact, both of the perpetrators interviewed for or analyzed by the texts I explore in part 1 (Adolf Eichmann and Franz Stangl) stood trial for their participation in the crimes of the Holocaust; Arendt, Mulisch, and Sereny were alerted to their very existence by virtue of the men's public notoriety. The relative absence of trials between the late 1960s and the first decade of the twenty-first century (when creative interpretation of German law made new trials possible) meant that in the interim fewer perpetrators were publicly identified. (A notable exception to this trend is the convoluted history of highly publicized legal cases concerning the culpability of John Demjanjuk that began in 1977 and ended in 2012.) The second reason is the gradual aging and death of the perpetrator generations, with the result that there have been fewer living perpetrators to interview and that those who are still alive are of advanced age (a problem to which, as I point out in my introduction to part 1, a number of recent documentary films have developed creative strategies for responding). In this, the discourse on Holocaust perpetrators must negotiate a problem analogous to the challenges posed by the passing of the final generation of Holocaust survivors, whereby the dominance of nonfictional forms, such as testimony and memoir, is gradually superseded by fictions and imaginative depictions. As I see it, the gradual but perceptible transition from nonfiction to fiction in the literature of the Holocaust writ large is also at work in the subgenre of representations of the mindset and motivations of perpetrators.

Narrative Strategies and Fiction

I discern between the wave of nonfiction that probes the mental states of real-life perpetrators and fictional texts that do the same through the means of autodiegetic narration not only a *historical* connection but also an *aesthetic* one. In fact, the fictional texts I investigate in this part take up some of the narrative strategies of nonfiction in their depiction of the interiority of their perpetrator-narrators and transform them into flexible devices that allow for the same dialectical movement between familiarization and estrangement, empathy and judgment, and intimate cohabitation of perspective and broader historical context that plays out in the nonfictional portraits. In particular, Edgar Hilsenrath's *The Nazi and the Barber*, Jonathan Littell's *The Kindly Ones*, and Martin Amis's *Time's Arrow* and *The Zone of Interest* all employ a filtering strategy that constitutes the fictional analogue of a critical filter found in the nonfictional texts, namely, the mediating voice of the author. The nonfictional texts I analyze in part 1—Arendt's *Eichmann in Jerusalem*, Mulisch's *Criminal Case 40/61*, Hull's *The Struggle for a Soul*, and Sereny's *Into That Darkness*—all feature homodiegetic narrators or intradiegetic figures who become protagonists or interventional voices in the narratives they relate; their intersubjective engagement with the minds of the perpetrators they analyze thus becomes an important part of their narratives. In this way, while the former Holocaust perpetrator is the overt subject of representation, each text also contains a second, inferred subject in the figure of the authorial persona, who, in his or her reaction to and interpretation of the man in question, becomes a crucial mediating figure who communicates the perpetrator's statements, translates his mental and emotional states, and signals to readers how they should evaluate his story. Our access to the inner experience of each of the perpetrators in these nonfictional representations is thus regulated and shaped by the authors' own affective, cognitive, and ethical investment in their projects.

Fictional representations of perpetrators can, of course, reproduce this authorial persona with a heterodiegetic (or third-person) narrator who exists outside the story he or she tells or with a homodiegetic (first-person) narrator who is not the perpetrator but who tells the perpetrator's story from within the storyworld. To be sure, the canon of "perpetrator fiction" includes texts that feature such external or internal interpreter-narrators. An example of the former (heterodiegetic narration) includes Patrick Hicks's 2014 novel *The Commandant of Lubizec*, which depicts a fictional Operation Reinhard killing center. As the blurb on its jacket reports, the novel is "told as an historical account in a documentary style" that "probes into the mind of its commandant"; its narrator thus assumes the impersonal, heterodiegetic form of the apparently objective historian. An example of the latter (homodiegetic narration) is Bernhard Schlink's 1995 novel *Der Vorleser* (*The Reader*, 1997), which is narrated by Michael Berg, the onetime lover of Hanna Schmitz, a woman who turns out to have been a perpetrator. As I have previously argued,

> Hanna's entire story—her relationship with Michael, her prehistory as a camp guard, her trial for her crimes during the Holocaust, her years in prison, and her suicide—is filtered through Michael's narrow, egocentric, and often self-serving perspective.... Michael (as narrator) thus provides an exclusively objective view of Hanna that is not counterbalanced by her own voice. ("Theorizing the Perpetrator" 216–17)

In both these cases, the mind of the perpetrator is mediated through an external or indirect narrating instance. My study here, by contrast, is limited to fictions that are narrated autodiegetically—in other words, self-narrated—by the perpetrators themselves, which ostensibly offer what Pettitt calls "direct access to the thoughts and feelings of the perpetrator" (2), a mode of representation of the Holocaust that, as Rau reminds us, continues to be "the most subversive choice" (94). However, the texts I investigate here, although narrated in the first person, each mitigate the reader's "direct access"; in these works, the function of the mediating authorial persona in nonfiction is translated via fictional means into some version of an externalized or internalized narratorial double that functions to buffer the perpetrator's mind. With *The Nazi and the Barber*, *The Kindly Ones*, and *Time's Arrow*, all of which contain to a greater or lesser extent some antimimetic features, the phenomenon of doubling, which, according to Gomel, "generates a paradoxical and uncanny double self" (xxxviii), takes place within the narrator himself, producing a sort of internalized external perspective that, not unlike a nonfictional authorial persona, serves to filter and selectively mediate the perpetrator's consciousness. In Hilsenrath's novel, such filtering takes place as a result of a vocal breach, in which the perpetrator, Max Schulz, assumes the identity and narrative voice of his victim, Itzig Finkelstein, and conducts a dialogue in the second person both *with* the effaced Itzig and *as* Itzig. The double in this case is the antithetical voice of the victim, who resides within the perpetrator as an internal Other. In Littell's novel, the narrator, Max Aue, is in a sense tripled in that he produces discrete, contradictory narrative discourses that create three iterations of the same narrating figure; as Stefan Iversen puts it, "The attribution of desires and beliefs to Aue is at times obstructed and disfigured by the particular narrative features of the novel" (155–56). In Amis's *Time's Arrow*, the most antimimetic of the four texts I interpret, the narration is provided by the perpetrator figure's soul, which has become uncoupled from the body that houses it and that engages physically with the storyworld and which further experiences the perpetrator's actions through perception of a reversed temporality. With Amis's *The Zone of Interest*, by contrast, a mimetically more conventional novel, doubling happens with the distribution of the narrative voice across three figures, two of which are perpetrators; by featuring the monologues of multiple narrators, the novel thus provides an external antipode to the authoritative narration of each of the two perpetrator figures. In these cases—and in several texts I do not analyze, such as Borges's "Deutsches Requiem" or Gary's *The Dance of Genghis Cohn*[5]—the filtering mechanism provided by an external or internal counterpart to the narrating perpetrator both animates the reader to immerse in the narrator's experience and mental state and at the same time impedes such processes of identification. In each case, the text in question generates a fictional variant of the critical counter-perspective constituted by the authorial voice in nonfictional engagements with perpetrators, which both reveals and occludes the interiority of the perpetrator and yields and withholds insight into his motivations.

Hilsenrath, Littell, and Amis thus revamp for their own ends a prominent strategy utilized by nonfictional portraits of perpetrators. At the same time, however, each of the four novels illustrates what Stefan Iversen calls "the experiential power" of fiction "to do what no historical, sociological or psychological approach has ever really succeeded in doing," namely, to construct "through very thick descriptions of motivations, dispositions, emotions and thoughts" (155) the consciousness of the Holocaust perpetrator.[6] In other words, the aim of these novels is not simply to reproduce mimetically the strategies and insights of nonfictional texts but rather to exploit the particular properties of fiction in their construction of the idiosyncratic narrative voices of their protagonists. In this, novelists not only enjoy a degree of flexibility with regard to referentiality (although, with the depiction of the historical Holocaust, the leash is still somewhat short) but also have at their fingertips the full range of fictional strategies, devices, and

---

5 In Borges's story, the filter is constituted by the function of the extradiegetic editor, who in typical Borgesian fashion provides footnotes to the narrator's account. In Gary's novel, much like Hilsenrath's, the filter is the internalized voice of the victim, who resides as a dybbuk within the perpetrator.

6 While I agree with Iversen that fiction offers particular inroads to readers' comprehension of the consciousness of perpetrators of violence, it does not follow that "no historical, sociological or psychological approach has every really succeeded" in explaining the mental states of perpetrators. Rather, as the extremely insightful work of scholars such as Christopher Browning, Thomas Kühne, Mark Roseman, Hilary Earl, Johannes Lang, Harald Welzer, James Waller, Ervin Staub, Katharina von Kellenbach, Rachel MacNair, Björn Krondorfer, and many others has demonstrated, the scholarly study of real-life perpetrators, taken as a whole, produces an incredibly sophisticated portrait of the men (and women) implicated in the crimes of the Holocaust. It is important for me, as a literary scholar, to acknowledge the value of their considerable contributions (just as it is important that they value the work on representation that I do).

techniques. While the novels investigated in this part utilize a heterogenous mixture of formal strategies, including experimentation with voice (as I indicate above), focalization, temporal structure, causality, genre, intertextuality, and paratextual framing, two particular dynamics shape both the novels' representations and my readings of them and therefore deserve special mention here.

The first is the phenomenon of unreliable narration, a concept generally associated with the rhetorical approach to narrative developed by Wayne Booth, James Phelan, Peter Rabinowitz, and others. According to Phelan, whose theory of unreliability I find to be most useful for my readings of the four novels,

> The rhetorical approach conceives of narrative as a purposive communicative act. In this view, narrative is not just a representation of events but is also itself an event—one in which someone is doing something with a representation of events. . . . The focus on purposes includes a recognition that narrative communication is a multi-layered event, one in which tellers seek to engage and influence their audiences' cognition, emotions, and values. Moreover, the approach recognizes that, in telling what happened, narrators give accounts of characters whose interactions with each other have an ethical dimension and that the acts of telling and receiving these accounts also have an ethical dimension. Consequently, the rhetorical approach attends to both an ethics of the told and an ethics of the telling. ("Rhetoric/ethics" 203)

For my purposes here, the attention to the ethical dimension of the narrator on the part of rhetorical narratology is particularly important, given not only my explicit focus on the function of the autodiegetic narrators in the novels I examine but also the extreme extent of their ethical entanglement in violence. Moreover, the rhetorical approach's emphasis on the role of the reader in the narrative's act of communication is also valuable. As readers, we are at the mercy of the text's narrator for our understanding and evaluation of the events it depicts, but as the rhetorical approach stresses, we also play a powerful role in the communicative act constituted by the narrative. In particular, our role—our readerly duty, one might say—is to assess the narrator's account of the events of the Holocaust and his implication in them (among other matters) and to decide where it is candid, trustworthy, and useful to us and where it is deficient or deceptive. We do this by establishing the relative reliability or unreliability of the narrator. As Phelan points out, all narrators are to some extent unreliable, just as they are to some degree reliable. The question of reliability (or unreliability) is thus not a digital "on" or "off" button but a spectrum that shifts at different stages of the narrative and of the reading process.

Narrators, according to Phelan, "perform three main roles—reporting, interpreting, and evaluating; sometimes they perform the roles simultaneously and sometimes sequentially" (*Living to Tell about It* 50). These functions correspond to what Phelan calls the three axes of communication in narrative: "the axis of characters, facts, and events," "the axis of knowledge and perception," and "the axis of ethics and evaluation" (50). In other words, narrators not only give (or withhold) information but also mediate to us what they know (or do not know) and how they perceive (or fail to perceive) events and further how they judge the meaning and ethical implication of events. When narrators are unreliable, their unreliability thus manifests on one of the three axes:

> They can **misreport** (by, for example, distorting what happened, getting the order of events wrong, or even outright lying); they can **misread or misinterpret** (naïve narrators demonstrate their naïveté by misreading); and they can **misregard or misevaluate** (judging evil characters to be good, and vice versa). We can add another layer of precision to this taxonomy by noting that sometimes a narrator's report, reading, or regarding is reliable as far as it goes, though it clearly does not go far enough. This observation yields three other kinds of unreliability: underreporting, underreading, and underregarding. (Phelan, "The Ethics and Aesthetics of Backward Narration" 127)

Phelan's taxonomy helps us to determine precisely what the narrator is attempting to accomplish when we sense the operation of unreliability in his account, which in turn can assist us in locating, understanding, and interpreting the aspects of his narration that trouble or confuse us. Further, his taxonomy is useful for comprehending the sophisticated interplay between the various forms of unreliability that may occur in a text; while some narrators may demonstrate a single type of unreliability, the variants often work in tandem with each other to magnify or exacerbate the overall unreliable effect. Thus, for example, as Phelan writes in his astute analysis of unreliable narration in *Time's Arrow*, "Amis makes unreliability the default condition of the narration, because Soul is reporting events in the wrong order and compounding that misreporting with a misreading of the relations between cause and effect" ("The Ethics and Aesthetics of Backward Narration" 127). Finally, particular deployments of unreliability can have disparate effects on the reader; Phelan distinguishes in this regard between bonding unreliability, which serves to minimize the distance between narrator and reader, and estranging reliability, which emphasizes or increases this distance ("Estranging Unreliability, Bonding Unreliability" 223–24). Unreliability can thus both draw readers in and alienate them; it can also serve both in the interest of the narrator or against it.

The question of reliability inheres in texts that feature perpetrator-narrators, whose accounts we receive from the beginning with skepticism by virtue of their very status as victimizer; as Ansgar Nünning argues, "Narrators who violate agreed-upon moral and ethical norms or the standards that a given culture holds to be constitutive of normal psychological behaviour are generally taken to be unreliable" (497). Dan Shen proposes the term "dispositionally unreliable" to refer to narrators who are untrustworthy by virtue of their character or values, a label that aptly describes narrators known to be Holocaust perpetrators, whom the reader identifies a priori as less than credible. Moreover, the reader's recognition of the Holocaust perpetrator as a violator of moral and ethical standards relies at least in part on the knowledge she brings to the text, which allows her to compare the perpetrator's description and interpretation of the events with those of the victims and with historians' accounts and to identify moments in which the perpetrator fudges the facts, mischaracterizes the events, or downplays particular experiences to defer responsibility for them. For this reason, issues of unreliability in texts narrated by Holocaust perpetrators are what Per Krogh Hansen has identified as extratextual in nature in that they rely on the reader's ability to recognize "the narrator's misinterpretation of commonly known historical facts" (334). At the same time, however, the texts I analyze in part 2 also contain aspects of intratextual unreliability—for example, internal tensions generated by the discrepancy between the narrator's professed account and interpretation of the events and cues supplied through his narration by the implied author that call his version into question—which means that these narratives are subject to the same principles of narrative reliability that govern homodiegetic narration in general. As my reading of the variable manifestations of unreliable narration in the four novels I investigate will demonstrate, unreliability constitutes in these texts a further variant of filtering in the representation of the perpetrator's mind.

The second narrative dynamic that is integral for my discussion is the tension between mimetic and antimimetic representational modes in the texts' construction of the consciousness of their narrators and the disparate effects each mode can have on readers. Antimimetic or "unnatural" narrative, as it is generally understood by narrative theorists, is a heuristic—not essential or fixed—category for describing representational conventions of fiction that depart from the norms of mimetic or realist narrative in a given historical moment and cultural and literary context. (In the present moment, in which the conventions of literary representation are still substantially shaped by realism and literary modernism, aspects of the unnatural and antimimetic are often—but not exclusively—found in postmodernist fiction.) Unnatural narratives, according to Brian Richardson, "transgress mimetic expectations, the canons of realism, and the conventions of natural narrative" ("What Is Unnatural Narrative Theory?" 23) as well as "the conventions of nonfictional narratives and of fiction that closely resembles nonfiction" ("Unnatural Narrative Theory" 385); such violation of established representational modes can take place both "in the fictional storyworld and in the narrative discourse" (389). In Jan Alber's view, "The unnatural involves the representation of impossibilities" ("Unnatural Narratology" 450); thus, "the represented scenarios or events [in unnatural narrative] have to be impossible according to the known laws governing the physical world, accepted principles of logic (such as the principle of non-contradiction), or standard human limitations of knowledge" ("Unnatural Narratology" 449). In other words, while realist or mimetic

Imagining the Mind of the Holocaust Perpetrator in Fiction | 189 narrative "attempts to provide narrators, characters, events, and settings that more or less resemble those of our quotidian experience," "antimimetic or antirealist modes of narrative representation play with, exaggerate, or parody the conventions of mimetic representation; often they foreground narrative elements and events that are wildly implausible or palpably impossible in the real world" (Richardson, "Antimimetic, Unnatural, and Postmodern Narrative Theory" 20).[7] Importantly, the line between mimetic or realist narrative and unnatural or antimimetic narrative is a shifting one that is established according to the prevalent representational conventions of the moment; strategies that at one time may be considered antimimetic can be naturalized into conventions culturally and historically regarded as mimetic.[8] Moreover, narratives considered in a particular context to be mimetic and those seen as antimimetic both make reference to *and* depart from the real world; just as the most realist of fictional narratives imaginatively transform to some extent the world they reference, all unnatural narratives "are in some sense based on the world we know" (Pettersson 85) and thus "typically contain 'natural' elements (based on real-world parameters) and unnatural components at the same time" (Alber, "Unnatural Narrative"). For that reason, "in some sense or at some level every work of literature engages in realism," while "the unnatural is a quality that can be found in almost every work of fiction" (Richardson, "What Is Unnatural Narrative Theory?" 37).[9] It is therefore important, when using the terms "mimetic/realist" and "antimimetic/unnatural," to avoid erecting a

---

7 Richardson further distinguishes the antimimetic or natural from what he calls the nonmimetic, which includes "conventional fairy tales, animal fables, ghost stories, and other kinds of fiction that invoke magical or supernatural elements. Such narratives employ consistent storyworlds and obey established generic conventions or, in some cases, merely add a single supernatural component to an otherwise naturalistic world. By contrast, unnatural texts do not attempt to extend the boundaries of the mimetic, but rather play with the very conventions of mimesis" ("Unnatural Narrative Theory" 386).
8 According to Jan Alber, "During the course of literary history, numerous unnatural scenarios and events have already been integrated into our fictional encyclopedias, i.e., our knowledge of particular genres" ("Unnatural Narratology" 451).
9 As Richardson argues, "Unnatural or antimimetic elements can be found in a wide range of ostensibly realist fictions, though they are often ignored because they can be quickly subsumed within the works' general mimetic frame" ("Unnatural Narrative Theory" 399).

strict dichotomy between them; rather, it is more useful to think of the two categories as "flexible narrative models" (Pettersson 76) that exist "on a continuum" (Alber, "Unnatural Narratology" 450).[10]

For its part, realist and mimetic fiction, by positing a close correspondence between the storyworld and the real world and by mimicking the conventions of nonfictional narrative, offers readers an immersive experience, whereby, according to Werner Wolf, they "seem to *experience representations* as if in real life, i.e. *in analogous ways to real-life experience*" (11–12). While "readers are always to some extent aware of the fictionality of fiction" (Polvinen 94), even when reading decidedly realist texts, highly mimetic texts can streamline the pathways toward immersion, particularly through their adherence to generic conventions, their facilitation of what Wolf terms "aesthetic illusion," and their accessibility:

> The *consistency* and *life-likeness* (or verisimilitude) of proto- typically illusionist representations such as realist novels are actually facets of a more general quality of illusionist worlds, namely their *accessibility*. . . . It is obvious that enhanced accessibility facilitates illusionist immersion, and that therefore illusionist works tend to lower the threshold of access as much as possible. In realism, this recipient-friendly tendency towards effortlessness (which is typical of illusionism in general and sometimes criticized as trivializing) is manifest in the construction and presentation of fictional

---

10 Richardson has convincingly argued that classical (and much postclassical) narratology has attempted to "wrest [unnatural works] into a more familiar framework and forcibly conventionalize them" ("What Is Unnatural Narrative Theory?" 32). He advocates for a "capacious narratology" that "recognize[s] the anti-mimetic as such, and resist[s] impulses to deny its protean essence and unexpected effects" ("What Is Unnatural Narrative Theory?" 33). At the same time, he also stresses that "we will be most effective as narrative theorists if we reject models that, based on categories derived from linguistic or natural narrative, insist on firm distinctions, binary oppositions, fixed hierarchies, or impermeable categories" (*Unnatural Voices* 139). Further, he points out that, for unnatural narratologists, "the word 'unnatural' has no extranarrative connotations"; it thus is not used in ways that pertain to "any cultural practices, individual actions, or sexual preferences commonly designated as unnatural by society" ("Unnatural Narrative Theory" 393). Its normative potential is thus limited to the possibilities and structures of narrative.

worlds that seem to be a mimetic extension of the recipients' real world in terms of spatial, temporal (contemporary) and social settings but also, e.g., in terms of norms, ideals and epistemological preconceptions about the "readability" of reality. (Wolf 40)

Through their construction of aesthetic illusion and their accessible appeal, realist or mimetic texts "manage to draw their readers into their worlds in a particularly easily [sic] way because they successfully maintain a feeling of verisimilitude and life-like experience while minimizing aesthetic distance" (Wolf 35). Further, as Wolf points out, there is a "link between immersion and emotion" (54), meaning that, during highly immersive experiences, readers can develop emotional, empathetic, or identificatory bonds, whereby they regard, at least provisionally and through the dynamics of aesthetic illusion, "characters as possible people" and "the narrative world as like our own, that is, hypothetically or conceptually possible" (Phelan, *Experiencing Fiction* 5). Issues of reader identification and empathy are particularly important with regard to texts that immerse their readers through their construction of mimetic or illusionist worlds and characters.

Antimimetic or unnatural narratives also facilitate to some extent aesthetic illusion, but at the same time, they work to "compromise" "the experience of immersion in a storyworld" (Richardson, "Unnatural Narrative Theory" 393) through estrangement effects; as Richardson argues, "An antimimetic or unnatural fiction requires a partial belief in the fictional world and also sabotages that belief" ("Unnatural Narrative Theory" 393). In fact, one of the markers of unnatural narrative is its particular capacity to facilitate the process of defamiliarization, as theorized by Viktor Shklovsky: "The technique of art is to make objects 'unfamiliar,' to make forms difficult, to increase the difficulty and length of perception because the process of perception is an aesthetic end in itself and must be prolonged" (778). While Shklovsky attributes the dynamics of defamiliarization more generally to works that call attention to their formal properties ("defamiliarization is found almost everywhere form is found" [781]), his employment of the concept, according to Alber, describes well the effects produced by unnatural techniques: "For Shklovsky, the term 'defamiliarization' has three specific senses, namely the deviation from conventionalized forms of representation; the disruption of automated patterns of cognition; and the alienation of familiar objects, concepts, and forms" ("Unnatural Narratology" 458). Unnatural narratives interrupt readers' immersion through defamiliarization or, to use Wolf's term, "distance," meaning the "latent, rational and observational awareness 'from without,' namely that the illusion-inducing trigger is an artefact and a 'mere' representation (this is a metacommunicative and hence a metareferential awareness)" (22); they thus work to weaken readers' emotional bonds while increasing their cognitive interest in narrative form and function and in the contradictions and impossibilities foregrounded by antimimetic elements and their effects. In markedly unnatural narratives, readers' investment is thus more epistemological than emotional; the reading process is directed in the main toward understanding and explaining the defamiliarized, unnatural world of the text and its narration. It is important to note that the concepts of immersion and distance/defamiliarization, while often posited as polar opposites, are, as Anderson and Iversen point out, part of a more fluid, complex, and interdependent dynamic.

Keeping in mind that these representational modes exist on a continuum rather than as an antithetical binary, I nevertheless find the structural opposition between antimimetic and mimetic narration useful for thinking about how the authors represented in this study go about rendering perpetrator consciousness and how these modes can be deployed as filtering mechanisms. Each of the four novels has one foot in the "natural" world, if only by virtue of its referentiality to the Holocaust. In other words, for its Holocaust perpetrator to be legible as such, its storyworld needs to be realist to the extent that readers recognize it as a setting for the events of the Holocaust. Moreover, these four novels, through generic convention, intertextual reference, or substantial paratextual explanation, each mimic or allude to nonfictional genres of Holocaust writing (primary bureaucratic document, testimony, interview, survivor memoir, historical scholarship); in this way they all model themselves to some extent on the nonfictional conventions that undergird realist representation. At the same time, however, three of the four texts also overtly employ what—from our present cultural moment—we recognize as unnatural or antimimetic devices; they thus transform to some extent the historical framework and defamiliarize it through a variety of antimimetic means. The fourth novel, by contrast, utilizes mostly natural conventions but avoids the psychological realism associated with full mimeticism by taking advantage of distancing elements such as satire. In this way, all four of the novels can be positioned at discrete points on the antimimetic-mimetic spectrum. Amis's two texts, one of which is markedly antimimetic and the other of which is decidedly realist, inhabit the outlying ends of the continuum. On the one side resides *Time's Arrow*, which, through its use of antinomic or reverse temporality and its bisection of narrative voice, defamiliarizes both the natural causal relationship between the events of the Holocaust and the ethical interpretation that proceeds from such a distorted causality. Located on the other end is *The Zone of Interest*, which presents Auschwitz through realist narrative conventions, including narration by three narrators that resembles nonfictional genres (testimony, diary, and retrospective memoir). Inhabiting the rough middle are both *The Nazi and the Barber* and *The Kindly Ones*. Hilsenrath's novel is written as a sort of autobiographical confessional that nevertheless disrupts its own mimetic effects through its use of second-person narration, "an artificial mode that does not normally occur in natural narrative" (Richardson, *Unnatural Voices* 19), and through satire and the grotesque. For its part, Littell's text models itself on the documentary eyewitness report but controverts the authenticity effects of that mode with hallucinatory narration and logically impossible events. Hilsenrath's and Littell's novels thus avail themselves of the advantages of both a realist framework and the imaginative possibilities of the unnatural.

Taken as a whole, the four novels I investigate in the following chapters not only show the capacity and malleability of fiction for representing mental states and experiences that are inaccessible to the methodologies of nonfiction; they also demonstrate the ways in which such depictions, rather than providing "direct access" to the minds of their narrators, deploy a heterogeneous arsenal of techniques and devices to filter, mitigate, and regulate their apparent transparency. As indicated by their adoption and transformation of particular strategies, namely, the creation of an alternate perspective through the doubling of the narrative voice, the adept use of the dynamics of unreliable narration, and the tensional relationship between mimetic and antimimetic modes of representation, these texts manifest the creative lengths their writers go to in their attempt to write in the voice of the Holocaust perpetrator and at the same time to provide a critical counter-discourse to his narrative.

3

Perpetrators on the Run

Edgar Hilsenrath's *The Nazi and the Barber* and Jonathan Littell's *The Kindly Ones*

Doing the Math

Near the beginning of Edgar Hilsenrath's satirical novel *The Nazi and the Barber* (published in English translation in 1971 and in the original German, *Der Nazi und der Friseur*, in 1977), the autodiegetic (first-person) narrator, Max Schulz, a former member of the SS who was deployed in an Einsatzgruppe and served as a guard in the fictional concentration camp Laubwalde, describes to his audience in the space of a few pages the extent of his implication in the crimes of the Holocaust:

> It only began to get gory when the march into Russia started. Mobile Killing Unit D in the South Russia section. But that was later, in 1941.
>
> Have you any idea how one shoots thirty thousand Jews in a forest? And do you know what that does to a non-smoker? It's there that I learned to smoke.

> Can you do arithmetic in your head? Are you good at figures? If you are, then you'll know that sort of thing is not easy.
>
> In the beginning I counted the victims; although the way I did it was rather like the way I used to count the flagstones as a child when we were playing hopscotch—and it's easy to make a mistake in counting. Later that method didn't work. It was too laborious.
>
> Yes, and what happened next? Well, I had a little heart attack and I found myself transferred into the hinterland. [. . .]
>
> Do you know the concentration camp Laubwalde? At one time the place had a Polish name. But we gave it a new name: Laubwalde. It was a wonderfully beautiful place, surrounded by woods.
>
> There were two hundred thousand Jews in Laubwalde. We killed them all. Two hundred thousand! Even so, that was a small camp because most of the prisoners were done away with almost as soon as they'd come in. That was practical. It meant that we never had to keep guard over too many of them. As I said: it was a small camp.
>
> Two hundred thousand. That's a number with five zeros. Do you know how to knock off a zero? Or two zeros? Or three zeros? Or four zeros? Or five zeros? Can you imagine how a man knocks off a zero? And in the end the number two also . . . even though that is no zero? Do you know how that's done?
>
> I know, since I was one of those who were involved, even though today I can't remember what happened too exactly, and can't remember exactly how many prisoners I shot, or beat to death, or hanged. (72–74)

In this long dialogical passage, which nevertheless consists of less than a dozen very short paragraphs, Max Schulz describes a momentous period of his life that lasted roughly three and a half years. During this time—as he admits with an impudent candor that, as will be discussed later in this chapter, characterizes his narration—he actively perpetrated murderous violence on an almost unimaginable scale. However, rather than narrate his participation in genocide in the form of a conventional autobiographical chronicle, he expresses his egregious history of violence in the guise of an imaginative exercise regarding the running tally of his victims, whereby the mathematical amplitude of the number of murdered Jews is somehow meant to indicate the extremity of his actions. Schulz's numerous victims, whom he freely admits to beating, hanging, and shooting with his own hand (even as he attempts—in the original German at least—to qualify his participation, obliquely conceding that he merely "was, as it were, 'involved'" ["sozusagen 'mitbeteiligt' war," *Der Nazi und der Friseur* 79, my translation]), are not acknowledged as humans, each of whom had a unique identity and subjectivity; on the contrary, he remembers them as a statistical aggregate whose plurality was numerical rather than qualitative. Expressed by Schulz as a raw total, the victims reveal nothing about themselves; they serve in his recollection and narration only to illuminate him and his own experience. Although as casualties of genocidal violence they were subtracted from the totality of the living human community, Schulz expresses them here not as losses but as positive numbers meant to indicate something beyond themselves, namely, the staggering extent of Schulz's violent transgressions. Moreover, he derives these numbers of murder victims—a prodigious thirty thousand in a mass shooting, a colossal two hundred thousand in Laubwalde—not from his own count but from official tallies of the violence collectively perpetrated by him and his comrades, figures that astound and shock by virtue of the multitudinous deaths that they denote. He himself, as he readily admits, lost count of his personal total long ago;[1] akin to the failure of memory in a repetitive children's game (Schulz's outrageous and offensive choice of analogy for the perpetration of mass killing), his mind simply could not keep track of the extent of his recurrent commission of violence, as it had become a daily routine that necessitated no particular mnemonic exertion. Indeed, he can longer "remember what happened too exactly."

For Schulz, the shockingly high numbers of people who were murdered—whether by his own hand or by that of his colleagues in the shared temporal

---

[1] Later in the book, when pressed on the issue, Schulz hazards a guess as to how many people he personally killed: "Approximately ten thousand. But it could have been a few more. Or a few less. But to give you a round figure, ten thousand!" (*The Nazi and the Barber* 388).

and spatial coordinates of the mass killings of the Einsatzgruppe and the concentration camp—function further as signifiers of a negatively sublime cumulative excess. In other words, Max is titillated by the sheer magnitude and unalloyed transgression—"the nexus of transcendence and violence" (Gomel xxvii)—manifested by the numerical signs; he appears to fetishize them as trophies of a sort and even to exalt them as indicators of pure negativity, the inscrutable enigma of which he attempts to penetrate by carefully parsing the totals. By asking his audience how one goes about "knocking off"—or, as the original German "durchstreichen" (*Der Nazi und der Friseur* 79) connotes, "crossing out"—each zero of the latter number, he performatively dissevers the total, feeling out each digit and considering—one might even say negatively *savoring*—the exponential increase in deaths it denotes. He thereby not only recounts (both in the narrative and in the enumerative sense) these murders but also rhetorically reenacts them one decimal point at a time, distending the number to its full conceptual capability and its negative potential. Moreover, in the original German, Schulz's exercise of the mathematical imagination takes an additional step: Not only does he attempt to "cross out" each digit that represents the cumulative mass murder in Laubwalde (an exercise that constitutes on the discursive level a sort of echo effect of the original murders themselves), but he also suggests "annulling the nulls" ("Nullen annulier[en]," *Der Nazi und der Friseur* 79), which is tantamount to a kind of double negation. In other words, by deconstructing the number of murders in Laubwalde—by disaggregating and then nullifying each of the zeros—Schulz attempts in a sense to undo by rhetorical means his crimes, even as he shockingly acknowledges their monstrous extent. In this way, although in this passage he discomfitingly admits to his outsized role in the genocide (even if, as Corey Twitchell points out, he deftly employs the pronoun "wir" in lieu of "I" at critical moments [94]), he also works discursively to efface it. His disingenuously candid recounting of the stupendous murders in which he was both directly and indirectly involved thus functions as a narrative and numeric game of smoke and mirrors—to wit, as a kind of filtering strategy—that allows him on the surface to acknowledge his crimes and at the same time to disavow or evade responsibility for them on a more subterranean level.

Jonathan Littell's 2006 novel *Les Bienveillantes*, which appeared in English in 2009 as *The Kindly Ones*, features the autodiegetic narration of another

Max—Maximilien Aue, also an SS officer who was part of an Einsatzgruppe (in this case, Einsatzgruppe C, whose field of genocidal operations was northern and central Ukraine, in contrast to Schulz's Einsatzgruppe D, which perpetrated massacres in southern Ukraine, the Crimea, and the Caucasus) and who was charged late in the war with identifying ways of extending the life expectancy of the massive slave labor force at Auschwitz and other concentration and labor camps. In the prefatory chapter ("Toccata") of his account, which he narrates from his postwar position as the manager of a lace factory in northern France, Aue, like Schulz, attempts to reckon with the almost unfathomable numbers of victims—both Jewish and non-Jewish—of the war of annihilation waged by the German forces against the Soviet Union. At the beginning of an extended section (from which I can quote only small excerpts), Aue, in dialogue—like Schulz—with his audience, reflects,

> The television bombards us with numbers, impressive numbers, in the seven- or even eight-figure range; but who among you has ever seriously stopped to think about these numbers? Who among you has ever even tried to count all the people he knows or has known in his life, and to compare that laughable number with the numbers he hears on television, those famous *six million*, or *twenty million*? Let's do some math. Math is useful; it gives one perspective, refreshes the soul. It can be a very instructive exercise. Be a little patient, then, and pay attention. I will consider only the two theaters of operations where I played a role, however minute: the war against the Soviet Union, and the extermination program officially referred to in our documents as "The Final Solution of the Jewish Question," *die Endlösung der Judenfrage*, to cite that fine euphemism. On the Western front, in any case, the losses were relatively minor, a few hundred thousand here or there at the most. (13)

Like Max Schulz, Max Aue is disquietingly frank about the prodigious violence unleashed by the Nazi regime in its "total war" (18) in the East; indeed, rather than downplay its extent, he forthrightly concedes it and even proposes to "do some math" to explore the ambit of its body count.

Also like Schulz, he displays a fascination with the inconceivably high number of deaths caused by that violence, although while Schulz focuses his mathematical rumination on the immediate victims of the contexts (the mass shooting, the concentration camp) in which he took part as a perpetrator, Aue chooses to broaden the scope of his inquiry to encompass the entire military and genocidal offensives in which he, as one among millions of German troops, played what he terms a "minute" role. He includes in the scope of his "exercise" victims of initiatives of which he was not—and could not logically have been—remotely a part; therefore, in contrast to the tens or hundreds of thousands of deaths on which Schulz ponders, Aue contemplates a death count that numbers into the millions and even tens of millions. In this way, Aue's reflections relate not to his own personal commission of or implication in violence (as do Schulz's) but to the larger collective culpability of the German forces. Moreover, whereas the number "two hundred thousand" is for Schulz almost sublime in its signification of extremity and excess, in Aue's view, as the last sentence of his quote indicates, a mere "few hundred thousand" is a "relatively minor" matter, especially in comparison to the millions involved in the "Final Solution" and Operation Barbarossa. The extremity of the latter is so stupendous that one could contemplate it in perpetuum, or at least "until the ground opens up beneath your feet" (16).

As part of his "instructive exercise," Aue spends the next several pages discussing various estimates posited by historians of the total loss of human life in the German campaign against the Soviet Union and in the Judeocide (including the "Soviet dead," the "German dead," and the "*Endlösung*" [15]), deciding on a combined sum of 26.6 million. Using this number, he performs a feat of creative calculation, imagining how such a mind-boggling figure might be conceptualized on a more conceivable scale:

> Thus for the overall total in my field of activities we have an average of 572,043 dead per month, 131,410 dead per week, 18,722 dead per day, 782 per hour, and 13.04 dead per minute, every minute of every hour of every day of every week of every month of every year of the given period, which is, if you will recall, 3 years, 10 months, 16 days, 20 hours, and 1 minute. Let those who smirked at that admittedly somewhat pedantic

extra minute please consider that it is worth an additional 13.04 dead, on average, and imagine, if they can, 13 people from their circle of friends killed in 1 minute. You can also calculate the length of time it takes to generate a fresh corpse: this gives us on average a dead German every 40.8 seconds, a dead Jew every 24 seconds, and a dead Bolshevik (Soviet Jews included) every 6.12 seconds, or on the whole a new dead body on average every 4.6 seconds, for the entirety of said period. You are now in a position to carry out, based on these numbers, concrete exercises of imagination. For example, stopwatch in hand, count off 1 death, 2 deaths, 3 deaths, etc., every 4.6 seconds (or every 6.12 seconds, or every 24 seconds, or every 40.8 seconds, if you have a marked preference), while trying to picture them lying there in front of you, those 1, 2, 3 dead. You'll find it's a good meditation exercise. (15–16)

In a manner not unlike that of Schulz, Aue takes the astounding number of all the deaths that occurred in the Nazis' war of annihilation in the East and pulls it apart, attempting thereby to reduce it to a conceivable scale. He asks his audience to project what it would be like to witness (although not to perpetrate) the death of a person—even a friend—every fifth second for a full minute and to imagine that frequency of death happening every minute for the entirety of the phase of the war that began on 22 June 1941 (a total of 2,040,241 minutes, as he calculates earlier in this section). Such "concrete exercises of imagination," as Aue conceives them, "generate" corpses; in conceptual terms, they thus function in an analogous way to Max Schulz's musings. Rather than denoting the subduction of actual lives and communities through the extreme violence of which Aue was a part, his mathematical conjectures engender a positive number of mortalities that confounds with its radical sublimity. For Aue, as for Schulz, the obsessive fixation on calculating the numbers of the dead manifests a salacious fascination with the transgressive character and seemingly ineffable scope of the genocidal violence of the German war in the occupied territories, which in terms of the pace and frequency of killing—not to mention the methods and the brutal character—exceeded both historical models and our conventional imaginative capacity.

Further, through his "mediation exercise," Aue not only compels us to contemplate the drastic number of deaths and the extraordinary regularity of the killing in his "field of activities" but also demands that we visualize the corpses "generated" by such an operation. Thereby, he presents us with an imaginative scenario that simulates the atmosphere in which he himself lived during the German invasion of the Soviet Union, in the course of which—as we will learn later in the novel—he transitioned from a witness to the pandemic violence against civilians, especially Jews, to a perpetrator of it.[2] The corpses—both the not insignificant number killed by Aue himself and the much greater number whose slaughter he observes—pile up over the course of the narrative, becoming part of the global toll at which he marvels. He attempts here in a sense to replicate not only the physical omnipresence of the bodies of the victims, which at times he saw lying literally in front of him, but also their ubiquity in the narrative, which teems with them from beginning to end. With astonishing candor, he thus conjures for his audience an unsparing image of the incessant brutality in "the two theaters of operations" in which he "played a role," where the killing of civilians was wholesale and incessant and where the corpses of murder victims aggregated with unprecedented and inconceivable speed. However, at the same time, Aue's exercise in the imagination is disingenuous; though he refers explicitly to the comprehensive total of victims produced by the German war of annihilation, he declines to count—or indeed to account for—his contribution to that total through his own acts of killing. About that number—about that phenomenon in general—he is decisively reticent, at least in this opening chapter, in which, with his nebulous reference to his part in the prodigious killings—"And then came the war, I served, and I found myself at the heart of terrible things, atrocities" (24)—he skirts the question of his culpability. Aue thus appears to tackle candidly the topic of the war in which he, as a member of the SS, played a not insignificant role, but in fact he uses his mathematical exercise of imagination to circumvent rather than acknowledge his own personal fraction of the atrocious numbers that so captivate him. In this way, he filters his personal history of

---

2 As Leona Toker argues, "There is a gradation within Aue's participation in the regime's atrocities, from intelligence work, to observation of mass killings, to administering *coups de grâce*, to getting into the flow of the work of destruction though without exactly developing an addiction to it" (158).

violence through an abstract, generalized thought experiment, which he employs to diffuse and diminish his accountability for his own part in the death toll. Moreover, by requiring us, his audience, to visualize the corpses that he "generates" with his speculation, he additionally pushes onto us—or at least compels us to share a part of—his complicity, which constitutes a further instance in which he evades his crimes rhetorically.

With their mutual, although disparately articulated, preoccupation with the numbers of war casualties and victims of genocide in the Second World War and the Holocaust, Max Schulz and Max Aue thus both manifest a critical feature endemic to the fictional perpetrator's narration of his own history of violence: the filtering of that experience through various narrative, rhetorical, and conceptual stratagems, in this case, the framework of the mathematical exercise. Schulz and Aue disconcert and disarm their audience with their frank, even flagrant discourse about the genocidal crimes of the Nazi regime and their hard-boiled breakdown of the numbers of victims; they neither deny nor downplay the mind-boggling extent of the mass murder, nor are they reticent about the cruelty of its violence. Both narrators style themselves—in implicit contrast to the prevalent image of the Holocaust perpetrator as taciturn, dishonest, or resistant to accepting responsibility—as brutally candid and unconventionally aboveboard; in their willingness to mediate in unsparing detail the unparalleled extent and singular character of the crimes of the genocide and war of annihilation they were involved in waging, they thus lay claim to an openness and veracity about the crimes of the Holocaust that seem anomalous or even unprecedented in the history of perpetrator discourse. At the same time, however, Schulz and Aue also capitalize on their tone of candor in order to gloss over or even efface their own accountability for the violence. Their apparent frankness maintains thereby an antithetical function, operating simultaneously as a means of acknowledgment and a strategy of evasion and equivocation.

Acts of Narrative Evasion

Edgar Hilsenrath's *The Nazi and the Barber* and Jonathan Littell's *The Kindly Ones* each depict the events of the Holocaust through the first-person narration of one its perpetrators, thereby granting the reader extended access to the consciousness and discourse of a character whose perspective, by virtue of his abhorrent actions, is conventionally regarded as ethically anathematic and epistemologically inscrutable. In their construction of the narrative voice of their singular protagonists—Max Schulz and Max Aue—the two novels, though far from interchangeable or homologous, are congruent in several respects (beyond the shared given name and military membership of their protagonists) to the extent that they invite comparison—or at least parallel reading. This is true of the texts' reception, their narrative and generic properties, and the construction of their central characters.

Although each text emerged at a different moment in the historical development of the discourse on the Holocaust (Hilsenrath's novel in the early 1970s, at the beginning of what Annette Wieviorka terms "the era of the witness" and the widespread social acknowledgment of the Holocaust, Littell's in the first decade of the twenty-first century, after a certain master narrative of the Holocaust had become a fundamental feature of mainstream Western popular culture), each novel became a media sensation in its day on account of its controversial decision to feature the perspective of a character who not only supports the Nazis' genocide of the European Jews but also actively commits murder as a part of the "Final Solution." Moreover, both texts were hailed in their respective eras as innovative and even transgressive depictions of the Holocaust, although Hilsenrath's text, after achieving notoriety in the 1970s (a phenomenon I will briefly discuss in a moment), largely disappeared from the transnational canon of Holocaust literature, only recently reemerging in scholarly discourse (and particularly in the wake of the appearance of Littell's text) following the "turn toward the figure of the perpetrator in recent historical fiction" (Crownshaw 75). Furthermore, Hilsenrath portrays Max Schulz's story through the genre of satire or "black comedy" (Fuchs 166), while Littell avoids Hilsenrath's satirical stance to produce, according to Jenni Adams, "what is for the most part a meticulously researched and historically realist text" ("Reading (as) Violence" 41) that distends, in LaCapra's words, into "traumatic realism or even hyperrealism" ("Historical and Literary Approaches" 72). However, despite their divergence with regard to their respective principal generic orientations, the two novels both contain elements of the picaresque (a genre that, with its "technique of narrative confession," has been "recycled in German literature as a means of representing Nazism" [Coquio

84]), the grotesque, and "the literature of excess and radical transgression" (LaCapra, "Historical and Literary Approaches" 72), including scenes of exaggerated violence, aberrant sexual encounters, and abject or mutilated bodies. In addition, both books feature the sustained first-person perspective (or, to use Martin von Koppenfels's term, "infamous first person" ["*Kommissbrot*" 929]) of shockingly violent perpetrators over profuse pages (Hilsenrath's novel totals in the original German to almost five hundred pages, while Littell's runs to almost double that), immersing the reader for an uncomfortably extended period in their protagonists' respective worlds and worldviews. In fact, the narrators of both texts develop a markedly and self-consciously constructed dialogical relationship with their readers, a strategy that, according to Stephanie Bird, "invit[es] complicity with their view" (168–69).

In terms of the qualities of the central characters themselves, while Max Schulz and Max Aue do not resemble each other with regard to either personality or social status (Schulz is portrayed as a simpleton from the lower middle class who serves during the war as a foot soldier in the SS,[3] while Aue is a former lawyer educated in classical and modern literature and an elite officer in the SD, the security and intelligence arm of the SS), they both witness, abet, and even participate in widespread violence and mass killings; they also each commit acts of individual homicide as well. Further, although Schulz and Aue experience the war and the genocide from different vantage points as a result of their status, they manifest roughly similar trajectories both as characters within the diegesis and as narrators of it. At the end of the war (and, in Schulz's case, its aftermath), both characters spend a not insignificant stretch of the narrative on the run, attempting to evade accountability for their crimes. In particular, because of their notorious status as members of the SS, both figures are compelled to flee the advancing Soviet army; additionally, Schulz takes inordinate measures to thwart postwar attempts to bring him to justice for his genocidal crimes, while Aue tries to elude apprehension for the intimate murders he commits. At the same time, as indicated by my analysis of the quotes that open this chapter, as narrators who depict their respective histories of perpetration

---

3 In an interview from 2008 with Volker Dittrich, Hilsenrath himself designated Schulz "a would-be intellectual" ("ein verhinderter Intellektueller," my translation).

"from a position of safety" (Bird 168) and from a temporal standpoint long after the war,[4] Schulz and Aue pursue strategies of evasion as well, whereby they seek—through their narrative authority and function—to elude accountability for their part in genocide even as they unabashedly chronicle that experience in uncommonly candid and graphic detail.

The following analysis of *The Nazi and the Barber* and *The Kindly Ones* will focus in particular on this latter phenomenon, namely, the ways in which autodiegetic narration—the mediation of the mind of the perpetrator through the first-person fictional perspective—enables a complex filtering process that both yields an innovative glimpse into the projected minds of men who commit unspeakable violence and at the same time manages that seemingly transparent view through buffering strategies. Hilsenrath's text pursues its approach to the construction of the consciousness of its perpetrator through a radical act of narrative evasion, whereby Max Schulz narrates much of his story through the assumed identity and perspective of one of his victims. Littell's text, on the other hand, posits a triad of mutually incommensurate discourses that mitigate the reliability of the historical eyewitness Max Aue claims to be; in this way, Max engages in a form of narrative flight as well. Through their respective filtering strategies, the two novels thus alternately compel and foreclose the reader's investment in the narrator's account, allowing her both to identify and to repudiate each perpetrator's understanding of his violent past.

"I, Itzig Finkelstein, Alias the Mass Murderer Max Schulz or Vice Versa"

Jonathan Littell's *The Kindly Ones* has been dubbed "the first important work of fiction to narrate the Holocaust from the perpetrators' perspective" (von Koppenfels, "The Infamous 'I'" 133). However, fully twenty-five years before its appearance in 2006, Edgar Hilsenrath published *The Nazi and the*

---

[4] Nathan Bracher terms this narrative dynamic, whereby the former perpetrator reviews his past from a temporal position years after the war, "a sort of 'double helix' arrangement," in which the "narrative of one set of traumatic events of the World War II past is closely and interactively woven with the story of the author/narrator's own very personal quest to uncover the truth about that past and decipher its meaning for the present" (6). One of his examples for this concept is Littell's text.

Barber, a dazzling satirical novel narrated by Max Schulz, a former member of the SS who confesses to the reader the genocidal murder he committed during the Second World War. Hilsenrath (1926–2018), a German-Jewish survivor of the Holocaust who was interned in the Moghilov-Podolsk ghetto in the Transnistria from 1941 to 1944, completed his extraordinary novel in German in 1968. Unable to find a German publisher for his novel because of what I have termed the "narrative transgression" of its firstperson depiction of a Holocaust perpetrator ("Narrative Transgression" 233–35) and its employment of black humor, the grotesque, and the abject,[5] Hilsenrath published the text first in English translation in 1971; it sold over a million copies within five years and enjoyed a "resounding echo" in the American press.[6] In 1977, after being rejected by over sixty German publishing houses,[7] the novel finally appeared in the original German as *Der Nazi und der Friseur* (Braun 46). Initially causing with its irreverent

---

5   Fritz Rumler calls it "a bloody picaresque, grotesque, bizarre and at times brutally laconic" ("Ein blutiger Schelmenroman, grotesk, bizarre und zuweilen von grausamer Lakonik," 69, my translation).

6   "ein breites Echo" (Braun 44, my translation). For analysis of the elements of satire, black comedy, and the grotesque in *The Nazi and the Barber*, see Hans Otto Horch, Jens Birkmeyer, Astrid Klocke, Jennifer Bjornstad, Stephanie Bird, and Georg-Michael Schulz. Rupert Kalkofen and Bernhard Malkmus consider the properties of the picaresque in the novel, while Anne Fuchs addresses the function of abjection, particularly with regard to gender. Hilsenrath further appropriates and subverts the German genres of the Bildungsroman and the fairy tale, aspects addressed by Jennifer Taylor and Peter Arnds.

7   Helmut Braun, the original German publisher of *Der Nazi und der Friseur*, gives an excellent overview of its convoluted publication history in German, which he attributes generally to the calcified public discourse about the Holocaust in West Germany in the 1960s and early 1970s and more specifically to a rigid and reflexive philosemitism on the part of the German publishing industry. According to Braun, "[The German publishing scene] was in agreement that a working-through of the Shoah in the form of a bitterly angry, pitchblack satire—and exclusively from the perpetrator's perspective at that—was completely inappropriate and therefore forbidden. To put it in a nutshell: 'the bookmakers' sitting in the publishing houses reserved the right to dictate to the survivor how the Shoah should be represented literarily and to determine where the limits for such a representation would lie" ("so war man sich nun einig, daß eine Aufarbeitung der Shoah in Form einer bitterbösen, pechschwarzen Satire—noch dazu ausschließlich aus der Täterperspektive geschrieben—völlig unangemessen und deshalb unzulässig sei. Auf den Punkt gebracht: Die in Verlagen sitzenden 'Büchermacher' beanspruchten, dem Opfer vorzuschreiben, wie die Shoah literarisch darzustellen sei, beziehungsweise festzulegen, wo die Grenzen für eine solche Darstellung lägen," 46–47, my translation). Patricia

narrative style and its taboo-breaking depiction of the consciousness of a Holocaust perpetrator a small scandal in a West German society that preferred not to peer too closely into the psyche of former Nazi criminals, Hilsenrath's novel has since achieved limited recognition as one of the most original works of German literature about the Holocaust and one that, on account of its shocking narrative perspective and its grotesque and even pornographic content, is of particular challenge to readers. At the same time, however, in the media sensation that followed the publication of *The Kindly Ones*, Hilsenrath's achievement was almost completely forgotten, even in the German-language reception of Littell's novel. Because the road to publication and critical recognition of *The Nazi and the Barber* (particularly in Germany) was so long and circuitous, and because Hilsenrath, despite having published ten acclaimed novels in German, is still seen as somewhat of an outsider to the canon of German contemporary literature (which regards him at best as a "German-Jewish" author but certainly not as a mainstream "German" one), it is disheartening that precisely *German* scholars and critics such as von Koppenfels and Iris Radisch are so eager to claim unprecedented status for Littell's adoption of the first-person perspective in *The Kindly Ones* and neglect to acknowledge Hilsenrath's innovative and masterly use of the same technique.[8] When Littell's novel

---

Vahsen gives an exhaustive account of the novel's difficult publication and reception history in her 2008 monograph.

8 Radisch writes, "But the Jewish author Jonathan Littell has done what no one has dared to do in earnest.... He does not describe the Nazi perpetrator—that's been done by many—he explores what perpetration feels like from the inside. The detailed report of the decades-past war experiences of the SS man Dr. Max Aue, who fled to France, fills a gap in the media that strangely no one had noticed" ("Doch der jüdische Autor Jonathan Littell hat getan, was in der Tat noch niemand gewagt hat. . . . Er beschreibt den NS-Täter nicht—das haben schon viele getan—, er erkundet, wie sich Täterschaft von innen anfühlt. Der detaillierte Bericht des nach Frankreich geflohenen SS-Mannes Dr. Max Aue über seine Jahrzehnte zurückliegenden Kriegserlebnisse füllt eine publizistische Lücke, die merkwürdigerweise noch niemandem aufgefallen war," my translation). During the uproar over Littell's novel, Jan Süselbeck was one of the few critics to call attention to Hilsenrath's novel: "Radisch and her ilk in fact believe that Littell attempts to conceal his literary inability with a breach of taboo, a hitherto unprecedented 'provocation.' But if criticism always means comparison, then one will have to point to a fact that up to now very few have recalled in the general excitement: There is a complex history of Holocaust literature. . . . Littell has predecessors and role models. If literary criticism claims that [Littell] had crossed a 'red line' with his decision to take on the

appeared in German translation in 2008, Hilsenrath was put in the position of having to once again fight for recognition of his book. In an interview with Volker Dittrich, he states,

> The publicity for [Littell's] book has been unbelievable. And it's been claimed again and again that it's the first account written from the perspective of an executioner. That's not quite true. My novel *Der Nazi und der Friseur* was published in America back in 1971 and then in the 1970s in England, France and Italy and in 1977 in Germany. In *Der Nazi und der Friseur*, I described the mass extermination from the point of view of a perpetrator.[9]

At the same time that he consciously links his own earlier novel to Littell's book, however, Hilsenrath rejects comparisons between the two texts, arguing that, besides the first-person perspective, they share little in common; *The Kindly Ones*, in his view, is a "thoroughly realistic novel," while *The Nazi and the Barber*, on the other hand, is "a literary grotesque."[10]

---

perspective of an SS mass murderer . . . then that is nonsense. Edgar Hilsenrath dealt with the subject with his work *The Nazi & the Barber* already in the 1970s on a world literary level—in a way even more radical than Littell, because he dared to write about the Shoah in the form of a satire" ("Zwar meinten Radisch & Co., Littell versuche, seine literarische Unfähigkeit mit einem Tabubruch, einer bisher noch nicht dagewesenen 'Provokation' zu kaschieren. Doch wenn Kritisieren immer auch Vergleichen heißt, dann wird man auf eine Tatsache hinweisen müssen, an die bisher in der allgemeinen Aufregung nur ganz wenige erinnert haben: Es gibt eine komplexe Shoah-Literaturgeschichte. . . . Littell hat Vorgänger und Vorbilder. Wenn die Literaturkritik behauptet, [Littell] habe mit der Entscheidung, die Perspektive eines SS-Massenmörders einzunehmen, eine 'rote Linie' überschritten . . . dann ist das Unsinn. Edgar Hilsenrath erledigte das Thema mit seinem Werk *Der Nazi & der Friseur* bereits in den 1970er-Jahren auf weltliterarischem Niveau—in gewisser Weise sogar radikaler als Littell, da er es wagte, über die Shoah in der Form einer Satire zu schreiben," my translation).

9 "Das Buch is unglaublich lanciert worden. Und es wird ja immer wieder behauptet, dass es der erste Bericht aus der Perspektive eines Henkers ist. Das stimmt so nicht. Mein Roman *Der Nazi & der Friseur* ist ja schon 1971 in Amerika veröffentlicht worden und dann in den siebziger Jahren in England, Frankreich, Italien und 1977 auch in Deutschland. In *Der Nazi & der Friseur* habe ich die Massenvernichtungen aus der Sicht eines Täters beschrieben" (Dittrich, my translation).

10 "einen ganz realistischen Roman"; "eine literarische Groteske" (Dittrich, my translation).

Hilsenrath's descriptor "grotesque" pertains in particular to the novel's autodiegetic narrator, Max Schulz, and to his discourse, which is by turns impudent, scurrilous, implausible, and outlandish, qualities that inhere in the very first sentences of the text. Schulz begins his autobiographical account in *The Nazi and the Barber* with a preposterous description of his birth in 1907 in the town of Wieshalle, East Prussia:

> I am Max Schulz, illegitimate though purely Aryan son of Minna Schulz ... who at the time of my birth was a maid in the house of the Jewish fur dealer Abramowitz. There can be no doubt of my pure Aryan origin, since the family tree of my mother, Minna Schulz, while it does not go back to the Battle of Teutoburger Forest, nevertheless has roots which reach back to Frederick the Great. Who my father was I cannot tell you with any certainty, but he must definitely have been one of five men: the butcher, Hubert Nagler; the locksmith, Franz Heinrich Wieland; the builder's mate, Hans Huber; the coachman, Wilhelm Hopfenstange; or the butler, Adolf Hennemann.
>
> I have had the family trees of my five fathers carefully looked into and I can assure you, the Aryan origin of all five can be certified beyond doubt. (7–8)

With this singular opening passage, Hilsenrath establishes Schulz's voice in the novel as a picaresque combination of the hyperbolic and the banal, the confessional and the implausible.[11] This particular narratorial configuration draws the reader into Schulz's idiosyncratic perspective and at the same time alerts her to his likely unreliability, an issue that Schulz himself addresses head-on when he senses the reader's incredulity

---

11 Fuchs argues that "the entire novel is conceived as a first-person narrative and confessional in the tradition of Jean Jacques Rousseau's *Confessions*. But whereas Rousseau's autobiography and the ensuing literary tradition articulate the genesis of an innocent and authentic subjectivity which is constituted through the act of writing, Hilsenrath's satirical novel undermines such an idealistic conception" (170). In this, the novel uncannily resembles the confessional performances about which Leigh A. Payne writes (and which I discuss in chapter 2).

regarding his authoritative descriptions of his life as an infant: "This is probably the place where you will ask yourself how it is that I know all this so exactly, but with the best will in the world I can't tell you" (13). As this quote demonstrates, Schulz is not remotely interested in giving the reader evidence for his implausible stories. In fact, he pokes fun here at the reader's expectation that he will do so, flaunting his control of the narrative and his command of the reader's attention. According to Jennifer Bjornstad, "Max is fully aware of the power that is invested in him as narrator through poetic license, an inherent monopoly on perspective, and the sole ability to speak, and he is not afraid to exploit this power thoroughly" (54); he thus functions as "the conduit through which all information is conveyed" (60). While these aspects, of course, apply to the function of autodiegetic narrators more generally, in this specific case, Schulz makes his reader aware of the ways in which he capitalizes on and even takes advantage of the authority vested in him as narrator. Through his unreliability, he regulates the frameworks through which his reader is to receive his narrative.

As demonstrated by his address to a "you" in the second paragraph, Schulz further fashions his narration in part as a dialogue with an implied reader, whom he sets up to reflect back to him a discordant and unreliable image of his function as narrator. Twitchell argues that Schulz's overt gesture toward dialogism, whereby "he feigns engaging in a dialogue with his audience" (75), functions as an additional stratagem, whereby he "assert[s] (or reassert[s]) monologic control over the narration" (75) and thus works both to conceal and to consolidate his narrative dominance.[12] An example of Schulz's manipulative employment of the dialogical mode occurs after he narrates an episode that supposedly took place shortly after his birth, when his mother, having witnessed the ritual circumcision of the infant son of the town's Jewish barber (who was born two minutes after Max Schulz), tries to castrate her own son. At this point, the narrator exclaims:

---

12 Twitchell's insightful analysis of Schulz's narration builds its argument in part in reference to my 2007 article on the novel and to an earlier and shorter version of this chapter that I published in 2014. My citation of Twitchell's work here thus constitutes part of an ongoing, recursive, and intellectually invigorating dialogue between the two of us about Hilsenrath's book.

> You're probably thinking I'm pulling your leg? Or perhaps that's not what you think, maybe you're just saying to yourself: Max Schulz has a screw loose! He's got a mania that somebody wanted to kill him ... because he was a bastard ... and all done under the disguise of a circumcision, executed, as is the custom among Jews, on the eighth day after birth. What is Max Schulz up to? What's he trying to say to me? Who is he trying to blame? His mother? The Jews? Or God? (14–15)

Not only does Schulz figure himself in this passage as the original victim of violence, a claim that conflicts to some extent with his self-identification just a few pages earlier as a "mass-murderer" (11), but he also models to the reader how she should consume his text: with skepticism as to its veracity and with an awareness of his psychological and narratorial instability. Andreas Graf has written insightfully about the "pathology of the narrative perspective" in *The Nazi and the Barber*;[13] however, this narrative disease is not just an external critical diagnosis of Hilsenrath's text but also a condition of which Schulz himself is aware. Moreover, as evident in the quote above, in which he indicates his own propensity toward "mania" or fantasy, Schulz himself proposes the notion of pathological narration as the appropriate interpretive framework for understanding his story. Beginning with the first sentences of the novel, I argue, Schulz self-consciously and with surprising adeptness constructs his own elaborate narrative pathology in the form of a markedly self-conscious unreliability that runs the full gamut of James Phelan's taxonomy of unreliable narration, which I introduced in the introduction to part 2, ranging from underreporting and misreporting, which have to do with Schulz's faulty record of the facts (particularly pertaining to—returning to my opening reading—the number of victims he claims to have personally murdered); to underreading and misreading, which concern the reliability of his perception; to underregarding and misregarding, which relate to his questionable ethical interpretation. Furthermore, key features of Schulz's diseased narrative include his deliberate manipulation of narrative perspective and his employment of a strategy

---

13 "Pathologie der Erzählperspektive" (Graf, my translation).

of obscuration, both of which allow him to withhold from the reader his relationship to and motivations for his crimes.

In the first of the novel's six books, Schulz describes his childhood and youth in Wieshalle, focusing in particular on the horrific physical and sexual abuse he experiences at the hands of his stepfather, Anton Slavitzki, and his intense friendship with Itzig Finkelstein, the son of the Jewish barber, Chaim Finkelstein. Chaim accepts Schulz as an affiliated member of the Finkelstein family, teaches him Yiddish and Jewish customs, and eventually takes him on, along with Itzig, as an apprentice barber. Itzig and Max are inseparable throughout their time in school—where Itzig, a superior student, helps Max, who has a "hole in his head" and a "bastard brain" (34),[14] complete his coursework—and their apprenticeship; the lives of the two boys are, as Jonathan Schorsch argues, "intertwined in semi-mythical fashion" (144).[15] However, in the early 1930s, Schulz, a young man at this point, converts to Nazism after attending a speech by Hitler (an event that Hilsenrath satirically locates on the "Mount of Olives" [in the original German, "Ölberg"] outside of Wieshalle) and joins the SS. We then learn in the novel's second book, which takes place after the war, of Schulz's service during the war, first in the Einsatzgruppe and then in Laubwalde. At that "extermination camp without gas chambers,"[16] Schulz claims to have personally killed (as he tells us at the very end of the novel) as many as ten thousand Jewish prisoners (388), a grotesque assertion that is but one example of Max's exaggerated mode of narration. In the third book, Schulz,

---

14 Twitchell develops an excellent analysis of the motifs of Schulz's "hole in the head" and his "loose screw" (*The Nazi and the Barber* 27), which he connects to Schulz's abuse by his stepfather when he was an infant: "Slavitzki's gargantuan penis struck the baby's developing brain from the inside during the act of anal rape, and as a result the boy Max has a 'Dachschaden,' i.e. a hole in his roof, i.e. in his head. Max's injury is the literal manifestation of a figure of speech— a joke in itself. The 'Dachschaden' also operates synecdochally here, representing the physical, mental and emotional damage that Max has incurred" (87).

15 Stephan Braese reads the symbiotic relationship between Max and Itzig, along with its destruction by virtue of the former's murder of the latter, as a "satirical frontal assault" ("satirische[r] Frontalangriff," 430, my translation) on the institutionalized discourse of philosemitism in postwar Germany and its fantasy of an erstwhile "German-Jewish symbiosis."

16 "Das Vernichtungslager ohne Gaskammer" (*Der Nazi und der Friseur* 122, my translation). The 1971 English translation of Hilsenrath's novel by Andrew White, which is in general quite good, curiously omits the short section in which Max claims that Laubwalde did not have gas chambers.

on the run as a wanted mass murderer, has himself circumcised and tattooed with an Auschwitz number and then appropriates the identity of Itzig Finkelstein, who, as Schulz quasi confesses at the end of *The Nazi and the Barber*,[17] was murdered in Laubwalde by none other than his childhood friend Max. In the last half of Hilsenrath's novel, Schulz travels as Itzig, under Itzig's name, and in Itzig's place to Palestine (a trip financed by a sack of gold teeth looted from his victims in Laubwalde), where he helps found the Jewish state, becomes a model Israeli citizen, marries a Holocaust survivor, and composes—even if only mentally—his confessional autobiography: the very text, in fact, that we have been reading all along.

By murdering Itzig, assuming Itzig's identity, and living out the life that he brutally robbed of Itzig, Schulz commits a particularly vituperative act of identity theft, a brutal expropriation of the life of one individual that functions as a synecdoche for both his massacre of multiple victims and the Nazis' project of destroying and effacing from memory millions of European Jews; "in this way," asserts Sebastian Meixner, "the murderer posthumously dispossesses the victim of the Shoah of his identity."[18] Further, as Rupert Kalkofen argues, picking up on the mathematical metaphor with which I began this chapter, by positioning the reader as a witness to Schulz's outrageous transformation, the novel implicates its audience in this process:

> When the I-narrator "changes sides" after a little more than a third of the novel, the readers land purely arithmetically rather on the right side again. But this double negation does not nullify itself; rather, it involves the readers in an offense in which the murderer of thousands of Jews, evading both detection and punishment, helps establish the Jewish state and develops a Jewish-Israeli identity. The function of this change of sides, which not only is performed by the

---

17 Schulz's "confession," which he delivers as an old man in Israel to his friend, the former German judge Wolfgang Richter, is not so much an acknowledgment of culpability as a bare statement of truth, albeit a convoluted, mediated, and disguised one. He performs this rhetorical act not as Max Schulz but from his assumed identity as Itzig Finkelstein, who tells the story of Max's murder of Itzig as a sort of imagined hypothetical (*The Nazi and the Barber* 374).
18 "Auf diese Art und Weise raubt der Mörder dem Opfer der Shoah posthum seine Identität" (Meixner 255, my translation).

protagonist but also must be suffered by the readers, is one of the most decisive moments in the comprehension of the novel.[19]

Schulz's violations not only consist of the crimes he commits in the story-world of the text but also include transgressions he commits as a narrator. As I have previously argued,

> Critics have labeled Hilsenrath's novel an anti-*Bildungsroman*, the inversion of the classical novel of development. Like the hero of the *Bildungsroman*, Max achieves something in the course of the novel. However, this achievement is not the development of a harmonious identity, but the radical rewriting of his own murderous history as the diametrically opposite tale of survival and heroism. Max's transgressions as a character are many—he murders thousands of European Jews; he evades all judicial accountability for his crimes; he inverts moral accountability by passing himself off as a victim; he identifies himself unproblematically as a Jew, announces his solidarity with other Jews and commits himself to Judaism and the creation of a Jewish state; and he steals the identity of his former best friend. As a narrator, however, his transgression is singular: it is the hubristic, radical assumption of the voice of the victim by the perpetrator. In this way, Max thumbs his nose at the project of autobiography (especially Holocaust autobiography) and its ostensible pact of authenticity with the reader. ("Narrative Transgression" 224)

---

[19] "Wenn der Ich-Erzähler nach etwas mehr als dem ersten Drittel des Romans seinen Seitenwechsel vornimmt, landen die Leser rein arithmetisch eigentlich wieder auf der richtigen Seite, doch hebt sich diese doppelte Negation nicht auf, sondern beteiligt die Leser vielmehr an dem Skandalon, dass ein tausendfacher Mörder von Juden unentdeckt und unbestraft den Judenstaat mit aufbaut und ein jüdisch-israelisches Selbstbewussstein entwickelt. Die Funktion des Seitenwechsels, den einerseits der Held und andererseits die Leser vollziehen müssen, ist eines der entscheidenden Momente für das Verständnis des Romans" (Kalkofen 49, my translation).

By inserting himself in the position of Itzig's I-narrator and by framing his history of murder in Itzig's voice, Schulz thus vacates the narrative position of the perpetrator and slips into that of the victim. Thereby he accrues both within the diegesis and—to a more limited extent—on the level of narration the advantages that attend the position of the blameless victim, not the least of which is the abdication of culpability; as Twitchell argues, "Max strives to force open an interstice between the categories of victim and perpetrator . . . for the purpose of deferring rhetorically the repercussions of accepting responsibility for his crimes" (69).

At the same time, however, Schulz's relocation of identity from his old perpetrator-self (Max) to an invented survivor-self (Itzig) is not a one-time, unidirectional process. Rather, the two selves exist in perpetual tension with each other; according to Kalkofen, "The I-narrator is both Max Schulz and Itzig Finkelstein, sometimes one, sometimes the other, and the two identities do not always exist in the same relationship to one another."[20] This ambiguous movement of identities not only occurs within the storyworld; it also—and more prominently—takes place within the narration itself. Schulz performs his act of identity theft repetitively and ritualistically throughout his narration, as evident in such frequent utterances as "I, Itzig Finkelstein, at that time still Max Schulz" (15), "I, Itzig Finkelstein, alias the mass murderer Max Schulz or vice versa" (310), and "I, Itzig Finkelstein or the mass-murderer Max Schulz" (362); with each iterative variant of this statement of cannibalized identity he performatively reproduces his original crime of murder, thus not only regenerating his crimes (and thereby, as Twitchell argues, "reanimat[ing] the dynamics of perpetration" [98]) but also leaving behind traces of it in his narration.

Moreover, not only does Schulz's identity go through a complex transformation over the course of the novel, but his relationship to his narration changes as well. While Schulz occupies the position of the autodiegetic narrator for the greater part of the novel, book 2, which is set in the immediate postwar period, before Schulz assumes Itzig's identity, is narrated by an anonymous heterodiegetic (third-person) narrator who

---

20 "Der Ich-Erzähler ist beides, Max Schulz und Itzig Finkelstein, mal der eine, mal der andere, und nicht immer stehen die beiden Identitäten im selben Verhältnis zueinander" (Kalkofen 50, my translation).

focalizes much of the action through the perspective of Frau Holle, the one-legged widow of one of Schulz's SS comrades. However, although this book gives us an external perspective of Schulz (we, like Frau Holle, experience him as a stranger who suddenly arrives on her doorstep), the bulk of the chapter features Schulz telling Frau Holle about his flight from the Red Army and Polish partisans at the end of the war. In this way, even when Max is patently absent as the diegetic narrator in this part of the novel, he is recuperated as an intradiegetic (interior) narrator and thus, in a more alienated fashion, still controls the text's narration. Further, as Jennifer Bjornstad argues,

> It makes the most sense to consider Book Two as a continuation of Max's narration, since the thematic and formal features of the narration are all the same as what one finds throughout the rest of the novel: mockery, grotesque comparisons, crass imagery, extensive ellipsis, stilted dialog, and simplified syntax. In any case, it serves the narrative purpose of filling in some of the details Max left out of Book One and moving the plot further, toward Max's crucial transformation into Itzig Finkelstein. (56)

While we as readers encounter in book 2 a narrator who is heterodiegetic and thus technically implicated in neither Schulz's physical flight nor his narrative evasion, we are also encouraged by the text's intricate embedding of Schulz's vocal authority and its reproduction of his idiosyncratic linguistic style to attribute this apparently unconnected narration to Schulz himself. Andreas Graf reads this complex aberration in the novel's vocal structure as part of its "pathology of narrative perspective," a description that likely draws on Gérard Genette's observations on the phenomenon of the abrupt (and unexplained) change in vocal perspective in otherwise mimetic or "natural" narrative, a dynamic that Genette claims results from "a narrative pathology" (246).[21] As Graf writes of book 2,

---

21 According to Genette, "An even more glaring violation is the shift in grammatical person to designate the same character ... such effects obviously result from a sort of narrative pathology, explicable by last-minute reshufflings and states of textual incompleteness" (*Narrative Discourse* 246).

The auctorial narrator of the second book is in all probability identical with the I-narrator of the other books. But his I, his self-confident manner of speaking, is temporarily missing. . . . By means of this detour [Max's narration to Frau Holle about his escape] the I-narration finds its way back into the text and thus significantly relativizes the auctorial diegesis, which is degraded to the status of narrative frame.²²

Graf argues convincingly that the narrative anomaly of book 2 represents a variant, however alienated, of Schulz's function as a pathological narrator. However, whereas Graf sees this aberrant narration as evidence of a gradual process in which Schulz is able to dissolve, by means of "a grotesque internally fictitious fiction,"²³ his two identities as perpetrator and survivor and forge a third, narratively constructed harmonious self, I contend that even on the narrative level, Schulz practices the same sort of evasion that he utilizes diegetically to circumvent punishment' for his crimes. As I see it, rather than creating a new, fictive self through what Graf calls the "therapeutic function of writing,"²⁴ Schulz manipulates until the end the text's ambiguous narrative perspective, jumping reflexively and repeatedly from one narrative position to the other without either fixing permanently on one of the two poles of identity or forging a third one.²⁵

---

22 "Allerdings ist der auktoriale Erzähler dieses zweiten Buches aller Wahrscheinlichkeit nach mit dem Ich-Erzähler der übrigen Bücher identisch. Doch sein Ich, die selbstbewußte Redeweise, ist im vorübergehend abhanden gekommen . . . auf diesem Umweg hält nun doch wieder die Ich-Erzählung Einzug in den Text und relativiert damit die auktoriale Haltung" (Graf 143, my translation).
23 "mit einer grotesken innerfiktiven Fiktion" (Graf 147, my translation).
24 "die therapeutische Funktion des Schreibens" (Graf 147, my translation).
25 "Seen in this light," writes Twitchell, "the second book provides additional contours to Max's pathological narration: he disguises himself on the diegetic level as Itzig Finkelstein and acts as ventriloquist on the extradiegetic level, masquerading as an unnamed third-person narrator who ostensibly does not participate in the events of the story world" (96). Twitchell further connects the idea of Schulz's narrative pathology to his "hole in the head" and his "loose screw": "Taking Graf's and McGlothlin's taxonomy of pathology and disease as a point of departure, I propose the further expansion of the bio-medical metaphor to discuss Max's narration as an 'injured' one" (88). In Twitchell's view, "Max wants us to believe . . . that his loose screw is a reason for his becoming a perpetrator later in life. It is important to note that he does not explicitly make

In book 4, which chronicles Max/Itzig's journey by sea from Europe to Palestine, Schulz displays his slippery vocal identity as well, alternating between the first-person singular and first-person plural and a second-person address to Itzig. However, the referent of the "you" of the address is ambiguous; at times "you" designates Schulz's former friend and his murder victim, with whom Schulz conducts an imagined, one-sided dialogue:[26]

> Dear Itzig. This is not a letter. Or: These are not letters. I am not even writing in my diary. I am not even writing at all. I am just thinking. Or I think I am thinking. I am imagining I am writing to you. To whom? To you! The dead man!
> Itzig! Come! Talk to me! Or let me talk. Listen. That's how it is. That's how it must be and can't be otherwise. Come with me to Jerusalem, let me take you with me. (208)

In such cases, as Twitchell argues, Schulz's "monologue resembles, at least structurally, an extradiegetic dialogue between two speaking partners," one that can, however, only "mimic, but not constitute, dialogue between two

---

this claim; instead, he employs rhetorical strategies available to him as narrator so that we might arrive at this conclusion through the process of reading" (89). Thus, "Max's injured narration allows him to perform the role of mentally unstable criminal in the diegesis and psychologically disturbed narrator in the extradiegesis—even if the narrating-I is, as I suspect, not in fact 'crazy' and is in fact extremely clever and conscious of the rhetorical strategies he deploys for evading guilt and responsibility" (93).

26 Twitchell maintains that Max's address to Itzig in this book constitutes a kind of narrative metalepsis: "Max reconfigures the character of Itzig Finkelstein from the novel's fabula and situates him in the role of narratee. Disregarding the (ostensible) distinction between the realm of the narrator and that of the story world and the fact that Itzig is dead, Max reorders the narrative's ontology. Max plucks the character of Itzig—or at least the memory of him—out of the story world that is under Max's narratorial control and reshapes him into a passive listener" (100). Following Twitchell's argument, one might propose that Hilsenrath threatens here to transgress the limits of his mimetic narrative and to push his novel into the realm of the "unnatural" or antimimetic narrative, which, according to Jan Alber, "violates physical laws, logical principles, or standard anthropomorphic limitations of knowledge by representing storytelling scenarios, narrators, characters, temporalities, or spaces that could not exist in the actual world" ("Unnatural Narrative"). I will address the question of unnatural narrative with regard to fictional representations of the mind of the Holocaust perpetrator in the next chapter.

discrete subjective entities" (103). Twitchell therefore proposes the designation "monologic dialogue" (103) to designate these moments. At other times, the "you" to whom the narrator speaks is his own newly forged Itzig-self: "If Itzig Finkelstein were mad . . . who would be the one to talk nonsense then? Me or you? Be careful, Itzig! Don't quarrel with me! We have to get on well with each other! The two of us! You and I!" (245). The referent of the second-person address in this book it thus doubled, designating not only Schulz's imaginary discourse with a deceased narratee who is clearly a separate character but also the dialogue the protagonist conducts with himself, a narrative situation that further complicates the novel's already extremely complex narrative structure and framework of identity. Added to this Byzantine vocal structure is the fact that, in those instances in which Schulz's second-person address is formulated as a self-dialogue (and not to the deceased Itzig as an imaginary interlocutor), the "you" to which it is directed is not his Max-self but rather his newly figured Itzig-self—the self that is produced by his cannibalization of an Other and that seems to reside uncomfortably beside or within his Max-self. In this way, although Schulz has incorporated Itzig's identity into his own, at the same time, on the level of pronominal reference and in the act of narration, Itzig and Max remain radically unintegrated, a condition made all the more evident by Schulz's disingenuous second-person address to the deceased Itzig, whose identity he has hijacked. Hilsenrath's text thus demonstrates a particularly pathological and almost literal version of Bakhtin's notion of double-voiced discourse (Bakhtin 324), whereby Schulz not only claims two speaking selves, one that has devoured the identity of the other, but also, with his second-person narration, reproduces this cannibalization with his address to himself.

Given the already established vocal promiscuity of *The Nazi and the Barber*, it should perhaps not be surprising to us that Schulz should avail himself of the expanded possibilities for evasion provided by second-person narration, which, according to Brian Richardson, "is an artificial mode that does not normally occur in natural narrative" (*Unnatural Voices* 19). Second-person narrative, as Richardson argues, "is admirably suited to express the unstable nature and intersubjective constitution of the self" (36) and in particular is adept at "revealing a mind in flux," "disclosing the sense of intimate unfamiliarity present" in an addled brain, and indicating "suppressed subjectivity and silenced speech" (35–36). By virtue of its highly constructed, artificial, and mutable mode and because, as Richardson writes, "its very essence is to eschew a fixed essence" (19), second-person narration seems tailor-made for Schulz, a narrator who is nothing if not polymorphic and synthetic. The "you" of his narration in book 4 is as unstable and protean as the "I" in the rest of the novel.

In my analysis of *The Nazi and the Barber*, the narrative situation thus functions as an analogue to the novel's plot, reproducing on the text's narrative level the interminable processes of equivocal transmutation and escape that Schulz undergoes as a character, which, according to Twitchell, manifest "physically and psychologically" (69).[27] In the end, Schulz's "I" is a non-locatable entity, a narrative voice in flight, like the perpetrator himself, from a perspective that would unequivocally pin the self to its murderous autobiography. As Twitchell contends,

> While Max's manipulation of narration and performance of multiple identities are certainly not tantamount to the original crime of murder, his self-contradicting narratorial habit of switching between opposing subject positions for the purpose of evading guilt reinforces for the reader his status as mass murderer and war criminal, thus reaffirming his identity as perpetrator. (70)

On account of Schulz's frequent and frenetic ping-ponging between vocal positions throughout the novel—a phenomenon Twitchell terms his "narrative tic" (71)—the pathological "I" in Hilsenrath's text is, narratively speaking, a moving target, and as such, it functions as a filtering barrier to his consciousness, distorting with its perpetual motion the narrative interface between Schulz's mind and the reader who wishes to understand his autobiographical construction of his violent history. Rather than compelling the reader's identification with the perpetrator's motives, mindset,

---

27 "Max demonstrates over the course of the novel a tendency toward flight, both physically and psychologically. He flees the permanence of and culpability involved with self-identification as a perpetrator by cycling back and forth between identities and subject positions, a tactic that assists him in claiming at various points in the novel status as both Holocaust perpetrator and Holocaust survivor" (Twitchell 68–69).

and worldview, *The Nazi and the Barber* deploys the filtering strategy of Schulz's non-locatable "I" to impede the reader's affective attachment to its perpetrator-protagonist. After all, in Hilsenrath's text, there is nary a narrator with whom the reader can identify; Schulz makes sure that, narratively speaking, there's no "there" there. In this way, with its heterogenous narrative strategy that exploits the ambiguities of vocal perspective and focalization, Hilsenrath's text self-consciously highlights both its construction of this filter and Schulz's hubristic assumption of the voice of the victim to narrate his own history of violence as a perpetrator.

"Directed at the Darkness"

The Kindly Ones famously commences with an address by its autodiegetic narrator to his audience:

> Oh my human brothers, let me tell you how it happened. I am not your brother, you'll retort, and I don't want to know. And it certainly is true that this is a bleak story, but an edifying one too, a real morality play, I assure you. You might find it a bit long—a lot of things happened, after all—but perhaps you're not in too much of a hurry; with a little luck you'll have some time to spare. And also, this concerns you: you'll see that this concerns you. (3)

With this singular opening, the novel's narrator, the former SS officer Maximilien Aue, makes a particular appeal to his readers. He asks us to admit him into the circle of human communication and to listen to the story of "how it happened," namely, how he evolved into a willing perpetrator of both the genocide of Europe's Jews and the homicide of individuals. Although he anticipates he will be met by a hostile response, Aue calls upon us to recognize his essential humanness and to identify with him as a confrere despite the monstrous story he will tell of his history of murderous violence. As he exclaims at the end of the "Toccata," "But I don't think I'm a devil. There were always reasons for what I did. Good reasons or bad reasons, I don't know, in any case human reasons. Those who kill are humans, just like those who are killed, that's what's terrible. . . . I am a man like other men, I am a man like you. I tell you I am just like you!" (24). By beginning his extremely lengthy and detailed account with this direct address to the reader, Aue attempts to accomplish three aims. First, he asserts his essential humanness and vigorously disputes those who would label him a "devil," a characterization that reflects widespread postwar public opinion about Holocaust perpetrators as monsters. Second, as Adams argues, he "insists upon the commonality of his own experience with the potential experience of the reader" ("Reading (as) Violence" 33), a rhetorical gesture that, according to Debarati Sanyal, summons the reader "into complicity in multiple senses of the word, as a partner in crime, but also as an intimate whose involvement will lead to understanding" (191). Third, he asks his readers to enter his mind and view the events of the Holocaust from his perspective in spite of our repugnance for his actions and our reluctance "to know." In short, Aue asks us to identify with him and to consider his "inner life" (23), an imaginative cohabitation of narrative perspective that he acknowledges is unprecedented and transgressive but that he claims is essential for understanding his crimes. He further compels us, as Hanna Meretoja describes it, "to live through the temporal process" in which he transforms into a genocidal killer (221). Sanyal (191), Meretoja (228), and Petra Rau (104) each view Aue's opening appeal as part of a "contract" that the narrator presents to his readers, whereby he promises to recount through an overtly confessional mode his criminal past in exchange for our recognition of the contingencies of his involvement in eliminationist warfare and genocide and our concomitant acknowledgment "that everyone, or nearly everyone, in a given set of circumstances, does what he is told to do" (20). Aue thus predicates his willingness to give a forthright account of his past on a mutually recognized homology and the potential for moral equivalence between narrator and audience: "But always keep this thought in mind: you might be luckier than I, but you're not a better person" (20).

Aue does not overtly signal in his opening address the kind of unreliability that Schulz flaunts at the beginning of his account. However, he endeavors in ways similar to Schulz—namely, through his insistence on his audience's assumption of what Meretoja calls the "uncomfortable position . . . of an implicated subject" (231) that would place it alongside him on the same continuum of potential culpability—to steer his readers toward particular frameworks for understanding it, thereby working through his own discursive power to manage their reception of his narration. Moreover, like Schulz, who gestures toward a dialogical mode but whose discourse is fundamentally circular, self-serving, and self-confirmatory (thus constituting what Twitchell terms a "monologic dialogue" [103]), Aue offers here an appeal that evinces what Rau calls a "mock-dialogical structure" (103), in that it announces a mode of interaction with the reader that it does not in fact actualize. Catherine Coquio reads Aue's address as a "fake plea to the other" (76) that "silenc[es] the reader by turning him or her into a spectator" (85). As she points out, Aue's address to and acknowledgment of the reader quickly disappear after "Toccata," resurfacing only briefly a couple of times as "another bad joke" (87). By "suspending a barely initiated dialogue," Aue thus "establishes the authority he wishes to hold over the reader" (85). Although he purports from the beginning to be committed to his announced objective to discharge his confession—a performative mode that, as I explained in my discussion of Franz Stangl's confession in chapter 2, requires a dialogical relationship with another who takes on the role of confessor—he erects a narrative pretense that at the same time allows him to circumvent the process of confession.

With its construction of what Sanyal terms "the beguiling intimacy of Aue's voice" (192), which Aurélie Barjonet and Liran Razinsky call "perhaps the most disturbing as well as the most innovative aspect of this novel" (9), *The Kindly Ones* has been credited with providing the most detailed and direct fictional representation of the mind of the Holocaust perpetrator to date.[28] Indeed, Littell's novel has become, in Ned Curthoys's words, "a *locus classicus* in perpetrator oriented fiction" (462) and, according to Robert Eaglestone, "has gone on to generate an academic mini-industry" (*The Broken Voice* 55). When it appeared in 2006, *The Kindly Ones* was awarded both France's Prix Goncourt and the prize of the Académie Française, but reception of the work has been mixed. Critics in France, Germany, the United States, and England have both praised and criticized the novel for being the first "real" attempt at an intimate representation of the perpetrator's mind, thereby ignoring a number of earlier texts that accomplish the same thing, including Hilsenrath's novel and Martin Amis's *Time's Arrow*,

---

28 Von Koppenfels writes, "The infamous first person provides the key to Littell's novel, the provocations of which mostly arise from perspective" ("*Kommissbrot*" 930).

the latter of which appeared fifteen years prior to great acclaim. Such claims that the novel provides an innovative and even unprecedented depiction of the psyche of the Holocaust perpetrator have been prompted not only by Littell's mostly "realist, immersive" (Meretoja 227) and mimetic approach but also by the apparent absence of a filtering device, such as Hilsenrath's satirical portrayal of the Holocaust through the voice of a radically dissociated I-narrator or Amis's inverted temporality (a phenomenon I will investigate in the next chapter). At the same time, however, in addition to its predominantly realist framework, *The Kindly Ones* also employs narrative strategies that urge "readings that diverge from straightforwardly realist ones" (Meretoja 227) and that operate as filtering mechanisms to mitigate the semblant transparency of its protagonist's mind via his narration. Chief among these is the novel's prohibitive length, which, with its sheer mass of repetitive detail and extended discourse, numbs the reader and paradoxically serves at times to screen the narrator's consciousness.[29] As Roberto Bui (writing under the pseudonym Wu Ming)[30] writes, picking up on Klaus Theweleit's praising assessment of the novel, "To read *The Kindly Ones* is to become the stunned witness of an *overflow*: drop after drop, trickle by trickle, the river gets swollen with data, anecdotes, memories, dreams and citations—the water rises on the sides until it *breaks out.*" The novel also contains a number of competing discourses, "intertextual emplotments" (Grethlein 573), and "non-conventional narrative elements" (Iversen 153), including techniques generally recognized as antimimetic or unnatural

---

29 A number of critics have referred to the excessive length of the novel as one of its chief deficiencies. Hilsenrath, for example, complains to Dittrich, "Much of it is tedious. On account of its length it was no pleasure to read" ("Vieles ist ermüdend. Es war schon wegen der Länge kein Vergnügen, es zu lesen," my translation). The book self-reflexively nods toward this issue when, late in the novel, Aue (in one of his few addresses to the reader) states, "You must be thinking: Ah, finally this story is over. But no, it still goes on" (913). Jenni Adams insightfully suggests that the novel exhibits "what might be termed a *realism of exhaustion*, carrying the realist project (in its accumulatory and archival dimensions) to an extreme which serves to problematize precisely these aspects of its practice, as well as their place in the compromised epistemological and representational project of modernity" ("Relationships to Realism in Post-Holocaust Fiction" 84–85).
30 Wu Ming is a group of Italian writers, each of whom writes under the pseudonym "Wu Ming" plus a number. Bui is known as Wu Ming 1 (http://www.wumingfoundation.com/english/biography.html).

(in the narratological sense), all of which not only rival with each other for the reader's attention but also to a certain extent contradict each other (thus calling into question the narrator's reliability and truth claims as a whole) and complicate its otherwise overarching realist, mimetic design. The friction between these discourses and narrative conventions, as Meretoja argues, has effected a similar divide in the novel's reception, whereby it "has mostly been read either 'mimetically,' as a representation of the Second World War that lends itself to a comparison with what we know about it from historical research, or 'anti-mimetically,' stressing its nature as an imaginative discourse and an aesthetic artifact" (218). Meretoja contends that the resistance of *The Kindly Ones* to precisely such unequivocal classification represents both its aesthetic challenge and its strength:

> Given the ways in which the novel underlines its own status as imaginative discourse—particularly through its abundant intertextuality and mythical framing—it clearly invites readings that diverge from straightforwardly realist ones. These elements introduce a self-reflexive level to the novel, one that works against its realist, immersive level. In my view, the mimetic/historical versus anti-mimetic/imaginative dichotomy is unhelpful in understanding this complex "both-and" quality that lies at the heart of the novel's narrative dynamic. (227)

My discussion of *The Kindly Ones* will explore some "both-and" aspects with regard not only to its simultaneous mimeticism and antimimeticism but also to the ways in which these representational frames intersect with the novel's construction of filtering strategies in its depiction of the consciousness of its perpetrator-protagonist Aue, whom Boswell calls "a monumentally divided character, representing both extreme 'otherness' and extreme 'ordinariness'" (191). In particular, I will focus on the disjunction between the novel's conflicting modes of narrative discourse, a dynamic that Sanyal terms "ironic complicity," whereby the narrative both "coerces the reader into solidarity with the narrator, yet simultaneously sabotages this identification through irony" (191). Through the construction of an ironic intermediary filter made possible by autodiegetic narration,

The Kindly Ones grants a certain degree of intimate access to Aue's mind and his responses to and subsequent understanding of his genocidal experience and at the same time works systematically to mitigate the cognitive and affective connections created through this connection.

Critics such as Barjonet and Razinsky, von Koppenfels, Susan Rubin Suleiman, Daniel Mendelsohn ("Transgression"), Richard J. Golsan, and Stefan Iversen are in general agreement that *The Kindly Ones* contains two major narrative orientations that organize the novel not only on the level of plot but also on that of generic framing, narrative style, epistemological authority, narrative reliability, and intertextual reticulation.[31]

---

31 Barjonet and Razinsky: "The presence of two strata within the plot—historical and personal—likewise invites various and possibly conflicting understandings. On the historical level, the Holocaust appears here as tragically human, resulting from a mere deviation of human rationality. The personal level, in contrast, pathologizes and particularizes historical events" (11); von Koppenfels: "The novel forces together two very distinct strands. On the one hand, there are the memoirs of a Nazi war criminal; on the other, the family history of a matricidal homosexual who has committed incest with his twin sister. If at all, this twisted coil is held together by the first-person narrator responsible for the story" ("*Kommissbrot*" 929–30); Suleiman: "It occurs to me, however, that one could read the two stories—the public history and the family tragedy—in counterpoint, without looking for causal connections between them. The two stories would then be related metaphorically, not logically or psychologically in terms of cause and effect. The metaphorical equivalence would hinge on the question of guilt and responsibility" ("When the Perpetrator Becomes a Reliable Witness" 18); Mendelsohn: "*The Kindly Ones* comprises two large structural elements intended to explore these questions. The first is the historical/documentary plot—that is to say, the meticulous chronological recreation of Maximilien Aue's wartime career from 1941 to 1945. . . . This itinerary allows Max to be both eyewitness to and participant in the atrocities—and, because this narrator is an educated, reasonable-seeming man, allows the reader some access to the mentality of a perpetrator. The second element is the mythic/sexual: that is, the entirety of the *Oresteia* story, superimposed on the primary narrative and consisting both of flashbacks to Max's earlier life and events transpiring in the wartime present, which establishes him as a latter-day Orestes. . . . All this is overlaid with increasingly elaborately narrated sexual fantasies and activities, culminating in an onanistic orgy at his sister's abandoned house as the Russians enter Pomerania. The surprise—and also a key to understanding the outrage Littell's book has provoked, and the reasons for its successes and its failures—is the way in which these structures are meant to tackle the large themes suggested by his Aeschylean title. For it is, in fact, the historical structure that is meant to shed light on the problem of human nature; while it is the mythic-fantasy element . . . which

The first and most prominent of the narrative discourses in the novel is Aue's eyewitness account of his experiences in the war and in the genocide of the Jews, which Suleiman calls "the genre of testimony" ("Performing a Perpetrator as Witness" 114). Aue is the ideal figure through which to represent a firsthand account of the Holocaust, for, as a member of the SD branch of the SS, he is a witness to and participant in a number of events: he serves in Ukraine in Einsatzkommando 4a and takes part in the mass execution of Jews at Babi Yar; he is present in Stalingrad during the final days of the siege, where he suffers a traumatic head injury and nearly dies; he is charged with improving the survival rate and labor potential of prisoners in a number of camps in occupied Poland, including Auschwitz, a role that "eventually puts Max in the bizarre position of having to value the lives of the Jews he had been obediently killing before" (Mendelsohn, "Transgression"); he is involved in the mass roundups of Hungarian Jews in 1944 (and in fact enters Budapest with Eichmann's contingent in March 1944); he witnesses the death marches from Auschwitz in January 1945; and he experiences the Soviet advance in Pomerania and the Fall of Berlin. He thus functions in the narrative as the ideal eyewitness—"a Nazi Zelig" (Moyn)—who is present at some of the most important events of the war and the "Final Solution"; his autodiegetic account, as Sanyal argues, "maps the itinerary of a pleasurable *flânerie* through the Third Reich's trajectory of conquest, occupation, and extermination" (201). As a "reflector character" (Curthoys 467) and "scanner" (LaCapra, "Historical and Literary Approaches" 78) figure, he also meets and discourses with both invented characters and important historical figures, such as Heinrich Himmler, Adolf Eichmann, Rudolf Höß, and Albert Speer; the lengthy and at times mind-numbingly tedious conversations he conducts with them (which he refers to as "these uninteresting bureaucratic episodes" [778])

[is] meant to explore the nature of crime, atrocity, and justice" ("Transgression"); Golsan: "One part chronicles the war, the Nazi bureaucracy, and the Holocaust itself, and the other concerns the entirely different matter of the sexual fantasies and excesses of a character some critics see as being straight out of Sade or Bataille" (178); Iversen: "The novel tells two stories about its protagonist. One is the story of the participation of an ambitious and bright young man in the Nazi genocide of the Jews. Aue is very much *ein Auge*, an eye, a witness, and this story is filled to the brim with the most detailed historical facts. The other story is the story of Aue's family life and of his sexuality" (153).

thus reproduce on a discursive level the collective mentality and criminal pathology of the Third Reich.[32]

For the most part, Aue reports on these historical events reliably and in great detail, referring to himself as "a veritable memory factory" (4). Although he claims to be as forthcoming as possible—to dedicate himself to "the search for truth" (5)—about his own participation in the genocide of the Jews without resorting to either sanctimonious contrition or myopic self-pity, he not infrequently deflects responsibility for crimes committed during the war and indulges in self-justification. As the much older narrating Aue tells us at the beginning of his account: "I am not pleading *Befehl[s]notstand*, the just-obeying-orders so highly valued by our good German lawyers. What I did, I did with my eyes open, believing that it was my duty and that it had to be done, disagreeable or unpleasant as it may have been" (18). We are thus dealing with a narrator who not only was witness to what Suleiman designates the "two spheres of activity—the killing by the *Einsatzgruppen* (mobile killing units) in the Soviet Union, and the system of the extermination camps in Poland—[that] can be said to constitute the essence of the historical event we know as the Holocaust"

---

32 Sanyal argues that Aue ventriloquizes a post-Holocaust archive of not only the discourse of the perpetrator but also that of the victims and survivors, a phenomenon that constitutes one of the novel's principal ethical challenges: "The greatest interpretive difficulty posed by *The Kindly Ones* is that the perpetrator's voice is fully mediated by the historical and testimonial archive of the Holocaust. . . . The novel's greatest transgression may well be the wall that it erects between its readers and the victims of the Shoah. Our only access to this traumatic history is a testimony whose archive is colonized by a perpetrator-accomplice's memory and voiced from within the roar of extermination" (189, 198). There are numerous instances, as Sanyal points out, of Littell's ventriloquism of victim testimony; one of the most notable, in my opinion, occurs in "Toccata," when, after his mathematical "exercises of imagination," he writes, "If you ever managed to make me cry, my tears would sear your face" (16). This statement constitutes an uncanny counterpart to the memorable moment in Lanzmann's *Shoah*, when Itzhak Zuckermann, survivor of the Warsaw Ghetto Uprising, says, "If you could lick my heart, it would poison you" (DVD disc 4, chap. 19). Von Koppenfels points out that this vast historical and testimonial archive undergirding Aue's experience and knowledge is an index of the heightened artifice of the character and his narration: "Littell takes Proust's overstretched 'I' to a paradoxical extreme as he seeks to combine the limited or even insane first-person perspective with a boundless gaze that sees everything historical research ever brought to light about the war of extermination waged in Eastern Europe" ("The Infamous 'I'" 141).

("When the Perpetrator Becomes a Reliable Witness" 6), but also, in long ethical and philosophical passages, resolutely tries to explain as best he can the how and why of his participation in these crimes. Suleiman argues that "this combination of participant status as a perpetrator with historical reliability, and with what I call moral witnessing, which Aue possesses, is a new phenomenon in fiction" ("When the Perpetrator Becomes a Reliable Witness" 5).[33] Thus we, as readers who have heretofore likely observed the events of the Holocaust chiefly through the eyes of the survivor-witnesses, must learn to rely on the perpetrator as our main witness to the events of the Holocaust, whose "confession and attempt at justification is a dark mirror of the victims' narrative and testimony" (von Koppenfels, "The Infamous 'I'" 140).[34]

Littell's text repeatedly underscores Aue's function as the historical eyewitness whose experience is expressed in frequent references to the act of seeing, especially in the first half of the novel, which chronicles Aue's experiences in Ukraine and the Caucasus. As Liran Razinsky argues, his ocular activity occurs both within the diegesis and in the narrative discourse: "Aue's function both in the novel and in the Nazi machine, is that of an eye" ("History, Excess and Testimony" 71).[35] In fact, it seems as if Aue himself—both the narrating self from his postwar vantage point and the former self he recounts—regards his primary duty as being to witness, to visually register the events that unfold before his eyes. Just a few pages into

---

33 Suleiman writes further, "This structure of simultaneous belonging and distance, so that Aue is at once wholly within the Nazi system and sufficiently outside it to see it for what it is, both historically and morally, is what defines his particular status as a perpetrator-witness. . . . As it happens, the structure of simultaneous but contradictory states that characterizes Aue as narrator also defines the psychological phenomenon of dissociation or splitting, whereby one part of the psyche 'knows' something that another part denies" ("When the Perpetrator Becomes a Reliable Witness" 15–16). As I demonstrated in my reading of Hilsenrath's novel, and as we will see in the discussion of Amis's text in the next chapter, the technique of dissociative splitting is not an uncommon representational strategy in fictional autodiegetic narratives of perpetrators.
34 For this reason, as Jakob Lothe argues, "for the reader of *The Kindly Ones*, it becomes essential to form an idea of an implied author whose authority can represent an ethical alternative to that of Aue as character and narrator" (106–7).
35 Both Razinsky ("Not the Witness We Wished For" 185) and Iversen (153) connect Littell's protagonist's family name—Aue—with the German word for "eye," *Auge*.

his account, he arrives in Lutsk and is forced to view a thousand corpses of Polish prisoners who had been shot by the retreating Soviets; this is his first glimpse of the aftermath of mass violence. He describes his reaction thus: "I wanted to close my eyes, or put my hand over my eyes, and at the same time I wanted to look, to look as much as I could, and by looking, try to understand, this incomprehensible thing, there, in front of me, this void for human thought" (34). Later, describing an *Aktion* that involves the murder of about 150 Ukrainian Jews and that constitutes his first encounter with the mass killings perpetrated by his own Einsatzkommando, he admits,

> One morning, Janssen suggested I come witness an action. That had to happen sooner or later, I knew it and had thought about it. I can in all honesty say that I had doubts about our methods: I had trouble grasping their logic. . . . Now, we were killing them. And undeniably, we were killing a lot of people. That seemed atrocious to me, even if it was inevitable and necessary. But one has to confront atrocity; one must always be ready to look inevitability and necessity in the face, and accept the consequences that result from them; closing your eyes is never an answer. (80–81)

Aue develops here a principle that will guide him throughout his service in the occupied territories of the Soviet Union: he consciously commits himself to watching the violence, to performing his duties "with eyes wide open" (96). Because of Aue's refusal to close his eyes to the atrocities that he observes and then later commits, he is thus able to provide for us an account of events in which there were no Jewish survivors in an eyewitness mode that Jason Burke calls "narrative photo-realism." Aue's willingness to closely observe the violence perpetrated in the occupied territories thus makes possible his capacity to narrate it.

Meretoja argues that "Aue is not merely an eyewitness, but also someone who perpetually reflects on the meaning of what he sees" (226). With regard to his ocular observation of the ubiquitous violence around him, however, the operations of seeing and reflecting do not produce understanding, despite his fervent hope that the repeated violence that he witnesses will yield insight. After months of witnessing—and participating in—mass executions, including the massacre at Babi Yar (at which his Einsatzkommando 4a shoots over thirty thousand Jews within a two-day period), he confesses that he is not better able to understand "this void for human thought" than he was before:

> Over the sidewalk in Kharkov, the hanged men swung slowly. There were, I knew, Jews, Russians, Gypsies there. All these dismal, bound men hanging made me think of sleeping chrysalises patiently waiting for metamorphosis. But there was still something I couldn't grasp. I was finally beginning to perceive that no matter how many dead people I might see, or people at the instant of their death, I would never manage to grasp death, that very moment, precisely in itself. It was one thing or the other: either you are dead, and then in any case there's nothing else to understand, or else you are not dead, and in that case, even with the rifle at the back of your head or the rope around your neck, death remains incomprehensible, a pure abstraction, this absurd idea that I, the only living person in the world, could disappear. Dying, we may already be dead, but we never die, that moment never comes, or rather it never stops coming, there it is, it's coming, and then it's still coming, and then it's already over, without ever having come. (170)

Here, Aue confesses that the act of repeatedly observing shooting after shooting, death after death, does not bring him the understanding that he seeks; the mountains of corpses that these acts "generate" (to recycle a word from the quote I discussed at the beginning of this chapter) represent his recurrent failure to derive either wisdom or meaning from the victims' deaths. However, Aue reveals with this passage much more than mere frustration with the perpetual gaze at the violence around him. He is not so much interested in functioning as the historical witness that readers (and critics) rely on him to be; rather, his impetus for watching is tied more to his own personal fascination with death and the existential puzzle that it poses.[36] In this, he is no different from the rank-and-file German soldiers who defy orders that forbid them "from attending, photographing, or participating in actions" (98) because, as Aue tells us, "the desire to see these things was also human" (98). Describing yet another public hanging, he tells us, "The people watched till the end. I watched too, full of an evil fascination. I eagerly examined the faces of the hanged men, of the condemned men before they were passed over the railing; these faces, these terrified or terrifyingly resigned eyes told me nothing" (168). Aue openly watches the mass violence and its aftermath in search of a fervently desired but unattainable enlightenment; the victims' bodies he visually consumes thus constitute for him solely a means for his own potential self-actualization. In this way, his function as a historical eyewitness for us as readers is shaped not only by what he sees (and what he then reports to us) but also by his very motivation for and interest in watching and interpreting the violence of which he is a part. This is what Sanyal means when she refers to "the coerced complicity with the perpetrator's gaze" (185); Aue functions as the exclusive optical instrument through which the events of the Holocaust are made manifest to us, but we, in turn, cannot disunite the prospect he provides from the psychological and ideological mindset that conditions his perspective. For this reason, "we do not see through the blindness of Aue's gaze into the victim's experience" (Sanyal 195–96); rather, we can only take note of the aperture between his rhetoric of open-eyed, undistorted eyewitnessing and the occlusion of the narrative lens with his own motivations and interpretations.

Alongside the narrative mode of historical witnessing in *The Kindly Ones*, which comprises Aue's painstaking—though not disinterested or dispassionate—documentary account of the "Final Solution," exists what critics have identified as a second discourse, that of Aue's personal and

---

36 Aue's fascination with death is tied to what he calls "the radicalism of the abyss": "True, I wasn't taking part in the executions, I wasn't commanding the firing squads; but that didn't change much, since I often attended them.... Ever since I was a child, I had been haunted by a passion for the absolute, for the overcoming of all limits; and now this passion had led me to the edge of the mass graves of the Ukraine. I had always wanted my thinking to be radical; and now the State, the nation had also chosen the radical and the absolute.... And if this radicalism was the radicalism of the abyss, and if the absolute turned out to be absolute evil, one still had to follow them to the end, with eyes wide open—of that at least I was utterly convinced" (95–96).

sexual relationships, encompassing in particular his hatred of his mother; his incestuous childhood relationship with his twin sister and his continued obsession with her; and his periodic anonymous and furtive sexual encounters with men, which he claims he engages in as a substitute for sex with his sister. In this part of his narration, which Suleiman calls "the genre of excess" ("Performing a Perpetrator as Witness" 114) and Mendelsohn calls the "mythic/sexual" plane, as it uses as an explanatory frame "the entirety of the *Oresteia* story" ("Transgression"), Aue relates in particularly graphic detail both true and fantasized sexual and violent encounters that become more scatological, erotogenic, and grotesque over the course of the novel. This account of Aue's emotional, sexual, and familial life, to which the narrator turns recurrently in intervals between descriptions of the larger historical events in which he participates, functions as an associated counterpart to the historical narrative. Indeed, the two are intimately entangled and mutually constitutive, as the personal narrative "pathologizes and particularizes historical events" (Barjonet and Razinsky 11), while the "lived experience of violence is displaced into erotic or somatic registers" (Sanyal 200). However, these personal interludes that occur in the interstices between segments of the historical account take place not just on the level of storytelling, for not only does Aue the narrator suspend his documentary discourse at times to shift to an account of his private familial and sexual affairs, but Aue the actor also periodically withdraws from the historical action and retreats to locations significant for his personal life, such as the south of France, where his mother and stepfather live, and Pomerania, the location of the family estate of his sister's husband. This last locale, to which an entire chapter ("Air") is devoted near the end of the book, functions as the site of the escalation of the sexual/personal narrative, in which Aue indulges in extended graphic fantasies of his sister, engages in what LaCapra calls "a masturbatory *Walpurgisnacht*" ("Historical and Literary Approaches" 77), and, as Aue himself describes it, succumbs to "the demented vision of a perfect coprophagic autarky" (886).[37] Much of

---

37 In an insightful reading of "Air," the chapter in which Aue narrates his extended masturbatory fantasy, Coquio argues that Aue, by drawing a connection between his sister and the Ukrainian woman whom he and his fellow SS hang in Kharkov, acknowledges—if only obliquely—his culpability in genocidal violence. In this moment, in Coquio's view, the "psychic catastrophe" and the "political catastrophe," that is, the "two levels of Aue's 'life' story," come together

the criticism of the novel has been directed at this narrative, for reviewers see it as somehow detracting from or even trivializing the larger historical account of the Holocaust. As Eaglestone summarizes this position,

> The novel has to look away from the evil in the "genocidal" strand and, as it were, excuse it or "redeem" it, in the sense of "paying it off," with the evil of the "family tragedy." Aue, despite his assertions on the first page that he is a man like us, is not: he is already a psychopath and/or a mythic figure, before becoming a genocidal perpetrator. Psychopaths and mythic figures, while they tell us about psychopathology and myth, tell us very little about the day-to-day evil of the perpetrators of Third Reich atrocities. (*The Broken Voice* 62)

At the same time, however, scholarly assessments by Suleiman and Razinsky argue that Littell explicitly turns to the French literary style of excess and transgression in the tradition of Sade, Bataille, and Genet as a counterpoint to the larger historical narrative; hence, "historical details are metabolized through Aue's deranged sexuality" (Razinsky, "History, Excess and Testimony" 75) and Aue's perspective represents "a brilliant push to the extreme, *ad absurdum* even, of something of the nature of the Holocaust itself, and of the idea of testimony bound with it" (80).[38] In this way, Littell's novel performs, on the narrative level, the excess and abjection that characterize the logic of the extreme violence inherent in the genocide. Although "the 'family' story and the 'genocidal' story work against each other" (Eaglestone, *The Broken Voice* 62) in essential ways, the former registers and amplifies the intensity and radicality of violence that in the latter is routine, bureaucratized, normalized, and coherently narrated.

---

(87). At the same time, as Suleiman points out, Aue goes on to murder four people after this point in the story, "which suggests that if he gained ethical insight and an awareness of 'the other' in that chapter, it didn't last very long" ("Performing a Perpetrator as Witness" 115).

[38] According to von Koppenfels, "Since the whole text of *Les Bienveillantes* is covered by that first-person narrator, there is no margin on which to present an ethically or even stylistically accountable authority outside of the text" ("*Kommissbrot*" 930). Meretoja, on the other hand, argues that the novel's abundant intertextual references function as an ethical counter-discourse external to Aue's perspective (229).

Alongside these two critically recognized, overarching narrative discourses in Littell's novel, namely, the historical/documentary and the personal/sexual/mythical, I posit a third order of discourse as well: the discourse of dreams, hallucinations, and repressed knowledge, which is especially connected to the personal narrative and, like it, gains traction particularly in the latter part of the novel. Not only is Aue shockingly transgressive in his desires, fantasies, and sexual proclivities, but he also gradually begins to lose a grip on reality when his fantasies slide into all-out hallucinations, which the narrating I recounts as if they were real.[39] The chapter describing his stay in Pomerania, in fact, can be characterized as one long hallucination from which he—in this case, both the narrating I and the experiencing I, who seem to be fused at this point (or, more precisely, the former is submerged into the latter)—surfaces only sporadically into consciousness. Moreover, Aue's gradual inability to distinguish between reality and fantasy also extends to a limited extent to his memory; although he is able to remember conversations, dates, and historical details with apparently perfect recall and to narrate the minute details of events over many pages, with regard to his personal life a few instances occur when he admits to us that some of his memories, especially of his sister, are dubious. Finally, he (and here I refer to both the narrating and the narrated selves) represses important knowledge about his personal life altogether, knowledge of which we, as readers, become gradually aware through various indices of his unreliability. Chief among these repressions is his brutal murder of his mother and stepfather, which takes place midway through the novel when, on recovery leave for his Stalingrad injury, he visits them in the south of France. Although he is investigated for these crimes throughout the rest of the novel by two persistent Berlin detectives (the furies alluded to in the novel's title),[40] he appears to be resolutely unaware of the fact that he

---

39 Peter Kuon points out that "when Aue gets involved in situations that psychologically overwhelm him a dream sequences follows" (38). Kuon's specific example is the incident of the hanging of a young woman in Kharkov, whose gaze at Aue shortly before her death causes him, in his reporting, to "burst into flames," whereupon his "remains [are] transformed into a salt statue" that collapses into "a pile of salt," which in turn is "swept away" by the wind (*The Kindly Ones* 179). This incident is one of the earliest in which hallucinations intrude into Aue's otherwise sober and realistic narration.

40 For excellent analyses of the function of the Euripidean hypotext in the novel, see Mendelsohn ("Transgression") and von Koppenfels ("*Kommissbrot*").

committed the crime, which "he seems to have [committed] unconsciously in a kind of psychotic trance" (von Koppenfels, "*Kommissbrot*" 936). Moreover, although it finally occurs to him late in the novel that the twin boys who were living with his mother and stepfather during this visit (children they claim are the sons of friends) are actually his sister's children, he never acknowledges the fact that he is likely their father.[41] These instances of hallucination and repression thus seriously compromise Aue's status for us as a reliable narrator, at least when it comes to his personal life. But does this unreliability call into question his apparent honesty about his participation in Holocaust crimes? For Suleiman, the reliability of Aue's memory threatens to undermine his entire narration of the war and the "Final Solution":

> Right to the end, Aue never "remembers" the action he committed; it is the two somewhat comical detectives, Weser and Clemens, who figure it out, by the usual methods of evidence gathering and deduction—methods similar to those of the historian, incidentally. But if Aue himself never recalls his act, how can we grant him—even fictively—the ability to recall and reliably report on the events in Kiev, Stalingrad, and other cities? Does his private memory hole undermine the project of historical witnessing that is the novel's major achievement? ("When the Perpetrator Becomes a Reliable Witness" 17)

In the end, Suleiman, who confesses that she is "still struggling with these questions" (18), decides that, while the novel flirts with this danger, it does not succumb to it: "By having Aue—at least the conscious, narrating Aue—remain dissociated from his act [the murder of his mother and

---

41 This is one example in which Aue's narration provides the reader with insight that Aue himself (as either narrator or character) does not consciously possess. In the introductory chapter, the narrating I, describing his present-day life and family, confesses, "In the meantime, I got married, rather reluctantly I must admit . . . I picked a woman from a good family . . . and I immediately got her with child, to keep her busy. Unfortunately, she had twins, it must run in the family, mine, I mean—one brat would have been more than enough for me" (11–12). Aue recognizes the affiliation between his own status as a twin and that of his postwar children, but he is unable to draw that connection with regard to the children in the care of his mother and stepfather.

stepfather] to the very end, Littell can preserve him as a reliable witness to the Holocaust, even while his memory hole about the family murder demonstrates the human ability to block out unbearable actions" (18).[42] In my opinion, however, the situation is more complex than Suleiman characterizes it, for Aue's murder of his family, while the text's major memory hole, is not the only one, nor do his dissociations remain exclusively in the personal narrative.[43] Rather, as I see it, the discourse of hallucinations occasionally infects the historical eyewitness discourse, which further complicates the larger historical narrative and the documentary effect it produces.

Although most of Aue's hallucinations occur in the personal/sexual narrative, there are a few instances in which they extend to his historical discourse as well, especially to his role as eyewitness. Rasson argues that Aue's hallucinations result from the head injury that he suffers in Stalingrad in early 1943, an event that, in his opinion, "constitutes a caesura in the novel" (107), as it alters Aue's narrative authority: "From Stalingrad on, the character's hallucinations tend to impose themselves, to the expense of accurate historical information. Perhaps a distinction should be made between a reliable narrator, writing up until the Stalingrad chapter, and an unreliable one who narrates thereafter" (107).[44] Rasson is certainly onto something with this suspicion; however, I think that the matter is less straightforward than he indicates, as it hinges on the distinctions between Aue's narrating I and his experiencing I. While the incident at Stalingrad is certainly significant for Aue's functions as a narrator (more on this in a

---

42 Suleiman revises her position somewhat in her 2012 essay, in which she writes, "Whereas Aue is a reliable narrator where the historical narrative is concerned—not only in the accuracy of his reporting but even in many of his judgments, to which the reader adheres—he is stunningly unreliable in recounting some major events of his personal story" ("Performing a Perpetrator as Witness" 112).

43 According to Razinsky, Aue's faulty memory is an index for the actual story that he will not (or cannot) narrate: "His true witnessing, experience, is carried out less through remembering, however, than through forgetting. The personal dimension is perforated with informational gaps. . . . His mode of witnessing is embodied, restricted, fragmented" ("Not the Witness We Wished For" 189–90).

44 Razinsky argues essentially the same thing: "Aue's third eye perhaps grants him better sight, yet this wound is also the point where his blindness starts" ("Not the Witness We Wished For" 185). However, as I contend here, this blindness—or in other words, this unreliability—begins earlier in the narrative, before the description of the Stalingrad injury.

moment), for Aue the character, the hallucinations originate much earlier in his experience, particularly in the critical months in the summer and fall of 1941, during which he is attached to the Einsatzgruppe. At the massacre at Babi Yar, for example, while engaging personally for the first time in a mass shooting, Aue experiences a dissociative delusion: "I kept shooting at her and her head exploded like a fruit, then my arm detached itself from me and went off all by itself down the ravine, shooting left and right, I ran after it, waving at it to wait with my other arm, but it didn't want to, it mocked me and shot at the wounded all by itself, without me" (130).[45] Shortly after the mass shooting at Babi Yar, while observing traffic on the Dnieper River with his colleague, Aue suddenly hallucinates the bodies of victims of the Battle of Smolensk, which took place over a century prior:

> Contemplating the long seaweed undulating beneath the surface, I suddenly had a kind of dual vision: I could clearly see the seaweed and at the same time I thought I saw the bodies of Napoleonic hussars, in apple-green, bottle-green, or yellow uniforms, with cockades and ostrich feathers waving, drifting with the current. This was very intense, and I must have spoken the emperor's name, since Osnabrugge suddenly said: "Napoleon?" (136–37)

Aue's hallucination is connected to the killings of which he is daily a part; in this case, even when he beholds a relatively benign prospect that is devoid of violence, Aue perceives corpses piling up all around him. Alongside other hallucinatory events, these examples demonstrate that Aue does not simply imagine unreal events as a part of a daydream; rather, he perceives such hallucinations to be real. The text strongly implies that Aue suffers from a significant degree of traumatic stress from his observation of and eventual participation in mass shootings, even if Aue himself—whether as character or as narrator—does not seem to connect his "bouts of nausea and

---

[45] According to Sanyal, this scene "cast[s] the perpetrator-accomplice as the subject of a trauma that is inflicted, paradoxically, *by* the victim" (195). Suleiman points out that "Aue appears here most definitely human: it is one instance in the novel where he significantly *fails* in his performance as an SS officer, since he breaks down and starts to cry" ("Performing a Perpetrator as Witness" 108–9).

vomiting" (305), his frequent dreams, and his "sudden, revealing visions blinding in their clarity and horror" (305) to the violence that he habitually witnesses and commits.[46] At the same time, however, Aue's trauma does not make itself known in an inability to tolerate the violence; on the contrary, he seems to seek out the violence to somehow cure himself of it. In a passage that occurs shortly after his repeated references to "sudden retchings, accompanied sometimes by painful and exhausting upwellings of gas" (162), he writes,

> My sleep was full of heavy, troubled dreams, not nightmares exactly, but like long underwater currents stirring up the mud in the depths while the surface remains smooth and calm. I should note that I went back regularly to witness the executions; no one required it, but I went of my own free will. I didn't shoot, but I studied the men who did, the officers especially, such as Häfner or Janssen, who had been there since the beginning and seemed now to have become perfectly hardened to their executioner's work. I must have been like them. By inflicting the piteous spectacle on myself, I felt, I wasn't trying to exhaust the scandal of it, the insurmountable feeling of a transgression, of a monstrous violation of the Good and the Beautiful, but rather this feeling of scandal came to wear out all by itself, one got used to it, and in the long run stopped feeling much; thus what I was trying, desperately but in vain, to regain was actually that

---

[46] Razinsky writes of the disconnect between Aue's symptoms and his obliviousness to their etiology: "As he centers his narration on his individual self, the perspective on the war becomes embodied and inseparable from his own gaze. The knowledge Aue attempts to convey is inextricably bound with his private, intimate, and irreducible experience. The more bizarre the fantasy, the more repulsive the somatic description, and the smellier the text, the more it seems inseparable from Aue's subjectivity. It all comes down to the body, and Aue's obsessive depictions of bodily functions serve the same purpose. This is especially so because Aue's response throughout the novel to the horrors he witnesses, his mode of metabolization of them, takes the form of literal defecation and vomiting, which inevitably amass metaphorical meanings. His body remembers and reacts, where his psyche remains passive and blind" ("Not the Witness We Wished For" 191).

> initial shock, that sensation of a rupture, an infinite distur-
> bance of my whole being; instead of that, I now felt only a
> dull, anxious kind of excitation, always briefer, more acrid,
> mixed with the fever and my physical symptoms, and thus,
> slowly, without truly realizing it, I was sinking into mud
> while searching for light. (178–79)

As a character, Aue thus finds himself entangled in the interminable loop of repetition compulsion: he experiences significant somatic and psychic consequences that result from his observation of and participation in the mass shootings, which he attempts to ameliorate by seeking out more violence, which he hopes will help him somehow find his way back to the first traumatic moment, "that initial shock, that sensation of a rupture, an infinite disturbance of my whole being," in order to unravel the effects of the traumatic breach.

The hallucinations that Aue as a character experiences eventually come to pollute the novel's narrative discourse as well; according to Meretoja, "the 'narrating I' and the 'experiencing I' become more and more entangled," an interfusion that "penetrates the very structure of narration" (241). As Rasson rightly points out, the novel's narration transforms after its depiction of the head injury suffered by Aue the character while fighting in the last days of the Stalingrad siege, when "eye and flesh unite" (Razinsky, "Not the Witness We Wished For" 185). As reported by the narrator, this wound, which was caused by a bullet, produces in him an irrevocable transformation:

> A hole went right through my head, a narrow circular corri-
> dor, a fabulous, closed shaft, inaccessible to thought, and if
> that were true, then nothing was the same again, how could
> it have been? My thinking about the world now had to re-
> organize itself around this hole. But the only concrete thing
> I could say was: I have awakened, and nothing will ever be
> the same again. (436)

Aue's traumatic head injury causes a crisis of sorts that destabilizes him and at the same time awakens him. As a result, he experiences a new way of seeing that allows him to perceive truths that are not visible to conventional modes of apprehension:

> Whenever I looked, the sight of ordinary life, the crowd in the trolleys or the S-Bahn, the laughter of an elegant woman, the satisfied creasing of a newspaper, struck me like contact with a sharp sliver of glass. I had the feeling that the hole in my forehead had opened up a third eye, a pineal eye, one not turned to the sun, not capable of contemplating the blinding light of the sun, but directed at the darkness, gifted with the power of looking at the bare face of death, and of grasping this face behind each face of flesh and blood, beneath the smiles, through the palest, healthiest skin, the most laughing eyes. The disaster was already there and they didn't realize it, since the disaster is the very idea of the disaster to come, which ruins everything long before term. (443)

By attributing his new mode of vision to a pineal, or third, eye, Aue accesses here a number of discourses in both Eastern and Western spiritual traditions that attribute heightened awareness, spiritual and psychological perception, and clairvoyance to an inner eye. Aue's pineal eye, which allows him to see "through the opacity of things" (470) to their essence, in particular to their dark, almost evil distillate, activates his apprehension of the perennial but latent catastrophe that he realizes is screened by the ephemeral normality of everyday life. His sensation of this heightened awareness is thus less a state of spiritual enlightenment than one of traumatic awareness; in fact, the expression of trauma seems to have migrated from the somatic to the perceptual: "I had no physical symptoms such as those I had experienced in the Ukraine or in Stalingrad: I wasn't overcome with nausea, I didn't vomit, my digestion was perfectly normal. Only, in the street, I felt as if I were walking on glass that was ready at any instant to shatter beneath my feet. Living required a sustained attention to things, which exhausted me" (444).

Aue's "pineal eye" remains with him throughout the rest of the narrative, and one could argue that it—meaning this change of consciousness that results from his head injury—is what causes his sexual hallucinations, which are narrated in abundance only in the second half of the novel. Importantly, however, his first extended perception with his pineal eye happens not with his fantasies of his sister but rather in his historical testimony when, during his recovery leave, he attends a speech given by Hitler, a scene that the narrator describes at length. When Hitler enters the room, Aue is shocked to see him clothed in the ritual garments of the Haredi Jew, complete with *tallis*, *tefillin*, and *peyes*. He notices immediately that he is the only one to perceive Hitler's apparel, for the prominent Nazi leaders present show no special reaction to the speech. Describing his dismay at the time, the narrator writes,

> I didn't know what to think. I scrutinized my neighbors: they were listening to the speech with solemn attention, the civil servant was studiously nodding his head. Didn't they notice anything? Was I the only one to see this unprecedented spectacle? I look at the dignitaries' stand: behind the Führer, I recognized Göring, Goebbels, Ley, the Reichsführer, Kaltenbrunner, other well-known leaders, high-ranking Wehrmacht officers; they were all contemplating the Führer's back or the audience, impassive. Maybe, I said to myself, panic-stricken, it's the story of the Emperor's New Clothes: everyone sees how it really is, but hides it, counting on his neighbor to do the same. No, I reasoned, I must be hallucinating, with a wound like mine, that's entirely possible. Yet I felt perfectly sound of mind. I was far from the platform, though, and the Führer was lit from the side; maybe it was simply an optical illusion? But I still saw it. Maybe my "pineal eye" was playing a trick on me? But there was nothing dreamlike about it. It was also possible that I had gone mad. (467)

In this passage, both the experiencing I and the narrating I appear aligned or even fused; Aue the character experiences an apparition that likewise perplexes Aue the narrator, who, from his retrospective position, fails to provide satisfactory contextualization, to hit on an adequate explanatory frame, or to discount the phenomenon altogether. While he acknowledges that he could be hallucinating or going "mad," he also insists on the sense of tangible reality of the perception and on the fact that he feels "perfectly sound of mind." Given that the text's heretofore dominant mode has been historical/documentary, that it has not until this point indulged in magical realism or other unnatural or antimimetic narrative elements, and that there exists no account of the referential Hitler appearing either publicly or privately in the ritual garments of Orthodox Jewry, the reader is likely to embrace the former interpretation, namely, that Aue's injury causes him to hallucinate (as opposed to the opposite conclusion, that Hitler has decided to appear publicly as a Jew). The narrating I, in contrast, comes down on neither one nor the other side of the divide, leaving the matter unsolved and indeterminate. The tension between the two unresolved possibilities within Aue's narration constitutes a particular narratorial variant of what Shlomith Rimmon-Kenan terms "narrative ambiguity" in that it presents "two mutually exclusive finalized hypotheses" (21), both of which the narrator endorses.[47] In Meretoja's words, Aue "loses his capacity for narrative sense-making" because "he can no longer link events to each other in the form of a narrative" (241). Not only is Aue unable to produce the sequential succession between events that underpins mimetic narration, but as his depiction of Hitler's speech indicates, he also lacks the ability to make the necessary interpretive decision between "multiple and mutually exclusive explanatory options" (Richardson, *Unlikely Stories* 43) that is integral to the establishment of causal factors for those events.[48]

This passage raises important questions for our understanding of the narrator and our apprehension of the text as a whole. What are we to do

---

[47] I stress that this is a variant of Rimmon-Kenan's concept, since she bases her definition on narratives that demonstrate the "coexistence of two mutually exclusive *fabulas* in one *sjuzhet*" (21). In this case, however, the reader suspects that there is one definite fabula, but the narrator himself insists on maintaining two mutually exclusive discursive possibilities for it.

[48] As Brian Richardson argues, "In many respects, interpretation and causality are two sides of the same coin. Confronted by multiple and mutually exclusive explanatory options, characters and readers alike are impelled to weigh the evidence, take hermeneutical stands, and adjust prior expectations to meet anomalous incidents. The more ambiguous, unlikely, or contradictory the causal agency appears to be, the greater the demand for interpretive accuracy becomes" (*Unlikely Stories* 43). Richardson's observation holds not only for characters and readers but for narrators as well. In this case, Aue cannot (or will not) take a "hermeneutical stand" to provide the necessary causal explanation for the scene.

with this hallucination? What does Aue see here with his pineal eye that cannot be penetrated by the gazes of the other observers? Are we to believe that he is really penetrating to Hitler's essence, which in this case would confirm the long-standing rumors of Hitler's possible Jewish ancestry? Or does Littell parody here the novel's dominantly documentary approach by having the narrative break down in its representation of Hitler, the transcendental signifier for Holocaust perpetration in particular and evil in general? I think there may be something to this last question, especially given that, at the end of the novel, in the last days of the war, Littell has Aue bite Hitler's nose as the latter awards the former a German Cross in Gold,[49] an action that represents either Aue's complete breakdown as narrator or character (or both) or Littell's last laugh at our attempts to reconcile such events with the novel's predominantly historical reliability.[50] But aside from these questions and the representation of Hitler in the novel, what is significant here is the novel's characterization of vision and seeing and how Aue—both as character and as narrator—transforms from the reliable documentary eyewitness he was in the first part of the novel to a witness who misperceives reality in his search for the essence or meaning behind things. It is unclear, however, whether this transformation of Aue's vision, which serves as a filter to documentary discourse, is inherently detrimental to the goals of the novel. Perhaps the novel suggests here that Aue's altered mode of seeing and the hallucinations it causes allow for a fresh perspective from which we can regard the Holocaust.[51] Or perhaps they offer an alternative

---

49 The depiction of this scene in the English translation of the novel ("So I leaned forward and bit into his bulbous nose, drawing blood" [*The Kindly Ones* 960]) differs slightly from its counterpart in the original French ("Avec un petit sourire sévère je tendis la main et lui pinçai le nez entre deux doigts repliés, lui secouant doucement la tête, comme on fait à un enfant qui s'est mal conduit" [*Les Bienveillantes* 880–81]). According to LaCapra, "During the ceremony he is disgusted by Hitler's fetid breath and bites the *Führer's* nose (a gesture toned down in the original French version where Aue 'tweaks' [pince] the nose and that Littell insisted be restored to 'bites' in all translations)" ("Historical and Literary Approaches" 77).

50 According to Suleiman, "We could see the growing loss of control in the narration [after the 'Air' chapter] as textually mirroring the disintegration of Berlin, bombed to smithereens, of the German army and bureaucracy, of Aue himself as he becomes another man—and also the disintegration of realist narrative, as Aue's narration becomes more hallucinatory and grotesque" ("Performing a Perpetrator as Witness" 116).

51 Klaus Theweleit reads the third eye as a sort of indicator of the implied or even the real author: "The author of the views of the third eye in the novel is, of

to conventional historical discourse, for each mode of vision has its appeal in particular epistemological inquiries: the documentary is important for ascertaining historical truth, while the search for the essential meaning behind historical fact is critical for determining a more existential truth. By having Aue embody both sorts of vision, Littell's novel attempts to tread the paths of both historical truth and imaginative representation, which is a difficult, though not entirely impossible, journey.

Through Aue's metaphor of the pineal eye, which becomes the lens through which we access the latter, *The Kindly Ones* provides its own metafictional justification for "the experiential power of a fictional narrative to do what no historical, sociological or psychological approach" (Iversen 155), by virtue of its epistemological limitations, is able to do, namely, to offer "a thought-adventure" (Boswell 195) that leads the reader into the otherwise impenetrable morass of the mind of a Holocaust perpetrator.

Narratorial Decomposition

In my reading, *The Kindly Ones* thus commences with an apparent absence of filtering strategies and then gradually accumulates them with the extreme friction between the various narrative discourses and with Aue's increasing unreliability as a narrator. Not only does the text vacillate between the historical/documentary, the "mythic/sexual," and the discourse of dreams, hallucinations, and repressed knowledge, but Aue as a narrator also flees from one discursive mode into the other in a movement not dissimilar to Max Schulz's frenetic ping-ponging between vocal positions in *The Nazi and the Barber*. The three discourses create, in a sense, three iterations of the same narrating figure, whose accounts are both complementary and contradictory, historically reliable and fantastically implausible, mimetic and antimimetic. This deviant narrative practice seals Aue's overall unreliability and causes us to at least question his apparent honesty about his participation in Holocaust crimes. If at first Maximilien Aue, in contrast to Max Schulz, provides an honest and accurate retrospective perspective on his experience (a narrative authority that Littell's novel takes pains—along with copious pages—to establish at the beginning), he gradually loses his

course, more Littell with his historical and analytic knowledge than his protagonist Aue" ("On the German Reaction" 26).

status as the narrative's reliable orientation point and ends up, not unlike Schulz, decamping from the narrative perspective he purports to represent. In this way, one could consider Aue's narration, like that of Hilsenrath's narrator, to be pathological. Although I do not endorse Michiko Kakutani's scathing review of Littell's book, I do agree with her assertion that Littell creates in Aue a monster.[52] As the novel constructs it, however, Aue's monstrousness is not a quality that inheres in his identity or behavior as a Holocaust perpetrator (conduct that, within the context of *The Kindly Ones*, is troublingly depicted as one of the less shocking experiences in Aue's history); rather, it emerges over the course of the novel in his increasingly aberrant narrative function.[53]

Aue's narratorial decomposition—or, in Meretoja's words, "the breakdown of narrative mastery" (241)—provokes a number of critical questions. Why does our candid narrator, who is forthright about the details of his participation in genocide and other crimes, devolve into an incoherent monster through the process of narrating? In other words, why does Littell, who takes such care to illuminate the consciousness of his protagonist, transform his representation of a perpetrator who is frank about his thoughts and motivations into the overused trope of the perpetrator as incomprehensible Other and mythically insane beast? Why does this much-acclaimed direct view into the mind of the perpetrator degenerate into the obscuration of its object, "as if the dark sun of the evil of the 'ordinary Nazi' is actually too much to bear" (Eaglestone, *The Broken Voice* 62)? The question that my reading of Littell's and Hilsenrath's novels raises is ultimately thus: Are

---

52 Kakutani writes, "Mr. Littell simply gives us a monster talking at monstrous length about his monstrous deeds, encouraging us to write off Nazis as cartoonish madmen" ("Unrepentant and Telling of Horrors Untellable").
53 According to Adams, "The narrative's unreliability raises the possibility that Aue's actions may be reassuringly accounted for by what Waller refers to as the 'mad Nazi theory.' . . . From another perspective, though, the unreliability of the narrative functions to dislodge the reader from a passive orientation towards the text, eliciting a questioning and interrogative form of reading that is valuable as a means of responding to the novel's ethical provocations" ("Reading (as) Violence" 42). Adam's argument about the novel's potential provocation of ethical reflection in the reader is seconded by Meretoja, who argues that *The Kindly Ones* "engenders an experience of moral implication through a narrative dynamic that simultaneously encourages immersion and critical distance," an "interplay [that] lies at the heart of the way the novel deals with the ethics of engaging with the legacy of the Holocaust" (231).

the filtering strategies I have identified in *The Nazi and the Barber* and *The Kindly Ones* ineluctable elements in autodiegetic narratives of Holocaust perpetration? One might well posit an answer to this question by imagining a novel that takes a radically opposed approach to that of Littell and Hilsenrath, namely, one that reduces all possible distance between the narrator and the reader and encourages rather than frustrates full identification with the perpetrator. Such a hypothetical text (which, as I have argued elsewhere, "exists only as a potentially dangerous but abstract specter and not as a likely possibility for the reader" ["Empathetic Identification" 264]) might indeed succeed at historicizing the cultural image of the Holocaust perpetrator, relocating him from the realm of myth into the sphere of human action and responsibility and allowing the reader to imagine that she, too, might, under similar circumstances, become involved in the perpetration of genocide. But such a novel would also run the real risk of encouraging the reader to assume the character's mental framework and to take on not only his ethical values but also his understanding of his participation in the Holocaust. By conjuring a highly mimetic representation of the perpetrator unmitigated by oppositional formal strategies, such a narrative would be unable to sustain any ethical or critical perspective external to the events he describes. Assuming, of course, that for writers and readers who share an interest in understanding the scope and nature of the Holocaust, including the role of the perpetrators, such an outcome is to be strenuously avoided, strategies for representing perpetrators in a manner that encourages critical reading are indispensable.

4

The Perpetrator Mind Divided | Martin Amis's *Time's Arrow* and *The Zone of Interest*

| On the Ramp

The Zone of Interest, Martin Amis's 2014 novel set in the vast concentrationary ecosystem of Auschwitz, depicts near its beginning a scene located on the infamous Auschwitz ramp, "an ominous place of life and death" (Gigliotti 179) that historically was the site of arrival for the Jewish deportees transported to the camp from the cities and ghettos of Europe.[1] By virtue of its memorable representation by such Auschwitz survivors as Primo Levi, Elie Wiesel, Ruth Klüger, Olga Lenyel, and Imre Kertész (among countless others), the Auschwitz ramp has become one of the most

---

1 Actually, there were three unloading ramps in the history of the Auschwitz camp complex: the first ramp, which was adjacent to the main camp; the second ramp or "Alte Judenrampe," which became the reception point for most of the transports of Jewish deportees that arrived between 1942 and May 1944; and the third ramp, which was located inside the Birkenau camp and was operative beginning in May 1944 in anticipation of the arrival of hundreds of thousands of Hungarian Jews (http://auschwitz.org/en/history/auschwitz-and-shoah/the-unloading-ramps-and-selections).

recognizable chronotopes not only of the Auschwitz experience in particular but also of the Holocaust in general. The violence, terror, disorientation, and familial rupture experienced by deportees on the receiving ramp signified their initial traumatic encounter with the world of Auschwitz. The ramp was also a prime locus of the process of *Selektion*,[2] whereby the newly arrived were wrenched from their loved ones and sorted into two groups: a smaller number of deportees deemed capable of work and thus allowed to enter the camp as inmates and a larger group sent directly to be killed in the gas chamber. In Amis's novel, however, the ramp is presented not from the viewpoint of the terrified and disoriented Jewish deportees who arrive there but from the perspective of a perpetrator, who obdurately receives them and purposively selects them for work or for death. One of the text's three narrators, the camp commandant Paul Doll, chronicles a day in August 1942 he spends on the receiving ramp (known historically as the "Alte Judenrampe" or "Old Jewish Ramp") located between the Auschwitz I and Birkenau (Auschwitz II) camps. Awaiting the arrival of a transport of Jews from France, who, he notes, "would be spending a mere 2 days in transit" (*The Zone of Interest* 22), Doll describes with pride the elaborate reception that he has prepared for them:

> Nobody can say that I don't cut a pretty imposing figure on the ramp: chest out, with sturdy fists planted on jodhpured hips, and the soles of my jackboots at least a metre apart. And look of what I disposed: I had with me my number 2, Wolfram Prufer [sic], 3 labour managers, 6 physicians and as many disinfectors, my trusty Sonderkommandofuhrer [sic], Szmul, with his 12-man team (3 of whom spoke French), 8 Kapos plus the hosing crew, and a full Storm of 96 troops under Captain Boris Eltz, reinforced by the 8-strong unit deploying the belt-fed, tripod-based heavy machine gun and the 2 flamethrowers. I had also called upon a) Senior Supervisor Grese and her platoon (Grese is admirably firm

---

2 While the experience of *Selektion* in Auschwitz is, in the contemporary popular imagination, almost exclusively tied to the process on the receiving ramp, Gigliotti writes that it was actually one manifestation of a larger overarching dynamic that operated throughout the camp complex (200).

with recalcitrant females), and b) the current "orchestra"—not the usual dog's breakfast of banjoes and accordions and didgeridoos, but a "septet" of 1st-rate violinists from Innsbruck. . . . We felt the hums and tremors in the rails, and I too felt a rush of energy and strength. . . . Oh yes, we bantered and smiled in the collegial fashion, but make no mistake: we were ready. (22–23)

Doll anticipates that the passengers of "Sonderzug 105" (21) will be "recalcitrant" with regard to the plans that he and his contingent have for them, namely, to murder forthwith the majority ("90% of them" [23]) in a gas chamber and to subject a small minority to grueling slave labor, enforced starvation, and disease. To greet them, he has carefully choreographed an imposing scene that includes both an impressive display of military might and pacific measures intended to soften the impact of the overwhelming demonstration of force on the newly arrived deportees. He savors the moment before the train arrives, taking pleasure in the exhibition of pure power that he has organized and assembled, a spectacle that aims to intimidate and subdue the passengers to the extent that they pose as little a challenge as possible to Doll's operation and to their intended demise. Doll admits that his planned reception on the ramp is somewhat disproportional to the situation, as the passengers themselves are unarmed and exhausted by their long involuntary journey. At the same time, however, he tells us that he was warned via telegram from a colleague that his "abilities" would be "tested to limits" by this particular transport, for which he should prepare with "extreme caution" (22). Thus, following his personal dictum, "*Fail to prepare? Prepare to fail!*," Doll "made [his] arrangements accordingly" (22) and convened as ostentatiously brutal a welcoming committee as possible to ensure that the arrival of the train would transpire without a hitch and the deportees could be "selected" and dispatched to their respective fates with minimal resistance.

As it turns out, however, Doll's colleague has played a practical joke on him, for the anticipated size, physical robustness, and capacity for defiance of the transport do not materialize. Rather, Doll observes, "A shipment of 1,000? Why, it comprised barely 100. As for the Selektion: all but a few were under 10 or over 60; and even the young adults among them were, so to speak, selected already" (*The Zone of Interest* 24). He complains that his prepared spectacle of staggering military might and immanent violence is thus wasted on "so light a load" and that, "in financial terms, ST 105 was something of a disaster," since not only does he mobilize far too many personnel for the operation, but he also unnecessarily authorizes the "costly use of the Little Brown Bower" (his euphemism for the gas chamber) when more economical methods of killing could be used on such a small and mostly infirm transport (28). Doll's pride at the outset of the train's arrival—his unqualified joy at the impressive spectacle of unadulterated power he has created on the ramp—is ultimately diminished by his administrative concern that the reception he planned for this particular transport turns out to be an inefficient waste of manpower and resources, for which he, as commandant, is ultimately responsible. Through the tension between these two preoccupations—his vanity at the "imposing figure" he cuts at the ramp and his pleasure at the expression of power under his command, on the one hand, and his bureaucratic commitment to the economic efficiency of the operation of mass murder, on the other hand—Doll reveals his particular investment in and perspective on the activities that take place on the ramp. Although he minimally acknowledges the fear experienced by the deportees (especially at the end of this particular scene, when the small group of French Jews inadvertently catches a glimpse of a truck filled with corpses—or in Doll's words, "the day's natural wastage" [26] from Auschwitz I—and bursts into a "helpless, quavering cry" [27]), he also convinces himself that he has prepared for them "a friendly and dignified reception" (26). Thus, in addition to his swaggering pride in his military muscle and his dispassionate, businesslike concern for the bottom line, Doll, in his perspective on the wrenching operation at the ramp, betrays obtuse denial and even disavowal of the experience of the deportees, to whom, once they have disembarked from the train, he jauntily shouts, "*Greetings, 1 and all*" (25).

Throughout the course of his narration in *The Zone of Interest*, Doll reports attending the reception of transports at the ramp (173, 177, 181, 189–90); in fact, the daily selections at the ramp form the routine background of his account, obliquely indicating not only the frequency of the transports arriving at Auschwitz but also the incessant conveyance of the deportees to the gas chambers. At times, he notes, the transports are a "nightmare" (180), particularly when several arrive all at once or the deportees interact directly with him (as when a little girl latches onto his hand or a woman smears his face with lice); Doll views these moments as a personal affront to his authority and frictionless supervision of the camp: "It seems, these days, these nights, that whenever I go to the ramp something dreadful happens—I mean to me personally" (177). At other times, he marvels at the harmonious functioning of the process:

> And it was going so well, it was going so well for once, and they were all calmly undressing, and it was quite warm in the Little Brown Bower, and Szmul was there, and his Sonders were darning their way through the throng, and it was all going so beautifully, and the birds outside were singing so prettily, and I found I even "believed" for a moist and misty interlude that we really were looking after these deeply inconvenienced folk, that we really were going to cleanse them and reclothe them and feed them and give them warm beds for the night, and I knew someone would spoil it, I knew someone would ruin it and madden my nightmares. (189–90)

During such peaceful, uneventful, almost idyllic incidents at the receiving ramp, when none of the "deeply inconvenienced" deportees in turn inconveniences him or obstructs the smooth, ineluctable path to death that he lays for them, Doll fantasizes that the rhetoric that he and his fellow SS officers routinely and cynically deploy to disarm and deceive the deportees—"*You're here to recuperate and then it's off to the farms with you, where there'll be honest work for honest board*" (25)—expresses the truth. In such moments, he chooses to fall for his own arts of deception, deluding himself that his mission consists of kind, humane acts of selfless consideration—as if he were running a charitable hostel for weary travelers—rather than underhanded pacification meant to disguise the genocidal violence that shortly awaits the exhausted, apprehensive, and disoriented deportees. Despite the extreme violence that he himself supervises and in which he daily participates, he prefers to picture here a ludicrous scenario—"a moist and misty interlude"—that is diametrically opposed to the superficially placid but latently brutal scene that plays out in reality before him. In this way, he radically reimagines his mission on the ramp as commensurate with the summery setting and apparent calm in which it unfolds, positing thereby a redemptive reinterpretation of his own consequential function in the dynamics of genocide. At the same time, however, he indicates that he is aware that "someone"—meaning, like the little girl who grasps his hand or the woman who defiantly besmirches him with lice, one of the Jewish deportees—has the capacity to "ruin" his idyllic fantasy with his or her unavoidable humanness and evident suffering, the latter of which he himself is in part the cause. His delusion, through which he tries to reinterpret his role at the receiving ramp as benign or even altruistic, is thus threatened by his confrontation with the very persons whom it concerns, who in the extremity of their plight refuse to conform to his happy fantasy.

Time's Arrow, or, The Nature of the Offense, which Amis wrote in 1991, almost a quarter of a century before he wrote *The Zone of Interest*, presents a strikingly similar scene. *Time's Arrow* is narrated as well from the point of view of a perpetrator (if not exactly in his voice, a complex issue that I will discuss later in this chapter), in this case, an SS doctor stationed at Auschwitz who, like Doll, discloses his own idiosyncratic perspective on the activities that take place on the receiving platform:

> These familial unions and arranged marriages, known as *selections on the ramp*, were the regular high points of the KZ routine. It is a commonplace to say that the triumph of Auschwitz was essentially organizational: we found the sacred fire that hides in the human heart—and built an autobahn that went there. But how to explain the divine synchronies of the ramp? At the very moment that the weak and young and old were brought from the Sprinkleroom to the railway station, as good as new, so their menfolk completed the appointed term of labor service and ventured forth to claim them, on the ramp, a trifle disheveled to be sure, but strong and sleek from their regime of hard work and strict diet. As matchmakers, we didn't know the meaning of the word *failure*; on the ramp, stunning successes were as cheap as spit. When the families coalesced, how their hands and eyes would plead for one another, under our indulgent

gaze. We toasted them far into the night. One guard, his knees bent and swaying, played an accordion. Actually we all drank like fiends. The stag party on the ramp, and the *Kapos*, like the groom's best friends, shoving the man into the waiting cart—freshly sprayed with trash and shit—for the journey home. (*Time's Arrow* 123)

Like Doll in *The Zone of Interest*, the unnamed narrator in *Time's Arrow* reinterprets the phenomenon of the Auschwitz ramp as a series of benign encounters, whereby the SS camp personnel provide constructive and even salutary assistance to the deportees. However, whereas Doll's fantasy is the result of his willful (but ultimately unsuccessful) exercise in self-deception and his denial of the terror experienced by the deportees, the delusion posited by the narrator in this case is less a question of psychological pathology than one of distorted perception. In *Time's Arrow*, as the title of the novel intimates, time is narrated backward in violation of the laws of classical physics, which means that events happen in the text in an order that we as readers recognize as retrograde. The narrator, however, perceives time as proceeding forward in the usual fashion; for him, the inverted order of events is natural, although, because it disrupts the logical connection between cause and effect, it also perplexes him. To reconcile the discordance, he is forced to engage in acts of sense making and interpretation that restore an uncorrupted causality to what he sees and experiences. As incomprehensible to a naive observer as the events that take place on the Auschwitz ramp are in classical, forward time, they make even less sense in backward time; the narrator is thus compelled to cast them in a meaningful narrative that explains what is happening. Like Doll, he chooses to apply a redemptive frame to what he observes; for the narrator in *Time's Arrow*, Auschwitz is an uncanny "triumph" of family "union," whereby husbands, wives, and children, in a succession of "divine synchronies," find each other at the exact same moment and go forth together into their lives. The role that the SS personnel play, in turn, is one of "indulgent" benevolence; as "matchmakers," they enable the perpetual acts of apparent conciliation, and intoxicated with alcohol and excitement, they cheer on these festive scenes of familial fusion. Like Doll, the narrator of *Time's Arrow* chooses to interpret the scenes on the ramp in as favorable a light as possible; whereas

Doll indulges for a brief moment in the belief that his job is to bring succor to frightened and exhausted travelers (since he and his colleagues systematically lie to the newly arrived deportees about their actual fate), here the narrator reads the frenetic activity and aggressive displays of power on the ramp as evidence of a bawdy bachelor party thrown by his macho but well-meaning colleagues.

In the accounts of the narrators in both of Amis's novels, the initial encounter between the Jewish deportees and the Auschwitz camp personnel is thus rewritten in self-serving ways that divest it of the cruel intent of the perpetrators, whose actions are self-interpreted as charitable toward and even beneficial to their victims, whom the personnel on the ramp kindly condescend to help. By fundamentally reframing the brutality enacted by the perpetrators as benevolent and resolutely refusing to perceive the apprehension, confusion, fear, and trauma experienced by the deportees, the narrators of both texts work to craft a narrative of the Auschwitz ramp—and of their own implication in its function—that recasts their own culpability in a positive light. In both cases, rather than remaining mute about what transpires on the receiving platform, the narrators draw attention to it; at the same time, however, by virtue of their concerted attempts to willfully misperceive and systematically misinterpret what happens there, they also highlight their own investment in the stories they relate as well as their unreliability as narrators, although each does so in a slightly different way. In the case of Paul Doll in *The Zone of Interest*, narrative unreliability inheres in the fact that, while he is fully aware of—and at times explicitly represents—the full dimension of malignity executed by him and his staff on the ramp, he cowardly wishes to downplay or avoid moral responsibility for this violence by indulging himself in a callow, fantastic fiction (a fabrication that, in his view, is continually and cruelly punctured only by the presence of the victims themselves). Viewed through the paradigm of unreliability posited by James Phelan, which I discussed in the introduction to part 2, Doll does not so much engage in misreporting or misinterpreting events as he does in misregarding them; his unreliability as a narrator lies not in a lack of knowledge of what is happening at the ramp or inadequate understanding of its implications but in his ethical deficiency and psychological disavowal of the moral dimensions of his role in the camp. His fantasies, which imagine an environment that is directly antithetical to the world of Auschwitz, in which the deportees are greeted kindly at the ramp and treated humanely in the camp, reveal a mind that is shockingly insensible to the moral enormity of the activities in which he plays a part daily and hourly. His inability to acknowledge (even to himself) the nature of his work on the ramp impedes readers' connection to him; for that reason, the challenge that his unreliability poses to the text's readers is in large part a question of empathetic identification. Amis's narrator in *Time's Arrow*, on the other hand, is unreliable across the spectrum—his inverted experience of time causes him to misreport the relationship between cause and effect, while he misregards the entire raison d'être of Auschwitz as one of unequivocally divine triumph—but his unreliability resides chiefly in his inability or unwillingness to adequately interpret the actions, relationships, emotions, and power dynamics that play out between the SS personnel and the Jewish families on the receiving platform. The readerly dynamics that result from his narration are thus chiefly a matter of readers' negotiation of his dubious understanding and deceptive narration of what occurs on the ramp and in the camp.

Amis and the Mimetic/Antimimetic Spectrum

Despite having authored two critically acclaimed novels set—at least in part—in the Auschwitz camp complex, the renowned British author Martin Amis is not typically thought of as a "Holocaust writer." To begin with, he does not manifest the biographical markers often associated with that admittedly ill-defined category, such as personal or familial connection to the Holocaust (whether as a survivor or as the offspring of survivors or perpetrators), Jewish identity (though his wife is half Jewish and, as he points out, his "daughters are Jewish because it comes down through the mother's side"), or German nationality or heritage (Battersby). Moreover, the Holocaust is one subject among many in Amis's works, which include more than two dozen novels, short story collections, screenplays, autobiographical texts, and assorted nonfictional texts. Amis's oeuvre focuses more generally on what Brian Finney calls "the sordid, ugly, threatening phenomenon of late capitalist Western civilization, a dying world in which love is also in its death-throws [*sic*]" ("What's Amis in Contemporary British Fiction?"), particularly as a result of fascist and communist dictatorships and the development of atomic weapons;[3] broadly speaking, he approaches this overarching complex of subjects and themes through a formal mix of postmodern play, satirical excess, "[a] rejection of realism, especially psychological realism, [an] exuberant use of figurative language, [a] punning allusiveness and [a] belief in the moral power of language used creatively" (Finney, "What's Amis in Contemporary British Fiction?"). The Holocaust thus constitutes but one event in a larger history of modern traumas and catastrophes to which Amis responds with his own particular aesthetic style; it is not the primary focus of his work or a predominant source of inspiration. In particular, Amis's impetus for writing the first of his two Holocaust novels, *Time's Arrow*, was less the result of an anterior, express interest in the ethical challenge posed by Holocaust perpetrators and more one of formal ambition; as he writes in the afterword to the novel, "Two summers ago I found myself considering the idea of telling the story of a man's life backward in time. Then, one afternoon, after a typically emotional encounter on the tennis court, [Robert Jay] Lifton gave me a copy of his book *The Nazi Doctors*. My novel would not and could not have been written without it" (*Time's Arrow* 167). In the case of *Time's Arrow*, the Holocaust thus became the subject that made itself immediately available to Amis's application of his aesthetic aims. In the twenty-three-year interval between *Time's Arrow* and *The Zone of Interest*, however, Amis's relationship to the Holocaust transformed; it became a more abiding preoccupation. As he writes in the acknowledgments and afterword to the latter novel,

> What is the unique difficulty in coming to terms with "that which happened" (in Paul Celan's coldly muted phrase)? Any attempt at an answer will necessarily be personal, and for this reason: "the Nazi genocide," as Michael André Bernstein has written, "is somehow central to our self-understanding." Not everyone will feel that way about the events in eastern Europe 1941–1945 (and I am reminded of W. G. Sebald's dry aside to the effect that no serious person

---

3 As Finney argues with regard to Amis's work, "Darkly comic, his novels attempt to undermine and embody the suicidal behavior of the modern world" ("Martin Amis's *Time's Arrow*" 102).

ever thinks about anything else). But I accede to Bernstein's formulation; it is surely one of the defining elements of the singularity. (*The Zone of Interest* 304)

With *The Zone of Interest*, the Holocaust thus moved to the center of Amis's literary focus; according to Mark Lawson, "*Time's Arrow* felt like a temporary diversion from the main direction of the writer's work, but it can now [with the publication of *The Zone of Interest*] be seen as the opening of a major new thoroughfare." As Amis himself describes his connection to the subject matter in a 2015 interview, "It is more as if it's chosen you rather than you've chosen it" (Seaman).

Perhaps more striking than the fact that Amis has written two novels about the Holocaust is his choice, in both texts, to depict that event from the perspective of its perpetrators, particularly given the relative rarity and taboo status of such a representational strategy within the established canon of Holocaust literature.[4] While one can think of a number of "Holocaust writers," such as Elie Wiesel, Primo Levi, Jorge Semprún, Imre Kertész, Ida Fink, and Aharon Appelfeld, who authored multiple fictional and non-fictional texts about the experience of the Holocaust from the viewpoint of the victims and survivors (and who were all, not coincidentally, survivors themselves), it is more difficult to produce a similar list of writers who have taken on the perspective of the perpetrator across multiple texts. (Apart from Amis, Günter Grass—with his bevy of variously implicated narrators in the Danzig trilogy and beyond, most of whom are not, strictly speaking, Holocaust perpetrators, and with his own history of complicity as a former member of the Waffen SS—is probably the only writer who would be a shoe-in for such a list.)[5] For this reason, Amis's two novels together present an interesting case study in the representation of the perspective and consciousness of the Holocaust perpetrator from two disparate positions within a single writer's oeuvre.

---

4 For discussion of the history of the taboo on the narrative focalization of the perpetrator, see McGlothlin, "Theorizing the Perpetrator" (212–14) and "Narrative Perspective and the Holocaust Perpetrator" (160–62), and Boswell, "Holocaust Literature and the Taboo" (188–92).

5 For an astute reading of the ethical dynamics in Grass's Danzig trilogy and his autobiographical writing, see Hanna Meretoja's chapter on Grass in *The Ethics of Storytelling*.

Furthermore, the stark contrast between *Time's Arrow* and *The Zone of Interest* with regard to how the mind of the Holocaust perpetrator is rendered formally and aesthetically produces a fruitful opportunity for exploring the varied functions of filtering. In particular, it provides an instructive exercise for considering the possibilities and limitations of antimimetic or unnatural narration, on the one hand, and mimetic or realist narrative, on the other hand. Amis's two novelistic presentations of perpetrator narration each approach their common subject matter from contrapositive points on the mimetic/antimimetic continuum, a representational phenomenon I analyze in detail in the introduction to part 2. This strategy enables in each text a very different construction of the storyworld of the Holocaust. Moreover, Amis exploits in each of the two novels the opportunity for facilitating varying degrees of readerly involvement enabled by the respective representational modes; whereas antimimetic techniques work to defamiliarize the reader, realist ones compel the experience of immersion. In *Time's Arrow*, Amis creates an unnatural narrative whose defamiliarizing strategies—namely, its inverted temporality and, as we shall shortly see, its impaired narrative voice—engage its readers in cognitive challenges whereby they not only are provoked to seek explanation for the estranged narration and inverted storyworld but also are prodded, by virtue of the narrator's radical misunderstanding and mischaracterization of what transpires around him in Auschwitz, to reflect more broadly on the role of interpretation in apprehending the events of the Holocaust.[6] For its part, *The Zone of Interest*, which Lawson describes as Amis's "notably more conventional novel," immerses the reader in the realist (if somewhat satirized) storyworld of Auschwitz; through its deft presentation of three radically different narrators (one of whom, Paul Doll, we have already encountered), the text involves its readers in a complex exercise in identification in which they are positioned to empathize with the ethically compromised position of a perpetrator. Taken together, the two novels highlight how the mind of the Holocaust perpetrator is rendered to disparate ends across two separate texts and from two distinct points on the mimetic/antimimetic continuum.

---

6 A number of interpreters of *Time's Arrow*, including Finney ("What's Amis in Contemporary British Fiction?"), Chatman, McCarthy, and María Jesús Martínez-Alfaro, connect the antimimetic narrative elements in the text to Shklovsky's concept of defamiliarization.

"While It Worked He and I Were One"

Martin Amis's 1991 novel *Time's Arrow, or, The Nature of the Offense* is a story of a Holocaust perpetrator—in this case, Odilo Unverdorben, an SS doctor who serves in Auschwitz—that begins its narration long after the war, at a time when the world seems to have reestablished a sense of normality and Odilo has likewise normalized into the American doctor Tod T. Friendly. Yet the novel's representation of the perpetrator's experience of the genocide takes place not by means of analeptic flashbacks of Odilo's past, as one might expect from a novel that attempts to portray the prehistory of its protagonist, but through the employment of the technique of inverted temporal narration, or what Brian Richardson terms "antinomic" temporality, whereby "the order of the *syuzhet* [or narrative presentation of events] is simply the opposite of the order of the *fabula* [or chronological order of events in the storyworld]" ("Beyond Story and Discourse" 49).[7] In a parody of the classical Bildungsroman,[8] *Time's Arrow* presents a retrograde story of an individual's development, beginning with the most recent temporal moment of Tod/Odilo's existence—that is to say, the moment of his death—and then moving backward through time as his life literally unfolds to his birth.[9] Amis's technique of reverse narration is often likened

---

7 "Antinomic" temporality is one of six strategies of "temporal reconstruction" that Richardson identifies in postmodern fiction and that, "though nonmimetic, . . . nevertheless bear a dialectical relationship to the concept of mimesis, since it is only through that concept that we can understand its violation" ("Beyond Story and Discourse" 48).
8 A number of scholars argue that, through its technique of inverted temporal narration, *Time's Arrow* attempts to deconstruct some of the generic conventions of the novel. Catherine Bernard (126) and Dermot McCarthy (294) term it an "inverted *Bildungsroman*," whereas Richard Menke describes it as a "postmodern unbildungsroman" (959). Further, John A. Dern calls it "Amis's most obvious anti-novel" (123), H. Porter Abbott describes it as "a kind of deranged narrative discourse" (17), and McCarthy describes it as "an autobiography told by an amnesiac" (294).
9 Actually, the protagonist of *Time's Arrow* bears four names over the course of the narrative: his birth name, Odilo Unverdorben, which he retains until he flees from Auschwitz at the end of the war, and three aliases that he takes in succession as a fugitive: Hamilton de Souza, John Young, and Tod T. Friendly. Of the three aliases, the last he keeps for the longest period of time, indicating the extent to which, after the relative insecurity of his first postwar years, he is able to conceal his criminal past.

to a film played backward,[10] and the novel presents the inverted temporality of its fictional world in as much physical detail as possible: rain rises to the clouds, earthquakes create cities instantly, and people walk backward and regurgitate their food. The novel's antinomic temporality gradually takes the protagonist from his postwar life in Boston and New York—where as a doctor he delivers babies to their mothers' wombs and wedges glass into his patients' skulls and then ships them off to car accidents, where the glass is suddenly yanked out and their wounds are instantly healed—back to Europe, where he becomes a fugitive who eventually returns to the scenes of his crimes:[11] Auschwitz, Treblinka, the killing fields of the Einsatzgruppen, and Schloss Hartheim, one of the Reich euthanasia facilities (and the institution at which, as I discussed in chapter 2, the real-life perpetrator Franz Stangl was posted).[12] At these sites of murder, just as in the American hospitals in which Tod is employed earlier in the text, the reverse narration unravels the historical product and the chain of cause and effect inherent to it; but in this case, rather than revoking the patients' healing and returning them to a state of sickness (as Tod does in his postwar role as a doctor), Odilo, now a doctor in Auschwitz, escorts multitudes of Jewish souls into their bodies and back to life, an inversion Sue Vice, following Robert J. Lifton, terms the "killing-healing paradox" (*Holocaust Fiction* 31). The brutal history of the Holocaust is thus, by way of chronological reversal, narratively undone, exposing an ironic disjunction between the historical event and its potential narration. This gap is made possible by readers' recognition that the novel remains historically accurate and at the same time performs, purely on the level of narrative technique, an act of radical

---

10 See Maya Slater (141), Ann Parry (253), James Diedrick (133), and Neil Easterbrook (53). The novel's narrator at one point also compares the way his life unfolds to a cinema of retrogression: "It just seems to me that the film is running backward" (*Time's Arrow* 8).

11 As Finney argues, "The boat taking [Odilo] from Europe to the States in its inverted form leaves 'no mark in the ocean, as if we are successfully covering our tracks' (99), which is precisely what the doctor was doing" ("What's Amis in Contemporary British Fiction?").

12 Sue Vice points out that the diversity of Unverdorben's experience and his service in Schloss Hartheim, in an Einsatzgruppe, and in Auschwitz make him the "archetypal Nazi perpetrator" (*Holocaust Fiction* 33). In this, he resembles Max Schulz in *The Nazi and the Barber* and Maximilien Aue in *The Kindly Ones*, both of whom also perpetrate violence in multiple Holocaust contexts.

historical revisionism.[13] Amis's novel takes the story of the perpetration of the Holocaust and rewrites it as an ironic tale in which the Nazis restore European Jewish life (33) and "genocide becomes genesis" (McCarthy 299) through the inversion of cause and effect.

The antinomic temporality of *Time's Arrow*, which "not only defamiliarizes the historical world it imitates, [but also] destabilizes the fundamental conventions of mimesis upon which all narrative relies" (McCarthy 303), is not, however, the only antimimetic element in the novel. As mentioned at the beginning of this chapter, *Time's Arrow* is told from the perspective of its perpetrator-protagonist, but not—and this is where the impossible quality of the unnatural comes into play—directly in his voice. Like the temporal framework of Amis's text, whose disintegration represents a pathological counterpart to the notion of progressive narrative time, the protagonist's voice is, from a narratological perspective, disjointed and diseased as well. As the reader learns early in the novel, although there is indubitably an "I" that tells Tod T. Friendly's story, and although this "I" inhabits Tod's body, the narrator is severed absolutely from Tod's consciousness and has no access to Tod's decisions, reactions, or reasoning (though he is able to register Tod's experience physically and emotionally).[14] The novel thus not only deforms the mimetic representation of time but also disfigures the conventional narratological conception of voice. According to Seymour Chatman, the narrator "is homodiegetic—he exists both as the narrating agent of his own story and the protagonist of his search through Tod's past. But in that search he is also the implicit heterodiegetic narrator of Odilo's story" (40). In this way, the narrator of the novel is a narrative oxymoron: the "I" of the text corresponds to neither the consciousness nor the name of the body in which he is housed and from which he perceives the world.

---

13 One might view *Time's Arrow* as the analeptic (i.e., told through flashback) counterpart to what Genette terms "novels of anticipation," which "belong fully to the prophetic genre" (*Narrative Discourse* 219). Amis's novel does not prophesize what will happen in the temporal future but rather hints at what will happen in the narrative future, which is, of course, the novel's temporal past.

14 Sue Vice argues that the narrator is "disembodied" (*Holocaust Fiction* 12) or "divided from his own body" (24). Given that the narrator perceives the world from inside Tod/Odilo's body—or, in Phelan's words, that "he is on the inside looking in" rather than "on the outside looking in" ("The Ethics and Aesthetics of Backward Narration" 124)—I argue that, rather than disunited from Tod/Odilo's body, he is exiled from Tod/Odilo's mind.

Rather, he functions as a supplemental mental and emotional substance that is slated, as "passenger or parasite" (*Time's Arrow* 8), to accompany the protagonist through life without being able to communicate with him: "We are in this together, absolutely. But it isn't good for him to be so alone. *His* isolation is complete. Because he doesn't know I'm here" (14). This unannexed narrator is a sort of Doppelgänger or, in James Diedrick's phrase, a "ghostly narrator" (139) who haunts the text, perpetually present but unable to act in the world around him.[15] Most critics regard the narrator as Tod/Odilo's soul, the sundered remnant of the protagonist's originally undivided consciousness. Amis's text itself suggests this interpretation; on the one hand, Irene, Tod's longtime lover, "tells Tod that he has no soul" (53), while on the other hand, the narrator himself gradually realizes that, despite his utter inability to affect Tod's thoughts or behavior, he is called upon to function as Tod's soul in absentia: "If I am his soul, and there were soul-loss or soul-death, would that stop him?" (88).

Critics further generally agree that we, as readers, are supposed to understand the cleavage between the protagonist (Tod/Odilo) and the narrator (whom both Chatman and Phelan ["The Ethics and Aesthetics of Backward Narration"] call "Soul") as the force that generates and drives the temporal distortion; in other words, the text intimates that the narrator and the protagonist each experience (and interpret) time differently.[16] Thus, while we encounter the happenings in the storyworld in retrograde order through and with the narrator (who, however, crucially does not perceive that time, as he lives it, flows in an unnatural direction), we also recognize that the narrator's discourse functions as a sort of reversed or mirrored representation of the fabula of Tod/Odilo's life, which, as we are to understand, unfolds in forward time in the conventional manner and which we have to reconstruct from the narrator's account. Phelan describes this readerly dynamic as "a progression that moves simultaneously along two different but interrelated tracks" and argues that it puts "a heavy cognitive load on us, one that requires extensive and often complex

---

15 See Diedrick (133), Dern (126), and Menke (960).
16 According to Horowitz, "Amis's observer soul reverses the flow of historical time, but only provisionally: as he moves backwards, the Nazi physician whose body he cohabits continues to move forward. Thus, just as the soul restores the damage caused by the body, the soul's acts of resurrection are perpetually undone by the doctor's acts of killing" (194).

interpretive judgments" ("The Ethics and Aesthetics of Backward Narration" 124). It also functions to foreground the critical operations of reconstruction and interpretation, which are decisive not only for the narrator but also for the text's readers, who, as Chatman argues, "must work to understand" (50) the defamiliarized events of the Holocaust as presented through the narrative discourse.

For his part, the narrator reads the events that take place at Auschwitz, Treblinka, and the killing fields in a way that is consonant with his earlier perception of cause and effect. However, in this case, instead of constituting the postwar "world of mistakes, of diametrical mistakes" (*Time's Arrow* 8), in which the American hospital "is an atrocity producing situation" (92) and doctors harm rather than heal their patients, "here in Auschwitz" the world "has a new habit. It makes sense" (129). In other words, with his inverted understanding of causal relationships produced by his experience of antinomic temporality, "the narrator radically misreads every event at Auschwitz" (Easterbrook 56), as, for example, in his description of the "divine synchronies" of the Auschwitz ramp. Unable—or, as I shall shortly argue, resolutely unwilling—to recognize or adjust to the illogical laws of his inverted temporality, he reads all of the actions and events through the lens of forward time. He thereby develops his own logic and chain of causal relationships to explain what he sees as the brutality of the postwar hospital and the messianic vision of Auschwitz, where Odilo and his colleagues "conjure a multitude from the sky above the river" (130), meaning the souls of Jews who are gathered "in the heavens—awaiting human form, and union" (123). In his reconstruction of the causality of events at Auschwitz and his characterization of himself as utopian dreamer who wishes to right the wrongness of the world, the narrator develops a profoundly false theory of the Nazi "redemption" (147) of Europe's Jews that mirrors the sinister, grandiose design of the "Final Solution." Through the narrator's revisionist reading of "an 'altruistic Holocaust'" (Vice, *Holocaust Fiction* 14) made possible by the unnatural narrative devices of antinomic temporality and vocal disfiguration and dissonance, Amis's text thus reveals a "bitterly ironic disparity" (Easterbrook 56) between the historical events and the narrator's professed understanding of them. However, to activate this irony, the text must stimulate the involvement of informed and perceptive readers profoundly aware of the true actual course of historical events.[17] The horrific character of the narrator's gross misreading of what happens in Auschwitz is thus predicated on readers' awareness of the real reasons for the camp's existence and their knowledge that in history, as opposed to in the narrator's account, the genocidal crimes of Auschwitz can never be undone.

In the logic of the narrative, the protagonist and his narrator-double are born cleaved when they come to life at the beginning of the novel (which is to say, at the moment of Tod's death); however, as the reader begins to understand the antinomic chrono-logic of the text and the idea that the narrator is hurtling blindly toward Odilo's unknown past (one imagines, as Sara Horowitz does, the narrator as the inverted counterpart to Walter Benjamin's reading of Paul Klee's "Angelus Novus" [194]), it becomes clear that this bifurcation is not an original state but an effect whose cause lies in the novel's narrative future. As Horowitz, Vice (*Holocaust Fiction*), Diedrick, and Richard Menke have separately argued, the protagonist's dissociative split is a direct result of his experience as a doctor in Auschwitz and, especially, as Diedrick points out, of his time at Schloss Hartheim, his chronologically first experience with state-sanctioned murder (138–39). "In a sense," writes Horowitz,

> Amis's device gives symbiotic existence to Robert J. Lifton's idea of the Nazi doctor's second self. In his psychological exploration of Nazi physicians who facilitated death and atrocity in concentration camps, Lifton posits a splitting of the Nazi perpetrator into two distinct selves—what he refers to as the normal and the Auschwitz self. (193)

---

17 According to Finney, "The implied reader is constantly required to supply the truth about historical events that the protagonist wants to repress and that the narrator misinterprets. . . . This is a risky strategy seeing that the younger generation, on Amis's own testimony, either do not know the facts about the Holocaust or see it as a myth. For those readers who discern the irony, the effect is contradictory. They simultaneously get pleasure from the conceits produced by the reversal of history and, forced to recollect the atrocities that actually occurred, recast the comedy as dark satire. . . . His use of irony compels a reader, in reversing the events and the narrator's interpretation of them, to enter the novel as a participant" (*Martin Amis* 56–57).

Seen in this way, the protagonist of *Time's Arrow* presents a fictional illustration of Lifton's theory of the doubling of the perpetrator-doctor, who, to be able to perform activities that pervert the Hippocratic oath to which he originally swore and at the same time "to continue to see himself as humane physician, husband, father" (Lifton 419), must disavow a part of himself through a kind of "Faustian bargain" (421). The Nazi doctors who served at the historical Auschwitz, according to Lifton, created a second self, an "Auschwitz self," in order to "function psychologically in an environment so antithetical to [their] previous ethical standards" (419); the doubled "Auschwitz self" took on the "'dirty work' for the entire self by rendering that work 'proper' and in that way protect[ed] the entire self from awareness of its own guilt" (422). By engaging in doubling, the Nazi doctors repudiated, according to Lifton,

> not reality itself—the individual doctor was aware of what he was doing via the Auschwitz self—but the meaning of that reality. The Nazi doctor knew that he selected, but did not interpret selections as murder. One level of disavowal, then, was the Auschwitz self's altering of the meaning of murder; and on another, the repudiation by the original self of *anything* done by the Auschwitz self. (422)

Integral to the process of doubling, in Lifton's view, was thus the doctor's reinterpretation of the meaning and moral significance of the acts attributed to the "Auschwitz self"; by divesting his actions of the ethical implications they would have borne outside the Auschwitz universe, the doctor was able to imagine that he was positively impacting his world through the purportedly hygienic measures he condoned and implemented at the camp. As Horowitz, Vice (*Holocaust Fiction*), Phelan ("Ethics and Aesthetics of Backwards Narration"), Menke, Finney ("Martin Amis's *Time's Arrow* and the Postmodern Sublime"), Chatman, Easterbrook, McCarthy, Badrideen ("The Soul in *Time's Arrow*"), Harris, Martínez-Alfaro, and Diedrick all argue (and as Amis himself suggests in the afterword to the novel), Lifton's theory of doubling accounts for the narrative pathology in *Time's Arrow*. According to this view, the narrator is the result of the doubling process and thus can be seen as a "vestigial conscience" (Menke 960) whose "attitude to the events is distinctly more humane than Tod's" (Chatman 41). Moreover, with its emphasis on the "killing-healing paradox" of "Auschwitz's institutional program of medicalized genocide" (Lifton 147), Lifton's theory also accounts for the narrator's acts of radical reinterpretation of cause and effect provoked by the antinomic temporality, whereby he sees his medical duties in the camp as part of a "war on death that now comes in many forms" (*Time's Arrow* 135).

At the same time, however, the way in which doubling occurs in the novel complicates its simple adoption of Lifton's paradigm. To begin with, the narrator's dissociation from Odilo's consciousness occurs not *during* his time at Auschwitz, as Lifton's theory of doubling holds that it should, but directly *before* and *after* his Holocaust experience.[18] At the beginning of chapter 5, which brings Odilo from his fugitive flight at the end of the war back to Auschwitz, the narrator makes a point of connecting for the first time the first-person pronoun to Odilo, the novel's protagonist-actor:

> I, Odilo Unverdorben, arrived in Auschwitz Central somewhat precipitately and by motorbike, with a wide twirl or frill of slush and mud, shortly after the Bolsheviks had entrained their ignoble withdrawal. *Now.* Was there a secret passenger on the backseat of the bike, or in some imaginary sidecar? No. I was one. . . . Auschwitz lay around me, miles and miles of it, like a somersaulted Vatican. Human life was all ripped and torn. But I was one now, fused for a preternatural purpose. (*Time's Arrow* 116)

As the narrator stresses, the experience of genocidal violence does not sunder the protagonist from his soul; rather, in the moment of the Auschwitz experience, the narrator-self (the soul) and the protagonist-self (the mind and body) are united in almost metaphysical harmony. Throughout this chapter and the next, rather than referring to Odilo as a separate entity, as

---

18 Greg Harris argues that "the narrative has the doppelgänger effect of a ghost consciousness haunting a body it used to call home (prior to the Nazi years)" (490–91). However, the narration of Odilo's childhood and youth takes the same shape as that of Tod's old age; in that part of the narrative as well, the narrator is split from the protagonist.

he has been wont to do until this point, the narrator uses "I" and "my" to refer to their consolidated identity and joint activities, the latter of which he regards not only with approval but also with wonder at their "sacred efficacy" (121). To be sure, he admits consternation about the atmosphere of the camp: "The Auschwitz universe, it has to be allowed, was fiercely coprocentric. It was *made* of shit" (123). However, the filth and chaotic unseemliness of his work environment do not in his view detract from the higher purpose to which he is committed:

> What tells me that this is right? What tells me that all the rest was wrong? Certainly not my aesthetic sense. I would never claim that Auschwitz-Birkenau-Monowitz was good to look at. Or to listen to, or to smell, or to taste, or to touch. There was, among my colleagues there, a general though desultory quest for greater elegance. I can understand that word, and all its yearning: *elegant*. Not for its elegance did I come to love the evening sky above the Vistula, hellish red with the gathering souls. *Hier ist kein warum*. Here there is no why. Here there is no when, no how, no where. Our preternatural purpose? To dream a race. To make a people from the weather. From thunder and from lightning. With gas, with electricity, with shit, with fire. (119–20)

Despite the "patina of cruelty, intense cruelty" (122) he perceives in Auschwitz, the world that the narrator previously experienced as upside down and counterintuitive begins to harmonize with his ethical ideals and with his lofty sense of his own role as a doctor. From his perspective, Tod was a murderous butcher in his postwar life as a doctor, but now he can see that Odilo is finally living up to the Hippocratic ideal to save lives and restore the sick to health. Accordingly, he feels fused with the body and consciousness from which he was heretofore exiled; he thus not only narrates but also acts from this position.

The narrator retains his identification with Odilo's body and mind throughout his experience of killing in Auschwitz, the Einsatzgruppe, and Schloss Hartheim, until the end of chapter 6, when he leaves Schloss Hartheim to enter his pre-Holocaust life. At this point, the narrator states,

He walks on, alone, Odilo Unverdorben. Fully alone.

    I who have no name and no body—I have slipped out from under him and am now scattered above like flakes of ash-blonde human hair. No longer can I bear with the ruined god, betrayed and beaten by his own magic. Calling on powers best left unsummoned, he took human beings apart—and then he put them back together again. For a while it worked (there was redemption); and while it worked he and I were one, on the banks of the Vistula. He put *us* back together. But of course you shouldn't be doing any of this kind of thing with human beings . . . The party is over. He lies there in the peeling pyramid of the attic bedroom, on his cot shaped like a gutter. A damp pink pillow is twisted in his fists. I'll always be here. But he's on his own. (*Time's Arrow* 147; ellipses in original)

At the end of his experience in the camps and killing fields of Eastern Europe—that is, at the beginning of what we recognize in forward time to be the initial events of the Holocaust—the narrator abandons the "preternatural" fusion with the protagonist and returns to the role he previously occupied in the postwar period as supplemental consciousness. Importantly, in the context of *Time's Arrow* as a whole, this fusion is a fleeting occurrence, occupying less than 20 percent of the novel. Perhaps for this reason, critics have taken the split protagonist to be the narrative norm and underestimated the significance of the brief period of identity. Sue Vice makes note of the narrator's assumption of the first-person pronoun with reference to Odilo but is suspicious of it because it would seem to contradict Lifton's theory. For this reason, she sees this part of the novel as an aberration and attributes it to a moment of unreliability on the narrator's part (*Holocaust Fiction* 24–25). Yet this incident of unreliability is not the exception in the novel; rather, from the first sentences of the text, the narrator is the quintessential unreliable narrator who insists on reading the backward events as if they were moving forward. As Phelan argues, unreliability is "the default condition of the narration, because Soul is reporting events in the wrong order and compounding that misreporting with a misreading of the relations between cause and effect" ("The Ethics and Aesthetics of Backward Narration" 127).[19] Moreover, the narrator reads his own existence and Odilo/Tod's work as a doctor both in Auschwitz and in postwar life from a reversed perspective. Just as the laws of time and of causality are inverted, the narrator inverts Lifton's theory as well; in this version, he and Odilo become whole again through Odilo's work at Auschwitz, where rather than participating in a grand plan in which Europe's Jews are systematically murdered, he is part of a diametrically opposite scheme to bring millions to life in an act of godly creation. In this inverted retelling of the Holocaust, the narrator parodically reverses the direction of Lifton's theory of doubling, choosing to become whole at the moment in which Lifton's doctors are forced to dissociate. In this way, he conforms less to Lifton's notion of doubling than he does to what James Waller, in his research on Holocaust perpetrators, calls the "unitary self-perspective" ("Perpetrators of the Holocaust" 12). According to Waller, when "we are troubled by inconsistencies between our overt behaviors and internal psychological constellations," we are "motivated to alleviate these inconsistencies to preserve the integrity of the self," usually through "fundamental alterations in the internal psychological constellation of a unitary self" (16). In other words, to reduce the cognitive dissonance between our "attitudes, beliefs, values, and morals" and "role-dictated behaviors" that are discrepant with them (21), we modify the former to harmonize with the latter rather than create a discontinuous, second self through doubling to which we relegate the problematic behaviors. The alteration of the unitary self in such situations involves accepting rather than rejecting the behavior, which in turn requires a reinterpretation of its meaning and consequences. The narrator's radical reversal of cause and effect in Auschwitz, his misreading of the violence that occurs there, and his revision of his own role in the genocide can thus be seen as the amplified literary expression of the processes of psychological revision and reinterpretation that allow one "to engage oneself systematically in evil actions while avoiding equally systematically a sense of one's own evil" (26).

Seen in this light, the narrator's stunning acts of misreading at Auschwitz, along with his overt identification with the body, mind, behaviors, and

---

[19] Or, as Menke sardonically writes, "This fictional soul is a supremely reliable narrator; he may be relied upon to get things diametrically, and often poignantly, wrong" (960).

motivations of Odilo Unverdorben, trouble the idea he is the straightforward product of the process of psychic doubling. They also call into question the notion that he functions in the text as "the moral and sympathetic consciousness which Odilo had to suppress in order to take on his inhumane work" (Badrideen, "The Soul in *Time's Arrow*" 57), which maintains a "childlike, life affirming innocence" and "possesses an unconditional love for others that is the only antidote for the horrors the novel unsparingly records" (Diedrick 141). Rather, as I argue, by presenting him as united with Odilo at Auschwitz and at other sites of atrocity as well as enthusiastically "'in it'" (*Time's Arrow* 135), the novel suggests a much more sinister reading of the narrator's role in the text, one that is redolent of Waller's unitary self-conception. Rather than represent an external ethical and narrative position that is uncorrupted (or, to use the German equivalent, *unverdorben*) by the genocidal environment in which he lives and functions, the narrator is fundamentally altered by it—in Waller's words, he "become[s] that to which [he is] exposed" ("Perpetrators of the Holocaust" 27)—and fully identifies with it psychologically, physically, and spiritually:

> Human beings want to be alive. They are dying to be alive. Twenty cubic centimeters of air—twenty cubic centimeters of nothing—is all you need to make the difference. So nobody thanks me as, with a hypodermic almost the size of a trombone and my right foot firmly stamped on the patient's chest, I continue to prosecute the war against nothing and air. (*Time's Arrow* 135)

As this quote demonstrates, at some moments the narrator's actions—when, for example, he plants his foot on the chest of a patient "dying to be alive"— are unequivocally violent whether viewed according to forward time or antinomically, a phenomenon that Phelan calls "pockets of reliability," whereby the narrator is "capable . . . of being wholly indifferent to" violence and pain ("The Ethics and Aesthetics of Backwards Narration" 127, 130). The narrator's obstinate mischaracterization of this violence is thus not merely a failure to recognize it; rather, it constitutes a cagey refusal to narrate it in a way that would reveal his actual agency in it. Through his recasting of this violence as an act of creation and of love, he is able to feign his own innocence, "remain convinced of his own morality" (Harris 495), and persuade the reader of the same.

Critics who maintain that the narrator represents the moral conscience that has split off from the protagonist, dividing the perpetrator neatly into a "prior, more humane, non-Auschwitz self" that has been "silenced and erased" and "a Hippocrates-free Auschwitz self" (Martínez-Alfaro 136–37), thus ignore not only the narrator's elation at being fused with the protagonist in the Holocaust experience but also the ways in which the self-conception and narration of the former are infected by the actions and behavior of the latter. Further, in their predilection to see the text as an exaggerated but largely unambiguous formal manifestation of Lifton's theory of doubling (which Lifton himself distinctly does *not* equate with pathological or clinical dissociation that may result in disorders such as dissociative identity or depersonalization but rather presents as a metaphor for psychological adaptation),[20] they take the narrator at his own word about both his relationship to the events that transpire at Auschwitz and his understanding of them. Such critics thus miss the way in which, as Harris astutely points out, "the narrator unimplicates himself in Nazi atrocity" (495) not only by remaining stubbornly and grossly insensible to the suffering and death caused by his "preternatural purpose" but also by providing a redemptive reading of the "triumph of Auschwitz" made possible by a willful misunderstanding of cause and effect and a crafty manipulation of the narrative enabled by it.[21]

---

20 According to Waller, "In his psychoanalytic analyses of evildoing, Lifton presents dissociation as the most frequent psychological adaptation utilized by the Nazi doctors. Lifton avoids the overgeneralization of a pathological condition to scores of perpetrators, however, by differentiating this dissociation from clinical dissociative disorders. The latter evidence a profoundly distinct and autonomous dissociation. . . . In contrast, Lifton presents the dissociation in evildoing as involving a dialectic (i.e., awareness) between the split selves" ("Perpetrators of the Holocaust" 14).

21 While a number of critics mention the narrator's unreliability, particularly with regard to his faulty understanding of events based on the antinomic temporality (a phenomenon that Phelan, in "The Ethics and Aesthetics of Backward Narration," investigates in detail with characteristic acuity), they are less skeptical about his purported honesty about how he understands the relationship between cause and effect in Auschwitz. Only Phelan and Harris question the narrator's implication and/or motives. According to Harris, who views the narrator as "the very conscience that Tod lost at some point in his repressed past" (495), "Of course, such denial is self-protective: it enables the narrator to transfer his Nazi activities on to his opposing self (which, to recall Lifton, he holds

At its extreme, such unqualified critical acceptance of the narrator's own account of how he (mis)understands his actions at Auschwitz can result in such astonishing readings of the book as that provided by Ahmed Badrideen, who, taking as a point of departure the generally accepted idea that the narrator is Tod/Odilo's soul, crafts the following interpretation:

> The notion of the narrator as a platonic or Judaeo-Christian soul may provide explanatory ground for the nature of the narrator's journey. . . . This re-encounter with, and undoing of, inhumanity, crime and sin evokes religious concepts of purgatory and purgation: soul's journey might be construed as a form of redress for Odilo's actions. Rather than being released into hell or heaven, the soul is redirected back into the body and expiates its moral debt by witnessing the Holocaust in reverse, when Jews, and other victims of the Nazis, are given their right to "life and love." Instead of being a silent witness to evil, the soul becomes an agent of good: "A parallel pleasure and comfort, for me at any rate, was to watch the Jews. The people I had helped to dream down from the heavens." This quotation also shows that, in contrast to Odilo's soul which remains on Earth, the souls of Holocaust victims attained heaven. ("The Soul in *Time's Arrow*" 61)

Badrideen proceeds from the assumption that a soul possesses "a strong moral sense" ("The Soul in *Time's Arrow*" 58) and an "inherent, 'heavenly'

---

in 'permanent disavowal'), a fossilized embodiment of the Auschwitz self. The narrator can, by contrast, remain convinced of his own morality. As a consequence, *no one is guilty*: the narrator unimplicates himself in Nazi atrocity" (495–96). Whereas Harris sees the narrator as "self-protective," however, I see him as deliberately feigning obtuseness in order to evade accountability. For his part, Phelan recognizes the narrator's identification with Odilo's ideological perspective while at Auschwitz: "We realize that the neatness of Soul's frequent dichotomy between those two selves cannot be sustained, since the 'other' narrated self actually shares traits and responses that Soul does not acknowledge, either because he cannot recognize them or because doing so would mean that he cannot claim ethical superiority over Tod/Unverdorben" ("The Ethics and Aesthetics of Backward Narration" 130).

sense of the good" (59); he also accepts without discrimination the narrator's claim to embody such a soul, his characterization of his own "inherent pacifism" (60), and his "rejoic[ing] in the lives of the Jews seemingly created by the death camps and who are now being generously assimilated into Germany" (60). Further, in spite of his claim to read the phenomenon of the narrator from the perspective of the "Judaeo-Christian tradition" (60), Badrideen considers the narrator exclusively from the perspective of Christian theology, since neither heaven nor hell nor purgatory is a central or even articulated concept in Judaism.[22] As a consequence of this perspective—and as a consequence of failing to recognize the narrator's extreme unreliability and his oblivious or even callous indifference to the suffering that exists around him—Badrideen sees the narrator as an unqualified "agent of good" that rescues and redeems the victims, thereby "expiat[ing] its moral debt." In my view, Badrideen's characterization of the narrator as a virtuous soul who strives for atonement is not only a gross misreading of the narrator's shrewd equivocality and the blatant ironies produced by Amis's text; it is also simply offensive in its suggestion that the "moral debt" of the Holocaust could be absolved or the souls of its perpetrators redeemed merely through the rewinding

---

22 Badrideen misrepresents Jewishness and Judaism at several points. His uncritical reading that the souls of the Jewish victims of the Holocaust "attained heaven"—in direct contradiction of Jewish belief (and in flagrant disregard of Amis's irony)—is reminiscent of the scandal that erupted in the 1990s and again in 2017, when it became known that members of the Church of Jesus Christ of Latter-day Saints were posthumously baptizing Jewish victims of the Holocaust with supercilious indifference to the religious convictions of the greater number of them. Badrideen further writes, "The narrator of *Time's Arrow* . . . is also a familiar compound ghost—in its nature as a spiritual entity—of broader cultural and intellectual traditions, dangerously diminished and marginalized by the Enlightenment and modernity: the dualistic conception of man and belief in metaphysical or supernatural realms, traditions which, it is important to note, are strongly associated with the Jewish people and Judaism: 'It's their [Jews'] eyes I admire. That glossy, heated look. An exoticism that points toward the transcendent' (Amis 160)" ("The Soul in *Time's Arrow*" 64). Not only does Badrideen assume here the narrator's historically and ethically questionable view of Jews as exotic, but, in his reification of Judaism and the Jewish people as "metaphysical or supernatural" (in other words, premodern and pre-Enlightenment), he also discounts the significant Jewish contribution to Enlightenment thought.

of time and the reversal of its causal relationships.[23] Badrideen's readiness to accept uncritically the narrator's take on his actions at Auschwitz not only erases the suffering of his victims but also effaces his role in causing it. In his reading of *Time's Arrow* as a post-Enlightenment "soul-cleansing narrative" (62), in which the existence of the narrator functions as a "quasi-purgatorial lingering to clear a moral debt" (63), Badrideen merges here completely with the narrator's perspective and ideological self-justification for his actions at Auschwitz, thereby not only missing the ironic thrust of Amis's rewriting of the Holocaust in reverse but also overlooking the disturbing ethical failings of the narrator's account of the violence in which he eagerly participates by characterizing it as something that can magically be expiated or undone through an act of antinomic narration.

Badrideen's reading, though anomalous in the scholarship on *Time's Arrow* and perhaps extreme in its identification with and uncritical acceptance of the narrator's self-professed function in the narrative, nevertheless demonstrates the tricky operations of interpretation raised by Amis's text, a dynamic to which all readers and interpreters are susceptible. Because of the bewilderment and defamiliarization caused by the text's deployment of unnatural devices, readers seek a stable point of orientation in the text, a role for which the narrator makes himself overtly available. Readers are compelled to become dependent on him, in spite of his rampant unreliability, for guidance through the storyworld; it is no wonder that they take him at least in part at his word, even when it is clear that his perspective is, in the "sense" that he distills from his Auschwitz experience, manipulatively disingenuous at best and malevolently deceptive at worst. Readers' reliance on him and his interpretation of the events in which he plays a part highlights the treacherous potential inherent to the enterprise of meaning making. According to Bernard,

---

23 When I teach *Time's Arrow* to undergraduates, I pair it with the Dan Pagis poem "Draft of a Reparations Agreement," which, with its similar temporal and causal inversions ("The smoke back to the tin chimney and further on and inside / back to the hollow of the bones, / and already you will be covered with skin and sinews and you will live, / look, you will have your lives back" [Pagis 35]), but without the perpetrator's perspective, "ironically prefigure[s]" (Chatman 54) *Time's Arrow*. Pagis's poem forcefully subverts the idea that the crimes of the Holocaust can ever be redeemed.

> By turning back the clock of time, Amis offers a literal allegory of the subversion of interpretation; by folding back the fabric of life and time, Amis questions the notion of teleology and the logic of interpretation. The position of the addressee is jeopardized by a text which reverses the notions of cause and effect and hurls the reader in a narrative black hole where he loses his bearings. (133)

Bernard refers here specifically to the narrator's grossly misconstrued interpretation of the physical laws and ethical implications of Auschwitz; however, the "allegory of the subversion of interpretation" holds true for the reader as well, who is forced—and at times fails—to adequately interpret the ethical implications of the narrator's interpretation. The "narrative black hole" to which Bernard refers is thus at times a confounding and unsettling void in which the narrator thrusts us and at other times a space of interpretive precarity into which we ourselves fall as a result of our credulous acceptance of his account.

Through its idiosyncratic depiction of the physics and ethics of Auschwitz, *Time's Arrow* provides an ironic aperture into the mind of the Holocaust perpetrator, a view that is nevertheless distorted by the novel's deployment of a pair of antimimetic narrative devices and filtered through a narrator who fails (or perhaps even flatly refuses) to correctly recognize, adequately acknowledge, or candidly narrate his role in the genocidal crimes that take place there and instead submits an exculpatory narrative of redemption that explains them in a positive light. In this way, according to Jenni Adams, the novel "presents an aspect of the perpetrator that cannot in any meaningful sense be held to account" ("Reading (as) Violence" 30). Further, by featuring the self-serving exculpatory narrative of an Auschwitz doctor—or at least his soul—who disingenuously rewrites mass murder as redemptive deliverance, Amis's novel not only provides a stark warning about the hazards attendant to the perpetrator's narration of his own experience but also models the dangers involved in readers' endeavors to interpret the perpetrator's perspective.

Zones of Interest

Amis's second novel about the Holocaust, *The Zone of Interest*, shares with the Auschwitz episodes in *Time's Arrow* the same geographical setting. However, it represents a vastly different fictional storyworld: while the world of the earlier text is unnatural in terms of the physical laws of temporality, that of the later novel renders the historical site of Auschwitz according to mostly mimetic conventions. In other words, the disparity in novelistic approach produces two very different representations of the Holocaust. In *Time's Arrow*, the concentration and death camp is rendered as a place of utopian—although "coprocentric"—redemption and creation, whose modus operandi is governed by a kind of negative sublime. In *The Zone of Interest*, by contrast, Auschwitz is the site of the everyday bureaucratic routine of genocidal murder, where "the *blinding* radicalism of the KL [*Konzentrationslager*, or concentration camp]" (*The Zone of Interest* 28), which has "no exemplum, no model, no precedent" (77), must also be organized, administered, and implemented and thus involves—for the perpetrators, at least—"complication and expense," "difficulties," and "'objective conditions'" (29). Moreover, while *Time's Arrow* focuses on a single perpetrator, who is partitioned in unnatural ways between a narrating consciousness and an acting protagonist (two entities that fuse in the retrograde ethical atmosphere of Auschwitz), *The Zone of Interest* departs from this strategy of disjunction within one perpetrator figure to distribute, in a much more mimetic manner, the narrative voice among three separate narrators—two perpetrators and one prisoner—each of whom occupies a discreet experiential position in the life-and-death habitat of the Auschwitz complex and accordingly depicts it in radically different ways than the other two. By conjuring the world of Auschwitz more mimetically through "the traditional historical novel" (Wood), Amis shifts the pressure points of the narrative strategy from one end of the antimimetic/mimetic spectrum to the other, that is, from defamiliarization through unnatural narrative devices to immersion through mimetic realism.

To be sure, while *The Zone of Interest* does not evince the postmodern, antirealist, and antimimetic character of *Time's Arrow* and some of Amis's other novels, such as *Money* (1984) and *London Fields* (1989), which use "excess and subversion of mimetic conventions to represent the modern world's self-alienation and sense of loss" (Finney, *Martin Amis* 119), in its commitment to mimetic realism it does carry over particular hallmarks of Amis's postmodern style, including a penchant for "dark satire" (Kakutani, "Ordinary, Everyday Monsters" C21), comic irreverence, linguistic play, and generic experimentation.[24] These potentially distancing elements thus mitigate to some degree the illusionist effect of the novel and prevent it from developing the full mimeticism associated with psychological realism.[25] At the same time, however, by abstaining in *The Zone of Interest* from the kind of metafictional, self-reflexive, and formally experimental strategies for which most of his fictional work is known, Amis mobilizes a natural narrative approach that favors "narrators, characters, events, and settings that more or less resemble those of our quotidian experience" (Richardson, "Antimimetic, Unnatural, and Postmodern Narrative Theory" 20), thereby positing "the mimetic extension of the recipients' real world" (Wolf 40). Of course, the concentrationary universe of Auschwitz is far from quotidian or coextensive with the social environment of the great majority of the novel's readers; however, by deploying "the conventions of nonfictional narratives and of fiction that closely resembles nonfiction" (Richardson, "Unnatural Narrative Theory" 385), particularly variations of autodiegetic narration that resemble private diary entries, testimony, and retrospective remembering, *The Zone of Interest* works to naturalize the world of the concentration and death camp, making it the setting of both everyday human encounters and the workaday administration of the excessive violence of genocide.

Within its mimetic frame, *The Zone of Interest* encompasses three discreet genres, each of which corresponds to one of its three narrators. With its focus on the everyday banality of the running of genocide, the first genre comprises what Sue Vice describes as "an office comedy about middle management, in which the office is Auschwitz" ("British Representation

---

24 For an excellent overview of Amis's stylistic signature, see Finney, *Martin Amis*, 116–53. Gavin Keulks provides a perceptive account of the representational shift in Amis's writing from the antimimetic to the mimetic, which he describes as "sanitized postmodernism" (160).

25 As Werner Wolf points out, "Comedy and laughter always imply emotional distance, and this runs counter to the strong affinity between emotional involvement and aesthetic illusion" (41–42). However, while "comedies frequently have a bias towards the breaking of illusion" (42), illusionism may be maintained even in aesthetic works that feature the comic. Adam Kirsch describes *The Zone of Interest* as "comic realism."

of the Camps" 311). This generic direction is represented by Paul Doll, whom we encountered at the beginning of this chapter, the loutish and ideologically motivated commandant of Auschwitz and enthusiastic (if incompetent) *génocidaire*. Doll's account of the camp, which takes the form of diary entries written not long after the events they describe, narrates his experience of the day-to-day governance of the camp. In particular, it focuses on the unprecedented administrative challenges of running a vast institution of the kind and scale of Auschwitz, which, in its historical manifestation, included an extensive complex: the original concentration camp (Auschwitz I) designed to intern Poles; its expansion into Birkenau (Auschwitz II), which imprisoned in atrocious conditions first Soviet POWs and later Jews and eventually also became the location of the gassing and cremation facilities in which Jews from all over Europe were murdered; the labor camp Monowitz (Auschwitz III), the location of the huge Buna factory at which thousands of slave laborers toiled to produce synthetic rubber; and dozens of subcamps. Doll presides over this "Zone of Interest," a euphemism (*Interessengebiet KL Auschwitz*) that referred historically to the far-flung area in Silesia that encompassed this conglomeration of institutions; during the time in which the novel commences (summer 1942), Auschwitz, which up to this point has been far behind the Aktion Reinhard killing centers in terms of numbers of murdered deportees, is just beginning to ascend as a center of both slave labor and mass killing in occupied Poland. Doll's job in the novel is to make this transition possible, and the "comedy of errors" that constitutes his narration represents both his own inflated sense of his command ("my aura of infallible authority" [*The Zone of Interest* 60]) and his bungling attempts to solve the singular problems that arise from the unprecedented nature of the camp's activities (as demonstrated, e.g., by the initial scene on the ramp, in which he prepares a full battle-worthy contingent to greet a tiny transport of old, infirm, and orphaned French Jews). The ironic bite in this strand of the novel is generated in the discrepancy between the comic ineptitude and moral vacuity of Doll, who, according to Lawson, "embodies the buffoonery of evil," and the deadly organizational challenges with which he is charged, which include not only the coordination of the frequent incoming transports and the development of measures for deceiving the deportees on the ramp but also the logistical problems of burning the profuse number of decomposing corpses that have previously been buried, running an economically efficient program of mass killing, supervising the construction of the Monowitz camp, managing the various constituencies and competing interests in the "Zone of Interest," and reconciling the conflicting orders relayed to him from disparate institutions within the Third Reich. As Doll complains,

> I am someone caught between the devil and the deep blue sea. On the one hand, the Economic Administration Head Office is always after me to do everything I can to swell the labour strength (for the munitions industries); on the other, the Reich Central Security Department presses for the disposal of as many evacuees as possible, for obvious reasons of self defence (the Jews constituting a 5th column of intolerable proportions). (*The Zone of Interest* 72–73)

In Doll's account, according to Morten Høi Jensen, "nothing ever goes according to plan, and the bumbling Paul Doll—'The Old Boozer'—is forever dealing with some new mishap or failure." Tension is thus generated in the novel between, on the one hand, the bureaucratic slapstick of Doll's petty, self-inflated conception of himself and his maladroit management blunders, which avail themselves of conventional comic devices, and, on the other hand, the full moral and historical dimensions of his managerial portfolio, which resist the playfulness of comic representation. As Vice puts it, "It is hard to know how to approach Amis's grotesque, carnivalesque, and of course fictional version of the historical horror, at it might seem that representing the commandant of Auschwitz as a middle manager is to present a functionalist comedy, in which the structure holds responsibility for the escalation of the genocide" ("British Representation of the Camps" 312). In my view, Amis mitigates—but does not resolve—this tension by balancing out the comic with two additional generic frames.

The second genre employed by Amis's novel is the "love story" (Jensen), which is narrated retrospectively by Golo (Angelus) Thomsen, an SS-*Obersturmführer* and mid-ranking official at the Buna industrial works; a well-connected member of the Nazi elite (his uncle is Martin Bormann, the *Reichsleiter*, chief of the Nazi Party Chancellery, and, beginning in 1943, Hitler's private secretary); and—late in the novel—a onetime, nominal abettor of industrial sabotage, for which he is imprisoned. At the outset of the novel, Thomsen is an opportunistic philanderer known for seducing women throughout the "Zone of Interest" (including the sadistic camp guard Ilse Grese, a fictional composite of the notorious female perpetrator Irma Grese, who was a guard at Ravensbrück, Auschwitz, and Bergen-Belsen, and Ilse Koch, who, as the wife of the commandant of Buchenwald and Majdanek, was known as the "Bitch of Buchenwald"). He uses his position and connections less to achieve hegemonic aims than to pursue amatory ends:

> Now, *power corrupts*: this was not a metaphor. But *power attracts*, luckily (for me), was not a metaphor either; and I had derived much sexual advantage from my proximity to power. In wartime, women especially felt the gravitational pull of it; they would be needing all their friends and admirers, all their protectors. (*The Zone of Interest* 50)

At the very beginning of the novel, in a chapter titled "First Sight," Thomsen describes the moment in which he first beholds Hannah Doll, the wife of the commandant, and falls immediately in love with her:

> She was coming back from the Old Town with her two daughters, and they were already well within the Zone of Interest. Up ahead, waiting to receive them stretched an avenue—almost a colonnade—of maples, their branches and lobed leaves interlocking overhead. A late afternoon in midsummer, with minutely glinting midges . . .
> Tall, broad, and full, and yet light of foot, in a crenellated white ankle-length dress and a cream-coloured straw hat with a black band, and swinging a straw bag (the girls, also in white, had the straw hats and the straw bags), she moved in and out of pockets of fuzzy, fawny, leonine warmth. She laughed—head back, with tautened throat . . .
> Now the three of them crossed the drive of the Equestrian Academy. Teasingly circled by her children she moved past the ornamental windmill, the maypole, the three-wheeled

gallows, the carthorse slackly tethered to the iron pump, and then moved beyond.

Into the Kat Zet—into Kat Zet I.

Something happened at first sight. Lightning, thunder, cloudburst, sunshine, rainbow—the meteorology of first sight. (*The Zone of Interest* 3–4)

Thomsen's first encounter with Hannah—whom he pursues without success throughout the novel and on account of whom, the novel suggests, he is inspired to become involved in sabotage—is articulated wistfully in the pastoral lexicon of literary romance: the warm, bright summer day; the maples and midges; the windmill and maypole; the fresh, white dresses worn by mother and daughters; and the cataclysmic natural cycle of storm and peaceful aftermath. Through what Cynthia Ozick calls "this radiant painterly vision" of "the old world of romantic allusiveness" made possible by the sentimental capacities of his retrospective mode of narration, Thomsen thus contrives his initial glimpse of Hannah as a literary encounter, albeit a fairly formulaic one. At the same time, however, among its overblown bucolic and erotic signifiers, the halcyon scene of thunderbolt attraction he paints here also includes an incongruous element that not only is out of place in this "leafy idyll" (Ozick) but in fact is diametrically antithetical to it, namely, the wheeled gallows located between the maypole and the carthorse, which Thomsen seemingly blithely retains in his romantic description. Apart from the names "Zone of Interest" and "Kat Zet [sic],"[26]

---

[26] Amis renders the letters "KZ" (one of two possible acronyms for *Konzentrationslager*, or concentration camp, the other being "KL") not as they would be written in English to express German pronunciation—namely, "Ka-Tset"—but at "Kat-Zet" (*The Zone of Interest* 4). This is but one example of what to my mind is one of the weakest—and, to a reader fluent in German, most frustrating—aspects of *The Zone of Interest*, namely, its frequent but orthographically sloppy, grammatically incorrect, and semantically imprecise use of the German language. Perhaps to bolster the novel's realist effect, and because of Amis's belief in the importance of German for the particular historical conditions of his story (Thomsen asks whether "the story of National Socialism could have unfolded in any other language" [272], a curious assertion, as Wood points out, in a novel written in English), Amis "litter[s]" (Jensen) the narration of its characters—especially Doll but also Thomsen—with what Amis reductively refers to in the afterword as a "garnish of German" (306), "as if they were parsley on his linguistic canapés" (Menden, "als seien sie Petersilie auf

The Perpetrator Mind Divided | 283

which, the reader learns only later, refer respectively to the larger geography of the camp complex and the original Auschwitz *Stammlager* (main camp), this one object is the only indicator of the larger moral environment in which Thomsen's thunderbolt romantic epiphany about Hannah—the

---

seinen Sprachhäppchen," my translation). This includes words—not only Nazi jargon but also designations for everyday objects and concepts, such as "Nasenloch" (187, nostril) and "Sexualitat" (*sic*; 169, sexuality)—and phrases and even whole sentences, all of which are intended to somehow indicate that the narrator employing them is thinking in German. In fact, however, the effect is, according to Jensen, to "produc[e] a very tiresome, very jarring Anglo-German mulch." As Hofmann, a distinguished translator of some of the most admired translations of German literature of the past decades, acerbically puts it, "I haven't been confronted with so much German in ages in an English setting, not since the brazen Audi ads of the 1980s." The distracting effect of the pervasive use of German is heightened by the fact that the novel not only frequently misspells German words and gives them strange plurals (such as "Zigeunere" [124, gypsies, whose correct plural is *Zigeuner*] and "Zahnen" [186, teeth, whose correct form is *Zähne*]) but also omits all umlauts and eszetts (which are necessary, not optional, diacritics), even though it employs the correct diacritics for Polish and French words, which suggests that the oversight was not a mere printing error. (Oddly, however, it does employ umlauts in the afterword.) The novel further reproduces sentences that are either not possible in German (an egregious example is the curse "Blutig Holle" [192], which is not only grammatically incorrect [the correct form would be *blütige Hölle*] but also the direct translation of an English expletive that no German would ever utter) or grammatically monstrous, such as Thomsen's assertion that his colleagues "liked to say that 'Ich Wusste Nichts Uber Es' was the new national anthem (I Didn't Know Anything About It)" (281), whereas the correct form would be "Ich wusste nichts davon." The result is a strange kind of pidgin German that Amis appears to have invented with little more effort than brief consultation of a dictionary and that is somehow meant to indicate that some "words sound funny in German" (Jensen) and thus to otherize the language as a whole. Hans-Jost Weyandt argues with regard to the German translation of *The Zone of Interest* that the "countless inaccuracies" retained by the translator Werner Schmitz function as "alienation effects" ("Werner Schmitz . . . lässt . . . die zahllosen Ungenauigkeiten zu jenen Verfremdungseffekten werden," my translation), a claim that could be extended to the use of German in the English original as well. Vice argues essentially the same thing: "[The umlauts'] absence makes the novel's German quotations into what Mikhail Bakhtin calls the artistic image of a language and not the real thing, in another example of the novel's stylization of both literary and historical detail into a contemporary and Anglophone form" ("British Representation of the Camps" 314). In any case, the first time I read the novel, I put it down about fifty pages in because of the adulterated German and could not make myself pick it up again for another six months. Even then, I could convince myself to finish it only by allowing myself to pedantically correct all of the mistakes.

wife, after all, of the commandant of all Auschwitz—occurs; however, it defiles in its overt implication of violence his pastoral scene, which, it turns out, is set, in Lydia Millett's words, against "an active gas-chamber, human-extermination backdrop." The novel's activation of the generic frame of the retrospectively narrated love story is thus problematized from the very beginning; it turns out to be "a sham, the artful novelist's Potemkin village masking rot" (Ozick). Both Ozick and Millet excoriate *The Zone of Interest* for proffering the trite narrative of "love in a concentration camp" (which they quote from the book's promotional materials), in which the Holocaust is transmogrified into "another upstairs-downstairs drama, upstairs as usual plush and advantaged and lavishly expressive of feeling; downstairs a hill of skulls" (Ozick).[27] Like the formulaic farce of the office comedy, which, in its limited focus on the burlesque shtick of the bureaucratic blunder, turns the commandant of an extermination camp at which over a million people will be murdered into "a joke-figure, drunk, boorish, laughable" (Jensen), the genre of the love story—at least on its own—is unable to bear the weight of its setting. The instruments of mass murder invariably penetrate the bucolic frame.

The third genre featured in *The Zone of Interest* is that of the traumatic testimony, which is narrated in the present tense by Szmul, a Polish Jew who supervises the *Sonderkommandos*, the squad of Jewish prisoners formed in the historical Birkenau in July 1942 and forced into the physically and psychologically arduous work of operating the gas chambers and crematoria. In the time period in which the novel is set, Szmul is put in charge of digging up thousands of decomposed corpses and burning them in open-air fires. Unlike Doll, who fixates on the bureaucratic impediments involved in managing the camp (as well as on his own erotic frustrations with his wife), and in contrast to Thomsen, whose interest lies chiefly with Hannah, Szmul is focused on staying alive in an atmosphere in which death is not merely ubiquitous but in fact the axiomatic rule, as all of the members of the *Sonderkommando* expect to be eventually murdered themselves. His motivations for living are very specific:

---

27 Ozick's criticism is one that the novel itself anticipates; as Hannah, who after the war refuses to engage in a relationship with Thomsen, says to him, "Imagine how disgusting it would be if anything good came out of that place" (294).

> There persist three reasons, or excuses, for going on living: first, to bear witness, and, second, to exact mortal vengeance. I am bearing witness; but the magic looking glass does not show me a killer. Or not yet.
>
> Third, and most crucially, we save a life (or prolong a life) at the rate of one per transport. (*The Zone of Interest* 35)

Szmul, we learn, saw his own sons murdered at Chełmno, where, after dragging corpses to mass graves for "twelve hours under the lash" (*The Zone of Interest* 197), they were led to pits and shot; he further expects to never again see his wife, who he hopes is hiding in the Łódź Ghetto. His impetus to keep alive is thus not connected to either his own comfort or the hopes of seeing his family again. Rather, he wishes to make an impact more narrowly: by maximizing the opportunity to save a life (even if it is only ".01 per cent" [36] of the number murdered), by nursing an inner attitude of revenge, and, above all, by leaving some record of what he has experienced and witnessed, not unlike the testimony of a previous prisoner that Szmul and his fellow *Sonderkommandos* disinter from its hiding place in Doll's garden. Szmul's narration functions as that of immediate testimony; the shortest and most breviloquent of all the monologues of the three narrators, indicating that he has neither the time nor the opportunity to produce a longer text, it gives the impression of a surreptitiously written, desperately formulated, urgently expressed document of what is happening in the extermination camp in real time. In this, it is modeled on the historical manuscripts commonly referred to as the Scrolls of Auschwitz, a collection of five texts written by Auschwitz *Sonderkommandos*, buried in various locations in the camp and discovered between 1945 and 1980, all of which chronicle, according to Nicholas Chare and Dominic Williams, the experience of "being inside the event" (14). Szmul's narration is thus immediately recognizable as an exemplar of a genre that not only is associated with the Holocaust but also emerged out of the particular historical phenomenon in Auschwitz that he represents. Perhaps for this reason, some critics have seen the part of the novel that features his narration as more successful than the other two. As Ozick argues,

> [Amis's] Afterword, in combination with *Sonderkommando* Szmul, the novel's third interior voice, repudiates and

> virtually annuls all other voices, the farcical with the ahistorical; and nearly erases also the dominating voice of the novel itself. For Szmul, no suspension of disbelief, fiction's busy handmaiden, is required, and no element of caricature can touch him. He alone is immune to the reader's skepticism, he alone is safe from even the possibility of diminishment through parody; and this holds both within the novel's pliancy and in the tougher arena of historical truth. . . . Amis's crematorium raven flies out from the novel as its single invincibly convincing voice.[28]

As a generic frame, the testimony that Szmul's narration emulates thus corresponds to the novel's subject in ways that its other genres—the office comedy and the love story—cannot.

Given the jumble of conflicting genres in *The Zone of Interest*, it is no wonder that critics have found it difficult to pin the novel down. It is, as Jensen argues, "a novel desperately at odds with itself. It wants to be a satire in the classic Amis mold, but it also wants to bear witness, so to speak, to the documentary record on which it has been reared." The three parts of the text do not unify into a novelistic whole; according to Michael Hofmann, "the styles are rivalrous; the perspectives are incompatible," producing a narrative discord that disorients readers and interrupts their immersion in the text. At the same time, however, precisely through its "fractious" (Ozick) construction and the incommensurability between the three narrators and their heterogeneous discourses, Amis's novel presents what I see as a compelling exercise in the dynamics of reader immersion and in particular empathetic identification with the figure—or, in this case, figures—of the Holocaust perpetrator. As I see it, *The Zone of Interest* diverts readers' affective engagement so that they find themselves responding emotionally to the perpetrator almost in spite of themselves. Through its construction

---

[28] Joyce Carol Oates maintains a view that is quite different from Ozick's: "Far from being a vulture of the crematory, Szmul is a kind of saint of Auschwitz, ascetic and selfless. If he is not an altogether convincing character, it's a nearly impossible task to give a convincing voice to such a person (and such a person very likely existed)." Tova Reich holds a similar opinion: "*The Zone of Interest* is a novel of written testimonies. The least original is Szmul's, in which Amis is uncharacteristically cautious and deferential, as if treading on sacred ground."

of the love story between Golo Thomsen and Hannah Doll, and through its positioning of that story vis-à-vis Doll's comic narration, the novel activates an intricate process of empathetic alignment in which readers are forced into an unlikely alliance with Thomsen.

Through its narrative construction, *The Zone of Interest* overtly foregrounds the antithetical perspectives of Doll, Thomsen, and Szmul. Each of the numbered chapters in the novel provides in succession the three narrators' sometimes significantly divergent accounts of the same happenings, with Thomsen narrating alone a postwar epilogue entitled "Aftermath," which describes, among other things, the death of the other two (Szmul at the hands of Doll in 1943, Doll in a Nuremberg-adjudicated execution in 1947). Critics find this rigid narrative pattern disruptive to the reading experience; according to Joanne Pettitt, "The regimented nature of the structure, perpetually oscillating around this tripartite model, continually disrupts the flow of the narrative and instead gives the impression of leading the reader round the central point in concentric circles" (68). Hofmann is a bit less charitable:

> *The Zone of Interest* abolishes itself as it goes along, so that the book is continually heaving itself off the ground; it is the opposite of "building," in music, in architecture, in tension. Partly it is the difficulty of making any sort of showing against its chosen background, the Holocaust, but partly too it is Amis's structuring. Each chapter is narrated by one of the three principals in sequences; it is a mechanical rotation of three solo instruments, with each one rubbing out the one before, and this through six whole chapter cycles.

While I agree that the structure, along with the competing generic frames, temporal standpoints, and narrative voices, prevents the novel from achieving a harmonious whole, the juxtaposition of viewpoints on sometimes the same event or issue allows us to see the radical discordance between the perspectives of the perpetrators and that of the prisoners. All three characters intersect in the same "Zone of Interest," but they occupy two antipodal positions within it, namely, the antithetical identities of perpetrator and victim (with Thomsen, on account of his narrow involvement in sabotage and subsequent arrest and imprisonment, transitioning to a limited extent from the former to the latter). Although there are important differences in the scope of Doll's power and rank and that of Thomsen, both men enjoy unimaginable mastery over the lives of many thousands and thus reside in essentially the same area on the far end of the spectrum of power. On the diametrically opposite end exists Szmul, who laments, "We are of the Sonderkommando, the SK, the Special Squad, and we are the saddest men in the Lager. We are in fact the saddest men in the history of the world. And of all these very sad men I am the saddest" (*The Zone of Interest* 34). By including the voice of Szmul, "the moral conscience" of the book, who reveals "the horror of what is really going on" at Auschwitz (Kakutani, "Ordinary, Everyday Monsters" 25), *The Zone of Interest* attempts to impart the extreme experience of the victim and forced accomplice of genocidal violence as a pronounced counterpart to that of the perpetrator, a point of view that in *The Nazi and the Barber*, *The Kindly Ones*, and *Time's Arrow*, the three other fictional representations I investigate in this book, is evoked either obliquely or not at all. However, the novel's inclusion of Szmul's voice, a perspective that in particular supplements Doll's account of events, is not simply a strategy to create narrative symmetry, by which the perspective of the perpetrator is balanced by that of the victim; if that were the case, the novel would need only one narrator to occupy the perpetrator's role, a structure that would emphasize the gulf between victim and perpetrator with a stark binary and hinder reader identification with the perpetrator. Rather, I argue that the doubling of the narrative voice of the perpetrator with the perspectives of Thomsen and Doll, along with the inclusion of Szmul's perspective, works to create an imbalance, forcing the reader to focus more particularly on the nuances of one side of the spectrum, namely, on the differences between Thomsen and Doll. The novel's center of gravity, I argue, is situated between these two perpetrator-narrators, producing the dynamic that allows for readers' identification.[29]

Although Thomsen and Doll each play particular roles in both the storyworld and the plot and additionally function in divergent ways as narrators, readers' identification with them operates consonantly in several

---

[29] Ruth Franklin writes, "It's unclear what function Szmul serves in the novel, other than to demonstrate that Amis dares imaginatively to go places where almost no one else will venture."

respects. Both men's narratives stimulate the first two (out of five) modes of reader identification I lay out in the introduction, namely, "existential identification," meaning readers' basic recognition of the perpetrators' humanity, and "perspectival identification," or readers' willingness to adopt the perpetrators' viewpoints. The text accomplishes this through what Patrick Colm Hogan calls "a shift from what one might call 'objective mind' to 'subjective mind'" (138): "in literary terms, the more we come to know someone, the more we understand and respond to him/her as a subjective rather than objective mind, and the harder it is for us to view him or her as a villain" (138). For this reason, the very act of focalizing Doll's and Thomsen's perspectives compels some degree of empathetic identification on the part of the novel's readers. Further, readers depend heavily on Doll's and Thomsen's guidance through the dichotomous physical and social settings at Auschwitz (the infamous ramp, the SS officers' club, the spacious house Doll shares with his wife and young daughters) and their (often divergent) interpretations of the complex relationships of power that emerge in this concentrationary universe. The two men's fluid and apparently unselfconscious movement through this world, a motility also granted to the reader at least in part by these aspects of identification, actualizes the disquieting atmosphere of extreme domination that characterizes Auschwitz; we experience this setting through their privileged presence in it and thus uneasily come to identify, in part, with their positions of almost unlimited magisterial power—an identification that then becomes troubling as the contours of this world begin to crystallize.

Beyond these two modes of initial identification, however, the readers' relationships to the two respective perpetrator-narrators fork, advancing along distinct but at times strikingly analogous pathways. For his part, Doll emerges as a mostly churlish, resentful, and petty figure and "a strikingly one-dimensional character" (Badrideen, "The Banality of Good and Evil" 317), whose callow worldview and moral pusillanimity serve to mitigate the empathetic bond that readers develop with him. While his fatuous, childish behavior, especially in his petulant interactions with his wife, Hannah, humanizes him (and thus controverts his external status as almost omnipotent master), it also places decisive limits on readers' emotional identification with him. Moreover, Doll's narration resembles the bombastic self-justification and pronounced moral obtuseness displayed in the autobiography of Rudolf Höß, the historical commandant of Auschwitz and the figure on whom Amis bases his character. Doll's reflections about and rationalization of his role in the "Zone of Interest" comprise the superficial reiteration of Nazi discourse, exposing him as a sort of caricature of the banal bureaucrat à la Eichmann (or, in Jensen's words, "a caricature of a caricature") whose narration devolves into unaware self-parody and preventing the reader from inadvertently developing ideological admiration for or agreement with the power he wields. Furthermore, as a narrator, Doll is both extratextually and intratextually unreliable. As the man who orchestrates the daily genocidal murder of thousands of deportees and the violent subjugation of tens of thousands of prisoners (all the while insisting, "For I am a normal man with normal needs. I am *completely normal*" [*The Zone of Interest* 33]), he is the model for what Dan Shen terms "dispositional unreliability." Dispositional unreliability, as I explained in the introduction to part 2, refers to narrators who are untrustworthy by virtue of their character or values, a mode of unreliable narration that manifests chiefly in frequent instances of misinterpreting or misregarding (to return to Phelan's taxonomy of unreliability). But Doll also misreports or transfigures events to make himself appear in a more favorable light, a proclivity toward intratextual unreliability the reader discerns by comparing his account with those of Szmul and Thomsen. Readers thus develop without question an identificatory relationship to Doll, but this identification is far from unrestricted or unqualified. Moreover, while the text's mobilization of empathetic triggers and empathetic blockers ebbs and flows, allowing for sudden reversals or momentary empathic alignment, readers' initial identification (made possible by existential and perspectival identification) generally tends to weaken over the course of the novel. As Doll paradoxically says after a moment of rare introspection, "I must shut down a certain zone in my mind" (*The Zone of Interest* 217), a statement that instantiates rhetorically the limits on readers' identification with him.

Thomsen, on the other hand, at least with regard to his function as a reporter of events, is a far more reliable narrator than Doll. However, although the reader can generally credit Thomsen's account, she can be far less confident in his interpretation and evaluation of his environment, a factor that stems from his dispositional reliability as a perpetrator and has direct consequences for her emotional and ideological investment in him. While *The Zone of Interest* structures Thomsen in many respects as Doll's diametrical opposite (particularly in its erection of a love triangle between the two men and Hannah), in terms of his emotional and ideological appeal he is not so much Doll's antithesis as he is a marginally more palatable version of the commandant, despite both his status as the novel's chief romantic protagonist and his (admittedly fairly feeble) role in the sabotage plot. Thomsen is certainly not the narrow-minded, boorish bureaucrat concerned chiefly with making the machinery of genocide run more efficiently, but neither is he an admirable person, a resistance hero in the making, or a figure on whom the reader can rely to register on an emotional level the brutal violence that characterizes the storyworld. To be sure, some critics maintain that Thomsen is transformed over the course of the events depicted in the novel into a kind of "inner resister" by virtue of his feelings for Hannah (who herself, according to Ozick, is figured as "an internal dissident, a melancholy prisoner of circumstance: perhaps even as a highly privileged quasi-*Häftling* powerless to rebel"); as Julia M. Klein argues, "Thomsen's moral sense is stirred by his nascent love." Thomsen himself endorses such an interpretation, making a case to the reader that, despite appearances, he does not ideologically align himself with the Nazi regime but rather works to covertly undermine it:

> I put aside my ambivalence and after a false start or two established contact (by teletype and then by telephone) with an old friend of my father's in Berlin, Konrad Peters of the SD—the Sicherheitsdienst Reichsfuhrer-SS [sic], or Party Intelligence. Peters was formerly a professor of modern history at Humboldt; now he helped monitor the foes of National Socialism (sardonically specialising in the Freemasons)....
>
> Konrad Peters, although far more exalted, was like me. We were obstruktiv Mitlaufere [sic]. We went along. We went along, *we went along with*, doing all we could to drag our feet and scuff the carpets and scratch the parquet, but we went along. There were hundreds of thousands like us, maybe millions like us. (*The Zone of Interest* 147–48)[30]

---

30 This quote contains one of several unfortunate anachronisms in Amis's novel; until 1945, the oldest of Berlin's universities was named the

Thomsen labels himself and his colleague "obstructive fellow travelers" ("obstruktiv Mitlaufere," a grammatically monstrous variant of the correct form, "obstruktive Mitläufer"), meaning that, despite the clear privileges they enjoy as members of the SS, they are in reality undercover dissenters—in Millet's words, "only half-Nazi, possibly ironically Nazi, engaged in secret acts of subversion"—who work to decelerate the machinery of genocide. However, the mere fact that Thomsen puts himself on the same level of covert obstruction as a functionary in the SD—the SS security service and one of the chief bureaucratic agencies involved in the "Final Solution" (the historical Adolf Eichmann was a member of the SD, as is the fictional Maximilien Aue, the protagonist of Jonathan Littell's novel *The Kindly Ones*)—casts doubt on his reliability in this matter and indicates that his position is more implicated than he is wont to characterize it. While it is true that he is less ideologically committed to the goals and methods of National Socialism than Doll, he is much more invested in the Nazi regime itself and enjoys greater benefits as the nephew of Bormann, whom he continues to admire and love (and whose protection he enjoys while imprisoned) even after he experiences the superficial conversion that results from his love for Hannah. One could in fact argue essentially the opposite of the position held by Klein, namely, that Thomsen performs the role of resister—which would cast him as the antithesis of Doll— precisely to seduce Hannah. Moreover, throughout his time in Auschwitz, Thomsen seems on the whole disturbingly unaffected by the brutally violent atmosphere in which he lives and works; for him, the "Zone of Interest" is chiefly a source of potential erotic assignations that he, a womanizing playboy, is eager to exploit. What is more, he shows himself to be heavily implicated in the rampant oppression and exploitation of prisoners at the Buna factory at which he serves as an administrator, as demonstrated in a scene early in the book, when he argues in a meeting—possibly in an attempt to ingratiate himself to Doll—against a 20 percent increase in rations for forced laborers that could decrease the precipitate death rate

---

Friedrich-Wilhelms-Universität; in 1949, it was renamed the Humboldt-Universität zu Berlin. Another is Peters's use of the term "desk murderer" (*The Zone of Interest* 244), which, as Alan Milchman and Alan Rosenberg argue, was a postwar neologism that first emerged in the discourse on the Holocaust in the 1960s.

in Monowitz (*The Zone of Interest* 31). While it is true he is imprisoned toward the end of the war for committing industrial sabotage, his role in the offense is far from heroic, as he merely encourages an English prisoner of war to perform the subversive acts but undertakes no actions himself. One could in fact read Thomsen's presumption to the status of "obstructive fellow traveler" not as a position with which he identifies during the time of the events he describes but rather as an attempt in the postwar period to recast his wartime activities in a positive light, a reinterpretation made possible only retrospectively in consideration of his experience of imprisonment; as Hofmann sarcastically puts it, "Thomsen—he says it himself at the end, so it must be true—becomes a 'reformed character,' in every sense." For these reasons, Thomsen's role in the novel is far less heroic than it is ambivalent; much like the narrator in *Time's Arrow*, he overtly claims a moral integrity that is in fact belied by both his behavior and his narration.[31] He is thus only marginally a figure with whom the reader can identify emotionally or ethically, especially the reader who approaches the text with the desire to find the familiar but formulaic plot of Holocaust rescue and redemption, as embodied most notably in the heroic conversion of Nazi Party member Oskar Schindler into a selfless rescuer in Steven Spielberg's 1993 film *Schindler's List*.

However, despite the tenuous grounds for identification made available by Thomsen as both character and narrator, the text nevertheless positions him, I argue, as the ambivalent object of readers' identification. It does so not only through its construction of his marginal dissemblance to Doll and through its positioning of him in the novel's romantic plot but also through its exploitation of particular dynamic of empathy that Breithaupt

---

31 Ahmed Badrideen, with whose redemptive reading of the role of the narrator in *Time's Arrow* I vigorously disagree, has also written on *The Zone of Interest*. While I find his argument on the whole fairly persuasive, he tends to view Thomsen in similarly redemptive terms, although his assessment also acknowledges Thomsen's moral ambiguity: "Angelus Thomsen . . . appears to be something of a non-hero, or failed hero. . . . It is [his] willingness to break consensus, to cling to an indissoluble integrity—at least only internally—which casts Thomsen as an inheritor of the moral voice of *Time's Arrow* whose narrative imagines an alternative to the fascist reality" ("The Banality of Good and Evil" 320). Badrideen appears to conflate here the moral position of Amis's narrators with that of Amis himself, which perhaps accounts for his propensity to locate redemption in them.

terms "the three-person scenario" (1), to which "the basic situation of fiction corresponds" (6). According to Breithaupt's theory, empathy results from a triangular constellation whereby, in a conflict between two parties, an observer (in this case, the reader) takes sides—often automatically or semiconsciously—with one of the parties. In choosing a side, the observer then begins to "view the situation from the perspective of the chosen side" (5), to develop feelings of sympathy or care for the chosen party, and to seek internal and external justification for her decision to side with that party, all of which serve to reinforce the strength of the empathetic identification. With its duo of perpetrator-narrators, Amis's novel facilitates precisely such a triangular transaction of empathetic identification. Readers are encouraged in the first pages of the novel to side with Thomsen, the thunderstruck lover, against Doll, "the Old Boozer" (*The Zone of Interest* 4), and by thus determining Thomsen as the object of identification, they strengthen their empathetic attachment to him, despite his apparent ethical, emotional, and ideological shortcomings. In this way, Doll functions as the foil against which readers are persuaded to identify with Thomsen, a somewhat more sympathetic figure—not least on account of his love for Hannah, which contrasts with Doll's determination to have Szmul murder her. Critical to the novel's development of readers' identification with Thomsen is its ambivalent effect; readers are positioned to foster empathy for Thomsen, even though he does not really deserve it, for he does not emerge—as readers perhaps hope—as a hero who can be juxtaposed with Doll in starkly antithetical moral terms. On the contrary, while certainly less crass, murderous, self-delusional, and ideologically invested in the genocidal goals of Auschwitz than Doll, Thomsen is without question ethically dubious, even and particularly when he is transformed into an equivocal figure of resistance. Thomsen rather materializes over the course of the novel as an ambivalent figure whose burgeoning love for Hannah, nascent but inconsistently pursued anti-Nazi sentiments, and suffering during imprisonment create certain "zones of interest" or pathways to reader identification, even as his casual consumption of the spoils of domination over others that he enjoys as a favored child of the regime serves as an impediment to full empathetic alignment. With its triad of narrators and its careful manipulation of readers' identification, *The Zone of Interest* thus renders one of its perpetrator-narrators, at least, a very human figure, even if it resorts to portraying the other one with the standard vocabulary of banal evil to do so.

Exercises in Identification and Alienation

Through his two Holocaust fictions, both of which employ the autodiegetic narration of Holocaust perpetrators but do so from opposite sides of the mimetic/antimimetic continuum, Amis renders the mind of the perpetrator in ways that predicate disparate reading experiences. For its part, *Time's Arrow* deploys unnatural narrative devices to defamiliarize the Holocaust and its causal relationships, creating thereby a divided narrative voice that, in its failure to adequately interpret the violence that occurs around the protagonist, presents an ethically deficient representation of the Holocaust. In *Time's Arrow*, the mind of the perpetrator is occluded by a narrator who does not acknowledge his part in the genocide and instead creates a narrative of redemption that divests him of responsibility for it. In this way, the text relegates the question of interpretation to us, its readers, who are tasked with righting the wayward direction of time's arrow, reestablishing the proper relationship between cause and effect, and making the correct ethical judgment that the narrator is unable or refuses to make. With *The Zone of Interest*, Amis engages readers in a very different cognitive exercise, one that induces an identificatory response rather than an interpretive one. With its two implicated narrators, *The Zone of Interest* also doubles the voice of the perpetrator; however, in contrast to *Time's Arrow*, it does so through mimetic rather than antimimetic means. Rather than relying on unnatural devices to estrange readers and to defamiliarize the causality of the Holocaust, Amis's later text encourages readers to immerse themselves in the storyworld and to develop ambivalent empathetic connections to its perpetrator-protagonists, thereby facilitating a differential reading experience, one that stimulates the cognitive and affective processes of identification rather than the operations of interpretation. By activating a dynamic in which readers are compelled to align with Thomsen's self-understanding as a means of rejecting Doll's perspective, *The Zone of Interest*, like *Time's Arrow*, presents us with an ethical challenge. In this case, however, instead of tasking us with the job of rejecting inverted or redemptive readings of the Holocaust that rehabilitate the perpetrator's violent history and disavow his culpability, Amis's later novel invites us to enter into an empathetic relationship with a perpetrator without fully accepting his own framework for understanding and judging his implication in the genocide that takes place around him. By employing the vicissitudes of autodiegetic narration to alternately reveal and occlude the minds of their perpetrator-protagonists, both novels thus involve readers in carefully controlled exercises in identification and alienation, enabling them to engage in innovative ways with the uncomfortable moral questions provoked by considering the events of the Holocaust from the victimizer's point of view.

Epilogue

Throughout this book, I have limited my focus narrowly to literary and journalistic attempts to infer, inhabit, and represent the mind of the Holocaust perpetrator, consciously refraining thereby from examining representations of perpetrators of other historical traumas, instances of mass violence, or systematic oppression. I have done so for two major reasons. First, I consider myself a scholar of the Holocaust and its representation; this is not only my field of expertise, which I have spent decades developing, but also an area of academic inquiry that continues to fascinate and trouble me. The canon of Holocaust representation thus constitutes the abiding question of my scholarly life. Second, I believe that, while the historical perpetrators of the Holocaust themselves were neither anomalous nor unparalleled in their psychic makeup, their social behavior, or their criminal activity, the *image* of the perpetrator in the postwar and recent transnational cultural imagination does in fact demonstrate a singular history. By virtue of its association with extreme psychological depravity, mythical monstrousness, and intrinsic malignity, the figure of the Nazi perpetrator has been torn from the historical fabric and aggrandized as fundamentally evil and radically other. In this way, its function as a cultural trope displaces it from the historical conditions and behavior of the actual men on which it has been modeled and transports it to heterogeneous contexts in which it is called on to do very different representational work. The writers whose work I have examined in this study endeavor—to a greater or lesser extent—to reverse this process of reification through their attempts to imagine the mental interiority of the very human men who played a role in perpetrating the Holocaust. I believe that the story of their efforts is an important one to tell and that, by narrowing in particularly on the ways in which their texts construct the mind of the Holocaust perpetrator, we can come to understand the development and dissemination of this trope as well as its cultural functions. This phenomenon of representation, I contend, deserves to be studied in its own right.

At the same time, however, I emphatically reject the notion that one cannot make comparisons between perpetrators of the Holocaust—whether historical or imagined—and agents of other kinds of violence. I strongly believe that the Holocaust was an event that happened in human time and space, not in, as Elie Wiesel claims, "a universe outside the universe, a creation that exists parallel to creation" ("Trivializing Memory" 165). Nor was it an event so unique that, as Claude Lanzmann puts it, "it constructs a circle of flames around itself, the limit not to be broken because a certain absolute horror is not transmittable" (quoted in Roth 219). While we might feel at times that the sheer scope, duration, character, extremity, and effects of the "Final Solution," around which many of us are still trying to wrap our minds, somehow resist comparison to other historical events, this feeling is an expression of our helplessness and confusion in the face of such extreme violence rather than a condition to be accepted or even promoted. I firmly believe that the Holocaust not only allows but also demands that we knit it into human history, which means that we find linkages, continuities, resonances, and similarities between it and the seemingly endless chain of violent events and instances of systematic oppression that have taken place throughout human history—and that occur at this very moment. This does not mean that we should collapse historically diverse events into an undifferentiated mass of cruelty and suffering; our job as scholars is to make informed, nuanced, and responsible comparisons and to insist on differences and departures when we see them.

An example of the importance of the responsible practice of comparison emerged in a recent debate within the Holocaust Studies community. Responding to an official statement issued on 24 June 2019, by the United States Holocaust Memorial Museum (USHMM) condemning the use of analogies between the Holocaust and other historical events, Omer Bartov, Doris Bergen, Andrea Orzoff, Timothy Snyder, and Anika Walke authored an open letter.[1] Signed by hundreds of scholars of the Holocaust and other

---

1 According to a preface to the open letter by the editors of the *New York Review of Books*, "On June 17, [2019,] Representative Alexandria Ocasio-Cortez,

genocides (including me), the letter urged the USHMM to retract its statement:

> Scholars in the humanities and social sciences rely on careful and responsible analysis, contextualization, comparison, and argumentation to answer questions about the past and the present. By "unequivocally rejecting efforts to create analogies between the Holocaust and other events, whether historical or contemporary," the United States Holocaust Memorial Museum is taking a radical position that is far removed from mainstream scholarship on the Holocaust and genocide. And it makes learning from the past almost impossible. The Museum's decision to completely reject drawing any possible analogies to the Holocaust, or to the events leading up to it, is fundamentally ahistorical. . . . The very core of Holocaust education is to alert the public to dangerous developments that facilitate human rights violations and pain and suffering; pointing to similarities across time and space is essential for this task. (Bartov et al.)

As the authors of the letter point out, rigorous and conscientious comparisons of the Holocaust with other events (particularly contemporary ones) not only can shed light on those events and make us aware of their exigency and extremity but also can help us to better understand the dynamics of the Holocaust. Although the notion of the Holocaust's intrinsic uniqueness and incomparability was once axiomatic among many scholars of the Holocaust, in the last decade or two, rejection of this position within

---

Democrat of New York, posted an Instagram live video discussing the detention camps along the southern US border as 'concentration camps' in which she used the phrase 'Never Again.' This drew sharp criticism the following day from Representative Liz Cheney, Republican of Wyoming, and others for allegedly misappropriating a slogan associated with the Holocaust. After several days of heated media and political debate, the United States Holocaust Memorial Museum released a statement on June 24 condemning the use of Holocaust analogies. We received the following open letter addressed to the director of the museum, Sara J. Bloomfield, delivered by the signatories on July 1."

Holocaust Studies, as demonstrated by the widespread support for the letter, has become the norm.

In the spirit of such necessary comparison "across time and space" between the Holocaust and other instances of violence in our common world, I conclude my study by extending its consideration of the ethical and representational issues involved in depicting the perspective of men who perpetrated the Holocaust to a text that grapples with the legacy of a more recent instance of genocidal violence: Jessica Stern's 2020 work of nonfiction, *My War Criminal: Personal Encounters with an Architect of Genocide*. Stern's book engages in the same sort of mind-reading practices employed by the fictional and nonfictional narratives investigated in my study. In this case, however, the mind under examination belongs not to a Holocaust perpetrator such as Adolf Eichmann but to a man convicted by an international court in 2016 for genocide, crimes against humanity, and war crimes: Radovan Karadžić, the Bosnian Serb who served as the president of Republika Srpska during the Bosnian War. Along with the Army of Republika Srpska general Ratko Mladić, Karadžić was found guilty of the genocide of eight thousand Bosnian Muslims at Srebrenica in July 1995, an event described at its ten-year commemoration by then UN secretary-general Kofi Annan as "a terrible crime—the worst on European soil since the Second World War." Between 2014 and 2016, while Karadžić was awaiting the verdict of his trial, Stern, a counterterrorism expert and scholar of international relations, visited him numerous times in prison, meetings that she chronicles in *My War Criminal*.

The impetus for Stern's engagement with Karadžić is strikingly similar to Gitta Sereny's motivation for seeking out and interviewing the Treblinka commandant Franz Stangl (which I described in chapter 2); like Sereny, who feels a strong "need, a drive to know" (*The Healing Wound* 92) the psychological mindset of Stangl and other Holocaust perpetrators, Stern, the daughter of a Holocaust survivor, harbors "a deep curiosity about the causes of evil" as well as a desire to explore "people's underlying motivations for violence," particularly in the context of "genocidal wars" (xxxviii). In fact, Stern seems unconsciously to model her interview project after (or at the very least coincidentally to emulate) Sereny's; while Sereny fervently desires that Stangl "tell the truth" (*Into That Darkness* 362) about his role in genocide, Stern admits that, in her interactions with Karadžić, she "had been harboring a secret, megalomaniacal dream—that I was going to get him to apologize" (276).² At the same time, however, the two women follow decidedly divergent procedures in their interview projects. Sereny seeks to understand how Stangl and other perpetrators felt about their history of violence, but she also strenuously works "to retain distance—spiritual, emotional independence"—from her subjects by rigorously limiting her empathetic faculty ("Questioning the Perpetrators" 124). Stern, on the other hand, adopts a different principle: "Most of the time, when I interview a perpetrator, when the interview is going well, I enter an altered state in which my subject's feelings become more central to my experience than my own" (xlv). In her discussions with terrorists and perpetrators of war crimes, Stern follows "a painful process" (xlv), whereby she "embrac[es] the perpetrator's subjectivity," "follow[s] his moral logic so closely that it becomes my own," and transforms, in a sense, into "a fellow perpetrator" (xlv). Such fusing of the perpetrator's interiority with her own selfhood, Stern admits, occurred in her interactions with Karadžić during their prison visits: "He took up residence in my mind. I became a fellow prisoner, and he became 'my war criminal'" (xlvi). As a result of what she herself describes as a radical deployment of empathetic identification, Stern is able to find Karadžić "likeable," "magnetic," "charming" (278), and even, by virtue of his good looks, "a Byronic figure" (9).³ She comes to admire his educated, genteel manner and even at times seems desperate to seek his approval; at one point, in a chapter titled "The Mesmerist," she describes having allowed

---

2 Although Stern's text is uncannily similar to Sereny's well-known book in terms of impetus and structure, Stern does not appear to be aware of Sereny's prison interview with Stangl: "Since Nuremberg, there have been a number of international war crimes trials, but no researchers have been allowed into the detention units controlled by the international tribunals to write about the leaders tried for serious war crimes" (xxxix). Since Stangl was a leader neither tried for serious war crimes nor convicted by an international court, Stern's statement does not technically apply to Sereny's interview with him. However, given that Stern is a scholar of genocidal violence, it is surprising that she is unfamiliar with Sereny's text, a canonical text in the literature on perpetrators.
3 In contrast to, for example, Karadžić's brother Luka, who, according to Stern, radiates violence and has a "thuggish aspect" (87), Karadžić possesses in Stern's view an educated, genteel manner: "He had adopted the style and mannerisms of a Central European gentleman of indeterminate origin. In court, and with me, Radovan was unimpeachably polite, with an almost aristocratic bearing" (87).

him to demonstrate "his skill at bioenergetic healing" (1) by touching her palms and placing his hands above her head. Initially unable to perceive any effect of these actions, she confesses, "A shame-inducing thought floated into my mind: I wanted an A from this man. I had just received the first F of my life, and it stung. . . . Under his gaze, I regressed" (6).[4]

When it appeared in early 2020, *My War Criminal* immediately attracted a great deal of criticism for its unalloyed empathetic representation of Karadžić, which critics found "disturbing" (Zakaria), "indecent" (Kamm), and deeply "amoral" (Melonic). According to Janine di Giovanni, a human rights journalist who covered the war in Bosnia, "By humanizing a mass murderer, Stern has done a massive injustice to a country that is bleeding today." However, to my mind, what is troubling about Stern's portrayal of Karadžić is not that she sees him as a fully human agent but rather that she does quite the opposite: she "romanticizes" (Melonic) him, uncritically reproduces his own self-image as both "martyr for Serbia" and "mythic hero" (*My War Criminal* 211), and thereby equates him with the tragic figures in Serbian epic poetry whom both she and Karadžić admire. In short, she transforms him into myth rather than revealing him to be a fully human agent who deliberately nurtured among the Bosnian Serbs an environment of hatred toward and fear of Bosnian Muslims and developed a genocidal policy to eliminate the latter group. Her depiction of him as a tragic hero, although adulatory, thus functions not unlike representations of Holocaust perpetrators that characterize them as preternatural demons. Such aggrandization, both positive and negative, serves to reinforce the notion of perpetrators as somehow radically apart from—rather than emerging from within—the human community.

Even more troublingly, in her construction of this myth, Stern adopts Karadžić's own narrative framework for understanding the dynamics that led to Serbian violence against the Bosnian Muslim population. She writes,

> For large periods of time, it felt to me as if we were a research team, working together on the project of explaining what

---

4 A number of critics cite this scene as evidence of the ways in which Stern falls prey to Karadžić's hypnotic seduction. According to Melonic, "Stern indulges in utter eroticization of not only a war criminal but also what she believes is her relationship with him."

motivated Radovan Karadžić. My impossible task involved the effort to stay open to Karadžić's explication of why he behaved as he did, rather than blindly accepting the common narrative—that the Serbs were evil genocidaires and the Muslims guileless victims. I felt committed to taking in his account, his version of history. (195–96)

By committing herself fully to Karadžić's "version of history," by not "cross[ing] my war criminal in any way" (53) via provocative questions or culpatory evidence, and by not balancing his version of events with the testimony of survivors of the genocide (as Sereny does, e.g., in her portrait of Stangl), Stern thus rejects "the common narrative" put forth by survivors, eyewitnesses such as di Giovanni, and historians such as Edina Bećirević. Instead, she not only accepts his account as authoritative but also filters her representation of his culpability through his own "tortured excuses and grotesque fantasies" (Szalai). Chief among these are the "false moral equivalence" (Bećirević) that propagates the notion "that today's evil perpetrators were yesterday's guileless victims" (*My War Criminal* 137)—meaning that the genocide committed by Serbs against Bosnian Muslims could be characterized as a direct, logical, and related consequence of the suppression of Serbs under Ottoman rule from the fifteenth to the nineteenth centuries—and the exculpatory and historically specious explanation that Serbs engaged in mass atrocities against their Bosnian Muslim neighbors out of a legitimate fear that the latter were working to construct a sharia state. In claiming to "be objective and fair to all sides" (*My War Criminal* 137) in her reproduction of Karadžić's self-serving and historically disputable interpretation of history, Stern thus, in Emina Melonic's words, "continuously minimizes the genocide against Bosnian Muslims." Taken to its logical conclusion, Stern's application of "what sounds terribly like a 'both sides' argument to a genocide that was clearly engineered by one" (Zakaria) has the effect, according to an open letter written by prominent members of the Bosnian American community, of "almost leading one to believe that *the genocide was justified*" (Delkic et al.).[5]

---

5 A number of critics associate Stern's book with the alarming emergence of public denial of the genocide of Bosnian Muslims exemplified most notoriously in the bestowal of the 2019 Nobel Prize for Literature on Peter Handke, who has

In the last paragraph of their open letter, which was issued on 27 January 2020, the authors write, "Today, on International Holocaust Remembrance Day, we are reminded of what evildoers such as Hitler, Karadžić, and those alike were capable of. To our detriment, their vile legacy continues to live and inspire, thanks in part to the likes of Dr. Stern" (Delkic et al.). Through this reference to the context of the Holocaust and its commemoration, the authors of the open letter thus craft a rhetorical appeal that explicitly conjoins what they see as "Stern's hagiography" of Karadžić to a more universally recognized example of mass violence and human malevolence in the history of the Holocaust. Moreover, in so doing, they also implicitly link Stern's project to the long-standing discourse on Holocaust representation—in particular, the representation of Holocaust perpetrators. Their express analogy between Stern's historically dubious narrative of Karadžić's culpability and the "vile legacy" of Holocaust perpetrators makes clear that the phenomenon of the former—the attempt to depict the mind of the architect of the Bosnian genocide—poses some of the same challenges that plague the portrayal of the latter. Although the authors do not further explore this comparison, their juxtaposition of Stern's book alongside the canon of representation of the "evildoers" of the Third Reich and the Holocaust not only reminds us of their shared characteristics (despite their critical divergences) but also suggests the ways in which the figure of the Holocaust perpetrator can be deployed strategically as a framework—or, to use a concept I have proposed over the course of this book, a filtering mechanism—for representing and interpreting the narratives of perpetrators of genocidal violence beyond the Holocaust.

The uproar over Stern's problematic portrait of Karadžić puts into sharp relief some of the concerns presented in this book, providing a critical counterpoint to the texts I analyze here and illustrating the high risks that continue to attend the project of probing the mind of perpetrators of mass violence. Even while, as I have argued, more recent representations of the inner life of Holocaust perpetrators have come to humanize them and thereby to imagine them as complex and contradictory individuals, we continue to be challenged by the larger ethical and representational questions of how to depict the mindset of agents of mass violence without

---

long been known for his whitewashing of Serb violence and his outright denial of the genocide.

reifying them as incomprehensible monsters—or, as in the case of Karadžić, as mythic heroes. What the debate over Stern's book demonstrates in this regard is that the cultural discourse on perpetrators of violence is not progressive, unidirectional, or teleological; on the contrary, it is cyclical, dialectical, and recursive. It is thus imperative that we work to understand it, both with regard to the past and in our present.

The figure of the Holocaust perpetrator is not the apotheosis of evil, nor is it evil's unique, unparalleled manifestation. Rather, it represents a particularly well-studied and ubiquitously represented historical, conceptual, and aesthetic phenomenon that moreover finds compelling resonance with and correspondence to agents of other instances of violence and oppression. For this reason, far from representing an anomalous or singular case of radical evil, the representation of the mind of the Holocaust perpetrator—in fiction and in nonfiction, along historical lines and along aesthetic ones—gives us an important model not only for understanding "evil" but also for understanding *how* we understand it.

Works Cited

Abbott, H. Porter. *The Cambridge Introduction to Narrative*. 2nd ed. Cambridge: Cambridge UP, 2008.
Abrams, Lynn. *Oral History Theory*. 2nd ed. London: Routledge, 2016.
Adams, Jenni. "Glossary of Major Terms and Concepts." *The Bloomsbury Companion to Holocaust Literature*, ed. Jenni Adams. London: Bloomsbury, 2014, 297–334.
———. "Introduction." *Representing Perpetrators in Holocaust Literature and Film*, ed. Jenni Adams and Sue Vice. London: Vallentine Mitchell, 2013, 1–10.
———. "Reading (as) Violence in Jonathan Littell's *The Kindly Ones*." *Representing Holocaust Perpetrators in Literature and Film*, ed. Jenni Adams and Sue Vice. London: Vallentine Mitchell, 2013, 25–46.
———. "Relationships to Realism in Post-Holocaust Fiction." *The Bloomsbury Companion to Holocaust Literature*, ed. Jenni Adams. London: Bloomsbury, 2014, 81–101.
Agamben, Giorgio. *Remnants of Auschwitz: The Witness and the Archive*. Trans. Daniel Heller-Roazen. New York: Zone Books, 2002.
Alber, Jan. "Unnatural Narrative." *the living handbook of narratology*, ed. Peter Hühn et al. Hamburg: Hamburg University, 2014. https://www.lhn.uni-hamburg.de/node/104.html. Accessed 7 July 2019.
———. "Unnatural Narratology: The Systematic Study of Anti-Mimeticism." *Literature Compass* 10, no. 5 (2013): 449–60.
Alley, Gary. "The Roots of Jerusalem Cornerstone (1936–1961): Birth of a Nation and a Vision." *Jerusalem Cornerstone Foundation*. http://jcf-newsletters.s3.amazonaws.com/June%202003.pdf. Accessed 5 Feb. 2019.
Amis, Martin. *Time's Arrow, or, The Nature of the Offense*. New York: Vintage, 1991.
———. *The Zone of Interest*. New York: Knopf, 2014.

Anderson, Kate T. "Intersubjectivity." *The Sage Encyclopedia of Qualitative Research Methods*, ed. Lisa M. Given. Thousand Oaks, CA: Sage Publications, 2008, 468.

Anderson, Miranda, and Stefan Iversen. "Immersion and Defamiliarization: Experiencing Literature and World." *Poetics Today* 39, no. 3 (2018): 569–95.

Annan, Kofi. "Secretary-General's Message to Ceremony Marking the 10th Anniversary of the Srebrenica Massacre." *United Nations*. https://www.un.org/sg/en/content/sg/statement/2005-07-11/secretary-generals-message-ceremony-marking-10th-anniversary. Accessed 1 May 2020.

Arendt, Hannah. *Eichmann in Jerusalem: A Report on the Banality of Evil*. New York: Viking Penguin, 1963.

———. "'Eichmann in Jerusalem': An Exchange of Letters between Gershom Scholem and Hannah Arendt." *Encounter* 22, no. 1 (1964): 51–56.

Ariel, Yaakov. *Evangelizing the Chosen People: Missions to the Jewish in America, 1880–2000*. Chapel Hill: U of North Carolina P, 2000.

Arnds, Peter. "On the Awful German Fairy Tale: Breaking Taboos in Representations of Nazi Euthanasia and the Holocaust in Günter Grass's *Die Blechtrommel*, Edgar Hilsenrath's *Der Nazi & der Friseur*, and Anselm Kiefer's Visual Art." *The German Quarterly* 75, no. 4 (2002): 422–39.

Badrideen, Ahmed. "The Banality of Good and Evil in *The Zone of Interest*." *English* 66, no. 255 (2017): 311–27.

———. "The Soul in *Time's Arrow*: A Post-Enlightenment Presence." *Journal of European Studies* 48, no. 1 (2018): 56–68.

Bajohr, Frank. "Neuere Täterforschung." *Docupedia-Zeitgeschichte*, 18 June 2013. http://docupedia.de/zg/bajohr_neuere_taeterforschung_v1_de_2013. Accessed 8 Apr. 2019.

Bakhtin, Mikhail. "Discourse in the Novel." *The Dialogic Imagination: Four Essays*. Trans. Michael Holquist and Caryl Emerson. Austin: U of Texas P, 1981, 259–422.

Barjonet, Aurélie, and Liran Razinsky. "Introduction." *Writing the Holocaust Today: Critical Perspectives on Jonathan Littell's "The Kindly Ones,"* ed. Aurélie Barjonet and Liran Razinsky. Amsterdam: Rodopi, 2012, 7–16.

Barrett, Lisa Feldman. *How Emotions Are Made: The Secret Life of the Brain*. Boston: Houghton Mifflin Harcourt, 2017.

Barton, George. *Angels of the Battlefield: A History of the Labors of the Catholic Sisterhood in the Late Civil War*. Philadelphia: Catholic Art Publishing, 1897.

Bartov, Omer, Doris Bergen, Andrea Orzoff, Timothy Snyder, and Anika Walke. "An Open Letter to the Director of the US Holocaust Memorial Museum." *The New York Review of Books*, 1 July 2019. https://www.nybooks.com/daily/2019/

07/01/an-open-letter-to-the-director-of-the-holocaust-memorial-museum/. Accessed 5 Aug. 2019.

Battersby, Eileen. "The Thinker." *Irish Times*, 13 Oct. 2006, https://www.irishtimes.com/culture/the-thinker-1.1015227. Accessed 14 Aug. 2020.

Bauman, Zygmunt. *Modernity and the Holocaust*. Ithaca, NY: Cornell UP, 1989.

Bax, Sander. "'The Loneliest Spot on Earth': Harry Mulisch's Literary Experiment in *Criminal Case 40/61*." *werkwinkel* 7, no. 1 (2012): 33–60.

Bećirević, Edina. "How Radovan Karadzic Led an American Scholar into a Labyrinth of Genocide Denial." *The Intercept*, 29 Jan. 2020. https://theintercept.com/2020/01/29/radovan-karadzic-book-bosnia-jessica-stern/. Accessed 3 May 2020.

Benhabib, Seyla. "Arendt's *Eichmann in Jerusalem*." *The Cambridge Companion to Hannah Arendt*, ed. Dana Villa. Cambridge: Cambridge UP, 2001, 65–85.

———. "Whose Trial? Adolf Eichmann's or Hannah Arendt's? The Eichmann Controversy Revisited." *The Trial That Never Ends: Hannah Arendt's "Eichmann in Jerusalem" in Retrospect*, ed. Richard J. Golsan and Sarah M. Misemer. Toronto: U of Toronto P, 2017, 209–28.

Berding, Joop. "Devastating Irony: Hannah Arendt and Harry Mulisch on the Eichmann Trial." *Back to the Core: Rethinking Core Texts in Liberal Arts and Sciences Education in Europe*. Wilmington, DE: Vernon Press, 2017, 335–47.

Berenstein, Tatiana, ed. *Faschismus—Getto—Massenmord: Dokumentation über Ausrottung und Widerstand der Juden in Polen während des Zweiten Weltkrieges*. Berlin: Rütten & Loening, 1960.

Bernard, Catherine. "Dismembering/Remembering Mimesis: Martin Amis, Graham Swift." *British Postmodern Fiction*, ed. Theo D'haen and Hans Bertens. Amsterdam: Rodopi, 1993, 121–44.

Bernstein, Michael André. *Foregone Conclusions: Against Apocalyptic History*. Berkeley: U of California P, 1994.

Bernstein, Richard J. "Did Hannah Arendt Change Her Mind? From Radical Evil to the Banality of Evil." *Hannah Arendt: Twenty Years Later*, ed. Larry May and Jerome Kohn. Cambridge, MA: MIT P, 1996, 127–46.

Bettelheim, Bruno. "Their Specialty Was Murder." *The New York Times Book Review*, 5 Oct. 1986, 1, 60–61.

Bilsky, Leora. "Truth and Judgment in Arendt's Writing." *The Trial That Never Ends: Hannah Arendt's "Eichmann in Jerusalem" in Retrospect*, ed. Richard J. Golsan and Sarah M. Misemer. Toronto: U of Toronto P, 2017, 161–90.

Bird, Stephanie. *Comedy and Trauma in Germany and Austria after 1945: The Inner Side of Mourning*. Cambridge: Legenda, 2016.

Birkmeyer, Jens. "Die Infamie der Schuld: Vom Briefroman zur Tätergroteske: Edgar Hilsenraths *Der Nazi & der Friseur*." *Verliebt in die deutsche Sprache: Die Odyssee des Edgar Hilsenrath*, ed. Helmut Braun. Berlin: Dittrich Verlag, 2005, 51–67.

Bjornstad, Jennifer. *Functions of Humor in German Holocaust Literature: Edgar Hilsenrath, Günter Grass and Jurek Becker*. Ann Arbor: UMI, 2002, PhD dissertation.

Blucher, Av Richard. "How Helpful Is Hannah Arendt in Looking 'Into that Darkness'"? *Pacem* 10, no. 2 (2007): 49–57.

Bolens, Guillemette. *The Style of Gestures: Embodiment and Cognition in Literary Narrative*. Baltimore: Johns Hopkins UP, 2012.

Borges, Jorge Luis. "Deutsches Requiem." Trans. Julian Palley. *Labyrinths: Selected Stories and Other Writings*, ed. Donald A. Yates and James E. Irby. New York: New Directions, 1964, 141–47.

Boswell, Matthew. "Holocaust Literature and the Taboo." *The Bloomsbury Companion to Holocaust Literature*, ed. Jenni Adams. London: Bloomsbury, 2014, 179–97.

Bracher, Nathan. "Timely Representations: Writing the Past in the First-Person Present Imperfect." *History & Memory* 28, no. 1 (2016): 3–35.

Braese, Stephan. *Die andere Erinnerung: Jüdische Autoren in der westdeutschen Nachkriegsliteratur*. Berlin: Philo Verlag, 2001.

Braun, Helmut. "Entstehungs- und Publikationsgeschichte des Romans *Der Nazi & der Friseur*." *Verliebt in die deutsche Sprache: Die Odyssee des Edgar Hilsenrath*, ed. Helmut Braun. Berlin: Dittrich Verlag, 2005, 41–49.

Breithaupt, Fritz. "The Blocking of Empathy, Narrative Empathy, and a Three-Person Model of Empathy." *Emotion Review* 20, no. 1 (2011): 1–8.

Brockmeier, Jens. "Fact and Fiction: Exploring the Narrative Mind." *The Travelling Concepts of Narrative*, ed. Matti Hyvärin, Mari Hatavara, and Lars-Christer Hydén. Amsterdam: John Benjamins, 2013, 121–40.

Brooks, Peter. *Troubling Confessions: Speaking Guilt in Law and Literature*. Chicago: U of Chicago P, 2000.

Browder, George C. *Hitler's Enforcers: The Gestapo and the SS Security Service in the Nazi Revolution*. New York: Oxford UP, 1996.

———. "Perpetrator Character and Motivation: An Emerging Consensus?" *Holocaust and Genocide Studies* 17, no. 3 (2003): 480–97.

Browning, Christopher. *Collected Memories: Holocaust History and Postwar Testimony*. Madison: U of Wisconsin P, 2003.

———. "German Memory, Judicial Interrogation, and Historical Reconstruction: Writing Perpetrator History from Postwar Testimony." *Probing the Limits of Representation: Nazism and the "Final Solution,"* ed. Saul Friedlander. Cambridge, MA: Harvard UP, 1992.

Bruner, Jerome. "Life as Narrative." *Social Research* 54, no. 1 (1987): 11–32.

Brunner, José. "Eichmann's Mind: Psychological, Philosophical, and Legal Perspectives." *Theoretical Inquiries in Law* 1, no. 2 (2008): 1–35.

Bubandt, Nils, and Rane Willerslev. "The Dark Side of Empathy: Mimesis, Deception, and the Magic of Alterity." *Comparative Studies in Society and History* 57, no. 1 (2015): 5–34.

Bui, Roberto. "None of Us Is Immune from Becoming a 'Nazi." *Wu Ming Foundation*, 30 Sept. 2007. http://www.wumingfoundation.com/english/outtakes/the_kindly_ones.htm. Accessed 20 July 2019.

Burke, Jason. "The Evil That Ordinary Men Can Do." *The Guardian*, 22 Feb. 2009. http://www.guardian.co.uk/books/2009/feb/22/history-holocaust-books-jonathan-littell?INTCMP=SRCH. Accessed 20 July 2019.

Cantor, Jay. "Death and the Image." *Beyond Document: Essays on Nonfiction Film*, ed. Charles Warren. Hanover, NH: UP of New England, 1996, 23–49.

Catalog of Copyright Entries Third Series: Books and Pamphlets. 17.1.1 (January–June 1963). Washington: Library of Congress Copyright Office, 1964.

Cesarani, David. *Becoming Eichmann: Rethinking the Life, Crimes, and Trial of a "Desk Murderer."* Cambridge, MA: Da Capo Press, 2004.

Chare, Nicholas, and Dominic Williams. *Matters of Testimony: Interpreting the Scrolls of Auschwitz.* New York: Berghahn, 2016.

Chatman, Seymour. "Backwards." *Narrative* 17, no. 1 (2009): 31–55.

Childs, Harwood L. Preface to *The Nazi Primer: Official Handbook for Schooling the Hitler Youth.* New York: Harper and Brothers, 1938.

Clendinnen, Inga. *Reading the Holocaust.* Cambridge: Cambridge UP, 1999.

"Converting Eichmann." *Time*, 18 May 1962, 76.

Conway, Daniel. "Banality, Again." *The Trial That Never Ends: Hannah Arendt's "Eichmann in Jerusalem" in Retrospect*, ed. Richard J. Golsan and Sarah M. Misemer. Toronto: U of Toronto P, 2017, 67–91.

Coquio, Catherine. "'Oh My Human Brothers, Let Me Tell You How It Happened.' (Who Is the Perpetrator Talking To?)." *Writing the Holocaust Today: Critical Perspectives on Jonathan Littell's "The Kindly Ones,"* ed. Aurélie Barjonet and Liran Razinsky. Amsterdam: Editions Rodopi, 2012, 75–96.

Corduwener, Pepijn. "'Eichmann Is My Father': Harry Mulisch, the Eichmann Trial and the Question of Guilt." *Journal of War & Culture Studies* 7, no. 2 (2014): 133–46.

Critchell, Kara, Susanne C. Knittel, Emiliano Perra, and Uğur Ümit Üngör. "Editors' Introduction." *Journal of Perpetrator Research* 1, no. 1 (2017): 1–27.

Crownshaw, Richard. "Perpetrator Fictions and Transcultural Memory." *parallax* 17, no. 4 (2011): 75–89.

Curthoys, Ned. "Evaluating Risk in Perpetrator Narratives: Resituating Jonathan Littell's *The Kindly Ones* as Historical Fiction." *Textual Practice* 31, no. 3 (2017): 457–75.

... *dann bin ich ja ein Mörder!* Dir. Walter Manoschek. Walter Manoschek, 2012.

de Goeij, Bart. "Briefwisseling van Hannah Arendt en Harry Mulisch." *Harry-Mulisch.nl*, 16 Oct. 2014. http://www.harry-mulisch.nl/briefwisseling-van-hannah-arendt-en-harry-mulisch/. Accessed 23 Jan. 2019.

Delkic, Ajla, et al. "Open Letter Regarding Dr. Jessica Stern's Book Titled *My War Criminal: Personal Encounters with an Architect of Genocide*." *Advisory Council for Bosnia and Herzegovina*, 27 Jan. 2020. https://www.acbih.org/open-letter-dr-jessica-sterns-book-my-war-criminal/. Accessed 3 May 2020.

Dern, John A. *Martians, Monsters and Madonna: Fiction and Form in the World of Martin Amis*. New York: Peter Lang, 2000.

Diedrick, James. *Understanding Martin Amis*. Columbia: U of South Carolina P, 2004.

di Giovanni, Janine. "I Can Never Forget the Bosnian Genocide: But Others Are Trying to Rewrite History." *The Washington Post*, 3 Feb. 2020. https://www.washingtonpost.com/opinions/2020/02/03/i-can-never-forget-bosnian-genocide-others-are-trying-rewrite-history/. Accessed 3 May 2020.

Dittrich, Volker. "'Es ist mir ein Rätsel': Ein Gespräch mit Edgar Hilsenrath über Jonathan Littells Roman *Die Wohlgesinnten*." *literarturkritik.de* 5 (2008). http://www.literarturkritik.de/public/rezension.php?rez_id=11904. Accessed 14 Aug. 2020.

Dvash, Jonathan, and Simone G. Shamay-Tsoory. "Theory of Mind and Empathy as Multidimensional Constructs Neurological Foundations." *Topics in Language Disorders* 34, no. 4 (2014): 282–95.

Dwork, Debórah. Foreword to *Criminal Case 40/61, the Trial of Adolf Eichmann: An Eyewitness Account* by Harry Mulisch. Trans. Robert Naborn. Philadelphia: U of Pennsylvania P, 2005, ix–xxiv.

Eaglestone, Robert. *The Broken Voice: Reading Post-Holocaust Literature*. Oxford: Oxford UP, 2017.

———. "Reading Perpetrator Testimony." *The Future of Memory*, ed. Richard Crownshaw, Jane Kilby, and Antony Rowland. New York: Berghahn, 2010, 123–34.

Easterbrook, Neil. "'I Know That It Is to Do with Trash and Shit, and That It Is Wrong in Time': Narrative Reversal in Martin Amis' *Time's Arrow*." *CCTE Studies* 55 (1995): 52–61.

Evans, Richard. *The Third Reich at War*. New York: Penguin, 2009.
Fackenheim, Emil L. "Philosophical Considerations and the Teaching of the Holocaust." *Jewish Philosophy and the Academy*, ed. Emil L. Fackenheim and Raphael Jospe. London: Associated University Presses, 1996, 191–203.
Felman, Shoshana. "Theaters of Justice: Arendt in Jerusalem, the Eichmann Trial, and the Redefinition of Legal Meaning in the Wake of the Holocaust." *Critical Inquiry* 27, no. 2 (2001): 201–38.
Finney, Brian. *Martin Amis*. London: Routledge, 2008.
———. "Martin Amis's *Time's Arrow* and the Postmodern Sublime." *Martin Amis: Postmodernism and Beyond*, ed. Gavin Keulks. New York: Palgrave, 2006, 101–16.
———. "What's Amis in Contemporary British Fiction? Martin Amis's *Money* and *Time's Arrow*." California State University Long Beach. http://web.csulb.edu/~bhfinney/amismoney.html. Accessed 1 Aug. 2019.
Fludernik, Monika. "Factual Narrative: A Missing Narratological Paradigm." *Germanisch-Romanische Monatsschrift* 63, no. 1 (2013): 117–34.
Foucault, Michel. *The History of Sexuality. Vol. 1: An Introduction*. Trans. Robert Hurley. New York: Random House, 1978.
Franklin, Ruth. "Viper's Nest: Martin Amis's *Zone of Interest*." *The New York Times*, 5 Oct. 2014, A15.
Fuchs, Anne. *A Space of Anxiety: Dislocation and Abjection in Modern German-Jewish Literature*. Amsterdam: Rodopi, 1999.
Gellately, Robert. "Introduction." *The Nuremberg Interviews*. Conducted by Leon Goldensohn. New York: Knopf, 2004, vii–xxix.
Genette, Gérard. *Narrative Discourse: An Essay in Method*. Trans. Jane E. Lewin. Ithaca, NY: Cornell UP, 1980.
Gerlach, Christian. "The Eichmann Interrogations in Holocaust Historiography." *Holocaust and Genocide Studies* 15, no. 3 (2001): 428–52.
Gigliotti, Simone. *The Train Journey: Transit, Captivity, and Witnessing in the Holocaust*. New York: Berghahn, 2009.
Gill, Jo, editor. *Modern Confessional Writing: New Critical Essays*. London: Routledge, 2006.
Golsan, Richard J. "The American Reception of Max Aue." *SubStance* 121, no. 39 (2010): 174–83.
Golsan, Richard J., and Sarah M. Misemer. "Arendt in Jerusalem: The Eichmann Trial, the Banality of Evil, and the Meaning of Justice Fifty Years On." *The Trial That Never Ends: Hannah Arendt's "Eichmann in Jerusalem" in Retrospect*, ed. Richard J. Golsan and Sarah M. Misemer. Toronto: U of Toronto P, 2017, 11–21.

Gomel, Elana. *Bloodscripts: Writing the Violent Subject*. Columbus: Ohio State UP, 2003.

Graf, Andreas. "Mörderisches Ich: Zur Pathologie der Erzählperspektive in Edgar Hilsenraths Roman *Der Nazi und der Friseur*." *Edgar Hilsenrath: Das Unerzählbare erzählen*, ed. Thomas Kraft. Munich: Piper, 1996, 135–49.

Gray, Richard T. *About Face: German Physiognomic Thought from Lavater to Auschwitz*. Detroit: Wayne State UP, 2004.

Grethlein, Jonas. "S.S. Officers as Tragic Heroes? Jonathan Littell's *Les Bienveillantes* and the Narrative Representation of the Shoah." *Style* 44, no. 4 (2010): 566–85.

Hansen, Per Krogh. "First Person, Present Tense: Authorial Presence and Unreliable Narration in Simultaneous Narration." *Narrative Unreliability in the Twentieth-Century First-Person Novel*, ed. Elke D'hoker and Gunther Martens. Berlin: de Gruyter, 2008, 317–38.

Harris, Greg. "Men Giving Birth to New World Orders: Martin Amis's *Time's Arrow*." *Studies in the Novel* 31, no. 4 (1999): 489–505.

Hartouni, Valerie. *Visualizing Atrocity: Arendt, Evil, and the Optics of Thoughtlessness*. New York: New York UP, 2102.

Hausner, Gideon. "Eichmann and His Trial." Part 1 of 3. *The Saturday Evening Post*, Nov. 1962, 19–25.

Herman, David. "Introduction." *The Emergence of Mind: Representations of Consciousness in Narrative Discourses in English*, ed. David Herman. Lincoln: U of Nebraska P, 2011, 1–42.

———. "Storytelling and the Sciences of Mind: Cognitive Narratology, Discursive Psychology, and Narratives in Face-to-Face Interaction." *Narrative* 15, no. 3 (2007): 306–34.

Hicks, Patrick. *The Commandant of Lubizec*. Hanover, NH: Steerforth Press, 2014.

Hilberg, Raul. *Perpetrators Victims Bystanders: The Jewish Catastrophe, 1933–1945*. New York: Harper Perennial, 1992.

Hilsenrath, Edgar. *Der Nazi und der Friseur*. Berlin/Köln: Dittrich Verlag, 2004.

———. *The Nazi and the Barber*. Trans. Andrew White. Berlin: Barber Press, 2013.

Hoffman, Louise E. "American Psychologists and Wartime Research on Germany, 1941–1945." *American Psychologist* 47, no. 2 (1992): 264–73.

Hofmann, Michael. "Splashing through the Puddles." *London Review of Books* 36, no. 20 (2014): 3–5. https://www-lrb-co-uk.libproxy.wustl.edu/v36/n20/michael-hofmann/splashing-through-the-puddles. Accessed 10 Aug. 2019.

Hogan, Patrick Colm. "The Epilogue of Suffering: Heroism, Empathy, Ethics." *SubStance* 94/95 (2001): 119–43.

Horan, Geraldine. "Er zog sich die 'neue Sprache' des 'Dritten Reiches' über wie ein Kleidungsstück: Communities of Practice and Performativity in National Socialist Discourse." *Linguistik online* 30, no. 1 (2007). https://bop.unibe.ch/linguistik-online/article/view/549/927. Accessed 20 June 2018.

Horch, Hans Otto. "Grauen und Groteske: Zu Edgar Hilsenraths Romanen." *Verliebt in die deutsche Sprache: Die Odyssee des Edgar Hilsenrath*, ed. Helmut Braun. Berlin: Dittrich Verlag, 2005, 19–32.

Horowitz, Sara R. *Voicing the Void: Muteness and Memory in Holocaust Fiction*. Albany: State U of New York P, 1997.

Horsman, Yasco. *Theaters of Justice: Judging, Staging and Working Through in Arendt, Brecht and Delbo*. Stanford: Stanford UP, 2011.

Hughes, Judith M. *The Holocaust and the Revival of Psychological History*. New York: Cambridge UP, 2015.

Hühn, Peter. "The Detective as Reader: Narrativity and Reading Concepts in Detective Fiction." *Modern Fiction Studies* 33, no. 3 (1987): 451–66.

Hull, William L. *The Struggle for a Soul*. Garden City, NY: Doubleday, 1963.

Iversen, Stefan. "Broken or Unnatural? On the Distinction of Fiction in Non-Conventional First Person Narration." *The Travelling Concepts of Narrative*, ed. Matti Hyvärin, Mari Hatavara, and Lars-Christer Hydén. Amsterdam: John Benjamins, 2013, 141–62.

Jensen, Morten Høi. "The Hilarity of Evil." *Los Angeles Review of Books*, 18 Nov. 2014. https://lareviewofbooks.org/article/hilarity-evil/. Accessed 10 Aug. 2019.

Kakutani, Michiko. "Ordinary, Everyday Monsters." *The New York Times*, 3 Oct. 2014, C21, C25.

———. "Unrepentant and Telling of Horrors Untellable." *The New York Times*, 24 Feb. 2009. http://www.nytimes.com/2009/02/24/books/24kaku.html?_r=0. Accessed 20 July 2019.

Kalkofen, Rupert. "Nach dem Ende auf die andere Seite: Edgar Hilsenraths *Der Nazi & der Friseur*." *Erwartung des Endes: Apokalypsen in der Literatur des 20. Jahrhunderts*, ed. Christian Uhlig and Rupert Kalkofen. Bern: Peter Lang, 2000, 41–62.

Kamm, Oliver. "An Indecent Depiction of Evil." *CapX*, 24 Jan. 2020. https://capx.co/an-indecent-depiction-of-evil/. Accessed 4 May 2020.

Kärkkäinen, Veli-Matti. "Pentecostal Mission and Encounter with Religions." *The Cambridge Companion to Pentecostalism*, ed. Cecil M. Robeck Jr. and Amos Yong. Cambridge: Cambridge UP, 2014, 294–312.

Keen, Suzanne. "Life Writing and the Empathetic Circle." *Concentric: Literary and Cultural Studies* 42, no. 2 (2016): 9–26.

Kekes, John. *The Roots of Evil*. Ithaca, NY: Cornell UP, 2005.

Kettner, Fabian. "Ein Handlungsreisender in Sachen 'Endlösung der Judenfrage': Die Rolle Adolf Eichmanns für das Bild von der Moderne." *Kritiknetz—Zeitschrift für Kritische Theorie der Gesellschaft*, 1 Nov. 2006. https://www.kritiknetz.de/wissenschaftrezensionen/277-einhandlungsreisenderinsachenendloesungderjudenfrage. Accessed 27 Jan. 2019.

Keulks, Gavin. "W(h)ither Postmodernism: Late Amis." *Martin Amis: Postmodernism and Beyond*, ed. Gavin Keulks. Houndsmills, Basingstoke, Hampshire: Palgrave MacMillan, 2006, 158–79.

Kidd, Thomas S. *American Christians and Islam: Evangelical Culture and Muslims from the Colonial Period to the Age of Terrorism*. Princeton: Princeton UP, 2009.

Kieser, Hans-Lukas. *Nearest East: American Millennialism and Mission to the Middle East*. Philadelphia: Temple UP, 2010.

Kirsch, Adam. "Martin Amis and Howard Jacobson Get the Holocaust Backwards, From Different Angles." *Tablet Magazine*, 8 Oct. 2014. https://www.tabletmag.com/jewish-arts-and-culture/books/186117/amis-jacobson-holocaust. Accessed 10 Aug. 2019.

Klein, Julia M. "Review: *The Zone of Interest* by Martin Amis." *Chicago Tribune*, 26 Sept. 2014. https://www.chicagotribune.com/entertainment/books/ct-prj-zone-of-interest-martin-amis-20140926-story.html. Accessed 28 July 2019.

Klocke, Astrid. "Subverting Satire: Edgar Hilsenrath's Novel *Der Nazi und der Friseur* and Charlie Chaplin's Film *The Great Dictator*." *Holocaust and Genocide Studies* 22, no. 3 (2008): 497–513.

von Koppenfels, Martin. "The Infamous 'I': Notes on Littell and Céline." *Writing the Holocaust Today: Critical Perspectives on Jonathan Littell's "The Kindly Ones,"* ed. Aurélie Barjonet and Liran Razinsky. Amsterdam: Rodopi, 2012, 133–52.

———. "*Kommissbrot*: Jonathan Littell's Glossary." *MLN* 125, no. 4 (2010): 927–40.

Kulcsar, Istvan S. "Ich habe immer Angst gehabt: Test- und Untersuchungsbefunde zur Persönlichkeit Adolf Eichmanns." *Der Spiegel* 47 (1966): 176–82.

Kuon, Peter. "From 'Kitsch' to 'Splatter': The Aesthetics of Violence in *The Kindly Ones*." *Writing the Holocaust Today: Critical Perspectives on Jonathan Littell's "The Kindly Ones,"* ed. Aurélie Barjonet and Liran Razinsky. Amsterdam: Editions Rodopi, 2012, 33–45.

LaCapra, Dominick. "Historical and Literary Approaches to the 'Final Solution': Saul Friedländer and Jonathan Littell." *History and Theory* 50, no. 1 (2011): 71–97.

———. "Lanzmann's *Shoah*: 'Here There Is No Why.'" *Critical Inquiry* 23, no. 2 (1997): 231–69.

Landsman, Stephan. Review of *Criminal Case 40/61, the Trial of Adolf Eichmann: An Eyewitness Account* by Harry Mulisch. *Human Rights Quarterly* 28, no. 4 (2006): 1074–78.

Lang, Johannes. "Questioning Dehumanization: Intersubjective Dimensions of Violence in the Nazi Concentration and Death Camps." *Holocaust and Genocide Studies* 24, no. 2 (2010): 225–46.

Lanzmann, Claude. *Le lièvre de Patagonie*. Paris: Éditions Gallimard, 2009.

———. *The Patagonian Hare: A Memoir*. Trans. Frank Wynne. New York: Farrar, Straus and Giroux, 2012.

Lawson, Mark. "Return to Kat Zet." *Literary Review* 424 (2014). https://literaryreview.co.uk/return-to-kat-zet. Accessed 30 July 2019.

Leake, Eric. "Humanizing the Inhumane: The Value of Difficult Empathy." *Rethinking Empathy through Literature*, ed. Meghan Marie Hammond and Sue J. Kim. New York: Routledge, 2014, 175–85.

Le Chagrin et la Pitié. Dir. Marcel Ophüls. Norddeutscher Rundfunk, Société Suisse, De Radiodiffusion, 1969.

Lehman, Daniel W. *Matters of Fact: Reading Nonfiction over the Edge*. Columbus: Ohio State UP, 1997.

Less, Avner. "Introduction." Trans. Joel Agee. *Eichmann Interrogated: Transcripts for the Archives of the Israeli Police*. Ed. Jochen von Lang in collaboration with Claus Sybill. Trans. Ralph Manheim. New York: Farrar, Straus and Giroux, 1983.

Lewy, Guenter. *Perpetrators: The World of the Holocaust Killers*. Oxford: Oxford UP, 2017.

Lifton, Robert Jay. *The Nazi Doctors: Medical Killing and the Psychology of Genocide*. New York: Basic Books, 1986.

Lilla, Mark. "The Defense of a Jewish Collaborator." *The New York Review of Books*, 5 Dec. 2013. http://www.nybooks.com/articles/2013/12/05/defense-jewish-collaborator/. Accessed 14 Aug. 2020.

Littell, Jonathan. *The Kindly Ones*. Trans. C. Mandell. New York: Harper, 2009.

———. *Les Bienveillantes*. Paris: Gallimard, 2006.

Löffelsender, Michael. "Der Mann im Glaskasten: Neuere Beiträge zu Adolf Eichmann und dem Jerusalemer Eichmann-Prozess." *Neue Politische Literatur* 58 (2013): 231–48.

Lothe, Jakob. "Authority, Reliability, and the Challenge of Reading: The Narrative Ethics of Jonathan Littell's *The Kindly Ones*." *Narrative Ethics*, ed. Jakob Lothe and Jeremy Hawthorn. Amsterdam: Rodopi, 2013, 103–18.

Lyotard, Jean-François. *The Differend: Phrases in Dispute*. Trans. Georges Van Den Abbeele. Minneapolis: U of Minnesota P, 1988.

Ma, Julie C. "Pentecostal Evangelism, Church Planting, and Church Growth." *Pentecostal Mission and Global Christianity*, ed. Wonsuk Ma, Veli Matti Karkkainen, and J. Kwabena Asamoah-Gyadu. Eugene, OR: Wipf and Stock, 2014, 87–106.

MacCannell, Juliet Flower. "Fascism and the Voice of Conscience." *Radical Evil*, ed. Joan Copjec. London: Verso, 1996, 46–73.

Magilow, Daniel H., Elizabeth Bridges, and Kristin Vander Lugt. *Nazisploitation! The Nazi Image in Low-Brow Cinema and Culture*. London: Continuum, 2012.

Malachy, Yona. *American Fundamentalism and Israel: The Relation of Fundamentalist Churches to Zionism and the State of Israel*. Jerusalem: Graph Press, 1978.

Malkmus, Bernhard. "Picaresque Narratology: Lazarillo de Tormes and Edgar Hilsenrath's *Der Nazi und der Friseur*." *Clowns, Fools and Picaros: Popular Forms in Theatre, Fiction and Film*, ed. David Robb. Amsterdam: Rodopi, 2007, 211–29.

Malle, Bertram F., and Jess Scon Holbrook, "Theory of Mind and Consciousness." *The Oxford Companion to Consciousness*, ed. Tim Bayne, Axel Cleeremans, and Patrick Wilken. Oxford: Oxford UP, 2009, 630–32.

Martínez-Alfaro, María Jesús. "Where Madness Lies: Holocaust Representation and the Ethics of Form in Martin Amis' *Time's Arrow*." *Ethics and Trauma in Contemporary British Fiction*, ed. Susana Onega and Jean-Michel Ganteau. Amsterdam: Rodopi, 2011, 127–54.

Matthäus, Jürgen. "Historiography and the Perpetrators of the Holocaust." *The Historiography of the Holocaust*, ed. Dan Stone. Houndsmills, Basingstoke, Hampshire: Palgrave Macmillan, 2004, 197–215.

May, Joshua. "Empathy and Intersubjectivity." *The Routledge Handbook of Philosophy of Empathy*, ed. Heidi L. Maibom. London: Routledge, 2017, 169–79.

McCarthy, Dermot. "The Limits of Irony: The Chronillogical World of Martin Amis' *Time's Arrow*." *War, Literature and the Arts* 11, no. 1 (1999): 294–320.

McGlothlin, Erin. "Empathetic Identification and the Mind of the Holocaust Perpetrator in Fiction: A Proposed Taxonomy of Response." *Narrative* 24, no. 3 (2016): 251–76.

———. "In Search of Suchomel in *Shoah*: Examining Claude Lanzmann's Postproduction Editing Practice." *The Construction of Testimony: Claude Lanzmann's "Shoah" and Its Outtakes*, ed. Erin McGlothlin, Brad Prager, and Markus Zisselsberger. Detroit: Wayne State University Press, 2020, 233–74.

———. "Listening to the Perpetrators in Claude Lanzmann's *Shoah*." *Colloquia Germanica* 43, no. 3 (2010; published 2013): 235–71.

———. "Narrative Perspective and the Holocaust Perpetrator in Edgar Hilsenrath's *The Nazi and the Barber* and Jonathan Littell's *The Kindly Ones*." *The Bloomsbury Companion to Holocaust Literature*, ed. Jenni Adams. London: Bloomsbury, 2014, 159–77.

———. "Narrative Transgression in Edgar Hilsenrath's *Der Nazi und der Friseur* and the Rhetoric of the Sacred in Holocaust Discourse." *German Quarterly* 80, no. 2 (2007): 220–39.

———. *Second-Generation Holocaust Literature: Legacies of Survival and Perpetration*. Rochester, NY: Camden House, 2006.

———. "Theorizing the Perpetrator in Bernhard Schlink's *The Reader* and Martin Amis's *Time's Arrow*." *After Representation?: The Holocaust, Literature, and Culture*, ed. R. Clifton Spargo and Robert M. Ehrenreich. New Brunswick, NJ: Rutgers UP, 2010, 210–30.

———. "The Voice of the Perpetrator, the Voices of the Survivors." *Persistent Legacy: The Holocaust and German Studies*, ed. Erin McGlothlin and Jennifer Kapczynski. Rochester, NY: Camden House, 2016, 1–16.

Meixner, Sebastian. "Edgar Hilsenrath: *Der Nazi und der Friseur*." *Handbuch des Antisemitismus: Judenfeindschaft in Geschichte und Gegenwart*. Vol. 8, ed. Wolfgang Benz. Berlin: DeGruyter, 2015, 254–56.

Melonic, Emina. "Jessica Stern's Denial of Evil." *Spectator USA*, 4 Feb. 2020. https://spectator.us/jessica-stern-denial-evil-war-criminal-architect-genocide/. Accessed 4 May 2020.

Mendelsohn, Daniel. "Transgression." *The New York Review of Books* 56, no. 5 (2009). http://www.nybooks.com/articles/archives/2009/mar/26/transgression/. Accessed 12 July 2019.

Menden, Alexander. "Provokation als Geschäftsmodell." *Süddeutsche Zeitung*, 18 Sept. 2014. https://www.sueddeutsche.de/kultur/roman-the-zone-of-interest-von-martin-amis-provokation-als-geschaeftsmodell-1.2133130. Accessed 10 Aug. 2019.

Menke, Richard. "Narrative Reversals and the Thermodynamics of History in Martin Amis's *Time's Arrow*." *Modern Fiction Studies* 44, no. 4 (1998): 959–80.

Meretoja, Hanna. *The Ethics of Storytelling: Narrative Hermeneutics, History, and the Possible*. Oxford: Oxford UP, 2018.

Metz, Jeremy. "Reading the Victimizer: Towards an Ethical Practice of Figuring the Traumatic Moment in Holocaust Literature." *Textual Practice* 26, no. 6 (2012): 1021–43.

Milchman, Alan, and Alan Rosenberg. "Hannah Arendt and the Etiology of the Desk Killer: The Holocaust as Portent." *History of European Ideas* 14, no. 2 (1992): 213–26.

Millet, Lydia. "Review: Martin Amis Takes on Nazi Love in *Zone of Interest*. Really." *Los Angeles Times*, 25 Sept. 2014. https://www.latimes.com/books/jacketcopy/la-ca-jc-martin-amis-20140928-story.html. Accessed 10 Aug. 2019.

Mohamed, Saira. "Of Monsters and Men: Perpetrator Trauma and Mass Atrocity." *Columbia Law Review* 115 (2015): 1157–216.

Morag, Raya. *Waltzing with Bashir: Perpetrator Trauma and Cinema*. London: I. B. Tauris, 2013.

Moyn, Samuel. "A Nazi Zelig: Jonathan Littell's *The Kindly Ones*." *The Nation*, 23 Mar. 2009. https://www.thenation.com/article/nazi-zelig-jonathan-littells-kindly-ones/. Accessed 20 July 2019.

Mulisch, Harry. *Criminal Case 40/61, the Trial of Adolf Eichmann: An Eyewitness Account*. Trans. Robert Naborn. Philadelphia: U of Pennsylvania P, 2005.

———. *De Zaak 40/61: Een Reportage*. Amsterdam: Uitgeverij de Bezige Bij, 1961.

Newmark, Catherine. "Er hat alle getäuscht: Gespräch mit Bettina Stangneth." *Philosophie Magazin* 114, no. 6 (2016): 114–20.

Norberg, Jakob. "The Banality of Narrative: Hannah Arendt's *Eichmann in Jerusalem*." *Textual Practice* 27, no. 5 (2013): 743–61.

Nünning, Ansgar. "Reliability." *Routledge Encyclopedia of Narrative Theory*, ed. David Herman, Manfred Jahn, and Marie-Laure Ryan. London: Routledge, 2010, 495–97.

Oates, Joyce Carol. "The Death Factory: Martin Amis's *The Zone of Interest*." *The New Yorker*, 29 Sept. 2014, 83–84.

Ozick, Cynthia. "There Were No Love Stories in Auschwitz. Is It Okay for a Novelist to Invent One?" Review of Martin Amis's *The Zone of Interest*. *New Republic*, 20 Oct. 2014. http://www.newrepublic.com/article/120029/zone-interest-review-it-ok-invent-holocaust-love-story. Accessed 22 Mar. 2015.

Pagis, Dan. *The Selected Poetry of Dan Pagis*. Trans. Stephen Mitchell. Berkeley: U of California P, 1989.

Parry, Ann. "The Caesura of the Holocaust in Martin Amis's *Time's Arrow* and Bernhard Schlink's *The Reader*." *Journal of European Studies* 29 (1999): 249–67.

Payne, Leigh A. "Confessional Performances: A Methodological Approach to Studying Perpetrators' Testimonies." *Assessing the Impact of Transitional Justice: Challenges for Empirical Research*, ed. Hugo van der Merwe, Victoria Baxter, and Audrey R. Chapman. Washington, DC: United States Institute of Peace, 2009, 227–47.

Pendas, Devin O. "*Eichmann in Jerusalem*, Arendt in Frankfurt: The Eichmann Trial, the Auschwitz Trial, and the Banality of Justice." *New German Critique* 100 (2007): 77–109.

Pettersson, Bo. "Beyond Anti-Mimetic Models: A Critique of Unnatural Narratology." *Rethinking Mimesis: Concepts and Practices of Literary Representation*, ed. Saija Isomaa, Sari Kivistö, Pirjo Lyytikäinen, Sanna Nyqvist, Merja Polvinen, and Riikka Rossi. Newcastle upon Tyne: Cambridge Scholars Publishing, 2012, 73–91.

Pettitt, Joanne. *Perpetrators in Holocaust Narratives: Encountering the Nazi Beast*. London: Palgrave MacMillan, 2017.

Phelan, James. "Estranging Unreliability, Bonding Unreliability, and the Ethics of *Lolita*." *Narrative* 15, no. 2 (2007): 222–38.

———. "The Ethics and Aesthetics of Backward Narration in Martin Amis's *Time's Arrow*." *After Testimony: The Ethics and Aesthetics of Holocaust Narrative for the Future*, ed. Jakob Lothe, Susan Rubin Suleiman, and James Phelan. Columbus: Ohio State UP, 2012, 120–39.

———. *Experiencing Fiction: Judgments, Progressions, and the Rhetorical Theory of Narrative*. Columbus: Ohio State UP, 2007.

———. *Living to Tell about It: A Rhetoric and Ethics of Character Narration*. Ithaca, NY: Cornell UP, 2005.

———. "Rhetoric/Ethics." *The Cambridge Companion to Narrative*, ed. David Herman. Cambridge: Cambridge UP, 2007, 203–16.

Pick, Daniel. *The Pursuit of the Nazi Mind: Hitler, Hess, and the Analysts*. Oxford: Oxford UP, 2012.

Polvinen, Merja. "Being Played: Mimesis, Fictionality, and Emotional Engagement." *Rethinking Mimesis: Concepts and Practices of Literary Representation*, ed. Saija Isomaa, Sari Kivistö, Pirjo Lyytikäinen, Sanna Nyqvist, Merja Polvinen, and Riikka Rossi. Newcastle upon Tyne: Cambridge Scholars Publishing, 2012, 93–112.

Postone, Moishe. "Reflections on Jewish History as General History: Hannah Arendt's *Eichmann in Jerusalem*." *Jüdische Geschichte als allgemeine Geschichte*, ed. Raphael Gross and Yfaat Weiss. Göttingen: Vandenhoeck und Ruprecht, 2006, 189–211.

Prager, Brad. "Bad Acting, from Adolf Eichmann to Paul Maria Hafner: Testimonial Performance and Nazi Perpetrators." *Performativity—Life. Stage, Screen: Reflections on a Transdisciplinary Concept*, ed. A. Dana Weber and Margaret E. Wright-Cleveland. Vienna: Lit Verlag, 2018, 71–92.

Radisch, Iris. "Am Anfang steht ein Missverständnis." *Die Zeit*, 14 February 2008. http://www.zeit.de/2008/08/L-Littell-Radisch. Accessed 13 July 2019.

Rasson, Luc. "How Nazis Undermine Their Own Point of View: Irony and Reliability in *The Kindly Ones*." *Writing the Holocaust Today: Critical*

Perspectives on Jonathan Littell's "The Kindly Ones," ed. Aurélie Barjonet and Liran Razinsky. Amsterdam: Rodopi, 2012, 97–110.

Rau, Petra. *Our Nazis: Representations of Fascism in Contemporary Literature and Film*. Edinburgh: Edinburgh UP, 2013.

Razinsky, Liran. "History, Excess and Testimony in Jonathan Littell's *Les Bienveillantes*." *French Forum* 33, no. 3 (2008): 69–87.

———. "Not the Witness We Wished For: Testimony in Jonathan Littell's *Kindly Ones*." *Modern Language Quarterly* 71, no. 2 (2010): 175–96.

Reeder, Glenn D., and David Trafimow. "Attributing Motives to Other People." *Other Minds: How Humans Bridge the Divide between Self and Others*, ed. Bertram F. Malle and Sara D. Hodges. New York: Guilford Press, 2005, 106–23.

Reich, Tova. "Book Review: *The Zone of Interest*, by Martin Amis." *Washington Post*, 25 Sept. 2014. https://www.washingtonpost.com/entertainment/books/book-review-the-zone-of-interest-by-martin-amis/2014/09/25/c61670fc-32c0-11e4-8f02-03c644b2d7d0_story.html. Accessed 22 Mar. 2015.

Reichman, Ravit. *The Affective Life of Law: Legal Modernism and the Literary Imagination*. Stanford: Stanford UP, 2009.

Richardson, Brian. "Antimimetic, Unnatural, and Postmodern Narrative Theory." *Narrative Theory: Core Concepts and Critical Debates*, ed. David Herman, James Phelan, Peter J. Rabinowitz, Brian Richardson, and Robyn Warhol. Columbus: Ohio State UP, 2012, 20–28.

———. "Beyond Story and Discourse: Narrative Time in Postmodern and Nonmimetic Fiction." *Narrative Dynamics: Essays on Time, Plot, Closure and Frames*, ed. Brian Richardson. Columbus: Ohio State UP, 2002, 47–63.

———. *Unlikely Stories: Causality and the Nature of Modern Narrative*. Newark: U of Delaware P, 1997.

———. "Unnatural Narrative Theory." *Style* 50, no. 4 (2016): 385–405.

———. *Unnatural Voices: Extreme Narration in Modern and Contemporary Fiction*. Columbus: Ohio State UP, 2006.

———. "What Is Unnatural Narrative Theory?" *Unnatural Narratives—Unnatural Narratology*, ed. Jan Alber and Rüdiger Heinze. Berlin: DeGruyter, 2011, 23–40.

Rimmon-Kenan, Shlomith. "Ambiguity and Narrative Levels: Christine Brooke-Rose's *Thru*." *Poetics Today* 3, no. 1 (1982): 21–32.

Rives, Rochelle. "Facing Wilde; or, Emotion's Image." *PMLA* 130, no. 5 (2015): 1363–80.

Rogovin, Or. "From 'German Wolfhounds' to 'Ordinary People': Characterizations of Holocaust Perpetrators in Israeli Fiction." *New German Critique* 46, no. 2 (2019): 65–89.

Ronnen, Meir. "Mass Murder by Timetable." *The Jerusalem Post*, 18 Aug. 2006, 27.
Roseman, Mark. "Beyond Conviction? Perpetrators, Ideas, and Action in the Holocaust in Historiographical Perspective." *Conflict, Catastrophe and Continuity: Essays on Modern German History*, ed. Frank Biess, Mark Roseman, and Hana Schissler. New York: Berghahn, 2007.
———. "Holocaust Perpetrators in Victims' Eyes." *Years of Persecution, Years of Extermination: Saul Friedländer and the Future of Holocaust Studies*, ed. Christian Wiese and Paul Betts. London: Continuum, 2010, 81–100.
Rosen, Alan. "Autobiography from the Other Side: The Reading of Nazi Memoirs and Confessional Ambiguity." *Biography* 24, no. 3 (2001): 553–69.
Rosenblum, Rachel. "Postponing Trauma: The Dangers of Telling." *The International Journal of Psychoanalysis* 90, no. 6 (2009): 1319–40.
Roth, Michael S. *The Ironist's Cage: Memory, Trauma and the Construction of History*. New York: Columbia UP, 1995.
Rumler, Fritz. "Max & Itzig." *Der Spiegel* 35 (1977): 137–39.
Sanyal, Debarati. *Memory and Complicity: Migrations of Holocaust Remembrance*. New York: Fordham UP, 2015.
"Satan in der Zelle." *Der Spiegel* 22 (1962): 51.
Schabert, Ina. "Fictional Biography, Factual Biography, and their Contaminations." *Biography* 5, no. 1 (1982): 1–16.
Schlant, Ernestine. *The Language of Silence: West German Literature and the Holocaust*. New York: Routledge, 1999.
Schmidt, Sybille. "Perpetrators' Knowledge: What and How Can We Learn from Perpetrator Testimony?" *Journal of Perpetrator Research* 1, no. 1 (2017): 85–104.
Schorsch, Jonathan. "Jewish Ghosts in Germany." *Jewish Social Studies* 9, no. 3 (2003): 139–69.
Schroer, Timothy L. "Civilization, Barbarism, and the Ethos of Self-Control among the Perpetrators." *German Studies Review* 35, no. 1 (2012): 33–54.
Schulz, Georg-Michael. "Schmerzerfüllte Kalauer: Das Komische bei George Tabori und Edgar Hilsenrath." *Wie die Welt lacht: Nationale Lachkulturen im Vergleich*, ed. Waltraud Wende. Würzburg: Königshausen und Neumann, 2008, 135–48.
Schwan, Gesine. "The 'Healing' Value of Truth-telling: Chances and Social Conditions in a Secularized World." *Social Research* 65, no. 4 (1998): 725–40.
Seaman, Donna. Interview with Martin Amis at the Chicago Humanities Festival. *Chicago Humanities Festival*. https://www.chicagohumanities.org/media/martin-amis-zone-interest/. 30 Oct. 2014. Accessed 29 July 2019.

Segal, Eyal. "Closure in Detective Fiction." *Poetics Today* 31, no. 2 (2010): 153–215.
Sereny, Gitta. *Am Abgrund: Eine Gewissensforschung*. Frankfurt am Main: Ullstein Verlag, 1979.
———. *Am Abgrund: Gespräche mit dem Henker*. Trans. Helmut Röhrling. Munich: Piper, 1995.
———. "Bekenntnisse eines Biedermanns." *Die Zeit*, 41, 8 Oct. 1971, 5–6.
———. "Colloquy with a Conscience." *The Daily Telegraph Magazine* 363, 8 Oct. 1971, 18–71.
———. "Es war Dantes Inferno." *Die Zeit* 43, 22 Oct. 1971, 5–6.
———. "Ich war gefangen in der Falle." *Die Zeit* 42, 15 Oct. 1971, 6–7.
———. *Into That Darkness: An Examination of Conscience*. New York: Vintage Books, 1974.
———. *Into That Darkness: From Mercy Killing to Mass Murder*. New York: McGraw Hill, 1974.
———. *The Healing Wound: Experiences and Reflections on Germany, 1938–2001*. New York: Norton, 2001.
———. "Questioning the Perpetrators: To Give and to Take." *NS-Täter aus interdisziplinärer Perspektive*, ed. Helgard Kramer. Munich: Martin Meidenbauer Verlagsbuchhandlung, 2006, 121–34.
———. "War Gott in Treblinka?" *Die Zeit* 44, 29 Oct. 1971, 10.
Shamir-de Leeuw, Elsje. "Harry Mulisch." *Holocaust Novelists: Dictionary of Literary Biography* 299, ed. Efraim Sicher. Farmington Hills, MI: Gale Cengage Learning, 2004, 245–52.
Shandler, Jeffrey. *While America Watches: Televising the Holocaust*. New York: Oxford UP, 1999.
Shen, Dan. "Unreliability." *the living handbook of narratology*, ed. Peter Hühn et al. Hamburg: Hamburg University, 2014. http://www.lhn.uni-hamburg.de/article/character. Accessed 28 July 2015.
Shklovsky, Viktor. "Art as Technique." *The Critical Tradition: Classic Texts and Contemporary Trends*, 3rd ed., ed. David H. Richter. Boston: Bedford/St. Martin's, 2006, 775–84.
Shoah. Dir. Claude Lanzmann. New Yorker Films, 1985. DVD.
Siertsema, Bettine. "Drie verslagen van het proces-Eichmann." *Voortgang* 30 (2012): 175–200.
Smith, Sidonie, and Julia Watson. *Reading Autobiography: A Guide for Interpreting Life Narratives*. Minneapolis: U of Minnesota P, 2001.
Slater, Maya. "Problems When Time Moves Backwards: Martin Amis's *Time's Arrow*." *English* 42, no. 173 (1993): 141–52.

Spiessens, Anneleen. "Voicing the Perpetrator's Perspective: Translation and Mediation in Jean Hatzfeld's *Une Saison des machettes*." *The Translator* 16, no. 2 (2010): 315–36.

Spolsky, Ellen. "Elaborated Knowledge: Reading Kinesis in Pictures." *Poetics Today* 17, no. 2 (1996): 157–80.

Stangneth, Bettina. *Eichmann Before Jerusalem: The Unexamined Life of a Mass Murderer*. Trans. Ruth Martin. New York: Knopf, 2014.

Staub, Ervin. "The Psychology of Perpetrators and Bystanders." *Political Psychology* 6, no. 1 (1985): 61–85.

Steitz, Kerstin. "And Hannah Laughed: The Role of Irony in Hannah Arendt's *Eichmann in Jerusalem*." *Studies in Contemporary Jewry* 29 (2016): 132–40.

Stern, Jessica. *My War Criminal: Personal Encounters with an Architect of Genocide*. New York: HarperCollins, 2020.

Suleiman, Susan Rubin. "Performing a Perpetrator as Witness: Jonathan Littell's *Les Bienveillantes*." *After Testimony: The Ethics and Aesthetics of Holocaust Narrative for the Future*, ed. Jakob Lothe, Susan Rubin Suleiman, and James Phelan. Columbus: Ohio State UP, 2012, 99–119.

———. "When the Perpetrator Becomes a Reliable Witness of the Holocaust: On Jonathan Littell's *Les bienveillantes*." *New German Critique* 36, no. 1 (2009): 1–19.

Süselbeck, Jan. "Nicht ohne Beispiel." *literaturkritik.de* 5 (2008). https://literaturkritik.de/id/11882. Accessed 13 July 2019.

Svendsen, Lars. *A Philosophy of Evil*. Trans. Kerri A. Pierce. Champaign, IL: Dalkey Archive Press, 2010.

Szalai, Jennifer. "In 'My War Criminal,' the Bad Guy Controls the Conversation." *The New York Times*, 23 Jan. 2020. https://www.nytimes.com/2020/01/23/books/review-my-war-criminal-jessica-stern.html. Accessed 3 May 2020.

Szejnmann, Claus-Christian W. "Perpetrators of the Holocaust: A Historiography." *Ordinary People as Mass Murderers: Perpetrators in Comparative Perspectives*, ed. Olaf Jensen and Claus-Christian W. Szejnmann. Houndsmills, Basingstoke, Hampshire: Palgrave Macmillan, 2008.

Taylor, Jennifer. "Writing as Revenge: Reading Edgar Hilsenrath's *Der Nazi und der Friseur* as a Shoah Survivor's Fantasy." *History of European Ideas* 20, nos. 1–3 (1995): 439–44.

Theweleit, Klaus. "On the German Reaction to Jonathan Littell's *Les bienveillantes*." Trans. Timothy Nunan. *New German Critique* 36, no. 1 (2009): 21–34.

Todorov, Tzevtan. *Facing the Extreme: Moral Life in the Concentration Camps*. Trans. Arthur Denner and Abigail Pollak. New York: Metropolitan Books, 1996.

———. "The Typology of Detective Fiction." *The Poetics of Prose*. Trans. Richard Howard. Ithaca, NY: Cornell UP, 1977.

Toker, Leona. "*The Kindly Ones* and the 'Scorched Earth' Principle." *Writing the Holocaust Today: Critical Perspectives on Jonathan Littell's "The Kindly Ones*," ed. Aurélie Barjonet and Liran Razinsky. Amsterdam: Rodopi, 2012, 153–63.

Torgovnick, Marianna. *The War Complex: World War II in Our Time*. Chicago: U of Chicago P, 2005.

Torte Bluma. Dir. Benjamin Ross. DMC Films and How Town Inc., 2005.

Tulloch, John. "Ethics, Trust and the First Person in the Narration of Long-Form Journalism." *Journalism* 15, no. 5 (2014): 629–38, 634.

Twitchell, Corey Lee. *The German Jewish Post-Holocaust Novel: Narrative and a Literary Language for Loss*. Arts & Sciences Electronic Theses and Dissertations 474 (2015). https://openscholarship.wustl.edu/art_sci_etds/474. Accessed 1 June 2019.

Vaessens, Thomas. "Making Overtures: Literature and Journalism, 1968 and 2011—A Dutch Perspective." *Literary Journalism Studies* 3, no. 2 (2011): 55–72.

Vahsen, Patricia. *Lesarten: Die Rezeption des Werks von Edgar Hilsenrath*. Tübingen: Max Niemeyer Verlag, 2008.

Vetlesen, Arne Johan. *Perception, Empathy and Judgment: An Inquiry into the Preconditions of Moral Performance*. University Park: Pennsylvania State UP, 1994.

Vice, Sue. "British Representation of the Camps." *Holocaust Studies* 22, nos. 2–3 (2016): 303–17.

———. *Holocaust Fiction*. New York: Routledge, 2000.

Waller, James E. *Becoming Evil: How Ordinary People Commit Genocide and Mass Killing*. 2nd ed. Oxford: Oxford UP, 2007.

———. "Perpetrators of the Holocaust: Divided and Unitary Self Conceptions of Evildoing." *Holocaust and Genocide Studies* 10, no. 1 (1996): 11–33.

Weinert, Matthew S. "Adolf Eichmann: Understanding Evil in Form and Content." *Human Rights & Human Welfare* 6 (2006): 179–92.

Welzer, Harald. "Mass Murder and Moral Code: Some Thoughts on an Easily Misunderstood Subject." *History of the Human Sciences* 17, nos. 2–3 (2004): 15–32.

Wennberg, Rebecca. "Between Sacred and the Profane: Holocaust Collaboration and 'Political Religion.'" *Religion Compass* 8, no. 1 (2014): 25–35.

Weyandt, Hans-Jost. "Auschwitz? Da lach ich doch." *Spiegel Online*, 4 Sept. 2015. https://www.spiegel.de/kultur/literatur/interessengebiet-von-martin-amis-auschwitz-da-lach-ich-doch-a-1050187.html. Accessed 10 Aug. 2019.

Wiesel, Elie. "Trivializing Memory." *From the Kingdom of Memory: Reminiscences*, by Elie Wiesel. New York: Summit Books, 1990, 165–72.

Wieviorka, Annette. *The Era of the Witness*. Trans. Jared Stark. Ithaca, NY: Cornell UP, 2006.

Wolf, Werner. "Aesthetic Illusion." *Immersion and Distance: Aesthetic Illusion in Literature and Other Media*, ed. Werner Wolf, Walter Bernhart, and Andreas Mahler. Amsterdam: Rodopi, 2013, 1–63.

Wood, Gaby. "*The Zone of Interest* by Martin Amis, Review: 'Bracingly Weird.'" *The Telegraph*, 28 Aug. 2014. https://www.telegraph.co.uk/culture/books/bookreviews/11061383/The-Zone-of-Interest-by-Martin-Amis-review-bracingly-weird.html. Accessed 10 Aug. 2019.

Yildiz, Yasemin. *Beyond the Mother Tongue: The Postmonolingual Condition*. New York: Fordham UP, 2012.

Your Job in Germany. Dir. Frank Capra. United States War Department, 1945.

Yow, Valerie. "'Do I Like Them Too Much?': Effects of the Oral History Interview on the Interviewer and Vice-Versa." *The Oral History Review* 24, no. 1 (1997): 55–79.

Zakaria, Rafia. "Empathy for the Devil." *The Baffler*, 21 Feb. 2020. https://thebaffler.com/alienated/empathy-for-the-devil-zakaria. Accessed 3 May 2020.

Zillmer, Eric A., Molly Harrower, Barry A. Rizler, and Robert P. Archer. *The Quest for the Nazi Personality: A Psychological Investigation of Nazi War Criminals*. Hillsdale, NJ: Lawrence Erlbaum, 1995.

Zlatav, Jordan, Timothy P. Racine, Chris Sinha, and Esa Itkonen. "Intersubjectivity: What Makes Us Human?" *The Shared Mind: Perspectives on Subjectivity*, ed. Jordan Zlatav, Timothy P. Racine, Chris Sinha, and Esa Itkonen. Amsterdam: John Benjamins, 2008, 1–14.

Zunshine, Lisa. *Why We Read Fiction: Theory of Mind and the Novel*. Columbus: Ohio State UP, 2006.

Index

Abbott, H. Porter, 58, 155, 261n8
Abrams, Lynn, 63
Adams, Jenni, 9, 11, 16, 36, 40, 204, 223, 225n29, 247n53, 277
Adorno, Theodor W.: *The Authoritarian Personality*, 51; "Freudian Theory and the Pattern of Fascist Propaganda," 51
affective processes, 15, 36, 39, 40, 41, 61, 63, 64, 80n18, 102, 139, 158, 183, 192–93, 222, 227, 279n25, 287, 290, 291, 292, 294, 296, 303
Albahari, David, *Götz and Meyer*, 180
Alber, Jan, 189, 190, 190n8, 191, 192, 219n26
Albert Speer: His Battle with the Truth (Sereny), 2, 17n5, 55
alienation, 37, 41, 42, 193, 283–84n26, 297
Alley, Gary, 111
Aly, Götz, *Endlösung*, 26n13
Amis, Martin, 30, 108n45, 257–59, 278–79; narrative strategies of, 185, 188; representation of the Holocaust, 179, 257–61. See also *Time's Arrow*; *Zone of Interest, The*
anagnorisis, 154–55, 163, 168, 170, 171n14, 172, 173
Anderson, Miranda, 193
Annan, Kofi, 302
Antelme, Robert, 52

antimimetic representation, 37, 45, 179, 184, 189–91, 190n7, 192–94, 219n26, 225–26, 244, 246, 260, 260n6, 263, 277, 278, 279n24, 296. See also mimetic representation; unnatural narrative
antinomic temporality, 194, 261–63, 261nn7–8, 265, 266, 268, 272, 273n21, 276. See also inverted temporality
antirealism, 179, 190, 278
Appelfeld, Aharon, 259
Arendt, Hannah, 43, 44, 57, 70, 70–71n5, 71–72, 72n7, 73–74n10, 76, 78n16, 79, 81n19, 82–83, 83n22, 84n23, 89–90n31, 94n35, 103, 113; on banality of evil, 68, 70, 71, 74–75, 75n12, 77, 80–83, 81–82n20, 82n21, 91, 93, 96; emotional investment of, 63, 80n18; empathy and, 64; *The Human Condition*, 90–91; influence of, 70–75, 71n6, 74n11, 77; ironic perspective of, 88n29; mind-reading and, 64, 75, 78, 84, 97; Harry Mulisch and, 94–98, 94n35; *The Origins of Totalitarianism*, 51; political philosophy of, 79, 93n34, 98; psychology and, 79–80, 79–80n17, 83, 83n22; on thoughtlessness, 70, 79, 83n22, 84n23, 87nn26–27, 88, 96. See also *Eichmann in Jerusalem*

331

Ariel, Yaakov, 120
Arnds, Peter, 207n6
aufhaltsame Aufstieg des Arturo Ui, Der (*The Resistible Rise of Arturo Ui*; Brecht), 176
Auschwitz, 52, 54, 110, 160, 249–50, 249n1, 250n2, 280, 282, 286, 291; in fiction, 30, 46, 171, 179, 194, 195, 214, 228, 250–57, 260, 261, 262, 262n12, 265–69, 271, 272, 273–74, 273–74n21, 276, 277, 278, 279–86, 289, 290, 293, 295
"Auschwitz self" (Lifton), 266–67, 273, 274n21
Auschwitz trials, 54
Austin, J. L., 76–77n14
authenticity, 143, 144, 164–66, 194, 215
Authoritarian Personality, The (Adorno, Frenkel-Brunswick, Levinson, and Sanford), 51
autobiography, 17, 31, 43, 52, 116, 124–25, 145, 154, 164, 167, 210n11, 257, 259n5, 291

"backshadowing" (Bernstein), 172–3
Badrideen, Ahmed, 267, 272, 274–76, 275n22, 290, 294n31
Bajohr, Frank, 56, 57
Bakhtin, Mikhail, 220
"banality of evil" (Arendt), 68, 70, 71, 74–75, 75n12, 77, 80–83, 81–82n20, 82n21, 91, 93, 96
Barjonet, Aurélie, 177, 224, 227, 227–28n31, 234
Barrett, Lisa Feldman, 102n41
Bauer, Yehuda, 16
Bauman, Zygmunt, 53
Bax, Sander, 98, 102
Bećirević, Edina, 305
Bełżec, 162
Bełżec trial, 54
Benhabib, Seyla, 71, 74n11, 80n18, 81–82n20

Berding, Joop, 62, 95, 108n46
Bergen-Belsen, 282
Bernard, Catherine, 261n8, 276–77
Bernstein, Michael André, 172–73, 258–59
Bernstein, Richard J., 81–82n20
Best, Werner, 57
Bettelheim, Bruno, 55n8
Beyer, Marcel, 176
Bienveillantes, Les (Littell). See *Kindly Ones, The*
Bildungsroman, 155, 207n6, 215, 261, 261n8
Bilsky, Leora, 78n16
Binet, Laurent, *HHhH*, 154, 180
Bird, Stephanie, 205, 206, 207n6
Birkenau, 249n1, 250, 280, 285; in fiction, 269. *See also* Auschwitz
Birkmeyer, Jens, 207n6
Bjornstad, Jennifer, 207n6, 211, 217
Blind Spot: Hitler's Secretary (Heller and Schmiderer). See *Im toten Winkel*
Blucher, Av Richard, 171n14
Bolens, Guillemette, 102
Böll, Heinrich, 176
Booth, Wayne, 186
Borges, Jorge Luis, "Deutsches Requiem," 177, 185, 185n5
Bosnian War, 302, 305–6n5
Boswell, Matthew, 11, 11n2, 21n8, 178, 226, 246, 259n4
Bracher, Nathan, 206n4
Braese, Stephan, 213n15
Braumann, Rony, *The Specialist*, 71
Braun, Helmut, 207–8n7
Brecht, Bertolt: *Der aufhaltsame Aufstieg des Arturo Ui*, 176; *Furcht und Elend im Dritten Reich*, 175
Breithaupt, Fritz, 37, 294–95
Bridges, Elizabeth, 176
Brockmeier, Jens, 60–61
Brooks, Peter, 124, 124n56, 164, 165, 166, 167, 168

332 | Index

Broszat, Martin, 26n12
Browder, George C., 72–73n9
Browning, Christopher, 26n13, 52, 56, 75, 76–77n14, 76n13, 185n6
Bruner, Jerome, 59–60
Brunner, José, 70–71n5, 71, 79–80n17, 83–84, 83n22, 84n23
Bubandt, Nils, 64
Buchenwald, 55n8, 107, 282
buffers. *See* filtering: strategies of
Bui, Roberto, 225
Butler, Judith, 71, 76–77n14

Cantor, Jay, 137–38
Capesius, der Auschwitzapotheker (Schlesak). *See Druggist of Auschwitz, The*
causality, 20, 22n9, 35, 38, 58, 61, 78, 154, 159, 186, 194, 227–28n31, 244, 244n48, 255, 265, 271, 276, 276n23, 296
Celan, Paul, 258
Cesarani, David, 68, 68n1, 69, 71–74, 72n7, 72–73n9, 89, 114
Chare, Nicholas, 286
Chatman, Seymour, 158n12, 260n6, 263, 264, 265, 267, 268, 276n23
Childs, Harwood L., *The Nazi Primer* (trans.), 48
Clendinnen, Inga, 138–39n3, 148–49
clichés, 86–88, 91–92
closure, 129, 155–56; confession and, 166, 169, 170, 171; death and, 173; desire for, 157n11; in detective story, 156–57, 157n10, 160, 163–64; lack of, 170–71
cognitive dissonance, 39, 162n13, 271
cognitive processes, 15, 28, 29, 33n17, 35, 59, 64, 101, 102, 296
cognitive science, 14, 32, 33, 34–35, 102n41
collaborative testimony, 153, 154
collective consciousness, 48–49, 51, 229

Commandant of Lubizec, The (Hicks), 183
confessional narrative, 15, 17n5, 44, 52n6, 76–77n14, 117, 120–21, 124–28, 124nn56–57, 137, 155, 156, 164–73, 171n14, 172n15, 177, 210n11, 224; in detective genre, 156n10; in fiction, 177, 194, 204, 210, 214, 214n17, 223, 224, 230; truth and, 164–65
contagion, fear of, 40
Conway, Daniel, 75n12, 79, 80, 81n19, 83n22, 84, 87, 88
Coquio, Catherine, 204, 224, 234–35n37
Corduwener, Pepijn, 96, 98, 98n38, 99, 99n39, 100n40
"Crimes of the Wehrmacht" exhibit (Hamburg Institute for Social Research), 26n13
Criminal Case 40/61, the Trial of Adolf Eichmann: An Eyewitness Account (*De Zaak 40/61: Een Reportage*; Mulisch), 15, 43, 54, 75, 94, 95–101, 102, 103n42, 104–10, 182
Critchell, Kara, 25, 68
Crownshaw, Richard, 12, 175, 176, 176n1, 178, 204
cultural construction, 10, 12
Curthoys, Ned, 12, 224

Dance of Genghis Cohn, The (*La Danse de Gengis Cohn*; Gary), 177, 185n5
Death Is My Trade (*La Morte est mon métier*; Merle), 177
defamiliarization, 192–94, 260, 260n6, 263, 265, 276, 278, 296. *See also* distance
de Goeij, Bart, 94n35
dehumanization, 89, 94, 145
Delbo, Charlotte, 52
Demjanjuk, John, 182
Dern, John A., 261n8
detective story, 15, 44, 155, 156–64, 156n10, 157n11, 158n12, 166, 168

Index | 333

"Deutsches Requiem" (Borges), 177, 185, 185n5
Diedrick, James, 262n10, 264, 264n15, 266, 267, 272
di Giovanni, Janine, 304, 305
discursive orientations, 7, 8, 13, 29, 30, 32
dissociation, 35, 36, 46, 225, 230n33, 238, 239, 266, 268, 271, 273, 273n20
distance, 3, 14, 37, 150–51, 194, 303; strategies for, 4; unnatural narration and, 193. *See also* defamiliarization; filtering
Dittrich, Volker, 205n3, 209, 209nn9–10, 225
Dora Bruder (Modiano), 154
double plot-structure, 158–59
double-voiced discourse, 220
doubling, 14, 45, 184, 194, 266, 267–68, 271–73, 289, 296
"Draft of a Reparations Agreement" (Pagis), 276n23
Druggist of Auschwitz, The (Capesius, der Auschwitzapotheker; Schlesak), 179
Dvash, Jonathan, 63–64
Dwork, Debórah, 94–95n36, 95, 96, 98

Eaglestone, Robert, 11, 17n5, 20, 21n8, 138–39n3, 157, 157n11, 160–61, 172n15, 175, 176, 176n1, 224, 235, 247; concept of "swerve," 16, 18, 20–21, 21n8; on evil, 8, 16–20, 21
Earl, Hilary, 185n6
Easterbrook, Neil, 262n10, 265, 267
Eichmann, Adolf, 11, 12, 26, 27, 43, 64, 71, 116, 130–31, 293; as archetype, 68, 69, 78; autobiographical writings of, 67, 72, 76–77n14, 76n13, 89–90n31, 90n32, 177; banality of, 68, 80–82, 81–82n20, 82n21, 83, 84, 96; books about, 43–44, 68n2, 71–72 (*see also individual works*); cultural image of, 12, 44, 54, 70–71n5, 70n4, 78n15, 84, 104; execution of, 116–17n51, 127; in fiction, 228; identification with National Socialism, 81, 89n29, 97; language of, 44, 84–94, 85n24, 89n29, 96, 112, 130; mentality of, 70, 75, 77, 78, 79, 79–80n17, 81n19, 84n23, 85, 111, 113, 114, 120, 122, 130; myth of, 68, 71–72, 78, 109, 131; performativity of, 44, 72–73, 72nn7–8, 72–73n9, 73–74n10, 76–77, 76–77n13, 84, 85, 87, 92, 96, 112, 122, 131; photographs of, 103, 104–8, 105, 108n45; physical descriptions of, 100–101, 103–4, 105n44, 108–9, 110n47, 130–31; portrayed as evil, by Hausner, 26, 70, 70n4, 70–71n5, 72, 81, 96, 110; religious beliefs of, 112, 112n48, 116, 121n55, 123, 125–30, 127–28n58; role of, in Holocaust, 67, 68nn1–2, 69, 78–79, 112n49; soul of, 44, 64, 77, 112, 114, 117, 119, 120, 121, 122, 123, 129, 130, 130n60, 131; thoughtlessness of, 70, 84n23, 87n26–27, 88, 96, 97. *See also Criminal Case 40/61*; *Eichmann in Jerusalem*; Eichmann trial; *Struggle for a Soul, The*
Eichmann in Jerusalem: A Report on the Banality of Evil (Arendt), 15, 43, 53–54, 78–94, 95–98, 103, 182; bias in, 80n18; influence of, 67–68, 70–71, 71n6, 74–75, 74n11, 77; narration and, 182; narrative voice of, 80n18; narrator presence in, 62; scope of, 78–79
Eichmann trial, 11, 26, 43, 44, 53–54, 56, 56n9, 62, 67–69, 68n2, 71–74, 71n6, 72–73n9, 73–74n10, 74n11, 75–76, 78–79, 78n16, 80n18, 84, 86, 88n28, 89–90n31, 90, 91–92, 94–96, 94n35, 99–101, 99n39, 103–4, 105n44, 108–9, 111, 112, 116, 117–18, 122, 126, 127, 130, 177, 181
Einsatzgruppe, 4, 5, 195, 198, 199, 213, 228, 229, 231, 232, 239, 262, 262n12, 269
Ellison, Ralph, 80n18
emotional alignment, 39. *See also* affective processes

empathy, 3, 18, 29, 33, 33–34n17, 36–42, 50, 87n27, 98n38, 99, 100, 135, 137, 149–50, 151, 152, 174, 182, 192, 260, 291, 294–95, 296, 303, 304; dangers of, 3, 36, 64, 127n58, 150; lack of empathy, 81, 84n23; mind-reading and, 63–64; reader immersion and, 192; resisting of, 55n8, 137–38; tactical, 64

English language, 81–82n20, 114, 116, 141–45, 147, 147n7, 181, 213n16, 245, 283–84n26

Enlightenment, 101, 138–40, 155, 174, 275n22, 276

Er ist wieder da (*Look Who's Back*; film; Wnendt), 27

Er ist wieder da (*Look Who's Back*; novel; Vermes), 27, 179

ethics, of identification, 14, 36, 39–40, 42, 42n18, 63, 127n58, 173, 294; Holocaust perpetrators and, 2, 4, 8, 14, 35, 38, 46, 52, 60, 65, 70, 79, 93n34, 130, 154, 157, 158, 188, 204, 212, 234–35n37, 248, 256, 258, 260, 267, 269, 272, 273–74n21, 275, 276, 295; of interpretation, 15n4, 41, 42n18, 136, 170, 187, 194, 212, 229n32, 247n53, 248, 277, 296; of interviews with Holocaust perpetrators, 2, 44, 50, 63, 120–21, 137, 149, 150, 152, 183; narration and, 15n4, 36, 37, 156, 156n10, 173, 186–87, 188, 212, 230n34, 235n38; of representation, 4, 9, 14, 15, 21, 30, 44, 247n53, 259n5, 277, 296, 302, 306–7

Evans, Richard, 72–73n9

evil, 2, 8, 10, 16–17, 18n6, 22, 70, 78n15, 80–83, 98, 103–4, 107–10, 112–14, 131, 176, 235, 242, 271, 273n20, 280, 299, 302; attempts to understand, 18–21, 138–39, 138–39n3, 302, 307; Hitler as embodying, 26n11, 27, 245; Holocaust perpetrators as archetypes of, 9, 27, 41, 44, 70, 75, 96, 176, 247, 299, 307. *See also* "banality of evil"

extratextuality, 39, 188–89, 291

fabula, 219n26, 244n47, 261, 264

Fackenheim, Emil, 19n7

Fear and Misery in the Third Reich (Brecht). See *Furcht und Elend im Dritten Reich*

Felman, Shoshana, 85, 91–92

fiction, 4, 8, 12, 13, 14, 16, 17, 18, 20, 28, 30, 45–46; conventions of nonfiction in, 30, 191, 193, 194, 279; empathetic identification and, 37–41; ethics of, 40; experiential power of, 185, 246; influence on nonfiction, 30–31, 102; mimetic and antimimetic representation in, 189–94; narrative strategies, 108n45, 182–94, 230n33, 261n7, 295; representation of Holocaust perpetrators in, history of, 11–13, 175–82, 204, 206, 224, 230; structural devices of, 40, 45; Theory of Mind and mind-reading in, 32, 32n16, 34, 35, 36, 302; trajectory from nonfiction, 13, 57–58, 175, 181–82; unreliable narration in, 186–89. *See also* fiction/nonfiction distinction; *and individual genres*

fiction/nonfiction distinction, 7, 13, 16, 18, 29–31, 29n15, 32, 32n16, 36, 60–61, 61n12, 189

filtering, 3, 4, 20–21, 21n8, 28, 46, 131, 203; absence of, 225; author mediation and, 15, 182–83; autodiegetic narration and, 19, 45, 46, 184, 185, 206, 221, 226, 248, 277; in fiction, 16, 45, 182, 184, 185, 185n5, 189, 194, 203; identification and, 41, 206; through narrative frames, 54, 131, 137, 173, 203; in nonfiction, 16, 45, 54, 77, 84, 114, 131, 137, 143, 173, 221–22, 245, 260, 305; strategies of, 3, 4, 8, 14–16, 21, 28, 41, 43, 45, 182, 194, 198, 206, 222, 226, 246, 248, 306; unreliability and, 189, 194

Index | 335

Fink, Ida, 259
Finney, Brian, 257–58, 258n3, 260n6, 262n11, 266n17, 267, 279, 279n24
first-person narration. *See* narration: autodiegetic; narration: homodiegetic
Fløgstad, Kjartan, *Grense Jakobselv*, 180n4
Fludernik, Monika, 31
focalization, 14, 28, 31, 36, 37–38, 45, 137, 186, 217, 222, 259n4, 290
foreshadowing, 163, 173
Foucault, Michel, 164–65, 168
Frank, Hans, 52
Franklin, Ruth, 289n29
Frenkel-Brunswick, Else, *The Authoritarian Personality*, 51
Freud, Sigmund, 49n4
"Freudian Theory and the Pattern of Fascist Propaganda" (Adorno), 51
Fuchs, Anne, 204, 207n6, 210n11
Furcht und Elend im Dritten Reich (*Fear and Misery in the Third Reich*; Brecht), 175

Gary, Romain, *The Dance of Genghis Cohn*, 177, 185n5
Gellately, Robert, 49–50; *The Nuremberg Interviews*, 50
Genette, Gérard, 158n12, 217, 217n21, 263n13
genre, 155–56, 186, 190n8, 193, 194, 279, 287; conventions of, 29, 31, 60, 137, 164, 190n7, 191, 193, 204, 261n8, 279; forms of, 14, 145, 155, 156n10; frames of, 59, 79–80n17, 98, 161, 227, 281, 285, 287, 288
Gerlach, Christian, 76, 76n13, 76–77n14
German language, 85, 85n24, 91–93, 141–45, 146–47, 147n7, 197, 198, 213, 230n35, 272; in *The Zone of Interest*, 283–84n26
German Life, A (Krönes et al.), 58n11

German literature, 88n28, 89, 93, 175–76, 204, 207–8, 207n6, 207–8n7
Gigliotti, Simone, 250n2
Gilbert, G. M.: *Nuremberg Diary*, 50; *The Psychology of Dictatorship*, 50
Gill, Jo, 166
Goldensohn, Leon, 50
Golsan, Richard J., 71n6, 72–73n9, 227, 227–28n31
Gomel, Elana, 11, 184
Götz and Meyer (Albahari), 180
Graf, Andreas, 212, 217–18, 218n25
Grass, Günter, 176, 259
Gray, Richard, 101
Grense Jakobselv (Fløgstad), 180n4
Grese, Irma, 282
Grossman, David, *See Under: Love*, 178, 178n3

Hafner, Paul Maria, 58n11, 240
Hafners Paradies (*Hafner's Paradise*; Schwaiger), 58n11
Handke, Peter, 305–6n5
Hannah Arendt (von Trotta), 71
Hansen, Per Krogh, 39, 188–89
Harris, Greg, 267, 268n18, 273, 273–74n21
Hartouni, Valerie, 83, 83n22
Hausner, Gideon, 26, 70, 70n4, 70–71n5, 72n8, 81, 84n23, 110
Healing Wound: Experiences and Reflections on Germany, 1938-2001, The (Sereny), 133–35
Heller, André, *Im toten Winkel*, 58n11
Herbert, Ulrich, *Best*, 57
Herman, David, 32, 32n16, 35
Heydrich, Reinhard, 72–73n9, 176
HHhH (Binet), 154, 180
Hicks, Patrick, *The Commandant of Lubizec*, 183
Hilberg, Raul, 19n7, 22n9, 23n10, 26n12
Hilsenrath, Edgar, 178, 207–9, 208–9n8, 225, 225n29; narrative strategies of, 185. *See also Nazi and the Barber, The*

Himmler, Heinrich, 26n12, 138–39n3; in fiction, 228
Hitler, Adolf, 26, 26nn11–12, 27–28, 47–48, 67, 138–39n3, 306; in fiction, 28, 176, 178, 179, 213, 243–45, 245n49; psychoanalytic study of, 49, 51. *See also* evil: Hitler as embodying
Hitler Youth, 48
Hoffman, Louise E., 49
Hofmann, Michael, 283–84n26, 287, 288, 294
Hogan, Patrick Colm, 37, 290
Holbrook, Jess Scon, 32–33, 33–34n17
Holocaust, analogies to, 300–302, 306
Holocaust discourse, 10, 22, 29, 42–43, 204; in Germany, 26n13, 30, 54, 55n8, 56, 133, 181, 207n7, 208, 213n15
Holocaust memory, 43, 53, 56, 56n9, 180
Holocaust perpetrators: archetype of, 9, 10, 27, 69, 78; autobiographies and memoirs of, 16–17, 43, 52–53, 52n6, 177, 259n5, 291 (*see also* Eichmann, Adolf: autobiographical writings of); axes of (Roseman), 24–27; compared to other perpetrators, 302, 306, 307; concept of, 23–24; in cultural imagination, 9, 53, 299; definitions of, 21–28; early analyses of, 49n4, 49–50n5, 50, 51; early fiction about, 175–76, 177; external views of, 10, 35, 62; fascination with, 53, 54, 68, 175, 180; female, 27n14, 282; in film, 12, 13, 16, 19n7, 27, 49–50n5, 55, 58n11, 71, 137, 152n9, 176, 182, 294; as filtering mechanisms, 306; historical research on, 10, 23–27, 26nn11–13, 27n14, 38, 51, 55n8, 56–57, 57n10, 68n2, 71–74, 71n6, 75, 144, 185n6; history of representation of, 11–13, 12n3, 30, 47–57, 175–82, 204, 206–9, 208–9n8, 300–301; humanization of, 9–10, 11, 27–28, 29–30, 37, 40, 178n3, 290–91, 306; identity outside victimization, 22n9, 39; interviewing of, 1–4, 13, 15, 17n5, 19n7, 35, 43, 50, 55, 55n7, 62, 63, 134–40, 144, 146–54, 158n12, 302–3, 303n2; as mythical construct, 10, 22, 27, 247–48, 299, 307 (*see also* Eichmann, Adolf: myth of); objectification of, 9, 11; as Other, 2, 8, 10, 84n23, 184, 226, 247, 273–74n21, 299; perspective of, 3, 4, 7, 8–9, 10, 11, 14–15, 21, 27n14, 28, 29, 36, 37–42, 88n28, 125, 137, 140, 146, 148–51, 173–74; perspective of, in fiction, 4, 8, 9, 16, 36, 45–46, 176n1, 207–8n7, 208–9n8, 224n28, 235n38, 240n50, 273–74n21, 276n23; psychological profiles of, 47–48n1, 49–51, 57, 176; in second-wave fiction, 177; seen as subjects, 2, 9, 42n18, 50, 55, 63–64, 102; subjectivity of, 9, 10, 11, 14, 20, 21, 290, 303; taxonomy of, 25–27; in third-wave fiction, 178–80. *See also* evil
Holocaust revisionism. *See* revisionism
Holocaust Studies, 55n8, 69, 77, 300–302
Holocaust survivors: autobiographies of, 52, 193, 249; ethical obligation to, 9; final generation of, 182; interviews with, 44, 141; narratives of, 30, 161, 178, 207–8n7, 229n32, 259; testimony of, 43, 52, 78n16, 157, 305
Horan, Geraldine, 89n29
Horch, Hans Otto, 207n6
Horowitz, Sara, 264n16, 266–67
Horsman, Yasco, 83n22, 90–91, 92
Höß, Rudolf, 52, 52n6, 177, 228, 291
Howe, Irving, 74n11
Hughes, Judith M., 51, 83, 83n22
Hühn, Peter, 158–60, 158n12
Hull, Lillian, 114–15n50, 114–16, 116–17n51, 119, 120, 121–22, 125

Index | 337

Hull, William L., 44, 62–63, 76, 77, 79, 111, 119n54, 121–22n55; empathy and, 64; impetus for writing *The Struggle for a Soul*, 111, 119; perspective on Eichmann, 76–77, 112n49, 113–14, 131; on salvation, 121–22n55, 121–23. See also *Struggle for a Soul, The*
humanization, 304. See also Holocaust perpetrators: humanization of

"I," 198, 229n32; experiencing, 4–5, 7, 116, 236, 237–39, 241–42, 243; narrating, 4–5, 116, 218–19n45, 221–22, 229, 230, 236, 237–39, 237n41, 241–42, 243, 244, 263, 269. See also narration: autodiegetic; narrators: autodiegetic
identification, 4, 8, 9, 15, 28, 41, 138–39n3, 185, 226, 294, 296; affective, 39, 287–88, 290; ambivalent, 11, 42, 46, 294, 295, 296; dangers of, 8, 14, 16, 36, 40, 41–42, 276; empathetic, 14, 29, 36–42, 42n18, 192, 257, 287–88, 290, 295, 297, 303–4; ethics of, 14, 260; existential, 37, 39, 290, 291; filtering strategies and, 15, 185, 221–22; ideological, 39–40; immersion and, 192; modalities of, 37–41, 290; perspectival, 37–38, 290, 291; reliability-dependent, 38–39. See also empathy; reader identification
immersion, of reader, 185, 191–93, 205, 225–26, 247n53, 260, 278, 287, 296
implied author, 39, 40, 189, 230n34
implied reader, 211, 266n17
Im toten Winkel: Hitlers Sekretärin (*Blind Spot: Hitler's Secretary*; Heller and Schmiderer), 58n11
incomprehensibility, 8, 18, 22, 35, 42n18, 60, 65, 160, 231–32, 247, 255, 307
Inglourious Basterds (Tarantino), 176
interiority, 6, 9, 12, 16, 20, 27n14, 32, 58, 101–2, 105, 108, 182, 185, 299, 303

interpreters, 13, 15, 16, 36, 130, 183; interventional role of, 43; as mediators, 65; mind-reading and, 35; relationships with subjects, 62; as structural device, 45. See also interviewers
intersubjectivity, 3, 30, 35–36, 44, 62–63, 76, 148, 182–83; balance and, 151; confession and, 168
interviewers, 13, 15, 16; functions of, 145, 147–48, 152; interventional role of, 43, 55; as mediators, 17n5, 57–58, 65; mind-reading and, 35, 140; as narrators, 137, 147, 151–52; neutrality of, 3–4; relationships with subjects, 62–63, 134, 144, 150; as structural device, 45, 57–58; techniques of, 148–49
Into That Darkness: An Examination of Conscience (Sereny), 2, 15, 133–74, 182, 303n2; confession and, 137, 164–74; detective story and, 137, 156–64, 168; editions of, 141–42, 145, 146–47; German translations of, 141–45, 146–47, 147n7; goals of, 135, 138–40, 154–55, 173–74; intersubjectivity in, 148–53, 168; masterplots in, 137, 155, 156, 160, 161, 168, 170, 171, 173–74; narration and, 137, 146–48, 151–52, 182; narrative closure in, 163, 169, 170, 171, 173; narrative construction of, 141, 144, 147–48, 156, 157, 159, 160, 161–64; narrative frames of, 137, 141, 155, 157–58, 160, 164, 171n14; narrative structure of, 153, 154, 174; publication history, 141–45; research for, 44, 54
intratextuality, 39, 189, 291
inverted temporality, 46, 184, 225, 255, 256, 257, 260, 261–63, 265, 271. See also antinomic temporality
ironic complicity, 226–27

irony, 64, 77, 88n28, 96, 108, 108n46, 121, 127–28n58, 226, 262–63, 265, 266n17, 275, 275n22, 276, 277, 280
Iversen, Stefan, 32n16, 61n12, 184, 185, 185n6, 193, 227, 227–28n31, 230n35

Jensen, Morten Høi, 281, 283–84n26, 285, 287, 291
journalistic discourse, 9, 12, 30, 43, 51, 54, 57, 98, 98n38, 102–3; objectivity and, 151
Junge, Traudl, 58n11

Kakutani, Michiko, 247, 247n56
Kalkofen, Rupert, 207n6, 214–15, 215n19, 216, 216n20
Karadžić, Radovan, 302–7, 303n3, 304n4
Kärkkäinen, Veli-Matti, 121
Keen, Suzanne, 30–31, 37
Kekes, John, 144–45, 144–45n6
Kelley, Douglas M., *22 Cells in Nuremberg*, 50
Kertész, Imre, 249, 259
Kettner, Fabian, 95
Keulks, Gavin, 279n24
Kieser, Hans-Lukas, 126
Kindly Ones, The (*Les Bienveillantes*; Littell), 4–8, 11–12, 13–14, 16, 21n8, 46, 179, 198–203, 289; antimimetic representation in, 184, 194, 225–26, 244; filtering and, 45, 182, 225, 226, 245, 246; hallucination in, 236–46, 236n39; narrative discourses, 46, 226, 228–35, 241, 245–46; narrative strategies, 45, 46, 184, 203–6, 222, 225–26, 227–30; reception of, 179, 180, 204, 206, 208–9, 208–9n8, 224–25, 226; repression in, 236–37; sexuality in, 234–35, 234–35n37, 242–43; structure of, 227–30; unreliable narration in, 206, 223, 226, 227, 236–39, 246–47; witnessing in, 230–33, 245

Kirsch, Adam, 279n25
Klein, Julia M., 292
Klocke, Astrid, 207n6
Klüger, Ruth, 249
Koch, Ilse, 282
Kramer, Robert, *Notre Nazi*, 55
Krondorfer, Björn, 185n6
Krönes, Christian, *A German Life*, 58n11
Kühne, Thomas, 185n6
Kulcsar, Istvan Shlomo, 89n29
Kulcsar, Shoshanna, 89n29
Kuon, Peter, 236

LaCapra, Dominick, 138, 234, 245n43
Lang, Johannes, 145, 185n6
Lanzmann, Claude, 26, 55, 55n7, 138–39n3, 138n2, 160, 300; *Shoah*, 13, 19n7, 137–38, 229n32; *The Patagonian Hare*, 138, 138n2
Last Days of Hitler, The (Trevor-Roper), 51
Lawson, Mark, 260, 280
Leake, Eric, 37
Lehman, Daniel W., 61
Lenyel, Olga, 249
Less, Avner, 85n24
Levi, Primo, 52, 160, 249, 259
Levinson, Daniel J., *The Authoritarian Personality*, 51
Lewy, Guenter, 51
Lidice (Mann), 176
Lifton, Robert Jay, 30, 258, 262, 266–68, 270, 271, 273, 273n20
Lilla, Mark, 74
Littell, Jonathan, 7, 185, 194, 235. See also *Kindly Ones, The*
Löffelsender, Michael, 71n6
Lost: A Search for Six of Six Million, The (Mendelsohn), 154
Lothe, Jakob, 180n4, 230n34
Lower, Wendy, 27n14
Lüdtke, Alf, 23
Luhmann, Susanne, 11, 27n14
Lyotard, Jean-François, 110

Ma, Julie C., 121
MacCannell, Juliet Flower, 91
MacMillan, Ian, *Village of a Million Spirits*, 179, 181
MacNair, Rachel, 185n6
Magilow, Daniel H., 176
Majdanek, 282
Malachy, Yona, 121–22n55
Malkmus, Bernhard, 207n6
Malle, Bertram F., 32–33, 33–34n17
Mann, Heinrich, *Lidice*, 176
Manoschek, Walter, *. . . dann bin ich ja ein Mörder!*, 58n11
Martínez-Alfaro, María Jesús, 260n6, 267, 273
masterplots, 14, 44, 60, 137, 155–56, 156n10, 161, 164, 165, 167, 168, 170, 171, 173–74
Matthäus, Jürgen, 22n9, 26nn12–13
Maus (Spiegelman), 153
McCarthy, Dermot, 260n6, 261n8, 263, 267
McGlothlin, Erin, 8, 10, 55n7, 218–19n25, 259n4
mediation: by authors, 17n5, 54, 57–58, 65, 75, 76, 131, 182–84; ethical, 152; through generic forms, 145, 158n12; by interpreters, 15, 16, 17n5; by interviewers, 13, 15, 16, 17n5, 18, 57, 147; linguistic, 116, 142–44, 147; of mental states, 5, 6, 7, 15, 32, 35, 36, 37, 75, 116, 137, 176, 206
Melonic, Emina, 305
memoir, 16, 31, 52, 76n13, 182, 193, 194. See also autobiography
Mendelsohn, Daniel, 227, 227–28n31, 228, 234, 236n40; *The Lost*, 154
Menden, Alexander, 283–84n26
Menke, Richard, 261n8, 266, 267
mens rea, 91–92
Meretoja, Hanna, 15, 15n4, 42n18, 60, 129, 129n59, 173, 174, 223, 225, 226, 231, 235n38, 241, 244, 247, 247n53, 259n5
Merle, Robert, *Death Is My Trade*, 177

Metz, Jeremy, 12
Milchman, Alan, 69n3, 292–93n30
Millett, Lydia, 285
Millu, Liana, 52
mimetic representation, 14, 16, 45, 46, 147, 184, 185, 189–92, 190n7, 190n9, 193–94, 217, 219n26, 225, 226, 244, 246, 248, 260, 263, 278–79, 279n24, 296. See also antimimetic representation
mind-reading, 8, 14–15, 29, 31–36, 49n2, 77, 79, 101, 110, 130, 302; empathy and, 63–64; in fiction, 58, 60, 176; functions of, 43; kinesic, 101–3, 107–9, 130; in nonfiction, 47, 60; in popular representations, 176. See also Theory of Mind
Misemer, Sarah M., 71n6, 72–73n9
Mladić, Ratko, 302
Modiano, Patrick, *Dora Bruder*, 154
Mohamed, Saira, 11
Mommsen, Hans, 26n12
"monolingual paradigm" (Yildiz), 143
"monologic dialogue" (Twitchell), 220, 224
Monowitz, 280, 281, 294. See also Auschwitz
monsters, Holocaust perpetrators as, 9, 11, 26n11, 42n18, 44, 53, 70, 75, 80, 84n23, 96, 99n39, 118, 134, 171n14, 178, 223, 247, 247n52, 299, 307
Morag, Raya, 17n5
moral equivalence, 223, 305
moral witnessing, 230
Morte est mon métier, La (Merle). See *Death Is My Trade*
Mulisch, Harry, 44, 77, 94–95, 94n35, 94–95n36, 99n39, 100n40, 113, 130–31; autobiography of, 94n36; on Eichmann's appearance, 77, 100–101; Eichmann trial coverage by, 75, 94–95; empathy and, 64, 100–101; perspective on Eichmann, 131. See also *Criminal Case 40/61*

Müller, Heinrich, 72–73n9
My War Criminal: Personal Encounters with an Architect of Genocide (Stern), 302–7

narration: autodiegetic, 6, 38, 46, 62, 177, 178–79, 180, 181, 182, 206, 226, 228, 230n33, 279, 296, 297; changing modes of, 216–17; heterodiegetic, 29, 38, 181, 183, 216–17; homodiegetic, 29, 38, 179, 180–81, 183, 189; reverse, 261–62; second-person, 194, 219, 220–21; techniques of, 14. *See also* narrative; narrators; unnatural narration; unreliable narration
narrative: axes of communication in (Phelan), 187; causality and, 38, 154, 186, 194, 244n48; conventions of, 15, 28, 43, 60, 62, 65, 102, 108, 156, 161, 164, 165, 168, 169, 173, 189–91, 193, 194, 226, 263, 278, 279; decomposition of, 246–47; devices of, 14, 16, 28, 37, 45, 58, 182, 185, 193, 194, 225, 265, 276, 277, 278, 296; evasion, 203–6, 217, 218, 220; factual, 31, 146; forms of, 141, 167; functions of, 14; hermeneutics, 15n4; pathology, 16, 46, 212, 217–18, 220, 221, 247, 263, 267; unnatural, 189–91, 192–94, 219n26, 265
narrative discourse, 116, 184, 189, 226, 228, 230, 236, 241, 246, 261n8, 265. See also *sjuzhet*
narrative theory, 28–31. *See also* narratology
narratology, 29, 30, 31, 32, 158n12, 180, 186–87, 191n10, 226, 263. *See also* narrative theory
narrators: autodiegetic, 6, 62, 184, 186, 195, 210, 211, 216, 222; divided, 46, 226, 230n33, 263–66, 268n18, 296; doubling and, 14, 45, 184, 194, 216, 266, 267–68, 270–71, 273, 289, 296;

heterodiegetic, 62, 179, 183, 216–17, 263; homodiegetic, 62, 182, 183, 263; interviewers as, 137, 147–48, 151–52; intradiegetic, 182, 217; mediation by, 183; multiple, 184; roles of, 187–88. *See also* unreliable narration
National Socialism. *See* Nazism
National Socialists. *See* Nazis
naturalization, 40, 41, 136, 190, 279
Nazi and the Barber, The (*Der Nazi und der Friseur*; Hilsenrath), 16, 178, 195–98, 208–9n, 210–22, 289; filtering in, 45, 182, 184, 185n5, 198, 203, 206, 221–22, 248–49; as grotesque, 194, 207–8, 209–10; mimetic and antimimetic representation in, 184, 194, 217, 219n26, 220–21; narrative strategies, 45–46, 184, 194, 203–6, 210–13, 221–22, 223–24, 225, 246–48; narrative structure of, 213–18, 220; publication history, 206–9, 207–8n7, 213n16; reception of, 204; unreliable narration in, 210–11, 212
"Nazi mind" (Pick), 47, 47–48n1, 48, 49n3, 51
"Nazi personality," 12, 47–48n1
Nazi Primer: Official Handbook for Schooling the Hitler Youth, The (Childs, trans.), 48
Nazis, 8, 9, 10, 12, 28, 30, 40, 49–51, 49–50n5, 55, 137–38, 151, 160, 247, 293, 299; cultural conceptions of, 50, 177n2; doctors, 266–67, 271, 273n20; fascination with, 176; female, 27n14; leadership, 26n11, 49–51, 243, 281
Nazism, 47, 100n40, 204–5; early efforts to explain, 47–48n1, 48–51, 100n40; language of, 44, 89, 91–92, 283–84n26, 291; as mental state, 47–48n1, 48, 175; simplification of, 26n11
"Nazisploitation" (Magilow, Bridges, Vander Lugt), 176

Index | 341

Nazi und der Friseur, Der (Hilsenrath). See *Nazi and the Barber, The*

new perpetrator research, 10, 26, 56–57, 57n10

Nir, Arieh, 111, 114, 121

nonfiction, 4, 8, 12, 13, 14, 15, 17–18, 20, 28, 42–43, 64–65, 182–83, 302; authorial persona in, 62; conventions of confession in, 124–26, 164–71; conventions of detective fiction in, 156–64; empathy in, 64–65; genres of, 102, 193, 194; influence on fiction, 30, 184–85, 191, 279; intersubjectivity in, 62–63; narrative strategies, 58–65, 185; poetics of, 31; representation of Holocaust perpetrators in, history of, 47–58; representation of life of real-world persons, 59; Theory of Mind and mind-reading in, 32, 32n16, 34, 35–36, 37, 63–64, 302; trajectory toward fiction, 13, 57–58, 175, 181–82. See also fiction/nonfiction distinction; and individual nonfiction genres

nonmimetic representation, 190n7, 261n7. See also antimimetic representation; antinomic temporality; mimetic representation

Norberg, Jakob, 89, 89–90n31, 90, 92

Nünning, Ansgar, 188

Nuremberg Diary (Gilbert), 50

Nuremberg Interviews: An American Psychiatrist's Conversations with the Defendants and Witnesses, The (Gellately), 50

Nuremberg trials, 26, 50, 51, 52, 53, 117, 161, 170, 288, 303n2

Oates, Joyce Carol, 287n28

objectivity, 127–28n58, 146, 151

Ogre, The (*Le Roi des aulnes*; Tournier), 178

Ophüls, Marcel, 55

Other, 2, 8, 10, 42n18, 84n23, 184, 220, 226, 234–35n37, 247, 273–74n21, 299

Ozick, Cynthia, 283, 285, 285n27, 286–87, 287n28, 292

Pagis, Dan: "Draft of a Reparations Agreement," 276n23; "Testimony," 176

parody, 85, 91, 190, 245, 261, 271, 287, 291

Patagonian Hare, The (Lanzmann), 138

Payne, Leigh A., 76–77n14, 167, 170, 210n11

Pendas, Devin O., 82n21, 87n27

perpetrator fiction, 12n3, 175, 176, 180, 181, 183; problematic nature of term, 176n1

perspective-taking, 42n18

Pettitt, Joanne, 11, 12n3, 175, 176–78, 176n1, 177n2, 180–81, 184, 288

Phelan, James, 186, 187–88, 192, 212, 256, 263n14, 264–65, 267, 270–71, 272, 273–74n21, 291

philosemitism, 207n7, 213n15

physiognomy, 44, 101–2, 105, 107–8, 109

picaresque, 204–5, 207nn5–6, 210

Pick, Daniel, 47, 47–48n1, 49, 49nn3–4

Picoult, Jodi, *The Storyteller*, 180

Pomsel, Brunhilde, 58n11

Postone, Moishe, 79

Prager, Brad, 11, 81n19, 83n22, 84, 100, 103

psychiatry, 30, 49n4, 49–50n5, 50–51, 79, 79–80n17, 89n29

psychoanalysis, 49, 49n4, 80n18, 165, 165, 273n20

psychology, 1, 10, 12, 33–34, 47–52, 49–50n5, 55–56, 55n8, 113, 137–38, 145, 160, 162, 162n13, 171, 176, 185, 185n6, 230n33, 246, 266; rejected by Arendt, 79–80, 79–80n17, 89n29, 101–2

Psychology of Dictatorship: Based on an Examination of the Leaders of Nazi Germany, The (Gilbert), 50

"Questioning the Perpetrators: To Give and to Take" (Sereny), 1

Rabinowitz, Peter, 186
Radisch, Iris, 208, 208–9n8
Rasson, Luc, 238, 241
Rau, Petra, 176, 177, 184, 223, 224
Ravensbrück, 282
Razinsky, Liran, 177, 224, 227, 227–28n31, 230, 230n35, 234, 235, 238nn43–44, 240n46, 241
reader: address to, 210–11, 222–24, 225n29; complicity and, 223, 226; as dialogical partner, 152–53, 161, 205, 211; expectations of, 155–56, 167, 170, 211; immersion and, 191–93, 205, 260, 287, 296; investment of, 193, 206; involvement of, 15, 52, 53, 139, 185, 210, 222, 244–45n48, 257, 260, 266n17, 276–77, 288, 296–97; role of, 186–87, 189; as witness, 214–15. *See also* implied reader; reader identification
Reader, The (*Der Vorleser*; Schlink), 180, 183
reader identification, 9, 14, 15, 28, 36–42, 185, 192, 221–23, 226–27, 248, 260, 289–91, 294–95, 296; impediments to, 4, 9, 14–15, 28, 37, 41, 185, 206, 222, 248, 289, 290–91, 294, 295, 297. *See also* identification
realism, 189–92, 190n9, 193–94, 204, 209, 225, 225n29, 226, 231, 236n39, 245n50, 258, 260, 278, 279, 279n25, 283–84n26
Reeder, Glenn R., 35
referentiality, 31, 61–62, 142, 143, 185, 193
Reich, Tova, 287n28

Reichman, Ravit, 79–80n17, 83n22
reliability, narrative. *See* unreliable narration
representational dynamics, 8, 14, 65
representational taboo, 9, 10–11, 11n2, 208, 208–9n8, 259, 259n4
Resistible Rise of Arturo Ui, The (Brecht). See *aufhaltsame Aufstieg des Arturo Ui, Der*
retranslation, 142–43, 147, 147n7
revisionism, 142n5, 263, 265
Richardson, Brian, 29n15, 189, 190, 190n7, 190n9, 191n10, 192, 194, 220–21, 244–45n48, 261, 261n7, 279
Rimmon-Kenan, Shlomith, 244, 244n51
Rise and Fall of the Third Reich, The (Shirer), 51
Rives, Rochelle, 101
Rogovin, Or, 178, 178n3
Röhrling, Helmut, 141, 145
Roi des aulnes, Le (Tournier). See *Ogre, The*
Ronnen, Meir, 105, 119
Roseman, Mark, 23–25, 27, 49n2, 50, 53, 55n8, 185n6
Rosenberg, Alan, 69n3, 292–93n30
Rosenblum, Rachel, 64, 149–50, 172n15
Ross, Benjamin, *Torte Bluma*, 152n9
Rumler, Fritz, 207n5

Sanford, R. Nevitt, *The Authoritarian Personality*, 51
Sanyal, Debarati, 11, 12, 56n9, 223, 224, 226, 228, 229n32, 233, 234, 239n45
Satan, 113, 114
satire, 37, 45, 178, 179, 194, 195, 204, 207–8nn6–7, 208–9n8, 210, 213, 213n15, 225, 258, 260, 266n17, 279, 287
Schabert, Ina, 31
Schindler's List (Spielberg), 294
Schlant, Ernestine, 176
Schlesak, Dieter, *The Druggist of Auschwitz*, 179

Index | 343

Schlink, Bernhard, 176; *The Reader*, 180, 183
Schloss Hartheim, 137, 138; in fiction, 262, 262n12, 266, 269
Schmiderer, Othmar, *Im toten Winkel*, 58n11
Schmidt, Sybille, 9
Schneider, Peter, 176
Scholem, Gershom, 82
Schorsch, Jonathan, 213
Schroer, Timothy, 57n10
Schulz, Hans-Georg, 207n6
Schwaiger, Günter, *Hafners Paradies*, 58n11
Schwan, Gesine, 171n14
Schwarz, Gudrun, 27n14
Scrolls of Auschwitz, 286
Sebald, W. G., 258–59
"second self" (Lifton), 266
See Under: Love (Grossman), 178, 178n3
Segal, Eyal, 156–57, 156n10
Semprún, Jorge, 259
Sereny, Gitta, 1, 7, 23, 26, 36, 43, 54, 57, 60; *Albert Speer*, 2, 4, 12, 13, 17n5, 54–55, 157; contrast to Claude Lanzmann, 137, 138–39n3; empathy and, 3, 64, 137, 148, 149–51, 152, 153, 174, 303; goals of, 133–34, 137, 138–39n3, 138–40, 154, 170, 173–74; *The Healing Wound*, 133–35; impact of interviews with Franz Stangl, 134–37, 146, 151n8; intersubjectivity and, 2, 44, 137, 148–53, 168, 171n14; as interviewer, 1, 3, 8, 12, 13, 54–55, 62, 63, 134, 140, 147–49, 150, 151, 152, 155, 173; motivations of, 133–34, 302–3; narrative roles of, 54, 62, 137, 145, 146–48, 149, 151–52, 155, 172; "Questioning the Perpetrators," 1–4, 24. See also *Into That Darkness*
Servatius, Robert, 111
Shadows Walking (Skopp), 179
Shamay-Tsoory, Simone G., 64
Shen, Dan, 188, 291
Shirer, William L., *The Rise and Fall of the Third Reich*, 51
Shklovsky, Viktor, 192–93, 260n6
Shoah (Lanzmann), 13, 19n7, 55, 137–38
Siertsema, Bettine, 95, 109n47
Sivan, Eyal, *The Specialist*, 71
sjuzhet, 244n47. See also narrative discourse
Skopp, Douglas, *Shadows Walking*, 179
Smith, Sidonie, 124
Sobibór, 1, 44, 54, 133, 137, 138
Sonderkommandos, 285–87, 289
Specialist, The (Braumann and Sivan), 71
speech act, 29n15, 76–77n14, 124, 164, 167
Speer, Albert, 1, 4, 12, 13, 17n5, 52, 54–55, 138–39n3, 157; as fictional character, 228
Spiegelman, Art, *Maus*, 153–54
Spielberg, Steven, *Schindler's List*, 294
Spiessens, Anneleen, 148
Spolsky, Ellen, 102
Stangl, Franz, 44, 54, 133–34, 138–39n3, 140, 152–53, 154, 157, 161, 173, 262, 302–3; as commandant of Treblinka and Sobibór, 135–37; confession and, 168–73; conviction of, 133, 140, 157, 303n2; crimes of, 159–60; death of, 133, 163, 172–73, 172n15; empathy for, 64, 137, 153; family of, 44, 141; guilt and, 169–70, 171n14; language and, 146–47, 147n7; role of, 1, 133, 137, 140n4; self-image of, 140; self-narrative of, 144–45; Sereny's interview with, 1, 12, 44, 133–34; Sereny's view of, 4; subjectivity and, 149–50, 157; trial of, 181; truth and, 161, 162, 163, 164, 168, 174. See also *Into That Darkness*
Stangneth, Bettina, 44, 68n2, 72–74, 72n8, 72–73n9, 73–74n10, 76, 76–77n14, 78n15, 90, 90n32, 120, 127–28n58

Staub, Ervin, 50, 185n6
Steitz, Kerstin, 62, 88n28
Stern, Jessica, *My War Criminal*, 302–7, 303n2, 304n4
Storyteller, The (Picoult), 180
storyworlds, 184, 189, 190n7, 215, 216, 261, 264, 276, 278, 289, 292; construction of, 260; immersion in, 191–93, 260, 296; narration in, 183; referentiality and, 191, 193
Struggle for a Soul, The (Hull), 15, 43–44, 54, 60, 75, 77–78, 111–30, 131–32; narration and, 182; rhetoric of confession in, 123–28; role of Lillian Hull in, 114–16, 114–15n50, 116–17n51; subsumptive narrative in, 128–30
"subsumptive practices" (Meretoja), 129–30, 129n59, 130, 173
Suchomel, Franz, 137, 137n1, 138
Suleiman, Susan Rubin, 4n1, 179, 227, 227–28n31, 228, 229–30, 230n33, 234, 234–35n37, 235, 237–38, 238n42, 239n45, 245n50
Süselbeck, Jan, 208–9n8
Svendsen, Lars, 18n6, 83n22, 171n14
swerve. *See* Eaglestone, Robert: concept of "swerve"
sympathy, 3, 9, 64, 75n12, 87n25, 127n58, 136, 149, 150, 295
Szejnmann, Claus-Christian W., 26n11, 26n13

Tarantino, Quentin, *Inglourious Basterds*, 176
Taylor, Jennifer, 207n6
"Testimony" (Pagis), 176
Theory of Mind (ToM), 29, 31–36, 33–34n17, 63–64, 102. *See also* mind-reading
Theweleit, Klaus, 225, 245n55
third-person narration. *See* narration: heterodiegetic

thoughtlessness. *See* Arendt, Hannah: on thoughtlessness
Time's Arrow, or, The Nature of the Offense (Amis), 16, 46, 178–79, 180, 254–57, 261–77, 278, 289, 294n31, 296–97; antimimetic representation in, 179, 184, 194, 260, 260n6, 263, 277, 278, 296; defamiliarization and, 260, 260n6, 263, 265, 276, 296; filtering and, 45, 181, 182, 260, 277; impetus for, 258; narrator of, 35, 62, 108n45, 184, 263–66, 267–77, 268, 270, 271n19, 274–76, 277, 294; reception of, 224–25; soul as narrator of, 108n45, 179, 184, 188, 264, 264n16, 268, 270, 271n19, 274–76, 277; temporality in, 255–56; unreliable narration in, 188, 256–57, 270, 271n19, 272, 273–74n21, 275, 276
Todorov, Tzevtan, 138–39n3, 151, 157–58, 158n12
Toker, Leona, 202n2
ToM. *See* Theory of Mind
Torgovnick, Marianna, 103–4
totalitarianism, 78–81, 93, 94, 97, 98
Tournier, Michel, *The Ogre*, 178
Trafimow, David, 35
transgression, 9, 11, 11n2, 36, 40, 45, 178, 189, 204, 205, 207, 215, 219n26, 223, 229n32, 235
translation, 91, 145, 181, 213n26, 245n49, 283–84n26; of Sereny's *Into That Darkness*, 141–45, 146–47, 147n7
transparency, 14, 32, 143, 147, 194, 206, 225
Treblinka, 1, 44, 54, 133, 136, 137, 137n1, 138, 152, 163, 302; in fiction, 262, 265
Treblinka trials, 54
Trevor-Roper, Hugh, *The Last Days of Hitler*, 51
Tulloch, John, 149, 151–52

22 Cells in Nuremberg: A Psychiatrist Examines the Nazi Criminals (Kelley), 50
Twitchell, Corey, 198, 211, 211n12, 213n14, 216, 218–19n25, 219–20, 219n26, 221, 221n27, 224

Ulm Einsatzkommando trial, 54
"unitary self" (Waller), 271, 272
United States Holocaust Memorial Museum, Washington, DC, 300–301, 300–301n1
unnatural narrative, 37, 189–94, 219n26, 225–26, 244, 260, 263, 264, 265, 276, 278, 296. *See also* antimimetic representation
unreliable narration, 28, 38–39, 45, 46, 186–89, 194, 206, 210–13, 223, 226, 227, 236–37, 238, 238n42, 238n44, 245, 246–47, 247n57, 256–57, 270, 271n19, 272, 273–74n21, 275, 276, 291, 293; axes of (Phelan), 187–88, 291; dispositional (Shen), 188, 291
unreliable narrators. *See* narrators: unreliable
US Office of Strategic Services, 49

Vaessens, Thomas, 102
Vahsen, Patricia, 207–8n7
Vander Lugt, Kristin T., 176
verisimilitude, 191, 192
Vermes, Timur, *Er ist wieder da*, 27, 179
Vetlesen, Arne Johan, 79–80, 80n18, 87n27
Vice, Sue, 11, 262, 262n12, 263n14, 265, 266, 267, 270, 279–80, 281, 284n26
Village of a Million Spirits: A Novel of the Treblinka Uprising (MacMillan), 179, 181
vocal structure, 217, 220
von Kellenbach, Katharina, 185n6

von Koppenfels, Martin, 179, 205, 206, 208, 224n28, 227, 227–28n31, 229n32, 230, 235n38, 236n40, 237
von Trotta, Margarete, 71
Vorleser, Der (Schlink). See *Reader, The*

Waller, James, 47–48n1, 162n13, 185n6, 247n57, 271, 272, 273n20
Watson, Julia, 124
Weinert, Matthew S., 95, 95n37
Weiss, Peter, 176
Welzer, Harald, 145, 171n14, 185n6
Wennberg, Rebecca, 10, 56
West Germany, 54
Weyandt, Hans-Jost, 283–84n26
Wiesel, Elie, 52, 249, 259, 300
Wieviorka, Annette, 204
Willerslev, Rane, 64
Williams, Dominic, 286
Wolf, Werner, 191–92, 279n25
Wood, Gaby, 278, 283–84n26

Yildiz, Yasemin, 143
Your Job in Germany (Capra), 49–50n5

Zaak 40/61: Een Reportage, De (Mulisch). See *Criminal Case 40/61*
Zone of Interest, The (Amis), 16, 46, 179–80, 249–54, 255, 258–59, 278–96, 297–98; empathetic identification and, 287–91, 294–96; filtering and, 45, 182, 260; generic frames of, 279–87, 288; German language in, 283–84n26, 293; mimetic representation and, 184, 194, 260, 278–80; narrative construction, 288; narrators in, 279–88; sexuality in, 282; structure of, 288; unreliable narration in, 256–57, 291, 293
Zunshine, Lisa, 34–35

About the Author

ERIN MCGLOTHLIN is professor of German and Jewish studies at Washington University in St. Louis. Her research focuses on Holocaust literature and film and German-Jewish literature. She is the author of *Second-Generation Holocaust Literature: Legacies of Survival and Perpetration* and coeditor of three volumes, *After the Digital Divide? German Aesthetic Theory in the Age of New Digital Media* (with Lutz Koepnick), *Persistent Legacy: The Holocaust and German Studies* (with Jennifer Kapczynski), and *The Construction of Testimony: Claude Lanzmann's Shoah and Its Outtakes* (Wayne State University Press, 2020, with Brad Prager and Markus Zisselsberger).

www.ingramcontent.com/pod-product-compliance
Lightning Source LLC
Chambersburg PA
CBHW021340300426
44114CB00012B/1022